ECONOMIC DIPLOMACY

Economic Diplomacy

THE EXPORT-IMPORT BANK AND AMERICAN FOREIGN POLICY 1934–1939

Frederick C. Adams

University of Missouri Press
1976

Library of Congress Cataloging in Publication Data

Adams, Frederick C   1941–
    Economic diplomacy.

    Bibliography: p.
    Includes index.
    1.   Export-Import Bank of the United States.
    2.   United States—Foreign economic relations—History.
    3.   United States—Foreign relations—1933–1945.
    I.   Title.
HG2613.W34E752   327.73   75-43758
ISBN 0-8262-0197-0

For my parents
Eda Chiodi Adams
John Paige Adams, Jr.

Preface

This monograph attempts to broaden understanding of American foreign policy during the 1930s by examining the activities of the Export-Import Bank of Washington. The Roosevelt administration created the bank in early 1934 to furnish governmental assistance for expansion of foreign commerce and for preservation of a multilateral pattern of world trade. By involving an agency of the federal government in the affairs of private enterprise, the bank represented one of the most important legacies of the New Deal. The institution has other significance.

The bank's objective of promoting foreign trade occasionally clashed with its goal of protecting the multilateral system. The resulting debate sheds light on the relationship between export-oriented interest groups and those individuals who formulated policy. In the case of the Export-Import Bank, export interests seldom played the decisive role in the decision-making process. Although traders initiated most requests for bank funds, officials in Washington exercised final authority. This is, however, an exceedingly complex issue. Even though they did not control decisions, interest groups helped define the major principles underlying the U. S. approach to international commercial relations and, therefore, often could compel a modification of these principles. To a degree, policymakers and foreign traders were in agreement on the type of world order most beneficial to the nation. Where they differed was on the question of perspective: exporters thought primarily in terms of immediate gains whereas State Department officers considered long-run implications.

An analysis of the bank's activities further reveals that the world crisis of the late 1930s prompted Washington to use the institution as an instrument for influencing overseas events. New Deal administrators believed that by the judicious provision of economic assistance they could counter those forces undermining the existing structure of international relations. The pursuit of this objective resulted in the manipulation of foreign business by the American government in ways which earlier administrations had rejected. Increased governmental participation in world affairs, furthermore, meant the United States was not following a policy of isolationism, if by this term one means a withdrawal from the international arena. American policy-makers chose not to rely on military force or to enter binding political alliances, but they did believe they could protect the nation's interests through economic diplomacy.

Finally, the Export-Import Bank provides another example of the way the New Deal concentrated power in the executive branch of government. During 1940, the Roosevelt administration obtained an important enlargement of the bank's lending authority. With this legislation, American policymakers could involve the nation in events around the globe without congressional approval. In effect, government officials insulated themselves from democratic pressures.

The study begins with an extended discussion of America's economic foreign policy during the 1920s. The First World War had thrust the United States into the fore as the world's leading commercial and financial power at the same time it signaled the end of the old European-dominated system of international politics. American officials, acutely aware of the magnitude of these changes, tried to create a new world order offering maximum protection and opportunity for their nation's interests. By analyzing the policies adopted by U. S. statesmen in the 1920s, I hope to provide the background necessary for an evaluation of the Export-Import Bank's actions for American foreign policy.

Acknowledgments

In the process of completing this project, I have received assistance from a number of sources. A fellowship from the Center for International Studies at Cornell University enabled me to do the initial research while in graduate school. On three separate occasions, Drake University provided funds which facilitated the final stages of research, writing, and typing. The helpfulness and cooperative attitude of the staffs of the National Archives, Manuscript Division of the Library of Congress, Franklin D. Roosevelt Presidential Library, Herbert Hoover Presidential Library, and Cowles Library of Drake University made research considerably easier. Chapter Eight is a slightly altered version of my article, "The Road to Pearl Harbor: A Reexamination of American Far Eastern Policy, July 1937–December 1938," that appeared in the June 1971 edition of the *Journal of American History*. Professor Martin Ridge, editor of the journal, gave me permission to use this material.

There are a number of individuals to whom I owe a special debt of gratitude. I profited immensely from my long talks with Professor William H. Beezley, now a member of the history department at North Carolina State University, when we were struggling to make the adjustment from graduate school to the rigors of the academic world. Professors Keach Johnson and Charles Nelson, members of the history department at Drake University, have been a constant source of support and encouragement. Julie Isenberg Wilkinson demonstrated great care and dedication when typing much of the manuscript. I am also indebted to the two readers for the University of Missouri Press who made several perceptive suggestions that improved the book. My greatest debt, however, belongs to Professor Walter LaFeber of Cornell University. In addition to overseeing this project when it was in the doctoral dissertation stage, he read the entire revised manuscript and made recommendations which strengthened it immeasurably. Besides this assistance, Professor LaFeber has continually provided encouragement and friendly advice. By his teaching and publications, moreover, he has set an example of professional excellence that I have found inspiring. Only those who have been fortunate enough to have worked with him realize what a truly remarkable individual he is.

Finally I would like to thank my wife, Ann, and daughters, Shavaun and Maura, for their patience and support.

F. C. A.
Des Moines, Iowa
January 1976

Contents

1

A New Era of
International Economic Relations
1920s

The First World War accelerated America's rise to a dominant position in the world economy. In responding to the needs of the Allies, American industrial and agricultural producers dramatically increased their output, expanding the nation's capacity for and dependence on foreign commerce. To pay for essential war supplies, the Allies borrowed heavily from the American public and, once the United States entered the war, from the American government. The flow of private capital was of sufficient magnitude to reverse the nation's international financial position; during the five years from 1914 to 1919, America moved from being a world debtor of $3.7 billion to being a world creditor of roughly the same amount. This transformation represented a gross capital outflow of nearly $7.5 billion. In addition, the American government loaned over $10 billion to the Allies. By the end of the second decade of the twentieth century, the United States not only possessed tremendous productive capacity but was also the world's major source of capital.[1]

The country's new position forced American political and economic leaders to reassess the nation's role in international affairs. Their analysis began with the supposition that the world was an economic unit in which American prosperity had become

1. Department of Commerce, *The United States in the World Economy*, Economic Series, no. 23, p. 148; Bureau of the Census, *Historical Statistics of the United States, 1789–1945*, p. 242: Milton Friedman and Anna J. Schwartz, *A Monetary History of the United States 1867–1960*, p. 199; Cleona Lewis, *America's Stake in International Investments*, chaps. 6, 17.

dependent on events throughout the globe.[2] At the base of this assumption lay a conviction that the phenomenal scientific and industrial advances which had taken place in the half century prior to the war had drawn the world together. The primary cause of the outbreak of fighting in 1914 had been the inability of nations to adjust their economic policies to reflect these new conditions. Future international stability, moreover, hinged on the ability of world leaders to accommodate the activities of their nations to the existing situation.[3] This view held tremendous significance for the United States. During the interwar years, American statesmen assumed that actions by other countries could exert a decisive influence on America's well-being. Although often at odds over the proper course for the nation to pursue, leading political and economic figures agreed that the United States had an important stake in the world community and should act to protect that stake. Consequently, when Norman H. Davis, one of the Democratic party's leading foreign policy advisers, criticized the Harding administration, he did not denounce it for pursuing a course of isolationism, which every-

2. See Woodrow Wilson, *A History of the American People*, 5 vols. (New York, 1902), 5:255; Wilson's message to Congress, May 20, 1919, *The Messages and Papers of Woodrow Wilson*, ed. Albert Shaw, 2:671–82; William Diamond, *The Economic Thought of Woodrow Wilson*, pp. 133–34, 166–72, 191–93; Cordell Hull, *The Memoirs of Cordell Hull*, 1:81–84; address to the Tennessee Society of New York, January 6, 1921, Container 91, Folder (1913) 1921–1923, Cordell Hull Papers (Library of Congress, Washington, D.C.); William C. Redfield, *Dependent America: A Study of the Economic Bases of Our International Relations* (Boston, 1926), pp. 1–16, 229–53; also see John S. Drum, "Survey of Economic Conditions," *Journal of the American Bankers' Association* 13, no. 11 (May 1921): 722–27; R. S. Hecht, "Premium on the Dollar a Barrier," *Journal of the American Bankers' Association* 14, no. 3 (September 1921): 107–8; Henry M. Robinson, "The United States As a Creditor Nation," *Bankers Magazine* 103 (August 1921): 261–68; and editorial, *New York Times*, January 23, 1921, sec. 2, p. 2. One of the best known presentations of the economic interdependence of the world was John Maynard Keynes, *The Economic Consequences of the Peace*; for an interesting critique of this book, see, J. A. M. de Sanchez, "Further Economic Consequences of the Peace," *Foreign Affairs* 1 (September 1922): 158–67.

3. For one of the best developments of this view, see the draft of a speech to be delivered by Norman Davis to the Council on Foreign Relations shortly after the French invasion of the Ruhr, Container 16a, Folder Dawes Plan, etc., Norman H. Davis Papers (Library of Congress, Washington, D.C.); also see Herbert Fraser, *Foreign Trade and World Politics*, pp. 162–66.

one recognized was no longer possible; he condemned the Republicans for acting unilaterally instead of multilaterally.[4]

The events of the immediate postwar period reinforced the consensus of an interrelated world. By early 1921, the U. S. economy was in the midst of one of the most dramatic tailspins in the country's history: wholesale prices for all commodities plunged by over 50 percent, unemployment soared, the number of bankruptcies rose sharply, and over 450,000 farmers lost their farms. Cordell Hull, a leading Democratic politician and later Franklin D. Roosevelt's secretary of state, interpreted the recession as a further indication that the world was a single economic unit. Hull maintained that America's difficulties were the product of a snowballing effect which began when the countries of central and eastern Europe did not receive the financial and moral support they needed to sustain economic growth. This downturn reduced the available markets for English, French, and Belgian goods so that the hard times spread to western Europe. In a similar fashion, depressed conditions emerged in the United States once its western European customers reduced their purchases of American products. The only way out of the impasse, Hull concluded, was for the United States to initiate a program to restore European stability.[5] Thus, the postwar recession added fuel to the ongoing debate over the nation's proper international posture.

Woodrow Wilson spent a great deal of time wrestling with precisely this question. The basic task was to design a program which would restore order to a badly disheveled world while preserving America's dominant position in the international economy.[6] The president opted for a course characterized by

4. Norman H. Davis, "Comments upon the Conference on Limitation of Armaments and Far Eastern Questions," February 17, 1922, Container 3, Folder 6, Hull Papers.

5. Friedman and Schwartz, *Monetary History of the United States*, pp. 223–36; George Soule, *Prosperity Decade from War to Depression*, pp. 96–106; address to the Tennessee Society of New York, January 6, 1921, Container 91, Folder (1913), 1921–1923, Hull Papers.

6. For an analysis of the steps taken by the Wilson administration to prepare the nation for its new role in world affairs, see Martin Sklar, "Woodrow Wilson and the Political Economy of Modern United States Liberalism," *Studies on the Left* 1 (Fall 1960): 17–47; Carl Parrini, *Heir to Empire*, chaps. 1, 2; N. Gordon Levin, Jr. *Woodrow Wilson and World Politics*, passim.

governmental participation in international political affairs and a reliance on private enterprise to sustain economic growth. The League of Nations lay at the heart of Wilson's approach, for only through such a body could nations achieve the political stability necessary for world rehabilitation. As Wilson later informed Norman Davis, American prosperity was so dependent on conditions abroad that enlightened self-interest alone dictated that the United States join the League. In addition to the League of Nations, the president wanted to moderate Allied reparations demands and formulate a war debts policy which would ensure that the Allies could meet the obligations without overtaxing their economies. Wilson also hoped to adjust America's tariff policy to reflect its new status as a creditor nation. High tariffs, he warned, would make it nearly impossible for Europe to repay the war debts and would "stand in the way of normal readjustment of business conditions throughout the world, which is as vital to the welfare of this country as to that of all the other nations." The United States could discharge the duty it owed itself and other countries "by widening, not by contracting, its world markets." Finally, following the lead of the Treasury Department as well as his own inclination, Wilson shifted the burden of reconstruction to private enterprise by withdrawing governmental controls from the economy and stopping the flow of public funds abroad.[7]

The president's attempts to implement these policies encountered many obstacles. The Senate refused to ratify the Versailles Treaty, thereby keeping the United States out of the League of Nations, and then combined with the House to pass an emergency tariff bill (over Wilson's veto) that raised the level of duties. The question of reparations and war debts remained unsettled as the French and, to a lesser degree, the British in-

7. Entry for March 10, 1921, Container 16a, Davis Diary, Davis Papers; Levin, *Wilson and World Politics*, pp. 140–50, 158–59, 175; Robert H. Van Meter, Jr., "American Foreign Policy and the Economic Reconstruction of Europe, 1918–1921," *Topic* 16 (Fall 1968): 49–50, 58–59, 60–62; Wilson, *Messages and Papers*, 2:1227–28; Colby to Hugh Wallace, September 17, 1920, Department of State, *Papers Relating to the Foreign Relations of the United States, 1920,* 1:96 (hereafter referred to as *Foreign Relations* for various dates); Paul P. Abrahams, "American Bankers and the Economic Tactics of Peace," *Journal of American History* 56 (December 1969): 572–73; Parrini, *Heir to Empire*, chap. 2; Ray Stannard Baker, *Woodrow Wilson and World Settlement*, 2:316–17, 329–32, 353–67.

sisted on placing heavy charges on Germany; and neither country was eager to conclude an agreement with the American government on the repayment of war and postwar loans.

The existence of these unresolved issues in combination with the normal caution of American bankers meant that the Wilson administration's plan to rely on private capital for the reconstruction of Europe did not work. The chief handicap facing both United States exporters and Europeans interested in purchasing American commodities was a shortage of dollars abroad. This condition placed a premium on the dollar, thereby curtailing American exports as effectively as if countries had raised protective tariffs. Even though most United States political and economic leaders could agree on the necessity of extending credits overseas, they had difficulty deciding on the proper way to go about it. A good deal of the indecision stemmed from the inadequacy of the American banking structure which was geared primarily to short-term domestic lending and not to the longer-term credits necessary for foreign trade. Furthermore, because American investors had only begun to deal extensively in foreign securities during the war, they preferred domestic issues unless interest rates on foreign obligations were high enough to attract attention.[8]

After the end of the war, leading American bankers such as Frank Vanderlip of First National City Bank of New York, Paul M. Warburg of Kuhn Loeb & Company, Henry P. Davison and Thomas Lamont of J. P. Morgan & Company, and Fred Kent of Bankers' Trust Company devised numerous proposals which in one way or another involved the American government underwriting a portion of foreign financing. The bankers believed that they could not attract private capital without governmental assistance. Officials in the Treasury Department, however, re-

8. Hecht, "Premium on the Dollar a Barrier," pp. 107–8; Drum, "Survey of Economic Conditions," pp. 725–27; Samuel MacClintock, "Foreign Credits," *Bankers Magazine* 102: 257–61; Arthur A. G. Laders, "Foreign Trade and its Relation to Domestic Business," ibid. 103 (July 1921): 73–76; Robinson, "The United States As a Creditor Nation," pp. 261–68; "Foreign Trade Outlook for United States," *Bankers Magazine* 102 (February 1921): 272–74; editorial, *New York Times*, January 20, 1921, p. 8; for the attitude of the National Foreign Trade Council, see *New York Times*, May 5, 1921, p. 26; John McHugh, "America's Foreign Trade Opportunity," *Bankers Magazine* 102 (January 1921): 19–20; Department of Commerce, *United States in the World Economy*, pp. 4, 98.

jected these proposals. Determined to reduce government expenditures, they insisted that private groups finance recovery. As an alternative to the recommendations of the big banking interests, Treasury Department officers supported passage of the Edge Act. This bill, which had the support of the influential American Bankers' Association, amended the Federal Reserve Act to allow the formation of private corporations to engage in foreign lending. The corporations either could discount short-term trade acceptances or they could undertake long-term investments. (A single corporation, however, could deal in only one form of financing.) Advocates of the bill counted on having the War Finance Corporation, an agency of the American government, supplement the flow of private capital by purchasing up to 20 percent of the debentures. In addition, national banks could contribute a portion of their assets to the foreign trade banks. The new institutions could have total obligations of up to a 10:1 ratio of their capital and surplus.[9]

After Congress passed the act, a committee of the American Bankers' Association met with committees from the United States Chamber of Commerce and the National Foreign Trade Council to draw up plans for a $100 million bank. On December 10 and 11, 1920, five hundred bankers, businessmen, and producers met at the Congress Hotel in Chicago to endorse the immediate formation of the Foreign Trade Financing Corporation. The convention also created a thirty-member permanent committee to organize the institution and raised $100,000 to cover preliminary expenses. The Chicago meeting represented the first time that American business and financial interests joined together to support a project designed to expand foreign commerce.[10]

9. Abrahams, "Bankers and Economic Tactics of Peace," pp. 574–78; Van Meter, "American Policy and the Reconstruction of Europe," pp. 50–57; McHugh, "America's Foreign Trade Opportunity," pp. 20–22; Charles A. Holder, "The Place of Foreign Trade Banks in Overseas Trade," *Bankers Magazine* 102 (April 1921): 595–96; Richard N. Owens, "The Hundred Million Dollar Foreign-Trade Financing Corporation," *Journal of Political Economy* 30 (June 1922): 346–47.

10. Owens, "Hundred Million Dollar Financing Corporation," pp. 346–51; the plan had the general support of bankers throughout the country, see McHugh, "America's Foreign Trade Opportunity," p. 21; "Foreign Trade Financing Corporation," *Bankers Magazine* 102 (January 1921): 17;

Although the bank's promoters had planned to begin business operations by March 1921, they were unable to raise the required capital because of continued financial uncertainties created by the recession. The plan was clearly in trouble by this point; before the year was over, it lost most of its initial supporters.[11] Notwithstanding this failure, the episode demonstrated that business and financial leaders recognized that the changed status of the nation required new policies. The failure also suggested that the government might have to assist in producing the international stability necessary for the return of prosperity.

Besides undermining the Foreign Trade Financing Corporation, the recession reinforced the position of those within the private sector of the economy who believed that exports were vital to the nation's well-being. "We have learned by recent experiences," commented a vice-president of the Guaranty Trust Company, "that the factories of America are today so huge and their output at full capacity is so great that the domestic market cannot regularly absorb it." Only by "a constant flow of overseas trade" could industry run full time all the time. A survey taken by the American Bankers' Association came to a similar conclusion: based on 1,000 replies, the poll indicated "indisputably" that bankers believed a serious fall in the foreign demand for U. S. goods had led to the recession. Export-oriented groups agreed with this analysis. The National Foreign Trade Council appealed to Congress for assistance in promoting foreign commerce. The chairman of the council, James A. Farrell, ex-president of U. S. Steel, sought government support to enable the nation to retain its new position as the world's leading economic power. "It is not too much to say," Farrell insisted, "that the welfare of every man, woman and child in America is linked up with a correct solution of these problems of international commerce." The New York State Chamber of Commerce echoed this plea for joint government-business action to promote the foreign trade needed to overcome the business decline. Wil-

---

"Financing Foreign Trade," *Journal of the American Bankers' Association* 13 (January 1921): 457.

11. "Financing Foreign Trade," p. 457; "American Banks and Foreign Trade," *Bankers Magazine* 103 (November 1921): 828; *New York Times*, January 27, 1922, p. 14; Parrini, *Heir to Empire*, pp. 83–100.

liam C. Redfield, president of the American Manufacturers' Export Association and former secretary of commerce under Woodrow Wilson, concisely stated the alternatives: "We must sell abroad or wither at home."[12]

When Warren G. Harding entered office, he faced a complex series of problems in the foreign and domestic arenas. Although agreeing with the Wilson administration on the necessity for establishing a world order compatible with America's interests, the Republican administration approached international relations in a manner quite different from that of its predecessors.[13] Instead of operating on a multilateral basis through the League of Nations, Republican leaders chose to act unilaterally, or as they put it, independently. Independent action, nonetheless, was not the same thing as isolationism, a point that Republican leaders were quick to make. Charles Evans Hughes, secretary of state from 1921 to 1925 and one of the leading architects of United States foreign policy during the 1920s, argued that because European nations had always been pounding on its doors, the country had never been isolated. American leaders traditionally had preserved the nation's independence of action by avoiding European alliances. Hughes further observed that the nature of America's interests made an isolationist policy unthinkable: "When we consider the vast extent of our interests, the amount and range of American investments, the reach of American enterprise and philanthropy, there is perhaps no people less isolated than ourselves." Henry Cabot Lodge, the powerful Republican senator from Massachusetts, chided Democratic critics

12. Willis H. Booth, "Foreign Trade and the Interior Bank," *Bankers Magazine* 102 (January 1921): 75; Drum, "Survey of Economic Conditions," p. 725; *New York Times*, January 11, 1921, p. 25; ibid., May 5, 1921, p. 28; Chamber of Commerce of the State of New York, *Bulletin of the Chamber of Commerce of the State of New York* 13 (June 1921): 8; *New York Times*, June 24, 1921, p. 21. For additional views on the importance of exports to domestic prosperity, skim *Bankers Magazine*, *Journal of the American Bankers' Association*, *Nation's Business*, and the *New York Times* for the 1920–1921 period.

13. For a full account of the difficulties bequeathed the new administration, see Robert K. Murray, *The Harding Era*, chap. 3; also see Merlo J. Pusey, *Charles Evans Hughes*, 2:411; for reappraisals of the foreign policy of the 1920s, see William A. Williams, "The Legend of Isolationism in the 1920's," *Science and Society* 18 (Winter 1954): 1–20; L. Ethan Ellis, *Republican Foreign Policy, 1922–1933*, passim.

by pointing out that there was a wide range of international activity which lay outside Europe and in which the Republicans had been active. Undersecretary of the Treasury Ogden Mills further clarified the Republican position by remarking that the United States did not wish to shirk its responsibility as a world power, "but we still maintain our right to define what those responsibilities are and to decide under what circumstances we shall use our power and our resources."[14]

Harding administration officials rejected a multilateral approach for two basic reasons. First, they adhered to the traditional view, which extended back to the time of George Washington, that Europe had a different set of interests from the United States. America should not become entangled in European political struggles, since they did not entail questions of great significance for this country. American involvement, moreover, would needlessly complicate issues. Second, Republican leaders believed that they could best serve the interests of world peace by acting unilaterally. Herbert Hoover, the new secretary of commerce, maintained that since the United States was the sole reservoir of the world's surplus capital, the country had to exert a firm control over the use of its resources. Before America could act, other nations would have to reduce armaments, lower taxes, and balance budgets. Following these steps, the United States "out of her own interests would join her economic strength to build the span on these firm piers so vital for economic progress. Without this foundation there is little for America to build upon: with this foundation America will not fail to do her part."[15]

14. Charles E. Hughes, *The Pathway of Peace*, pp. 143–44; Chamber of Commerce of the State of New York, *Bulletin of the Chamber of Commerce of the State of New York* 16 (April 1925): 10; Henry Cabot Lodge, "Foreign Relations of the United States, 1921–1924," *Foreign Affairs* 2 (June 1924): 525–39; Ogden L. Mills, "Our Foreign Policy: A Republican View," *Foreign Affairs* 6 (July 1928): 572.

15. Lodge, "Foreign Relations of the United States," pp. 538–39; Hughes, *Pathway of Peace*, pp. 140, 151–52; Theodore E. Burton, "American Foreign Policy: A Republican View," *Foreign Affairs* 3 (September 1924): 38–43; Herbert Hoover, address before the Union League Club of Chicago, February 22, 1922, Public Statements, 9, No. 208, Herbert Hoover Papers (Herbert Hoover Library, West Branch, Iowa); Mills, "Our Foreign Policy," p. 572.

The Republican approach to foreign policy, therefore, was characterized by a willingness to participate in international affairs as long as involvement did not produce binding political ties. As for international conferences, the Republicans favored working through small meetings that dealt with specific grievances. According to Hughes, conferences were successful in an inverse relationship to the number of participants and to the extent that the talks represented the common purpose of the few who were there. Similarly, Hoover assumed that nations could not solve all problems at once so that progress could come only through slow but assured steps.[16]

Republican leaders supported a tariff policy that differed significantly from the one advocated by the Wilson administration. While some within the Harding administration did believe that the nation would have to adjust tariff levels in the long run, they did not recommend an immediate reduction in duties. Again, Hoover was important in formulating the Republican position. Fearing that a vast influx of imports would cause unemployment by disrupting domestic markets, he questioned whether the United States should ever have a balanced merchandise trade. His desire to expand American exports as well as to rebuild Europe led Hoover to the conclusion that systematic foreign investment, rather than a tariff reduction, was the proper way to promote this country's welfare. He also believed that by guaranteeing a prosperous America, a protective tariff would increase the level of imports and, thus, stimulate economic growth in other regions of the world. Hoover likened the U. S. situation to that facing the British in 1860 when they began making permanent investments abroad in lieu of accepting the full value in commodities for exports.[17] Many bankers accepted the logic of this argument by opting for overseas investment as a means of maintaining an export surplus.[18]

16. Hughes, *Pathway of Peace*, p. 259; Hoover, address before Union League Club of Chicago, February 22, 1922, Public Statements, 9, No. 208, Hoover Papers.

17. Hoover, address to American Bankers' Association meeting, December 10, 1920, Public Statements, 5, No. 111, Hoover Papers; Joan Hoff Wilson, *American Business and Foreign Policy, 1920–1933*, pp. 87–92.

18. The attitude of bankers toward foreign investment can be found in Hecht, "Premium on the Dollar a Barrier," p. 108; Drum, "Survey of Economic Conditions," pp. 722–27; Robinson, "The United States As a

Even though they opposed joining the League of Nations and chose not to lower tariffs, Republicans did agree with Democrats that the private sector of the economy should provide the means for the restoration of international economic prosperity. Because the chaotic state of the postwar world continued to discourage private enterprise, one of the chief tasks confronting the new administration was to achieve that degree of political stability necessary to attract private capital.[19] The implementation of stabilization policies, furthermore, caused the American government to become more deeply involved in international affairs than it generally cared to admit.

Although conditions in Europe were the primary cause of world instability, Secretary of State Hughes moved first to ease the strains emanating from the Far East. The two regions were not distinct, however, since any East Asian settlement would have significance for the European nations with interests in the area. By 1921, the United States faced a complex situation in the Far East. The Japanese had taken advantage of the turmoil of the war and immediate postwar years to expand their influence on the Asian mainland and to seize certain islands in the Pacific. At Versailles, Wilson had tried unsuccessfully to reverse the Japanese movements. The Anglo-Japanese treaty further complicated matters by appearing to give tacit British support to Japan. Finally, the United States found itself entangled in a costly and potentially dangerous naval race with Great Britain and, to a lesser extent, Japan. Besides accentuating the unstable situation in the Far East, the naval race directed resources away from more productive uses and created inflationary conditions. Hoping to solve these issues, the Harding administration sponsored the Washington Conference, held from December 1921 through February 1922.

Creditor Nation," pp. 265–66; Laders, "Foreign Trade and its Relation to Domestic Business," pp. 74–76; McHugh, "American's Foreign Trade Opportunity," p. 24; "Financing Foreign Trade," pp. 458–59.

19. Hoover, address to annual convention of the Chamber of Commerce of the United States, May 16, 1922, Public Statements, 10, No. 228, Hoover Papers; Elmer H. Youngman, "America's International Banking and Financial Relations," *Bankers Magazine* 103 (September 1921): 402–5; "International Financial Problems," ibid. 104 (January 1922): 2–4; "The Forty-Eighth Annual Convention," *Journal of the American Bankers' Association* 15 (November 1922): 255; Thomas B. McAdams, "Address of the President," ibid., pp. 266–67.

To a surprising degree, the conferees settled most of the outstanding questions. The Five Power Naval Treaty brought a halt to the race in battleship construction. In return for accepting the short end of the battleship ratio (5:5:3), Japan received assurances that America would not build new fortifications west of Hawaii and that Britain would not erect additional fortifications on its Pacific islands. While these concessions gave Japan a preponderance of power in East Asia, U. S. officials hoped that the other treaties signed at the conference would protect America's interests in that region. Under the provisions of the Four Power Treaty, the Anglo-Japanese alliance was terminated and Great Britain, France, Japan, and the United States promised to respect each other's rights in the Pacific. The nations also consented to meet together to settle any disputes which might emerge among the contracting parties and to communicate with one another in the event of an act of aggression by a nonsignatory power. The key to the American position, however, was the Nine Power Treaty in which the signators agreed to observe the principles of equal commercial opportunity in China and of preserving that nation's political and administrative integrity. This accord marked the first time a group of nations had formally consented to the promises underlying the open door policy.[20] The Washington Conference represented the Republican approach to foreign affairs working in its most effective manner. The meeting involved a limited number of nations whose delegates were able to reach agreements on a specific range of topics. In addition, the conference had an importance that transcended the immediate issues, for, as Hoover noted, it led to the reconstruction of confidence everywhere. Without this, private enterprise would be unable to heal the world's ills.[21]

Under the direction of Cordell Hull and Norman Davis, the Democrats offered fundamental criticisms of the conference. Davis concentrated most of his fire on the Four Power Treaty, warning that this accord committed the United States to the formation of an alliance system. By becoming party to an agree-

20. For accounts of the conference, see Thomas H. Buckley, *The United States and the Washington Conference, 1921–1922*, passim; Ellis, *Republican Foreign Policy*, chap. 4; Pusey, *Hughes*, 2: chaps. 44–49.
21. Hoover, address to Union League Club of Chicago, February 22, 1922, Public Statements, 9, No. 208, Hoover Papers.

ment on Pacific questions that excluded other powers equally concerned (such as Germany and Russia), America would foster a situation in which the excluded nations might establish a counter-alliance. The end result would be a reversion to balance-of-power politics. Agreeing with Davis's charges, Hull further cautioned that the new treaty system forced the United States to disarm but enabled Japan to consolidate her hold on East Asia. As a consequence, the Japanese would be in a position to force American and British interests from that portion of the globe. The Democratic leaders hoped the Senate would modify the Four Power Treaty by including all nations with a stake in the Pacific as well as by making adherence to the pact contingent upon due observation by all parties to the pledges of the remaining treaties. They also wanted to provide means for dissolving the pact if one of the signators joined a separate alliance.[22] The Democrats were unsuccessful in their efforts, however, and had to settle for a pledge that the Four Power Treaty was not an alliance or commitment to use force.

Although the treaty system worked out at the Washington Conference collapsed during the following decade, in the short run, the accords did ease tensions in the Far East and enable American policymakers to turn their attention toward the difficulties plaguing Europe. The United States had a significant material interest in Europe since this area absorbed approximately 50 percent of America's total exports and was the prime purchaser of United States crude materials and foodstuffs. (In the period 1910 to 1914, European nations bought 83 percent of these exports.) Besides directly benefiting the American economy, a healthy Europe was essential for the return of world prosperity. By increased purchases from Latin America and Asia, a resurgent Europe would aid these regions and, in turn, make them a better market for U. S. products.[23]

22. Hull to Davis, December 15 and 22, 1921; Davis to Hull, December 20, 1921; Hull to Davis, December 22, 1921; Davis to Hull, February 23, 27, and March 8, 1922, Container 27, Folder, Hull, Cordell, ca. 1921–1927, Davis Papers; entries for December 10, 1921, and January 21, 1922, Container 16a, Davis Diary, Davis Papers; Davis to Hull, December 13, 1921, Container 2, Correspondence I, Hull Papers; Hull, *Memoirs*, 1:116.
23. Bureau of the Census, *Historical Statistics of the United States*, p. 250; Department of Commerce, *Foreign Commerce and Navigation of the*

Harding administration officials were acutely aware of the relationship between European stability and the well-being of other areas in the world. "The prosperity of the United States largely depends upon the economic settlements which may be made in Europe," Secretary of State Hughes informed the 1921 graduating class of Brown University, "and the key to the future is with those who make those settlements." A year and a half later the secretary told members of the American Historical Association that the economic conditions in Europe were receiving the administration's earnest consideration. "We cannot dispose of these problems by calling them European," he added, "for they are world problems and we cannot escape the injurious consequences of a failure to settle them."[24] Hoover similarly believed that the economic rehabilitation of Europe, especially eastern Europe, was of vital concern to the United States. Writing to Hughes and Benjamin Strong, the president of the New York Federal Reserve Bank, Hoover insisted that rebuilding a sound Europe was "of daily importance to every worker or farmer in our country and the whole world."[25]

Private groups involved in foreign enterprises concurred in these views. The National Foreign Trade Council stressed the significance of a stable Europe for American welfare. The council even suggested the cancellation or sharp reduction of war debts as a means of stimulating European recovery and of providing those nations with the exchange needed to purchase American products. The president of the American Bankers' Association urged the United States in 1922 to interest itself in European problems "in order that the world be saved and American happiness, prosperity, and security maintained." The American Bankers' Association itself passed a resolution calling on the government to formulate principles that could provide the co-

United States for the Calendar Year of 1924, p. LX; Julius Klein, Frontiers of Trade, pp. 144–46.

24. Quoted in Pusey, Hughes, 2:414; Hughes, Pathway of Peace, pp. 53–54; for two recent and highly illuminating analyses of the Republican approach to Europe, see Melvyn Leffler, "Political Isolationism: Economic Expansion or Diplomatic Realism?" Perspectives in American History 8 (1974): 413–61; and Frank C. Costigliola, "The Politics of Financial Stabilization" (Ph.D. dissertation, Cornell Univ., 1973), passim.

25. Hoover to Strong, August 30, 1921, and Hoover to Hughes, August 30, 1921, Records of Secretary of Commerce, Official File, Benjamin Strong, Hoover Papers.

operation necessary for the rehabilitation of Europe. Most leading bankers agreed that the nation could not achieve permanent prosperity until stability returned to Europe.[26]

At the heart of the issue lay the German question. Since the end of the war, American statesmen had argued that Europe's economic recovery was dependent on a thriving Germany. The revival of that country would also ease social conditions throughout the continent and thereby check the possible spread of bolshevism. Not surprisingly, Secretary Hughes devoted a good deal of attention to this matter, for, as he noted, "There can be no economic recuperation in Europe unless Germany recuperates." The first step taken by the secretary was to end the state of war that officially existed between the United States and the Central Powers. By so doing, America protected its rights and interests in what once had been Germany's overseas possessions, received payments for the costs of occupation, and terminated an anomalous situation. Hughes shrewdly worked out an arrangement whereby the United States received all the benefits accruing to the powers that signed the Versailles settlement but assumed none of the responsibilities. The Senate ratified the treaty in October 1922.[27]

One of the major problems standing in the way of a German recovery was the reparations issue. As a result of the American government's refusal to underwrite European recovery programs, Germany had to rely on private investors. In the early 1920s, the only groups with surplus capital were in America, but they would not extend loans pending a reparations settlement that did not overburden the German economy. A moder-

26. National Foreign Trade Council, "Report on European Conditions, 1923," pp. 3, 18–20; Thomas B. McAdams, "The Business Outlook for 1922," *Journal of the American Bankers' Association* 14 (January 1922): 495; "The Forty-Eighth Annual Convention," p. 255; Youngman, "America's International Banking and Financial Relations," pp. 401–5; McAdams, "Address of the President," pp. 263–67; Francis H. Sisson, "Must We Slow Down if Europe Does Not Come Back?" *Journal of the American Bankers' Association* 16 (January 1924): 414.

27. Davis to Hughes, March 12, 1921, Container 27, Folder, Hughes, Charles Evans, 1921, Davis Papers; Hughes, *Pathway of Peace*, p. 55; Pusey, *Hughes*, 2:440–42; also see Hoover, address to American Manufacturers' Export Association, October 6, 1921, Records of Secretary of Commerce, Personal File, HH Personal, Economic Situation in U.S., Hoover Papers.

ate settlement, therefore, became essential to gain investor confidence.[28]

Starting in the fall of 1922, Secretary Hughes began suggesting publicly that those nations whose well-being depended on a sound Germany form a commission of financial experts who would adjust reparations on the basis of Germany's capacity to pay. Because the members of the commission would not be governmental representatives, they could devote their attention solely to economic questions. The interested governments, moreover, would be free to accept or reject the recommendations, but they could be confident that the commissioners had acted knowledgeably and without prejudice. Hughes further observed that the nations indebted to the United States government could not accurately calculate their ability to pay until they knew the level of reparations. Thus the secretary came as close as any American statesman would to acknowledging officially a connection between war debts and reparations. Hughes did not receive a positive response to his proposal until the fall of 1923, when the massive German inflation in the wake of the French and Belgian invasion of the Ruhr Valley compelled European leaders to call for a meeting of experts.[29]

The most significant outcome of the meeting was the Dawes Plan. According to the terms of this agreement, the Allied governments based reparations on Germany's capacity to pay. Even though Germany was required to place payments in a special bank, the funds did not have to be transferred into foreign exchange unless the nation had a favorable balance of trade. By recognizing the important role that imported foodstuffs and raw materials played in the German economy, the Dawes committee placed greater emphasis on domestic conditions than on the payment of reparations. The commission of financial experts also

28. This problem is discussed in Davis to Hughes, March 12, 1921, Container 27, Folder, Hughes, Charles Evans, 1921, Davis Papers; Hoover's address to the American Manufacturers' Export Association, October 6, 1921, Records of Secretary of Commerce, Personal File, HH Personal, Economic Situation in U.S., Hoover Papers; press release, "Economic Situation in Europe" (December 1921), ibid.; Hoover to Harding, January 4, 1922, Records of Secretary of Commerce, Official File, Conferences, Genoa, 1922, Hoover Papers.

29. Pusey, *Hughes*, 2:580–81; Hughes, *Pathway of Peace*, pp. 53–58; S. Parker Gilbert, "The Meaning of the 'Dawes Plan'," *Foreign Affairs* 4 (April 1926, special supplement): iii–iv.

established a bank to regulate currency, handle reparations payments, and act as a fiscal agent for the German government. Finally, the commissioners recommended a foreign loan of $200 million to cover a portion of the coming year's reparations and for assistance in currency stabilization.[30]

The important role Hughes played during the negotiations indicated the degree to which the American government found itself involved in international affairs. Not only did the secretary participate in the selection of the United States delegates and then remain in close contact with them, he applied pressure on European officials to ensure their approval of the commission's recommendations. In the summer of 1924, Hughes sailed for London, ostensibly as part of a pilgrimmage to the Old World by American and Canadian lawyers, but primarily for the opportunity to talk with European leaders. Despite assertions that he was acting in an unofficial capacity, the secretary's warning to French, Belgian, and German leaders that they could not anticipate American support for reconstruction programs unless they cooperated with the commission's findings must have made Washington's position very clear.[31] Hughes had to do some persuading at home as well. Discovering that American bankers were slow in understanding the significance of the Dawes Plan, the secretary impressed upon J. P. Morgan and Thomas Lamont that the only alternative to American participation in the proposed loan was continued chaos. Once again, Hughes made his point as J. P. Morgan & Company floated the American portion of the loan.[32]

The Dawes Plan did not establish a final reparations settlement, but it helped restore confidence within Germany. Furthermore, the plan led to smoother political relations on the continent; and along with the withdrawal of the French troops from the Ruhr Valley, it paved the way for the Locarno Pact.[33] To a

30. For a full discussion of the details of the plan, see Harold G. Moulton, *The Reparation Plan*, pp. 1–94; also see Costigliola, "Politics of Financial Stabilization," chap. 2.

31. Betty Glad, *Charles Evans Hughes and the Illusions of Innocence*, pp. 224–29; Pusey, *Hughes*, 2:587–92; Leffler, "Political Isolationism," pp. 423–24.

32. Herbert Feis, *The Diplomacy of the Dollar, 1919–1932*, pp. 40–42; Lewis, *America's Stake in International Investments*, p. 620.

33. Moulton, *Reparation Plan*, pp. 116–18; Gilbert, "Meaning of the 'Dawes Plan'," pp. xi–xii; Glad, *Illusions of Innocence*, p. 230; also see

degree, this pact was the European counterpart to the Washington Conference: it involved a limited number of nations, it covered a specific set of issues, and it helped produce a political framework within which economic recovery could proceed. The Dawes Plan, consequently, was instrumental in aiding the return of European prosperity and stability.

The resumption of reparations payments facilitated the American government's efforts to reach agreements with its debtors. Even though few actions have attracted as much derision as the attempt to obtain war debt payments, the U. S. policy deserves a more careful analysis than it generally receives.[34] From the time of the Wilson administration, Washington refused to bow to foreign and domestic pressures to cancel the debt. In addition to arguing that the debts involved a matter of principle, American officials recognized that these obligations provided them with leverage over the debtors. In June 1921, Secretary of the Treasury Andrew Mellon asked Congress for blanket authority to carry out war debt negotiations. The secretary wanted permission to establish interest rates, determine the repayment period, and receive obligations from a third party in lieu of a direct commitment from the debtor. The last measure would have left open the possibility of the Allied nations using German reparations to pay off the American obligations. Congress did not grant Mellon's request; instead, it created the World War Debt Commission with carefully circumscribed powers. The commission had to ensure that each country repay the debt within twenty-five years, that the minimum interest rate would be 4.25 percent, and that debtor nations pay with their own obligations.

"The Condition of Business," *Journal of the American Bankers' Association* 17 (September 1924): 152–53; Walter Head, "The Beginning of a New Prosperity," ibid. 17 (October 1924): 195–96. At the time of the Locarno negotiations, U.S. officials hinted that European nations could not count on American financial aid unless they arranged a political accord, Leffler, "Political Isolationism," pp. 426–27.

34. For an interesting interpretation of United States-French negotiations, see Benjamin D. Rhodes, "Reassessing 'Uncle Shylock'," *Journal of American History* 55 (March 1969): 787–803; for a more traditional view of American handling of the war debts, see Wilson, *Business and Foreign Policy*, pp. 123–34; for a detailed description of the conflicting pressures on American officials, see Melvyn Leffler, "The Origins of Republican War Debt Policy, 1921–1923," *Journal of American History* 59 (December 1972): 585–601.

All settlements were to be final and not subject to later revision.[35]

As head of the commission, Secretary Mellon was the most important figure during the negotiations; a firm understanding of his approach to the debt question is vital for an appreciation of American policy. Mellon saw the settlements as one segment of the greater problem of restoring European prosperity and, thereby, expanding markets for American products. Since those nations that had not funded their debts were unable to obtain access to American money markets, Mellon was primarily interested in concluding arrangements so that foreign nations could borrow capital for their recovery programs. Though trying to obtain an equitable return, he used the capacity-to-pay principle to ensure that the payments would not place an undue strain on the debtors. Underlying Mellon's position was a conviction that foreign debtors were not worth as much to the American people as were prosperous customers.[36]

Governed by this reasoning, Mellon and his fellow commissioners ignored the congressional limitations, with the exception of the one banning the acceptance of obligations from a third country. By adjusting interest rates and lengthening the repayment period, the Debt Commission eased the burden of the debtors. The commissioners decided on a sixty-two year term and in nine of thirteen cases established 3.3 percent as the rate of interest. In the case of the other four nations, the interest rate ranged from 0.4 percent for Italy to 1.8 percent for Belgium. All agreements included provisions for a postponement of payment of principal in the event of unforeseen difficulties. The commissioners then completed their activities by gaining congressional approval of their actions. By the middle of the decade, most of the debtor nations had come to terms and had begun floating sizable loans in the United States. While the debt payments placed an additional strain on national budgets, it cannot be demonstrated that the load was intolerable or that the debtors had to struggle to meet the obligations.[37] The settlements did

35. Harold G. Moulton and Leo Pasvolsky, *War Debts and World Prosperity*, pp. 74–80; Harold G. Moulton and Leo Pasvolsky, *World War Debt Settlements*, pp. 111–12.

36. Moulton and Pasvolsky, *World War Debt Settlements*, pp. 140–42; see pp. 388–408 for Mellon's statements to Congress.

37. Ibid., pp. 93–97, 225–385; Moulton and Pasvolsky, *War Debts and World Prosperity*, p. 380. Hoover calculated that the yearly European

make American capital available to Europe; and, in conjunction with the Dawes Plan, helped lead to the resumption of a modified gold standard.

As part of its transition to become the world's leading economic power, the United States had gained control of a major portion of the global gold supply. Until Germany returned to the gold standard following the Dawes Plan, moreover, America was the only nation operating on the traditional medium of international exchange. As a result, the United States continued to hold large gold stocks which, during the early 1920s, increased in size. Because this situation created an inflationary threat for the domestic economy and promoted exchange rate instability abroad, American financial leaders were eager to help other nations resume gold payments.[38]

With the return of European stability and the growing number of debt settlements, Benjamin Strong, who dominated the Federal Reserve System during the 1920s by his control of the system's New York bank, seized the opportunity to push for the restoration of the international gold standard. During the second half of 1924, Strong persuaded the Federal Reserve System to pursue an easy money policy in order to counterbalance a mild domestic recession and, more importantly, to keep short-term interest rates in New York below those in London. The latter objective was crucial: it would aid England's resumption by drawing gold to London and it would assist American exporters by stimulating foreign borrowing. In December, Montagu Norman, the Governor of the Bank of England and a close friend of Strong's, arrived in New York for talks with officials of the Federal Reserve System and with Secretary Mellon. Norman and the Americans quickly agreed on the necessity for British resumption and worked out arrangements whereby the Federal Reserve Bank of New York and J. P. Morgan & Co. would extend support to the Bank of England and to the English government in case Great Britain encountered difficulties during the tran-

war debts payments were less than half the expenditures of American tourists in Europe, Hoover to Charles Hebberd, November 24, 1925, Records of Secretary of Commerce, Personal File, HH Personal, Economic Situation in Europe, Hoover Papers.

38. Lester V. Chandler, *Benjamin Strong, Central Banker*, pp. 248, 266; W. Randolph Burgess, ed., *Interpretations of Federal Reserve Policy in the Speeches and Writing of Benjamin Strong*, pp. 278–80.

sition period. With this pledge of assistance and the general improvement in world economic conditions, England returned to gold in April 1925.[39]

After this success, Strong began an extensive campaign to help other nations follow the British example. He usually worked with Norman, in part because Norman, as head of the Financial Committee of the League of Nations, provided a channel of communication to the continent. Strong preferred to operate in informal conferences with individual central bankers because it diminished the likelihood of political factors arising (which usually happened at larger meetings) and avoided the possibility of a hostile reaction by the American public. This method had the further advantage of ensuring that the United States would not find itself outvoted in situations in which it was the only lending power. Before extending assistance to any nation, Strong and Norman insisted that the government balance its budget, fund outstanding governmental obligations, adopt noninflationary policies, insure central bank autonomy from political control, and bring the foreign and domestic values of the currency into line. This strategy gave the two men a powerful influence on the monetary and fiscal policies of nations that desired to stabilize their exchanges but required outside aid to do so. Strong's efforts did not go unrewarded. Within a year of Britain's return to gold, more than thirty countries followed suit; by the time of Strong's death in 1928, most nations were operating on a gold exchange standard.[40] Because this development reduced the chance that depreciating foreign exchanges would hinder American exporters, Strong could explain to the House

39. Chandler, *Strong*, pp. 243–45, 308–11, 321; Elmus R. Wicker, *Federal Reserve Monetary Policy 1917–1933*, pp. 84–90; also see Costigliola, "Politics of Financial Stabilization," chap. 3.

40. Chandler, *Strong*, pp. 262–64, 279–86, 291–92. Although they generally saw eye-to-eye on financial affairs, Strong and Norman had a falling out over the question of aiding Poland and Rumania, and significantly, Strong's view prevailed, ibid., chap. 11; Richard H. Meyer, *Bankers' Diplomacy*, chaps. 4, 5. Costigliola, "Politics of Financial Stabilization," chap. 3. The gold exchange standard differed from a true gold standard in that central banks held large amounts of international reserves in the form of short-term claims on New York or London instead of actually holding bullion. As long as these obligations could be exchanged for gold, the system worked. However, this arrangement gave other central banks the potential to exert powerful influences on the New York and London money markets, see Chandler, *Strong*, pp. 289–90.

Banking and Currency Committee that the financial support which the United States extended to other countries served an important domestic function.[41]

In addition to dealing with questions about naval disarmament, reparations, war debts, and the gold exchange standard, American officials tried to adjust other policies to reflect the nation's new position in the world economy. One of these areas involved the tariff. Despite the great amount of criticism, some of which is justified, heaped on the Republicans' tariff policy, there is more to it than initially meets the eye. Inasmuch as they were traditionally a high tariff party, the Republicans were not likely to lower duty levels; nevertheless, the Fordney-McCumber Tariff of 1922 was high even by Republican standards. There were at least two major reasons for the increase in rates. First, the war had given birth to new industries that sought the same degree of protection other sheltered industries enjoyed. Second, Congress framed the tariff legislation during a period of tremendous uncertainty in international trade due to a worldwide collapse of prices and to sharply depreciated currencies. These conditions caused American industrial and political leaders to fear an onslaught of cheap foreign goods. Even though they responded to this situation by raising rates, some protectionists, like Senator Reed Smoot, saw the measure primarily as an emergency move and anticipated that Congress would lower the duty level once more normal conditions returned to international commerce.[42] As noted earlier, Republican leaders understood that the nation's new creditor status required some adjustment in tariff policy, but they could not agree on the nature of the changes. Hoover's solution was to retain high duties but to finance an export surplus, as well as to assist in European reconstruction and facilitate the payment of foreign debts, by placing the profits of foreign trade in permanent investments abroad. Others thought the United States eventually would have to adjust the tariff so that the country could accept an import surplus. They were uncertain, however, when the nation should make the transition.[43]

41. Burgess, *Interpretations of Federal Reserve Policy*, pp. 276–92.

42. Percy Bidwell, "The New American Tariff," *Foreign Affairs* 9 (October 1930): 15–16; Parrini, *Heir to Empire*, p. 219.

43. Moulton and Pasvolsky, *War Debts and World Prosperity*, pp. 405–

Under the best of circumstances, American policymakers would have faced major obstacles if they had suddenly tried to reverse the trade flow. The strength of the nation's industrial system, the emergence of war-spawned enterprises, the country's remarkable degree of self-sufficiency, the trade patterns which had evolved over a long period of years, and the large foreign demand for U. S. goods all worked against a rapid shift. Undoubtedly, the Republicans could have adjusted the trade balance by following a long-run policy of continued but declining investment coupled with positive efforts to promote imports. The 1920s witnessed the first condition but not the second.[44] Finally, there is reason to suspect that the level of tariffs did not exert the dominant influence on the flow of imports. Because the United States had had high duties in the prewar years, the new ones added little effective protection. Furthermore, some manufacturers, such as the automobile industry, did not receive protection and many others would have dominated the home market even without government help. Most imported goods consisted of raw materials and noncompeting products which came in duty free. In all probability, therefore, the major variable influencing the volume of imports was the strength of the domestic economy.[45]

To guarantee the protection of American enterprise, Congress authorized the president to equalize foreign and domestic costs of production by raising or lowering duties as much as 50 percent. Responding to pressure from the Harding administration, Congress also tried to ensure that U. S. products received equal

6; Department of Commerce, *Eleventh Annual Report of the Secretary of Commerce, 1923*, p. 10; Department of Commerce, *Fourteenth Annual Report of the Secretary of Commerce for the Fiscal Year Ended June 30, 1926*, p. 97.

44. Department of Commerce, *United States in the World Economy*, pp. 147–48; M. E. Falkus, "United States Economic Policy and the 'Dollar Gap' of the 1920's," *Economic History Review* 29 (November 1971): 599–605.

45. Department of Commerce, *United States in the World Economy*, pp. 39–41, 54, 199–200; Soule, *Prosperity Decade From War to Depression*, p. 267; Department of Commerce, *Tenth Annual Report of the Secretary of Commerce, 1922*, p. 20; Herbert Hoover, *The Memoirs of Herbert Hoover*, 2:29; Falkus, "United States Economic Policy," pp. 605–6, 618, 622–23; for a critique of Falkus, see Sean Glynn and Allan L. Lougheed, "A Comment on United States Economic Policy and the 'Dollar Gap' of the 1920's," *Economic History Review* 26 (November 1973): 692–94.

treatment in foreign markets. Section 317 of the Fordney-Mc-Cumber bill granted the president power to raise duties up to 50 percent on imports from countries discriminating against American goods.[46] This section provided the means for a fundamental change in United States foreign trade policy. At the urging of William S. Culbertson, acting chairman of the Tariff Commission, Secretary Hughes switched from the conditional to the unconditional most-favored-nation policy. America now unconditionally would extend the trade concessions which it negotiated with one nation to all countries that did not discriminate against United States trade. Conversely, America would receive similar treatment from the nations with whom it had treaties.[47]

Culbertson justified this departure by arguing that the vast increase in the nation's foreign trade and investment demanded a more aggressive policy. Hughes agreed that the "enlarged productive capacity developed during the World War has increased the need for assured equality of treatment of American commerce in foreign markets." Convinced that United States businessmen could hold their own throughout the world if they had equal opportunity, the secretary incorporated this principle in a new trade agreement with Germany which served as a model for the future.[48] Overall, the Republican approach to setting tariffs was directed toward attaining equal treatment, not in bargaining for reductions. Another significant feature of the

46. Frank W. Tausigg, *The Tariff History of the United States*, p. 479; Frank W. Tausigg, "The Tariff Controversy with France," *Foreign Affairs* 6 (January 1928): 181, 186; Chauncey Depew Snow, "What Will that New Tariff Do?" *Nation's Business* 10 (November 1922): 19.

47. Culbertson to Hughes, December 14, 1922, Department of State, *Foreign Relations*, 1923 1:121–26. Culbertson's role in the formulation of the tariff policy is described by Richard J. Snyder, "William Culbertson and the Formation of Modern American Commercial Policy, 1917–1925," *Kansas Historical Quarterly* (Winter 1929): 396–410. For a general discussion of the tariff see, Wilson, *Business and Foreign Policy*, pp. 68–86; Parrini, *Heir to Empire*, chap. 8.

48. Culbertson to Hughes, December 14, 1922, *Foreign Relations*, 1923, 1:121–26; Hughes to American Diplomatic Officers, August 18, 1923, ibid., pp. 131–33; Glad, *Illusions of Innocence*, pp. 315, 317; Pusey, *Hughes*, 2:570; Chamber of Commerce of the State of New York, *Bulletin of the Chamber of Commerce of the State of New York* 16 (April 1925, supplement): 6.

Republican policy was that it represented a trend toward removing tariff-making powers from Congress.[49] During the following decade, the Roosevelt administration tried to expand foreign commerce by combining a commitment to reduce tariff levels with these new principles.

The Republicans' tariff policy was consistent with their broader objective of promoting overseas trade and investment. Since he believed international problems were primarily economic in nature, Secretary Hughes assumed that the principal task of modern diplomacy was one of keeping open the highways of commerce.[50] The secretary, moreover, took it for granted that the nation's welfare was intimately tied up with foreign events. "Ability on our part to sell our surplus production, and thus to maintain a high degree of productive activity," he observed, "is the key to our prosperity"; hence, the expansion of exports was a matter of concern "primarily to our wage earners, who depend upon opportunities for employment, and secondarily to those engaged in the multitude of transactions incident to commercial exchanges."[51] To assist America's overseas economic expansion, Hughes moved along two fronts. He vigorously defended the rights and interests of American foreign enterprise by insisting that other nations fulfill their agreements. For a state to receive a place within the family of nations, it would have to enforce valid contracts. The confiscatory policies of the Soviet Union particularly concerned Hughes, since the spread of this form of economic nationalism would endanger the far-flung interests of the United States. The secretary also tried to pry open new areas for penetration by American enterprise. His principal method of achieving this objective was to apply the open door policy to the world at large. During his years in the State Department,

49. Parrini, *Heir to Empire*, pp. 227–41; Warren Adams Brown, Jr., *The United States and the Restoration of World Trade*, pp. 15–16; Hoover was a leading advocate of this movement, see Hoover, *Memoirs*, 2:292–93.

50. Hughes, *Pathway of Peace*, p. 257; Chamber of Commerce of the State of New York, *Bulletin of the Chamber of Commerce of the State of New York* 16 (April 1925, supplement): 5; Robert Carlyle Poole, "Charles Evans Hughes and the Protection of American Business Interests Abroad," (M.A. thesis, Univ. of Chicago, 1952), p. 4.

51. Charles Evans Hughes, *Our Relations to the Nations of the Western Hemisphere*, p. 54.

Hughes utilized this doctrine to justify American concern with the mandated islands of the Pacific, the oil-producing areas in the Near East, and the question of foreign concessions in Russia.[52]

The Department of Commerce acted in a manner that complemented State Department policies. Hoover reorganized the foreign service organs of his department to make them of more practical value to industry. In particular, Hoover and Julius Klein restructured the Bureau of Foreign and Domestic Commerce so that it could more effectively facilitate the expansion of trade. Under the direction of Klein, the bureau's foreign offices assisted exporters by seeking new markets, establishing credit ratings, and helping untangle local laws and customs.[53]

Hoover and Klein devoted a good deal of attention to the growing international cartel movement. Even though most of these arrangements grew out of attempts by European nations to rationalize their markets, they had anti-American undertones which caused Commerce Department officials to view them with some concern.[54] Members of the department primarily opposed cartels that restricted the sale of raw materials needed by American industry. Limitations on these products would raise manufacturing costs to the point where United States goods would no longer be competitive in foreign markets. Because pooling arrangements often led to governmental control of production and

52. Hughes, *Pathway of Peace*, pp. 53, 157–58, 254–55; Pusey, *Hughes*, 2:424–25, 445–49, 571–73; Poole, "Hughes and the Protection of American Interests," pp. 41, 56, as well as chaps. 4–8. Poole also notes that the open door would aid those American interests who were late in entering the race for overseas markets and sources of raw materials. It was not, therefore, merely a moral or legal principle, pp. 104–5; for a somewhat different view, see Wilson, *Business and Foreign Policy*, chap. 7.

53. Hoover, address before the annual convention of the Chamber of Commerce of the United States, May 16, 1922, Public Statements, 10, No. 228, Hoover Papers; Hoover, *Memoirs*, 2:79; Joseph Brandes, *Herbert Hoover and Economic Diplomacy*, pp. 4–10; Department of Commerce, *Tenth Annual Report, 1932*, pp. 2–5, 96–98; for a good example of Klein's views on American overseas expansion, see Klein, *Frontiers of Trade*, passim.

54. Julius Klein, "International Cartels," *Foreign Affairs* 6 (April 1928): 448; at the Paris Economic Conference in 1916, the Allies discussed policies which included a cartel movement that Washington interpreted as being directed against American interests, see Parrini, *Heir to Empire*, pp. 15–22, 37.

prices, Hoover feared that they would produce diplomatic pressures. To combat this trend, the secretary organized buying pools to steer purchasers away from government-dominated cartels and encouraged the development of new sources of raw materials. In addition, he tried to persuade the offending governments to halt their practices.[55]

American foreign trade principles received a limited endorsement from representatives attending two international economic conferences held at Geneva under the auspices of the League of Nations during the spring and fall of 1927. At the spring meeting, the delegates agreed that all nations should base their trade policies on the principles of equality of opportunity and unconditional most-favored-nation treatment. Furthermore, they accepted the American position that a high level of import duties did not disrupt trade as much as did frequent and abrupt alterations in rates. The United States gained additional support for its policies when the representatives accepted a strong statement condemning the creation of barriers on the export of raw materials. Although the first conference went on record against direct and indirect state subsidies, the members could not reach a common position on cartels. The American delegation, nevertheless, actively opposed pooling arrangements that entailed the participation of governmental bodies. The two conferences were the high water mark of progress toward removing discriminatory trade barriers during the interwar years, and they even produced a leveling off of tariff increases. U. S. interests fared particularly well since they stood to benefit from the abolition of a large number of restrictions but did not lose their own protective system.[56]

55. Klein, *Frontiers of Trade*, pp. 96–115; Hoover, *Memoirs*, 2:81–84; Brandes, *Hoover and Economic Diplomacy*, sec. 2; Julius Klein, "The Problem of Our Raw Materials Supplies," *Official Report of the Thirteenth National Foreign Trade Convention*, pp. 28–33.

56. Brown, *United States and Restoration of World Trade*, pp. 30–32, 37; Klein, *Frontiers of Trade*, pp. 79–80; Henry M. Robinson, "Some Lessons of the Economic Conference," *Foreign Affairs* 6 (October 1927): 14–21; Klein to Hoover, May 19, 1927, Records of Secretary of Commerce, Official File, Conferences, Economic, Geneva, 1927, Hoover Papers; Report of the Chairman of American Delegation to the International Economic Conference, June 10, 1927, *Foreign Relations, 1927*, 1:240–46; Kellogg to Wilson, October 17, 1927, ibid., pp. 264–66; Wilson to Kellogg, November 22, 1927, ibid., pp. 282–85.

During the 1920s, therefore, administration leaders went to considerable lengths to safeguard the nation's economic stake abroad. They maintained that the government should support American economic groups by ensuring their fair and equal treatment from other nations and by providing information on new opportunities. Nevertheless, Washington officials did believe there were limits beyond which they could not go: the government should not make contracts, use pressure to force concessions, or intervene in favor of one United States interest against another.[57] From time to time, business groups wanted the State Department to furnish them with the same degree of political backing which the British and French governments gave their nationals. Department officers generally refused to bend to this pressure, fearing that such steps would lead the American government to deep entanglement in the affairs of other nations. In addition, they argued that knowledge of Washington's unwillingness to participate in private business deals made foreigners more receptive to American enterprise. Secretary Hughes thought businessmen became so intent on their own immediate interests that they failed to see the adverse, long-run implications of their requests. Ironically, government leaders often exhibited more confidence in the ability of American enterprise to compete abroad than did industrial and financial spokesmen.[58]

In spite of its intentions, however, the State Department experienced difficulty remaining aloof from business transactions that involved sensitive interests.[59] It was one of the major dilem-

57. Hoover, address to the annual convention of the Chamber of Commerce of the United States, May 16, 1922, Public Statements, 10, No. 228, Hoover Papers; Department of Commerce, *Fourteenth Annual Report, 1926*, p. 29; Hughes, *Our Relations to Nations of the Western Hemisphere*, pp. 68–69; Chamber of Commerce of the State of New York, *Bulletin of the Chamber of Commerce of the State of New York* 16 (April 1925, supplement): 6–7. Hughes to Coolidge, November 8, 1923, *Foreign Relations, 1923* 2:717–18; William R. Castle, Jr. "The Department of State and American Enterprise Abroad," *Official Report of the Fifteenth National Foreign Trade Convention*, pp. 189–96.

58. Hughes to Coolidge, November 8, 1923, *Foreign Relations, 1923*, 2:717–18; an example of the cautious nature of American businessmen in the Near East can be seen in Poole, "Hughes and the Protection of American Interests," chap. 6.

59. As Poole points out, it required only a slight anxiety over oil to make official American policy identical to that of Standard Oil, Poole,

mas confronting American policymakers in this and later periods. Even though they did not wish to become embroiled in the affairs of other nations, department officials found they would have to act in order to safeguard interests that either they or others had defined as essential to the nation's welfare.

An important area of government-business relations which caused such a controversy was the control of foreign loans. By the summer of 1921, the Harding administration had concluded that the government would have to establish guidelines for overseas investment. In June, New York banking houses assured the State Department that they would inform Washington about negotiations for loans to other governments. But because some bankers did not abide by the agreement, the following spring, the administration required all bankers to consult with the government before completing their transactions. The government's purpose was neither to pass on the merits of the loans nor to assume responsibility for them but to see that the proposals did not conflict with national foreign policy objectives.[60]

The loan policy came under criticism from a number of quarters. Exporters were in general agreement that foreign investments were essential for the expansion of overseas commerce. Some foreign traders appear to have agreed with Hoover that a policy of sustained investment would enable the United States to have an export surplus, even though the nation was a world creditor and had a protective tariff. What concerned them about the administration's loan policy was the absence of any guarantee that foreign borrowers would spend the money in the United States. In many European nations, bankers, government officials, and manufacturers cooperated closely together to see that a percentage of the loans was used to purchase products from the lending country. During the 1920s, moreover, some European governments began providing financial aid to spur foreign commerce. American exporters were eager to have investment bankers provide for the expenditure of a portion of a loan in the United States. At one point, the National Foreign Trade Council

---

"Hughes and the Protection of American Interests," p. 128; also see Wilson, *Business and Foreign Policy*, pp. 192–99.

60. Young to Dearing, February 1, 1922, *Foreign Relations, 1922*, 1: 556–57; press release, March 3, 1922, ibid., pp. 557–58; Feis, *Diplomacy of the Dollar*, pp. 7–11.

urged the government to insist that foreign loan recipients spend 20 percent of the funds received on American products.[61]

American financial interests, however, objected to the administration's policy for reasons diametrically opposed to the exporters': the bankers did not want any controls whatsoever. Benjamin Strong gave the most forceful presentation of this position. As long as the dollar was at a premium, there was no need to earmark loans because borrowers would not find it profitable to take gold out of the country; the proceeds of loans would eventually be used to repay debts and to purchase goods. More significantly, Strong believed that New York had an opportunity to become the banking capital of the world. Loan restrictions might cause foreign borrowers to turn to London, which would both jeopardize this chance and harm export interests by reducing the volume of dollars abroad. John Foster Dulles, an expert on international financial affairs, echoed Strong's claims that loan controls would benefit London at the expense of New York.[62]

Secretary Hughes himself had mixed feelings about the poli-

---

61. Grosvenor Jones, "Comments of Mr. Hoover's Suggestion in Connection with Foreign Loans," n.d., Records of Secretary of Commerce, Official File, Foreign Loans, Miscellaneous, 1921–1922, Hoover Papers; Sameit to Hoover, July 26, 1922, Records of Secretary of Commerce, Official File, National Foreign Trade Council, Hoover Papers; Eugene P. Thomas, "The Foreign Trade Outlook," *Official Report of the Fifteenth National Foreign Trade Convention*, pp. 9–15; James A. Farrell, "An American Foreign Trade Policy," *Official Report of the Ninth National Foreign Trade Convention*, p. 576; James A. Farrell, "The Foreign Trade Outlook," *Official Report of the Twelfth National Foreign Trade Convention*, p. 17; "Report on American Foreign Trade Policy," *Official Report of the Eleventh National Foreign Trade Convention* (New York, 1924), pp. 186–87; Franklin Remington, "Foreign Loans a Trade Builder," ibid., pp. 170–76; the "Final Declaration" contains a typical statement on the need for bankers to be cognizant of exporters' interests, ibid., p. viii; Paul J. Kruesi, "Building Foreign Trade Through Foreign Loans," *Official Report of the Thirteenth National Foreign Trade Convention*, pp. 415–20.

62. Strong to Hughes, a copy sent to Hoover, April 20, 1922, Records of Secretary of Commerce, Official File, Foreign Loans, Miscellaneous, 1921–1922, Hoover Papers; John Foster Dulles, "Our Foreign Loan Policy," *Foreign Affairs* 5 (October 1926): 37–44; also see Henry M. Robinson, "American Banking and World Rehabilitation," *Official Report of the Twelfth National Foreign Trade Convention*, p. 153; J. T. Holdsworth, "A Foreign Loan Policy that will Enable Our Factories to get to Work," *Official Report of the Ninth National Foreign Trade Convention*, pp. 11–15.

cy. His major concern was that the screening process might result in the government implicitly assuming a degree of responsibility for the investments. If this situation did arise, Hughes realized that the door would be opened for diplomatic difficulties in the event of a default.[63] Other individuals attacked the concept of loan controls because they feared that the process delegated too much authority to the executive branch and that the policy would lead to American intervention in weaker nations to force repayment of the debt.[64]

With the assistance of Grosvenor Jones, head of the Finance Division of the Bureau of Foreign and Domestic Commerce, Herbert Hoover emerged as the leading defender of the administration's position. Hoover favored the supervision of loans for four principal reasons. First, by permitting only sound investments, the government would not have to intervene to recover bad debts. Second, because the United States was the last source of surplus capital, Washington had to be certain that the nation's funds did not go for nonproductive purposes, such as covering unbalanced budgets or building up armed forces. Third, the administration had a moral responsibility to inform American citizens of the financial condition of potential borrowers. Finally, the secretary argued that in their search for foreign investments, bankers were neglecting their responsibility to the domestic economy. By raising the last point, Hoover challenged the widely held belief that foreign loans aided the economy by fostering exports. "It is but partially true to say that goods exported as a result of foreign credits are an addition to our productivity and employment," Hoover insisted. "They may quite well displace goods that are needed in our domestic development." While not favoring the proposal of the National Foreign Trade Council, the secretary urged bankers to write into their loan contracts a clause giving U. S. interests an equal opportunity to compete for projects.[65]

63. Feis, *Diplomacy of the Dollar*, pp. 9–10; Wilson, *Business and Foreign Policy*, pp. 115–17; also see Herbert Feis, "The Export of American Capital," *Foreign Affairs* 3 (July 1933): 685.

64. Carter Glass, "Governmental Supervision of Foreign Loans," *Proceedings of Academy of Political Science* 12 (January 1928): 842–49; Lewis S. Gannet, "Foreign Investment and Public Policy," ibid., pp. 861–64.

65. For a lengthy discussion of these points, see Hoover to Hughes,

Those who opposed controls eventually triumphed: the government limited its review to an assessment of the effect a loan would have on foreign relations. Hoover fought a rearguard action by urging investors to extend assistance only for those projects that would produce additional wealth. His efforts were largely ineffective, and the quality of foreign loans floated in the American market deteriorated sharply throughout the decade. Given the role which foreign investment played in international economic relations, the failure to insist that financial groups limit their support to productive purposes added an unnecessary element of instability to world conditions.[66]

While many criticized the government's handling of the foreign loan issue, few found fault with the steps taken by the Federal Reserve System to promote overseas economic expansion. Benjamin Strong and other Federal Reserve officials often adjusted the nation's monetary policy because of conditions abroad. In 1924 and again in 1927, they followed an easy money policy primarily to ensure that interest rates in New York remained below those in London. By so doing, they hoped to keep New York as the world's leading money market and to provide the foreign loans needed for an expansion of exports. In 1924 and 1927, Americans were fortunate that conditions at home and overseas called for a reduction of interest rates; in later years, they were not equally fortunate.[67]

Throughout the postwar decade, therefore, United States policymakers tried various means to create a stable world order. At the base of their approach lay the assumption that an expanding American economy could achieve this objective without causing the nation to become entangled in the affairs of other countries. These years witnessed a tremendous outpour-

---

April 29, 1922, Records of Secretary of Commerce, Official File, Foreign Loans, Miscellaneous, 1921–1922, Hoover Papers.

66. Hoover, *Memoirs*, 2:88–90; Department of Commerce, *United States in the World Economy*, pp. 162, 168; Parrini, *Heir to Empire*, chap. 7, especially pp. 209–11; Wilson, *Business and Foreign Policy*, p. 122; Lewis, *America's Stake in International Investments*, pp. 379–82.

67. Elmus R. Wicker, "Federal Reserve Monetary Policy, 1923–33," *Journal of Political Economy* 73 (August 1965): 326–27, 329–37; Wicker, *Federal Reserve Monetary Policy*, pp. 77–102, chap. 8. Wicker argues that Federal Reserve officials made maintenance of the gold standard the predominant test for the expansion of credit.

ing of dollars that more than doubled the size of the United States foreign debt. Following the war, conditions were ripe for a vast growth of overseas investment: western European nations lacked the funds to support their development programs and when they looked to America, they encountered an investing public with surplus capital that had recently become accustomed to participating in international loans. With the exception of 1923, the net amount of foreign securities issued in the United States increased each year from 1919 to 1927. By 1929, American investors held portfolio investments of nearly $7.84 billion, of which a significant amount represented the obligations of foreign governments. In addition, United States direct investments grew from $3.88 billion in 1919 to $7.553 billion in 1929. At the end of the decade, American long-term overseas investment totaled $15.39 billion with the largest amount going to Latin America, followed by Europe and Canada.[68]

Besides acquiring a major role in long-term financing, the United States became a center for short-term transactions. In part, this reflected the success of Benjamin Strong's efforts to have American banks provide the commercial paper needed by U. S. exporters. Perhaps of greater significance was the fact that the nation's large gold stock made foreigners, particularly bankers, willing to hold short-term dollar balances as a portion of their total assets. This trend clearly indicated New York's ability to rival London as the banking capital of the world. When the depression began, the United States had increased its net creditor position on both the long- and short-term accounts to $8.8 billion.[69]

America's overseas commerce likewise grew significantly. The value of merchandise foreign trade, which did not include gold and silver shipments and reexports, grew from $7.9 billion in 1923 to $9.1 billion in 1926; after a brief slump in 1927, its value again rose to $9.6 billion in 1929. By the end of fiscal 1923, the United States was the world's foremost exporter and the second leading importer. This growth not only increased America's in-

68. Department of Commerce, *United States in the World Economy*, p. 91; Lewis, *America's Stake in International Investments*, pp. 605–6, Tables I and III; Feis, "The Export of American Capital," p. 673.
69. Department of Commerce, *United States in the World Economy*, pp. 113–14, 122, 151–52.

fluence in international relations, it also heightened the nation's dependence on events occurring beyond its borders.[70]

Thus, the expansion of the American economy committed the country to involvement in world affairs. Commerce Department figures illuminate this point: America's national income in 1929 was as great as that of the next twenty-three countries. Because of its vastness, the United States economy had a great impact on other nations; by the period from 1922 to 1924, America supplied 18 percent of the total foreign country imports (up from 12.4 percent in the years 1911 to 1913) and was the leading importer of primary products. In 1927/28, Americans consumed 39 percent of the nine principal raw materials and foodstuff items produced throughout the world. A report issued by the Commerce Department during the Second World War adequately summed up the U. S. position during the interwar period: "The impact of domestic economic developments on the rest of the world and the repercussions of its [America's] policies in the international sphere can scarcely be overrated."[71]

The changing composition of the nation's foreign trade was also extremely important. The postwar decade witnessed the culmination of an earlier trend in which the export of finished and semifinished manufactures grew at a faster rate than did the export of crude materials and foodstuffs.[72] While expecting the continuation of a heavy flow of manufactured products to Europe, Americans assumed that the areas of the world which lacked manufacturing capabilities would provide the best markets for the future.

By 1926, Commerce Department officials reported that notwithstanding a 62 percent increase over prewar figures in the value of exports to Europe, the value of items going to non-European areas had risen by 197 percent. In addition, the expansion of trade with regions outside Europe reflected the

70. The total value of foreign trade, including gold and silver shipments and reexports, was (in billions of dollars): 1923, $8.5; 1924, $8.8; 1925, $9.7; 1926, $9.7; 1927, $9.6; 1928, $10.1; 1929, $10.2, Bureau of the Census, *Historical Statistics of the United States*, p. 244; Department of Commerce, *Eleventh Annual Report*, 1923, p. 8.

71. Department of Commerce, *United States in the World Economy*, pp. 29, 31, 55.

72. Department of Commerce, *Foreign Commerce and Navigation*, 1924, p. LX.

growth of manufactures and semimanufactures. By 1928, finished and partially finished manufactured goods made up 59.1 percent of the country's exports with roughly 62 percent of these going to non-European nations. This pattern persisted throughout the decade with the result that in fiscal 1929, exports to Europe grew only 3 percent while those to the rest of the world increased 16.5 percent. Indicative of this change was the replacement of the United Kingdom by Canada as the leading foreign market for American products.[73] William F. Whiting, the new secretary of commerce, pulled together these various threads when he noted in February 1929 that the most conspicuous trend in the export trade had been "the swift expansion in sales of manufactured goods, and consequently, from the geographic standpoint, in shipments to countries which produce chiefly foodstuffs and raw materials and which are as yet but little developed in factory industry." As the secretary implied, the non-European areas could provide items needed by American industry and the consuming public at large.[74]

Accordingly, Americans directed a good deal of attention toward Latin America. The postwar years provided U. S. interests with an opportunity to expand their presence in the Western Hemisphere. While British investors retained their dominant position, United States long-term investments jumped from $1.649 billion in 1914 to $5.429 billion in 1929. Furthermore, America became the leading trader in Latin America, which absorbed nearly one-fifth of the nation's exports. In 1928, approximately 28 percent of the metals, machinery, manufactures, and vehicles exported from the United States went to nations in the Western Hemisphere. During the same year, the

73. Department of Commerce, *Fourteenth Annual Report, 1926*, pp. 32–33, see chart p. 32; Department of Commerce, *Foreign Commerce and Navigation of the United States for the Calendar Year of 1926*, 1:LXX; Department of Commerce, *Foreign Commerce and Navigation of the United States for the Calendar Year of 1928*, p. xxiii; Department of Commerce, *Seventeenth Annual Report of the Secretary of Commerce for the Fiscal Year Ended June 30, 1929*, p. xxv; Department of Commerce, *Sixteenth Annual Report of the Secretary of Commerce for the Fiscal Year Ended June 30, 1928*, p. xx.

74. Quoted by *New York Times*, February 13, 1929, p. 34; Department of Commerce, *Fifteenth Annual Report of the Secretary of Commerce for the Fiscal Year Ended June 30, 1927*, pp. xxii–xxiii; Grosvenor M. Jones, "Exporting American Capital," *Bankers Magazine* 106 (June 1923): 1059.

United States consumed over one-third of Latin America's exports. When the decade drew to a close, the volume of Latin America's commerce with the United States exceeded the combined total of its trade with Great Britain, Germany, and France.[75]

The Far East provided another region of interest to Americans even though the situation was complicated by the uncertainties accompanying the Chinese revolution. When the revolution moderated in 1928, United States exports to China rose by 50 percent compared to a 12 percent increase in exports to all of Asia. Nonetheless Japan remained the nation's leading Far Eastern market by purchasing $250 million worth of American goods, nearly twice the $130 million bought by the Chinese. While considerable capital did flow into Japan, the uncertain conditions in China coupled with the attractiveness of opportunities in Latin America and Europe meant that the total American investment in Asia remained low. Although the future of the Far East was cloudy, Julius Klein was sufficiently optimistic to conclude in 1928 that William Seward's earlier prediction that the richest trade areas in the world would eventually lie on the other side of the Pacific was on the verge of coming true.[76]

Considering the stake of the United States in the world economy, American leaders were substantially correct in insisting that the regions of the world had become interdependent. The American desire to create a world in which markets and raw materials were available to all nations on an equal basis made sense because this policy benefited those nations powerful enough to compete successfully with others. The open door principle also indirectly aided the United States by permitting

75. Lewis, *America's Stake in International Investments*, p. 606, Table III; "Record Year for U.S. Exports," *Bankers Magazine* 117 (December 1928): 1017; "United States and Latin America in Ever-Increasing Relations," ibid., p. 1068; "Our Commerce with Latin America," ibid. 118 (June 1929): 989, 991–93; Department of Commerce, *Foreign Commerce and Navigation, 1928*, p. lxiv.

76. The National Foreign Trade Council compiled the statistics, *New York Times*, January 1, 1929, p. 34; "New Year's Foreign Trade Report Shows Big Export Balance for United States," *Bankers Magazine* 118 (February 1929): 245; Lewis, *America's Stake in International Investments*, p. 627; O. K. Davis, "The Relation of Foreign Investment to the Flow of World Trade," *Proceedings of the Academy of Political Science* 12 (January 1928): 814–15; Klein, *Frontiers of Trade*, p. 293.

the emergence of triangular trade patterns. American leaders noted that while this country had an unfavorable balance of trade with Latin America, Latin American nations could use the surplus exchange to buy European goods, in turn permitting those countries to meet their unfavorable balance of trade with the United States. Because bilateral trade patterns and discriminatory trade arrangements endangered the free flow of commerce, American policymakers consistently opposed attempts by other nations to adopt those practices. Summing up a commonly held view, Julius Klein argued that the world's recovery, "politically as well as economically," depended on the restoration of trade and "the elimination of the old imperialistic trappings of politico-economic exploitations."[77]

In many ways, the United States did give the appearance by 1928 of entering a new era of prosperity, for not only were exports and foreign investments growing rapidly but the nation's industrial output had reached unprecedented heights. Nonetheless, a close analysis reveals that the New Era faced contradictions on both the international and national levels. Looking first at internal problems, American farmers suffered from high costs of production, heavy debt burdens, relatively low prices, and chronic overproduction. As the farmers' share of the nation's foreign commerce declined, Commerce Department officials assured them that they would profit from an expansion of manufactured exports by having larger domestic markets. Essentially, what the farming community heard was that its interests could be served best through the continued growth of the industrial sector. Although this argument was not necessarily incorrect nor did United States officials make it in bad faith, the failure of farm prices to regain their earlier levels and the continued decline of agriculture's share of the national income forced farm leaders to consider other means of achieving prosperity. Under the direction of George N. Peek and Hugh S. Johnson, farmers looked to the federal government for assistance. The two men devised a scheme whereby the government would protect domestic price levels by buying surplus crops and dumping them on the world market. During the late 1920s, Congress twice passed legislation, the so-called McNary-Haugen bill, incorpo-

77. Klein, *Frontiers of Trade*, p. 40, also see pp. 41–42, 58, 74–75, 146–47.

rating these principles, but President Calvin Coolidge vetoed the measure each time. Farm groups, therefore, could not seem to find a comfortable position within the New Era.[78]

Farmers were not the only ones in this predicament, however, as the industrial sector of the economy also contained several weaknesses. Even during the time of greatest prosperity, industry utilized existing plant and equipment at only 80 percent of capacity. The bituminous coal mining, textile, and shoe industries all experienced problems. Gains in productivity, moreover, were not matched by corresponding wage increases and price reductions. According to one estimate, as many as 85 percent of all Americans lived in families whose annual incomes were less than that required to maintain the "fair" level established by social measures. Although the incomes of the gainfully employed did increase, the per-man-hour index of productivity suggested that the increases should have been greater.[79] An analysis of the period from 1920 to 1929 undertaken by *Fortune* magazine revealed that output per-man-hour rose by 55 percent but hourly wage rates increased a mere 2 percent. To compound difficulties, income became concentrated in the upper levels with the top 1 percent of the population accounting for 12 percent of the disposable personal income (D.P.I.) in 1920 and 18 percent in 1929, while the top 5 percent of the population held 24 percent of the D.P.I. in 1920 and 33.5 percent in 1928. At the same time, income from profits, interest, and rent rose 45 percent while that from wages and salaries increased only 13 percent. If consumer prices had dropped enough to compensate for the discrepancy between the gains in productivity and the more slowly rising wages and salaries, real wages might have been sufficient to maintain domestic demand. But this did not occur as prices rose from 1922 to 1926 and fell only 3 percent from

78. Gilbert Fite, "The Farmers' Dilemma, 1919–1929," in *Change and Continuity in Twentieth Century America: The 1920's*, ed. John Braeman, Robert Bremner, and David Brody, pp. 67–96; Department of Commerce, *Fourteenth Annual Report, 1926*, p. 31; William E. Leuchtenburg, *The Perils of Prosperity, 1914–32*, pp. 100–103.

79. Edwin G. Norse, et al., *America's Capacity to Produce*, pp. 296–307, 425, 429–30; Rexford G. Tugwell, "The Paradox of Peace," *New Republic* 54 (April 18, 1928): 264; Rexford G. Tugwell, "Wage-Pressure and Efficiency," ibid. 55 (July 11, 1928): 197; Rexford G. Tugwell, "Hunger, Cold and Candidates," ibid. 54 (May 2, 1928): 324; Rexford G. Tugwell, "America's Wartime Socialism," *Nation* 124 (April 6, 1927): 366.

1926 to 1929. These dislocations in combination with depressed farm conditions were sufficient in themselves to cause the economy to experience a readjustment.[80]

Unfortunately, the economy was plagued by additional problems. The Federal Reserve's easy money policy of 1927, which it had followed primarily for international reasons, created a stockmarket boom that had an adverse internal effect and also attracted funds which had previously gone abroad. Beginning with the third quarter of 1928, the volume of long-term foreign portfolio investment declined by nearly 58 percent from the corresponding quarter in 1927. Although the amount of investment did increase in the fourth quarter of 1928, it remained 53 percent below the figure for the comparable quarter in 1927. After this point, the volume of foreign loans declined steadily. Inasmuch as the international economic structure was largely dependent on a constant supply of American dollars, the reduction of loans produced severe strains in the world economy. A temporary increase in the amount of United States direct investments and short-term credits eased these strains for a limited period. When the flow of these funds declined and when the American economy itself faltered, the result was that the economies of other nations were subjected to terrific pressures.[81]

The stresses emanating from the United States were complemented by difficulties in other countries. Starting in 1927, Australia and the Dutch East Indies underwent business downturns; and over the next year and a half, Germany, Finland, Brazil, Poland, Canada, and Argentina all slid into recessions. The dangerous state of overindebtedness by many borrowing nations, especially Germany and some Latin American countries, added to these problems, incidentally demonstrating the wisdom of Hoover's conviction that guidelines on foreign loans were needed. The uncertain financial atmosphere also kept American investors from sending additional funds overseas.[82]

80. Gilbert Burck and Charles Silberman, "What Caused the Great Depression," *Fortune*, February 1955, pp. 204, 206, and see pp. 96–97.

81. Paul D. Dickens, "Foreign Capital Issues Publicly Offered in the United States," *Commerce Reports* (January 27, 1930), p. 217; Department of Commerce, *United States in the World Economy*, pp. 98, 102–3, 161; Lewis, *America's Stake in International Investments*, p. 388.

82. Lewis, *America's Stake in International Investments*, pp. 376–88; Department of Commerce, *United States in the World Economy*, p. 162.

One of the major burdens facing the world economy was Europe's incomplete recovery from the effects of the war. As had been the case in the past, European troubles centered on the German question. Even though they agreed that a healthy Germany was important for their own well-being, Western European nations were not eager for the reappearance of German political and economic strength. These nations, as well as the United States, faced a dilemma: should they sponsor a prosperous Germany which could trade with them but would be highly competitive, or should they be satisfied with a weaker Germany which would not challenge them but which could produce a political and economic vacuum in central Europe.[83] The decision was not an easy one particularly since the countries of western Europe had already lost many of their traditional markets to American exporters. The multilateral trade patterns favored by Washington officials primarily benefited United States interests. "America has not left room for the triangular trade of Europe," commented the editor of the *Economist* "but has naturally endeavored with considerable success to fill these markets herself."[84] Consequently, European leaders did not relish the prospect of encountering additional competition in international markets.

By the fall of 1929, the world economy was sufficiently unstable that the shock waves associated with the collapse of the bull market on Wall Street and the ensuing slowdown in American business activity had global ramifications. The vastly diminished flow of dollars abroad strained already overburdened economies and resulted in a worldwide depression of unprecedented magnitude and duration.[85] The severity of the crisis vividly revealed the extent to which the welfare of all nations was intertwined and demonstrated the critical role played by the United States in the international economy. Since the war, American officials had assumed they could formulate a policy that would maximize opportunities for the expansion of private

83. Walter T. Laydon, "Europe's Future Role in World Trade," *Proceedings of the Academy of Political Science* 12 (January 1928): 947–50; Moulton, *The Reparation Plan*, pp. 107–10; Moulton and Pasvolsky, *War Debts and World Prosperity*, pp. 390–91.

84. Laydon, "Europe's Future in World Trade," pp. 958–60.

85. Department of Commerce, *United States in the World Economy*, pp. 12, 173–75.

enterprise yet minimize governmental involvement in foreign affairs and in the free enterprise system itself. By exposing the shortcomings of this logic, the depression caused United States leaders to review their original premises, and eventually led them to the conclusion that Washington would have to become more assertive in stimulating economic growth at home and overseas.

2

Collapse of the New Era
The Great Depression

The collapse of Wall Street in the fall of 1929 plunged the world economy into a prolonged descent lasting over three years in many areas of the world. Although a complex combination of circumstances produced the decline, the United States exerted a major depressing influence. The cessation of foreign investments and shrinking of imports caused by the slowdown of the American economy meant that the amount of dollars supplied to foreigners fell from $7.4 billion in 1929 to $2.4 billion in 1932. Because the fixed charges owed the United States remained constant, the currencies of some nations, especially those with unfavorable trade balances, came under pressure. With the spread of the depressed conditions, world trade decreased sharply. Part of this decline represented depressed prices, but a portion also reflected a reduction in the volume of goods traded—a highly unusual occurrence indicating the harshness of the economic difficulties. From 1929 to the middle of 1933, world trade fell approximately 40 percent in value, representing a 50 percent drop in price levels and a 25 percent reduction in volume.[1] Unlike previous depressions, this one affected virtually all areas of the globe, reinforcing the view that the world had become an economic unit in which the fate of all nations was interconnected. In general, agricultural areas bore the initial brunt of the depression, but by the last part of 1930 and early 1931, the predominantly manufacturing regions also began to experience major hardships.[2]

1. Department of Commerce, *United States in the World Economy*, Economic Series, no. 23, pp. 5–6, 173–75; League of Nations, *The Course and Phases of the World Economic Depression*, pp. 189–90; J. B. Condliffe, "Vanishing World Trade," *Foreign Affairs* 11 (July 1933): 645.

2. Edwin F. Gay, "The Great Depression," *Foreign Affairs* 10 (July

The economic crisis had a profound impact on trade patterns because those nations with unfavorable balances of payment devised techniques to shield themselves from the shock of international forces. As a first step, many countries raised tariffs; but when this move proved inadequate, they instituted tighter controls through preferential agreements, quotas, exchange restrictions, and licensing. Since one of the major objectives of all these measures was to buy from those nations who were one's customers, bilateral and regional trade patterns emerged in place of the multilateral system favored by the United States. Whether intentionally or not, these new arrangements reduced America's share of world commerce. Having been a net exporter throughout the prior decade, the United States now found that its export trade contracted when countries began to purchase primarily from their own leading customers. Moreover, bilateral and regional commercial policies prevented the increased internal purchasing power of other nations from spilling over into the American economy. Following the international crisis of 1931, these new restrictive arrangements dominated the full body of world trade and successfully impeded the flow of United States commerce. Trade figures told the story as America's share in all imports of foreign countries fell from 16.8 percent in 1929 to an average of 12.8 percent for the period from 1933 to 1938. In addition, by necessitating a high level of governmental participation in economic affairs, the new trade patterns violated a basic American belief that government should remain as aloof as possible from the economy and leave the major decisions to private groups.[3]

Consequently, the depression brought American policymakers a complex set of problems: they had to deal with immense internal difficulties and with an international trade system that was

---

1932): 531; League of Nations, *Course and Phases of the Depression*, pp. 190–98, 292; National Foreign Trade Council, *Foreign Trade in 1930: Official Report of the Seventeenth National Foreign Trade Convention* (New York, 1930), p. viii; Walter Lippmann and William O. Scroggs, *The United States in World Affairs*, p. 104. For a more detailed analysis of the trend, see Ilse Mintz, *Cyclical Fluctuations in the Exports of the United States since 1879*, Appendix A; also see the annual reports of the Department of Commerce for fiscal years 1930–1932.

3. Department of Commerce, *United States in the World Economy*, pp. 6–7, 12, 55–63, 170–86.

no longer compatible with United States interests. The depressed condition of the world economy, furthermore, created the potential for political upheavals that could jeopardize the existing world order. A final problem was that if the worldwide movement toward increased governmental involvement in the economy continued unabated, the United States might have to follow suit and thereby run the risk of infringing upon the freedom of enterprise deemed necessary for political liberty.

The task of coping with conditions spawned by the depression fell first to Herbert Hoover. Throughout his career as a public servant, Hoover guided his actions by a closely defined political philosophy that he thought explained the achievements of the American system.[4] Beginning with the assumption that spiritual and intellectual freedom could not exist without economic freedom, Hoover believed that an improving standard of living for all classes in society would provide the basis for an advancing civilization. Since he also believed that self-interest was the major motive force for production and leadership, Hoover concluded that the best society would be one in which individuals would have the maximum opportunity to further their interests. In the process of enhancing their self-interest, individuals would also improve the welfare of society. According to Hoover, the chief difference between America and other countries was that the absence of rigid class lines in the United States allowed people to rise as far as their talents would take them.[5]

Hoover recognized that unrestrained individualism contained unsavory aspects. To reduce the amount of waste associated with intense competition and to foster a sense of public service, he recommended that those with similar interests form organizations. For these reasons he supported the trade association movement of the 1920s, which he also believed would permit gains in

4. For more information on Hoover, see Richard Hofstadter, "Herbert Hoover and the Crisis of American Individualism," in *The American Political Tradition and the Men Who Made It*, pp. 279–310; William A. Williams, *The Contours of American History*, pp. 425–38; William A. Williams, "What this Country Needs. . . ," *New York Review of Books* 15 (November 5, 1970): 7–11; Murray N. Rothbard, "The Hoover Myth," reprinted in *For a New America*, ed. James Weinstein and David Eakins, pp. 162–79.

5. Herbert Hoover, *American Individualism*, pp. 9–10, 17, 32–35; Herbert Hoover, *The Memoirs of Herbert Hoover*, 2:28.

individuality while curbing selfishness. The government could provide a further check on rampant individualism by restraining those business forces that tried to destroy equality of opportunity. Fixing the boundaries of government-business relations was extremely difficult, however, and Hoover wrestled with this problem for many years. The major pitfall was that a governmental cure could be worse than the disease if it led to a sapping of initiative and diminished opportunities. The government could regulate business practices, but it should not become involved in fixing prices and wages or in the distribution of production inasmuch as these controls would create a fascist state. The primary function of government was to promote cooperation by private groups and to act as an impartial umpire in disputes.[6]

On foreign affairs, Hoover's views placed him on the fringe of the existing consensus. Although he accepted much of the analysis of the world as an economic unit, Hoover maintained that the United States was largely self-sufficient. Because the nation exported only 6 to 10 percent of its total productivity, it was the domestic economy that provided the key to prosperity. "We consume an average of about 90 percent of our own production of commodities," he explained in 1930. "If, for example, we assume a restored normal home consumptoin and held even our present reduced basis of exports, we should be upon 97 percent of normal business basis."[7] The changing nature of the export trade suggested that the nation would have greater flexibility in the future, especially vis-à-vis Europe. Manufactured exports would go primarily to non-European areas and would not be as important relative to the total volume of manufactures

6. Hoover, *American Individualism*, pp. 41–47, 51–62; Hoover, *Memoirs*, 2:167–74.

7. These points were developed more fully in the author's "Herbert Hoover and America's Role in World Affairs," a paper read at the spring 1971 meeting of the Missouri Valley Historical Convention; see Introduction to a Draft Letter, January 10 (no year given, but it was probably 1922 since Hoover was discussing the upcoming Genoa Conference), Personal File, Economic Recovery in Europe, Secretary of Commerce, Herbert Hoover Papers (Herbert Hoover Library, West Branch, Iowa); address to the annual convention of the Chamber of Commerce of the United States, May 16, 1922, Public Statements, Vol. 10, No. 228, Hoover Papers; "Causes of the Present Industrial Depression and Possible Contribution of Bankers in Solving Problems," October 2, 1930, Public Statements, Vol. 48, No. 1382, Hoover Papers.

as agricultural exports had been. If industry produced efficiently and faced sufficient competition to guarantee that gains in productivity went to workers and consumers, the country could manufacture and distribute all the goods required for a high standard of living. Because Hoover thought that the only military threat the nation need be concerned about was the possibility of an invasion, he concluded that the prosperity and security of the United States were not necessarily dependent upon events abroad.[8]

There was no contradiction, therefore, between his frequent assertion that international forces were the cause of the American depression and his belief that the country could find a domestic path to recovery. "I do not want to minimize the economic interdependence of the world," he told an audience in Indianapolis in June 1931, "but despite this, the potential and redeeming strength of the United States in the face of this situation is that we are economically more self-contained than any other great nation." Once temporary dislocations passed, the nation could "make a large measure of recovery irrespective of the rest of the world." As good times returned, Americans would stimulate production in other countries by increasing their volume of imports. The most important challenge facing American policymakers was the restoration of stability in the United States.[9]

On the domestic front, Hoover's actions were confined by his political philosophy. Nonetheless, within those areas where he thought action was possible, he was not afraid to move. The

8. Hoover, "Economic Prospects of 1924," Personal File, Economic Situation in U. S., Secretary of Commerce, Hoover Papers; Hoover, "The Future of Our Foreign Trade," March 16, 1926, Official File, Foreign Trade 1926, Secretary of Commerce, Hoover Papers; Hoover, "Our Future Economic Defense," September 18, 1940, in *Addresses Upon the American Road 1940–1941*, pp. 20–26; Hoover, "Should We Send Armies to Europe? And a Way to National Unity," November 19, 1941, Public Statements, Vol. 76, No. 2716, Hoover Papers; Hoover, "National Defense," May 27, 1940, in *Addresses Upon the American Road 1940–1941*, pp. 4–13; Hoover, "The Immediate Relation of the United States to this War," May 11, 1941, ibid., pp. 84–85; Hoover, "Our Foreign Relations," October 31, 1941, ibid., pp. 44–46; Hoover, "We Should Revise Our Foreign Policies," in *Addresses Upon the American Road 1950–1955*, pp. 13–17.

9. Hoover, "Business Depression and Policies of Government to It," June 15, 1931, Public Statements, Vol. 52, No. 1587, Hoover Papers; he repeated this theme in his annual address to Congress on December 8, 1931.

president tried to buoy public confidence and to stimulate people to take cooperative measures to meet the problems of the depression. While insisting on full action by state and local governments, Hoover was prepared to bring the strength of the federal government behind the people's organizations and their state and local governments. He held meetings, therefore, with industrial and labor leaders to seek their assistance in holding wages steady and avoiding strikes. He also increased the number of federal public works projects and encouraged state and local governments as well as private industry to increase capital investments. To afford some degree of coordination for the local relief organizations, Hoover created the President's Committee for Unemployment Relief. His most ambitious domestic actions, however, lay in attempts to ease credit restrictions. Because the government could act in this area without becoming involved in the marketplace, Hoover sponsored methods to bolster weak banks and to prevent further foreclosures. After attempts to achieve the voluntary cooperation of banks failed, he proposed, in December 1931, the formation of the Reconstruction Finance Corporation, the first direct governmental support of the credit system. This corporation was designed to lend funds to banks, railroads, building and loan associations, and similar institutions.[10]

Hoover's most dramatic moves came in foreign policy. In 1929, representatives from the Allied nations and the United States made what they hoped would be a final settlement of the reparations issue through an agreement known as the Young Plan (named after the American industrialist, Owen D. Young). This plan established the size and payment period of annual annuities and abolished foreign controls over the German economy. In addition, the delegates created the Bank for International Settlements to handle annuities, improve coordination among central banks, and help achieve currency and credit stability. The plan contained emergency provisions that enabled

10. Ray L. Wilbur and Arthur M. Hyde, *The Hoover Policies*, p. 362; Hoover, *Memoirs*, 3:32–36, 43–45, 53–56, 85–89, 107–8, 111–15, 150–58, 174–75; William E. Leuchtenburg, *The Perils of Prosperity, 1914–1932*, p. 257; Gerald D. Nash, "Herbert Hoover and the Origins of the Reconstruction Finance Corporation," *Mississippi Valley Historical Review* 46 (December 1959): 455–68.

Germany to forego for a year the transfer of a portion of the annual annuity, although the German government would continue to deposit reichsmarks at the Bank for International Settlements; if difficulties persisted beyond a year, Germany could suspend the transfer of all marks. The maximum period for any form of postponement was twenty-four months. The postponement provisions, however, afforded little immediate assistance since they limited relief during the first year to the balance of payments. Only in the second year did the Germans no longer have to make provisions for reparations.[11]

Quite clearly the Young Plan was not adequate to handle a crisis of the magnitude of the one that occurred in 1931. Although the Smoot-Hawley Tariff of 1930 increased the level of American duties and produced some retaliatory tariffs, it did not touch off a large-scale trading war, nor did it have as adverse an effect on the flow of imports into the United States as did the general business recession.[12] The chief difficulties facing the world in 1931 again came out of central Europe, especially Germany. Briefly stated, the chain of events leading up to the crisis went as follows: in September 1930, the conservative Heinrich Brüning government in Germany held elections which resulted in strong Nazi and Communist gains. Frightened by the growth of extremist groups, foreign investors began to withdraw funds; and the German government was able to check the outflow of capital only with the assistance of short-term funds from New York banks. Despite the return of stability in January 1931, the future was not bright because Germany found itself forced to rely heavily on short-term loans which nervous creditors

11. Thomas W. Lamont, "The Final Reparations Settlement," *Foreign Affairs* 8 (April 1930): 336–63; Shepard Morgan, "Constructive Functions of the International Bank," *Foreign Affairs* 9 (July 1931): 580–91; Harold G. Moulton and Leo Pasvolsky, *War Debts and World Prosperity*, pp. 188–203, 228–31. For a German view of the Young Plan, see Carl Bergmann, "Germany and the Young Plan," *Foreign Affairs* 8 (July 1930): 583–97. For a detailed analysis of the entire episode, see Frank C. Costigliola, "The Other Side of Isolationism," *Journal of American History* 59 (December 1972): 602–20; Frank C. Costigliola, "The Politics of Financial Stabilization" (Ph.D. dissertation, Cornell Univ., 1973), chap. 7.

12. Department of Commerce, *United States in the World Economy*, p. 172; Percy W. Bidwell, "Trade, Tariffs, and the Depression," *Foreign Affairs* 10 (April 1932): 396–97; Harris Gaylord Warren, *Herbert Hoover and the Great Depression*, pp. 93–96.

could withdraw quickly.[13] The flow of United States short-term funds into Germany had been so extensive, moreover, that the American banking structure had become dangerously dependent on the financial situation within that country. Toward the end of January, the American ambassador in Germany, Frederic Sackett, alerted Hoover to the size of America's financial involvement in Germany and to the need for some action to protect that stake. Sackett warned Hoover that U. S. interests could neither recall nor refuse to renew their notes without creating conditions that would endanger the financial situation in America. Sackett further noted that other countries would have to renew their loans in Germany in order to protect the American position.[14] The circumstances necessary for a standstill agreement on foreign credits in Germany, therefore, were present by the end of the first month of 1931.

The false calm was shattered in March when Germany and Austria announced their intention of forming a customs union. This announcement brought a strong reaction from the French, who believed the move to be merely the first step on the road to a political union, and led to a similar uneasiness in eastern Europe. Following the announcement, Austria encountered severe internal difficulties; in May, the government had to support the Kreditanstalt für Handel und Gewerbe, whose balances equaled 60 percent of all other Austrian banks. This news sent shock waves through central Europe. By the middle of May, Germany experienced such heavy withdrawals of capital that it became apparent she would need outside assistance to forestall a collapse. Chancellor Brüning, moreover, hoped to capitalize on the existing difficulties to obtain a significant reduction of the reparations payments. He informed the Allies that Germany could not meet her obligations without endangering both her own economy and the economy of the world.[15]

13. For the best coverage of European events during these months, see Edward W. Bennett, *Germany and the Diplomacy of the Financial Crisis, 1931*, passim; also see Lippmann and Scroggs, *United States in World Affairs*, p. 106.

14. Frederic Sackett to Stimson, January 21, 1931, Foreign Affairs, Germany, Presidential Papers, Hoover Papers; Louis Lochner, *Herbert Hoover and Germany*, pp. 115–16; see also Bennett, *Germany and the Diplomacy of the Financial Crisis*, pp. 38–39.

15. The coolness of British-French relations made it difficult for the two

President Hoover followed the events in Europe closely. After talking with Ambassador Sackett, who had returned to Washington for a short visit, he concluded in early June that the depression was so severe that nations did not have the capacity to pay intergovernmental debts. The president further decided that the United States should take the lead in trying to alleviate existing conditions.[16] Hoover had at least three primary considerations in mind. First, realizing that New York financial groups were in a panicky mood, he feared a European collapse would destroy what remained of Wall Street's confidence, thereby delivering a damaging blow to the nation's financial system. Hence, the president was not so much interested in bailing out New York financiers as he was in protecting the financial security of the entire country. A second consideration was that many nations had responded to the crisis by adopting trade practices that adversely affected United States markets. Finally, Hoover believed that an economic crisis in Germany would produce a revolution in which either the Communists or Nazis would gain control. Once unleashed, the forces of revolution could spread throughout the continent.[17]

Given the magnitude of the issues, Hoover could not easily have turned his back on them. On the other hand, if the United States participated in an international financial conference it might become enmeshed in Europe's problems and might face a united front of debtor nations. Undersecretary of the Treasury Ogden L. Mills pointed a way out of the impasse by noting that Hoover could act unilaterally to gain acceptance for the suspension of all intergovernmental debts. This move would have the advantage of contributing to prosperity without involving

---

countries to adopt a united front against Germany, Bennett, *Germany and the Diplomacy of the Financial Crisis*, pp. 51–101, 116; Lippmann and Scroggs, *United States in World Affairs*, pp. 124–25.

16. Entries for May 6, 11, 13, 19, and June 2, Diary of Developments of the Moratorium 6 May–22 July, 1931, Foreign Affairs, Presidential Papers, Hoover Papers.

17. Entries for June 6 and 9, ibid.; memorandum by Stimson, May 27, 1931, *Foreign Relations, 1931*, 1:1–2; Hoover, *Memoirs*, 3:64–66; British Prime Minister Ramsay MacDonald was particularly concerned about the revolutionary potential of the crisis, Ray Atherton to Stimson, June 8, 1931, *Foreign Relations, 1931*, 1:6–8; Atherton to Stimson, containing a letter from MacDonald to Hoover, June 8, 1931, ibid., pp. 11–14.

the United States in European political disputes.[18] Hoover received Mills's advice on June 18, the same day he learned from Secretary of the Treasury Mellon (visiting his son at Cambridge) that the situation in England was so grave that action by America was imperative. This information reinforced Hoover's own inclination to act and in all likelihood triggered his offer for a year-long moratorium on all intergovernmental debts.[19]

Hoover's hopes for the success of the moratorium were largely unrealized. The French created part of the problem with their attempts to amend the president's proposal. While negotiators tried to resolve the disputed points, the run on German banks continued. Although Hoover blamed the French for the moratorium's failure, the political and economic crisis was so immense that it is difficult to imagine what steps could have checked the downward spiral. Even without France's footdragging, events may well have been beyond control.[20] By the middle of July, the closing of most central and east European banks precipitated another financial crisis that had a direct impact on the United States because of the heavy American participation in German short-term credits. Hoover discovered to his dismay that certain large banks held huge quantities of German notes that were not supported with collateral. A loss of these notes would endanger the whole American banking structure. The president again assumed the initiative by securing a "standstill agreement" whereby banks holding short-term German bills would renew them when they fell due instead of trying to force payment (which the Brüning government could not have made).[21]

18. Mills to Hoover, June 18, 1931, Foreign Affairs, Financial Correspondence, Presidential Papers, Hoover Papers.

19. Since he had earlier opposed a moratorium, Mellon's message had added significance, Atherton to Stimson, June 18, 1931, *Foreign Relations, 1931*, 1:24–26; for a copy of the message, see Stimson to Walter Edge, June 20, 1931, ibid., pp. 33–35.

20. As Bennett has demonstrated, Hoover's analysis had weaknesses, Bennett, *Germany and the Diplomacy of the Financial Crisis*, pp. 166–203; also see Hoover, *Memoirs*, 3:72–73; entries for July 4, 5, and 6, 1931, Diary of Developments of the Moratorium, 6 May–22 July, 1931, Foreign Affairs, Presidential Papers, Hoover Papers.

21. The French again balked at the American proposal since they favored a long-term loan to which they could attach political strings, entries for July 17, 19, and 22, 1931, Diary of Developments of the Mora-

This move, however, could not stem the downward rush of the world economy, for the difficulties on the continent produced heavy gold drains from England and placed the British economy, which had never fully recovered from the war, under a heavy strain. Although it received assistance from the Federal Reserve Bank of New York and the Bank of France, the Bank of England was unable to protect the pound. The events of September and October 1931 made these among the worst months of the interwar years: Britain faced a mutiny in the Royal Navy and then had to suspend gold payments on September 21; soon other nations abandoned the gold standard; the United States experienced substantial gold outflows, causing the Federal Reserve to raise interest rates at a time when the domestic economy was contracting; and most ominous of all, Japanese troops initiated actions that culminated in the annexation of Manchuria. At the end of 1931, the postwar world order had virtually collapsed. Having repudiated the gold standard, most nations adopted protectionist trade policies that disrupted existing trade patterns and forced countries to rely on their own resources. The shattered state of the world economy also led some to conclude that the use of force to carve out a special sphere of influence was an acceptable procedure. England's rejection of the gold standard, her drift toward a protectionist policy, and the Japanese invasion of Manchuria most clearly marked the passing of the old order.[22]

---

torium, 6 May–22 July, 1931, Foreign Affairs, Presidential Papers, Hoover Papers; Hoover, *Memoirs*, 3:73–80; Sackett to Castle, July 11, 1931, Foreign Affairs, Financial Correspondence July 10–14, 1931, Presidential Papers, Hoover Papers; Castle to Edge, July 17, 1931, *Foreign Relations, 1931*, 1:275–78; Atherton to Castle, July 22, 1931, ibid., pp. 312–13. For an extended description of the moratorium and standstill agreement episodes, see Robert Ferrell, *American Diplomacy in the Great Depression*, chap. 7; Lochner, *Hoover and Germany*, chaps. 6, 7; Warren, *Hoover and the Depression*, chap. 10; Hoover, *Memoirs*, 3:chap. 7. For a critical appraisal of Hoover's policy, see Bernard V. Burke, "American Economic Diplomacy and the Weimar Republic," *Mid-America* 54 (October 1972): 211–33.

22. Hoover, *Memoirs*, 3:81–83; Elmus Wicker, *Federal Reserve Monetary Policy 1917–1933*, p. 164; Bennett, *Germany and the Diplomacy of the Financial Crisis*, pp. 243, 282–86; Lippmann and Scroggs, *United States in World Affairs*, chaps. 10, 11; Warren, *Hoover and the Depression*, pp. 94–96; Department of Commerce, *United States in the World Economy*, pp. 62–63.

The following year witnessed a continuation of these trends. With the adoption of the Imperial Preference System, the British officially renounced their traditional foreign trade policy.[23] At the Lausanne Conference, Allied nations agreed to reduce drastically German reparations if they could receive similar reductions on their United States obligations. As a result, the U. S. faced increased trade barriers and a united stance by the debtor countries. Throughout his remaining months in the White House, Hoover tried to reverse these events by offering to reduce war debts in return for lowering trade barriers and reinstating the gold standard. The president believed that if others would agree to his proposal, the recuperative powers of the U. S. economy were strong enough to restore prosperity. With this in mind, he agreed to participate in an international economic conference, a step he had been reluctant to take a few months earlier.[24]

Hoover's defeat in November 1932 made it difficult for him to act in foreign affairs; nevertheless, the pressures from abroad continued unabated. As the end of the moratorium year approached, Washington learned that many of the debtors either wished to extend the moratorium or to cancel the debts. In addition, the disarmament conference in London, the preparations for the world economic conference, and the difficulties in the Far East all pointed to the need for American action. Consequently, Hoover tried to obtain president-elect Franklin D. Roosevelt's support for his policies. The president was most concerned about European nations defaulting on their obligations before the United States could bargain for the resumption of the gold standard and the opening of markets to American products. Notwithstanding the exchange of several letters and telegrams and two face-to-face meetings, however, they failed

23. For a discussion of the British empire's movement toward protectionism, see Richard N. Kottman, *Reciprocity and the North Atlantic Triangle, 1932–1938,* chap. 1.

24. Hoover first proposed a world economic conference in the fall of 1931 but the French did not believe the time was ripe for a meeting. With the continued deterioration of world commerce, the British raised the subject again during the following spring. The leading trading nations eventually agreed to hold a conference in the late winter of 1933. Hoover, *Memoirs,* 3:130, 171–73; Hoover, address at Lincoln Day Dinner, February 13, 1933, Public Statements, Vol. 63, No. 2124, Hoover Papers; Stimson to Mellon, May 26, 1932, Foreign Affairs, Monetary and Economic Conference, Presidential Papers, Hoover Papers.

to reach an agreement. Roosevelt insisted on dealing with the issues separately as opposed to a quid pro quo approach.[25]

During the time Hoover's international plans were stalled, he encountered growing domestic difficulties. The continued hard times brought him under attack not only from those who were suffering physically but also from financial and business leaders who wanted assistance from the federal government. At the time of the standstill agreement, New York bankers had asked Hoover to take part in a large international loan to Germany. The president, however, insisted that since the bankers had overextended themselves, they, not the taxpayers, should shoulder the burden. He further discovered that financial groups wanted governmental aid for disabled banks in lieu of forming a private corporation to bail them out.[26] Besides seeking Washington's support, many within the banking community thought the present level of tariffs was too high and suggested a revision of the rates.[27] In addition, Hoover's instigation of a Senate investigation of stock exchange irregularities alienated bankers.

Disaffection with the president's policies found additional expression in the growing sentiment in business circles favoring

25. Roosevelt's refusal to cooperate with Hoover reflected personal and political considerations rather than fundamental policy differences. By the end of 1932, both men were deeply suspicious of one another and Roosevelt was reluctant to make any commitments that could limit his future domestic actions, Frank Freidel, *Franklin D. Roosevelt*, pp. 21–45, 102–36; Raymond Moley, *After Seven Years*, pp. 68–98; Raymond Moley, *The First New Deal*, pp. 22–61; Herbert Feis, *1933: Characters in Crisis*, pp. 15–86; Elliot Rosen, "Intranationalism vs. Internationalism," *Political Science Quarterly* 81 (June 1966): 274–97; Hoover, *Memoirs*, 3:176–87, 203–14; Rexford Tugwell, *The Brains Trust*, pp. xxi–xxiv, 44, 106, 423, 486, 512–20. Also see the Hoover-Roosevelt correspondence, President's Private File, Roosevelt, Franklin—Discussion with Roosevelt on Debts, November 12–January 27, 1933, Hoover Papers.

26. The Bonus Army of 1932 was the most pointed illustration of the plight of the poor; for Hoover's attitude toward the banking community, see Hoover, *Memoirs*, 3:77–78, 85–86.

27. "Help for International Trade," *Nation's Business* 19 (July 1931): 14; "Threats of Tariff Reprisals," *Bankers Magazine* 120 (June 1930): 763; "The New Tariff and Prosperity," ibid. 120 (August 1930): 167: "A Tariff Holiday," ibid. 123 (August 1931): 126–27; "New England Bankers on Business," ibid. 124 (May 1932): 531, 535; for a contrary view, see William Pickett Helm, "Tariff Walls, Past and Present," *Journal of the American Bankers' Association* 23 (July 1930): 12–13.

some type of planned economy. The United States Chamber of Commerce proposed one of the most significant of these plans: a three-to-five-member council that would organize an attack on the nation's economic problems. The council would cooperate with the government and trade associations to balance production with consumption and to stabilize prices and employment. To accomplish these objectives, Congress would have to amend the antitrust laws so that trade associations could enlarge their powers. When Henry I. Harriman, president of the Chamber of Commerce, urged Hoover to support the plan, the president refused to do so, fearing that the creation of monopolies would lead either directly to fascism or indirectly to socialism. Even Harriman's threat that failure to support the chamber's recommendations would cause powerful business leaders to support Roosevelt did not persuade the president to change his mind. By November 1932, Hoover's support had dwindled among businessmen.[28]

Franklin D. Roosevelt's approach to economic affairs differed sharply from his predecessor's on the critical issue of the use of governmental powers. Because he did not share Hoover's fear of government ownership and operation of some productive enterprises, Roosevelt was willing to adopt aggressive measures to correct what he perceived as weaknesses within society. Roosevelt preferred to have business handle its own problems, and he wanted to preserve equality of opportunity (which he considered a prerequisite for sustained growth), but he did not hesitate to act if business refused to reform itself. The new president, moreover, did not oppose governmental involvement in social welfare programs. As governor of New York, Roosevelt had sponsored the extension of workmen's compensation laws and had advocated old age pensions and unemployment insurance. He saw his actions as necessary to safeguard industrial capitalism from its own inadequacies. "The true conservative," the president once commented, "seeks to protect the system of private property and free enterprise by correcting such injustices and inequalities as arise from it. The most serious threat to our institutions comes from those who refuse to face the need for

28. "A Panorama of Economic Plannings," *Nation's Business* 20 (February 1932): 29–32; "Mr. Harriman's Business Platform," ibid. 20 (July 1932): 20; Hoover, *Memoirs*, 3:335.

change. Liberalism becomes the protection for the far-sighted conservative."[29]

As for the nation's role in international affairs, Roosevelt accepted the prevailing view of the world as an economic unit. Significantly, he was less certain about the ability of the United States to achieve full recovery on its own than was Hoover. In his second fireside chat, Roosevelt maintained that the internal situation was "inevitably and deeply tied in with the conditions in all of the other Nations of the world. In other words, we can get, in all probability, a fair measure of prosperity to return to the United States, but it will not be permanent unless we get a return to prosperity all over the world." The president's logic, therefore, easily led him to conclude that Washington should play a more active role in furthering the country's overseas economic expansion.[30]

Roosevelt took office at the darkest moment of the depression: the country was in the midst of a major banking panic, rural and urban unemployment stood at all-time highs; a harsh winter added to the general suffering; and talk of revolution was not uncommon.[31] Although these conditions caused the president to spend a great deal of time on domestic affairs, he did not ignore international events. Throughout the spring of 1933, Roosevelt tried to gain international acceptance of policies that would

29. Roosevelt accepted the older progressive view of the need for governmental intervention, Freidel, *Launching the New Deal*, pp. 64–65, 71–74. Also see Morris Edwards, "Roosevelt Talked Business with Me," *Nation's Business* 20 (December 1932): 14–16; Daniel R. Fusfeld, *The Economic Thought of Franklin D. Roosevelt and the Origins of the New Deal*, pp. 123–53, 163–65. Franklin D. Roosevelt, *The Public Papers and Addresses of Franklin D. Roosevelt*, ed. Samuel I. Rosenman, 1936:389 (hereafter cited as *PPAFDR*).

30. Willard D. Range, *Franklin D. Roosevelt's World Order*, pp. 3–4, 11–18, 52, 134, 140–60, 183–84; Roosevelt, *PPAFDR*, 1933:167. By the end of the 1930s, Roosevelt was arguing that world prosperity was a prerequisite for international peace and that the continued political, economic, and social independence of every nation was necessary for the preservation of America's safety and welfare, Roosevelt, *PPAFDR*, 1937: 436–37; 1939:191, 198.

31. William E. Leuchtenburg, *Franklin D. Roosevelt and the New Deal 1932–1940*, pp. 1–40; Department of Commerce, *World Economic Review 1933*, p. 3; Roosevelt was concerned about the possibility of a revolution if economic conditions did not improve shortly, see Tugwell, *The Brains Trust*, pp. 295–96, 358–59, 430–34; also see Roosevelt, *PPAFDR*, 1936:385–86.

aid prosperity and peace. The president also believed that America would not be able to achieve complete recovery until the volume of world trade increased. From the beginning, the New Deal was an attempt to attack the depression on the national and international levels. On some occasions, Roosevelt would find that the two goals would be in momentary conflict; and at times, he would devote more attention to one area than the other. He never lost sight, however, of his long-range goal of establishing order and prosperity on a worldwide basis.[32]

Roosevelt's chief objective during his first months in office was to raise prices. But before he could turn to this task, he had to deal with the banking crisis and the related gold drain. On March 10, the president prohibited the export of gold except by license. This move proved to be merely the first of several steps the administration took over the next month and a half that resulted in the United States abandoning the gold standard. Because it shielded the American financial structure from external disturbances, this measure enabled Roosevelt to tinker with the nation's monetary system. By causing the dollar to depreciate in international money markets, the action had the additional short-term advantages of stimulating exports as well as reducing imports.[33]

The backbone of the first New Deal recovery program was the Agricultural Adjustment Administration (A.A.A.) and the National Recovery Administration (N.R.A.). Through acreage limitation and outright crop and animal destruction, the A.A.A. tried to bring agricultural production more in line with consumption. The N.R.A. suspended the antitrust laws, empowered the president to sanction business agreements dealing with competitive and labor practices (such things as prices, wages, and hours), and allowed federal licensing to secure compliance with the agreements. Some hoped that the A.A.A. and N.R.A. would

32. Freidel, *Launching the New Deal*, pp. 102–17, 355–89; James R. Moore, "Sources of New Deal Economic Policy," *Journal of American History* 61 (December 1974): 728–30; Roosevelt, *PPAFDR*, 1933:14, 167; memorandum by Herbert Feis, April 3, 1934, in *Franklin D. Roosevelt and Foreign Affairs*, ed. Edgar B. Nixon, 1:35–39; Press Conference, May 26, 1933, ibid., pp. 169–72.

33. Freidel, *Launching the New Deal*, pp. 320–38; Moore, "Sources of New Deal Economic Policy," pp. 733–34; Department of Commerce, *World Economic Review 1933*, pp. 18, 53–55.

not remain solely as regulatory bodies but, with the assistance of the government, would plan the direction of the economy. These tactics appeared to improve economic conditions as wholesale prices and factory employment increased slowly and certain important indices pointed upward. Based on a figure of 100 for the years 1935–1939, the index of industrial production rose from 54 in March 1933 to 85 in July 1933, that of durable manufactures rose from 32 to 75, while the index of stock prices went from 45.6 to 85 over the same time period. Although the recovery was far from complete, the upward movement seemed hopeful and must have made the spring of 1933 a little more pleasant than the previous one.[34]

The apparent improvement in the economy largely governed the way the Roosevelt administration approached international economic relations during the summer. The president had to contend with two major foreign economic issues. One was the nagging problem of debts on which an installment was due in June. Because the likelihood of payment was slim, Roosevelt gave the appearance of trying to hold the line but, in fact, did not push the matter. Some countries made token remittances, yet within a year only the Finns continued to meet their obligations fully and on time. Following these defaults, the administration essentially gave up all hope of having the debts repaid.[35] The second problem facing the president was the proposed World Economic Conference. In a series of meetings with foreign representatives, he agreed to hold the conference in London beginning in the middle of June. As the opening date approached, Roosevelt seemed undecided about the purpose of the conference; and this uncertainty may have accounted for his peculiar selections for the American delegation, a motley group sadly lacking cohesion. Secretary of State Cordell Hull, the head of the delegation, wanted to use the conference to

34. Leuchtenburg, *Roosevelt and the New Deal*, pp. 48–50, 55–60; Arthur M. Schlesinger, Jr., *The Age of Roosevelt*, 2:27–54, 87–102; Rexford G. Tugwell, *The Democratic Roosevelt*, pp. 284, 289; Moley, *After Seven Years*, p. 369; Ellis Hawley, *The New Deal and the Problem of Monopoly*, chap. 1; Bureau of the Census, *Historical Statistics of the United States, 1789–1945*, appendices 3, 6, 7, 23, and 25.

35. William Phillips to Roosevelt, June 26, 1933, Nixon, *Roosevelt and Foreign Affairs*, 1:252–53; statement by Roosevelt, November 7, 1933, ibid., pp. 465–66; Roosevelt to Congress, June 1, 1935, ibid., 2:126–33.

obtain a general reduction of tariff barriers. While he was on the way to London, however, the president notified him that the administration would not submit the reciprocal trade agreements bill to the current session of Congress. Hull arrived in London empty-handed.[36]

In all probability Roosevelt should not have consented to hold the conference at that time.[37] Because he was currently engaged in attempting to raise domestic prices, he had little to gain from an agreement to stabilize exchanges, especially since stabilization at existing levels would have benefited those nations that had already devalued their currencies. The president was primarily interested in obtaining a series of commodity agreements that would raise prices, but there was little support for this position among other countries. The major difficulty at London was that all nations were unwilling to make concessions that might jeopardize their own domestic recovery programs. Once the conference headed even remotely in the direction of an exchange agreement, therefore, Roosevelt decided he had little choice but to reject the proposal, a step he undertook with considerable vigor.[38] Clearly, the torpedoing of the conference did not promote international cooperation, but there is little to suggest that the president's action undermined an otherwise promising movement toward an international solution of the depression. Similarly, there is no evidence to indicate that Roosevelt

36. Feis, *1933*, chap. 13, pp. 172–74; Roosevelt's message of May 16, 1933, Nixon, *Roosevelt and Foreign Affairs*, 1:126–28; Moley, *After Seven Years*, pp. 217–20; Schlesinger, *The Age of Roosevelt*, 2:208–9; Hull noted that he left for London with the highest hopes, "but arrived with empty hands," Cordell Hull, *The Memoirs of Cordell Hull*, 1:149–55.

37. In drafts of an intended letter to Ramsay MacDonald, Roosevelt admitted that the conference should not have been held for a few months, Moley, *The First New Deal*, p. 492; James Warburg's draft of proposed letter, July 24, 1933, Nixon, *Roosevelt and Foreign Affairs*, 1:327–28.

38. Freidel, *Launching the New Deal*, pp. 454–89; Moore, "Sources of New Deal Economic Policy," pp. 734–43; Tugwell, *The Democratic Roosevelt*, pp. 291–92; John M. Blum, *From the Morgenthau Diaries*, 1:64–65; Lloyd C. Gardner, *Economic Aspects of New Deal Diplomacy*, pp. 27, 29–30; press conference, July 5, 1933, Nixon, *Roosevelt and Foreign Affairs*, 1:273–79; Elmus Wicker, "Roosevelt's 1933 Monetary Experiment," *Journal of American History* 57 (March 1971): 874. Some accounts of the conference are Jeanette P. Nichols, "Roosevelt's Monetary Diplomacy in 1933," *American Historical Review* 56 (January 1951): 295–317; Schlesinger, *The Age of Roosevelt*, 2:chap. 13; Feis, *1933*, part 3; Moley, *After Seven Years*, chap. 7; Moley, *The First New Deal*, chap. 30.

saw his action as committing the United States to economic nationalism. At the proper moment, preferably one more propitious to the nation's interests, he would deal with questions involving the world economy.[39]

The rate of the domestic recovery began to slow down by the middle of July and soon a mild recession set in. Realizing that new measures were necessary to counteract the slump, Roosevelt initiated the Blue Eagle campaign in an effort to hasten the code-making process of N.R.A. Because the government lacked both the power sufficient to guarantee that individuals did not violate the codes and the will to use what powers it did have, businessmen who obeyed the rules often faced unfair competition from those who ignored them. Due to these violations and to a growing disenchantment by nearly all groups with N.R.A., Roosevelt began to look elsewhere for some means of restoring prosperity.[40]

One alternative to which he turned was a policy of controlled inflation. To bolster farm prices and to stave off a possible agrarian rebellion, the president adopted the gold-purchase scheme of George Warren, a Cornell University agricultural economist. Warren argued that raising the price of gold, which would reduce the gold value of the dollar, would increase the level of all prices of raw materials and consumer goods. Beginning in late October, the government purchased gold at ever-increasing prices. Not withstanding Warren's forecast, the general index of all farm prices fell off slightly in November and December, and the differential between agricultural and industrial prices remained.[41]

39. In the proposed letter to Ramsay MacDonald (see note 37), the administration's position was that rejection of the exchange agreement did not mean that the U.S. was adopting a policy of economic nationalism. Once a degree of internal stability returned, the United States would concentrate on international issues.

40. Roosevelt hoped that the Blue Eagle campaign would rally public support behind N.R.A. and thus give the administration the help it needed to force reluctant industrialists to sign codes. Bernard Sternsher, *Rexford Tugwell and the New Deal*, pp. 160–61; Tugwell, *The Democratic Roosevelt*, pp. 292, 308–9, 312; Schlesinger, *The Age of Roosevelt*, 2:108–10, 114–18.

41. Sternsher, *Tugwell and the New Deal*, p. 167; Tugwell, *The Democratic Roosevelt*, p. 312; Blum, *From the Morgenthau Diaries*, 1:61, 67–68, 72, 74–75; Wicker, "Roosevelt's 1933 Monetary Experiment," pp. 874–79.

By the end of 1933, the New Deal recovery attempts had stalled. The administration's actions had averted a complete collapse, but the July decline had punctured the earlier optimism. Even though the various economic indicators leveled off in December, they remained at a mark too low to warrant much enthusiasm. Although Roosevelt had indicated he would deal with international economic relations after he restored order in his own house, the persistence of the depression forced him to make the expansion of foreign trade a vital part of his recovery program. Once Roosevelt reached this decision, he committed himself to work not only for a New Deal at home but also for one abroad.[42]

Throughout 1933, certain influential groups inside and outside government continued to stress the importance of foreign commerce for domestic prosperity. Under the leadership of Cordell Hull, the State Department became a focal point for efforts to reduce world trade barriers. The secretary adhered doggedly to the view that the movement toward bilateral trade patterns would perpetuate the depression and ultimately lead to political and military disputes. With the exception of Raymond Moley, who resigned as assistant secretary of state in the fall of 1933, members of the department were in general agreement with Hull.[43] The Department of Commerce was another center of international trade interest. As in the 1920s, commerce officials reasoned that a healthy foreign trade was necessary for domestic prosperity and believed that the decline of overseas trade was a fundamental cause for the prolongation of the depression. The Bureau of Foreign and Domestic Commerce cooperated with the State Department to prevent "the establishment of discriminations against American trade and to assure for U. S. exporters an equitable share in markets subject to any form of restriction." At the request of the State Department, the bureau initiated studies of American trade with a number of individual countries as a background for the anticipated negotiation of reciprocal trade agreements.[44]

42. Gardner, *Economic Aspects of New Deal Diplomacy*, pp. viii, 26.
43. The State Department's trade program will be discussed in greater detail in chap. 3. For brief discussions of the members of the department, see Julius Pratt, *Cordell Hull, 1933–1944*, 1:16–22; Hull, *Memoirs*, 1:161, 180–83; Freidel, *Launching the New Deal*, pp. 359–65.
44. Department of Commerce, *Annual Report of the Secretary of Com-*

The attitudes and goals of certain private interest groups paralleled those of the state and commerce departments. Among manufacturers and exporters, the National Foreign Trade Council exerted pressure for expanded foreign trade. Speaking in October, James A. Farrell termed overseas commerce "a natural and indispensable element in the recovery of our national prosperity." In an article entitled "Let's Face the Facts About Foreign Trade," James D. Mooney, president of General Motors Export Company, wrote that the nation had to export its surpluses to insure a fair return to capital and high real wages for labor. If foreign markets were not found, Mooney predicted, the United States would undergo a series of readjustments that would mean suffering for many as well as prolonged business difficulties. The New York Chamber of Commerce repeated the familiar argument that, although foreign trade consumed only 10 percent of production, a decline in output by that amount meant a depression.[45] Many members of the financial community also expressed concern about the state of international economic affairs. In reply to the assertion that the U. S. should withdraw from foreign fields and mind its own business, an editorial in the March 1932 issue of *Bankers Magazine* stated that in view of America's heavy overseas investment, keeping an eye on its own business necessitated involvement in the world arena. Implying that strangled international trade was a major factor in producing the depression, other bankers urged the settlement of war debts and the institution of tariff reductions as steps needed to restore foreign commerce. The overseas banking machinery American financiers had established in the 1920s, moreover, continued to function as the number of banking establishments abroad increased from 218 in 1929 to 223 in April, 1933.[46] Nor

---

merce, *Fiscal Year 1933* (Washington, 1933), pp. ix, xvii, 32; Department of Commerce, *Annual Report of the Secretary of Commerce, Fiscal Year 1934*, p. xix.

45. *New York Times*, October 23, 1933, p. 24; James A. Farrell, "We Need Foreign Trade Too," *Nation's Business* 21 (September 1933): 13–15; James D. Mooney, "Let's Face the Facts about Foreign Trade," *Forbes* 31 (January 15, 1933): 7; Chamber of Commerce of the State of New York, *Monthly Bulletin* 24 (February 1933): 432–33.

46. Editorial, *Bankers Magazine* 124 (March 1932): 267; Winthrop Aldrich, "Causes of the Present Depression," ibid. 126 (April 1933): 339–44; "Two Roads—Which Shall We Take?" ibid. 126 (February 1933): 116–17; quote of Samuel Seabury, "What They Say," ibid., p. 192; for an

were business and economic groups the only ones interested in foreign commerce; in November 1933, the Social Science Research Council proposed a study of national policy in international economic relations.[47]

During the fall of 1933, government officials took steps to invigorate the nation's foreign commercial policy. In writing to a friend, Herbert Feis, the economic adviser for the State Department, effectively summed up the situation facing the Roosevelt administration. Feis noted that the government would have to deal with the country's surplus productive capacity through either the restoration of international trade or the regimentation of the industrial system. Since he opposed the second alternative, Feis helped set in motion a chain of events designed to provide greater coordination for the nation's overseas economic policy. To achieve this objective, he recommended the creation of one central authority over whose desk would pass all matters relating to international commerce. This movement culminated on November 11 when the president established the Executive Committee on Commercial Policy. Consisting of members from the State Department, the Treasury Department, N.R.A., A.A.A., the Reconstruction Finance Corporation, and the Tariff Commission, and chaired by a member of the State Department, the committee had to approve all actions that could affect foreign trade.[48]

Within nine days of its formation, the committee came to two general conclusions. Arguing that the recovery of export markets was necessary for the solution of many of the nation's

---

earlier indication of similar views, see "The Condition of Business," *Journal of the American Bankers' Association* 25 (August 1932): 59–60; editorial, ibid. 25 (September 1932): 28; "Our Foreign Trade Banking," ibid. 26 (October 1933): 25–26.

47. Roosevelt approved of the council's proposal, Roosevelt to Robert Crane, November 17, 1933, Nixon, *Roosevelt and Foreign Affairs*, 1:493; also see Commission of Inquiry into National Policy in International Economic Relations, *International Economic Relations*, pp. 1–21.

48. Feis's letter is partially reprinted in Feis, *1933*, p. 291; Hull to Feis, October 27, 1933, with enclosure, and Feis to Hull, October 26, 1933, Nixon, *Roosevelt and Foreign Affairs*, 1:440–42. George Peek, head of the A.A.A., also recommended the coordination of foreign economic policy, Frank Walker to Roosevelt, October 25, 1933, ibid., p. 437; Roosevelt to Hull, October 30, 1933, ibid., pp. 449–50; Roosevelt to Peek, November 11, 1933, ibid., pp. 482–83.

problems, committee members recommended that Congress grant the president authority to modify existing tariff duties upward or downward within specified limits. Executive control was absolutely necessary to provide unified direction for the trade program. The members also proposed the formation of a graded system that would divide industries into six groups on the basis of social and economic values. Those on top would receive highest priority in finding foreign markets while those on the bottom would have to face increased competition from imports. A month later, the committee completed a major report that omitted reference to the graded system but emphasized the necessity of granting the chief executive authority to set tariff rates. By so doing, the country could effectively integrate its economic life with that of other nations.[49]

The same day Roosevelt announced the formation of the new committee, Secretary Hull departed for the Montevideo Conference, where he informed the various Latin American delegates that the United States wanted to cooperate with them in the promotion of mutually beneficial economic and political programs. At the conference, Hull gained acceptance of a resolution calling for the liberalization of tariff barriers.[50] During the secretary's absence, Roosevelt removed George N. Peek from the head of A.A.A. and placed him in charge of a temporary committee to recommend a way to coordinate all governmental activities related to foreign trade. Although Peek and Hull disagreed strongly about the proper way to increase commerce, they had a common desire to find overseas markets for American products. In a speech to the Gridiron Club, Roosevelt gave additional evidence of the administration's intentions. "We hope for the stability of world currency," the president noted. "We hope for an increase in the exchange of goods and products— not with the thought of making one Nation rich at the expense

49. Memorandum by Feis, November 20, 1933, File No. 611.0031 Executive Committee 50, General Records of the Department of State, RG 59 (National Archives, Washington, D.C.); somebody leaked the section of the report on the graded system for industry to the *New York Herald Tribune*, see January 14, 1934, section 2, pp. 1, 7; Phillips to Roosevelt, December 22, 1933, Nixon, *Roosevelt and Foreign Affairs*, 1:544–46.

50. While favoring the principle, Roosevelt did not believe that world conditions were ripe for a general tariff reduction, Hull, *Memoirs*, 1:326, 331–32.

of another but of letting all nations participate in the profits of world trade."[51]

With the coming of the new year, Robert M. Hutchinson, president of the University of Chicago and head of the Social Science Research Council's committee studying the nation's international economic relations, posed the central question confronting the Roosevelt administration: "Can we plan our internal economic life without knowing in which direction we are moving in the international sphere."[52] At the end of January 1934, as a step toward clarifying America's position, Roosevelt stabilized the dollar at 60 percent of its old value. This move was necessary if the United States was to experience the benefits of devaluation. In addition, a continued rise in the price of gold would disrupt international trade by causing exchange fluctuations. From the profits of devaluation, Congress created a stabilization fund of $2 billion to protect the dollar by the purchase and sale of gold, foreign securities, and government securities. Henry Morgenthau, Jr., the acting secretary of the treasury, made heavy gold purchases in order to close the gap between the domestic and foreign price of gold. Within two months, he had succeeded in establishing the American price throughout the world.[53]

To counter the growth of trade barriers, Roosevelt introduced the Reciprocal Trade Agreements Act on March 2. The bill authorized the president to enter into accords with other nations to secure outlets for American products and enabled him to reduce tariffs by as much as 50 percent for bargaining purposes. Since the United States based its trade policy on the unconditional most-favored-nation principle, the administration would extend individual reductions to all nations that did not discriminate against American trade. The successful implementation of this program would help free world trade from discriminatory controls. The tariff differed from its predecessors by allowing the president to conclude treaties without having to obtain the con-

51. George N. Peek and Samuel Crowther, *Why Quit Our Own*, pp. 24, 26; Hull, *Memoirs*, 1:353–54; address to Gridiron Club, December 9, 1933, Nixon, *Roosevelt and Foreign Affairs*, 1:517–19; see chap. 3 for a discussion of the Hull-Peek controversy.

52. *New York Times*, January 5, 1934, p. 2.

53. Blum, *From the Morgenthau Diaries*, 1:120, 125.

currence of two-thirds of the Senate. After considerable debate, Congress passed the measure in June.

Besides advocating a new tariff policy, Roosevelt established the Export-Import Banks of Washington (soon merged into a single institution) in February and March 1934 to provide traders with governmental financial support. The disturbed conditions of international trade had forced commercial banks to stop handling certain types of foreign credits, particularly intermediate and long-term ones. Many exporters, moreover, faced blocked foreign exchanges, which meant that they did not receive immediate payment for their sales. Because of these conditions, some manufacturers either could not afford to sell abroad or were unwilling to do so. The availability of government credits would enable American businessmen to compete for foreign markets.

Beginning in the late fall of 1933, the Roosevelt administration placed increased emphasis on the need for an expanding foreign commerce. The formation of an executive committee on international trade affairs, the stabilization of the dollar, the passage of a new tariff bill, and the organization of government foreign trade banks were all part of this process. These actions were typical of the New Deal approach to the depression. Power was concentrated in Washington and, more specifically, within the executive branch. The Reciprocal Trade Agreements Act and the Export-Import Banks exemplify this trend. The banks, in addition, are an example of the New Deal tendency to rely on governmental funds to aid economic growth.[54]

On April 23, 1934, Cordell Hull reviewed the first year of the New Deal in a speech entitled "The Path to Recovery." The secretary noted that the government had adopted a two-pronged approach to the depression: one was intended to meet the immediate difficulties while the other aimed at fulfilling the long-run economic requirements of the country. Hull believed the problems of international commerce were at the very core of the country's economic dilemma, for if foreign trade was not

54. For a similar view, see Sternsher, *Tugwell and the New Deal*, p. 55; Gardner includes the build-up of the navy in the general trend toward increased emphasis on foreign commercial affairs, Gardner, *Economic Aspects of New Deal Diplomacy*, pp. 36–39; Schlesinger also notes that Roosevelt moved steadily toward involvement in world commerce, Schlesinger, *The Age of Roosevelt*, 2:253.

restored, the United States would have to place increased governmental restrictions on industry and agriculture. "It becomes all important as this nation emerges from panic conditions," Hull continued, "to combine with the permanent parts of the present domestic economic program a program of international economic cooperation, based on a more liberal commercial policy and steadily increasing mutually profitable trade with other nations."[55]

Hull's remarks provide an insight into the changing nature of the New Deal. The severity of the depression initially forced foreign trade considerations into the background. Following the logic laid out in his inaugural address, Roosevelt dealt first with the domestic crisis; but as the depression lingered, he devoted increased attention to the expansion of foreign commerce as a path to recovery. By the spring of 1934, the president placed the might of the federal government behind a program to remove the obstacles that shackled world trade. The Export-Import Banks were a product of this policy. The remainder of this study explores the activities of these banks as the New Deal attempted to rediscover domestic prosperity and promote international security.

55. Address to the Associated Press, April 22, 1934, *New York Times*, April 23, 1934, p. 16.

3

The Bank and
New Deal Foreign Commercial Policy

The shifting nature of the New Deal recovery program meant that the Roosevelt administration had to contend with the complex financial situation confronting American exporters. During the 1920s, foreign loans had underwritten much of the nation's export trade but the depression brought this floatation of bonds to a virtual halt. Not only did the volume of dollars going abroad drop off, but the disturbed conditions in Europe throughout the 1930s caused long-term capital to flow into the United States.[1] The commercial banking system, moreover, was not equipped to extend the longer-term credits generally required in foreign trade. Since Federal Reserve banks could not discount long-term notes, member banks had to deal primarily with short-term credits (up to ninety days) if they hoped to remain liquid. In the decade after the war, banks often granted successive extensions of short-term notes, but they soon had to stop this practice because of financial uncertainties created by the depression. The reliance on foreign exchange controls by nations with unfavorable trade balances posed a further difficulty for American trade. Exporters to these countries had trouble receiving private financing since bankers never knew when the importing nations would release exchange.[2]

Given these circumstances, businessmen and bankers looked to the government for assistance. The concept of governmental

1. Department of Commerce, *The United States in the World Economy*, Economic Series, no. 23, p. 188.

2. Charles E. Stuart, executive vice-president of the Export-Import Bank, spelled out these difficulties in a speech to the Export Managers Club of New York, August 21, 1934, General Correspondence File, Part 1, Records of the Reconstruction Finance Corporation, RG 234 (National Archives, Washington, D.C.); also see his speech to the National Foreign Trade Convention, November 19, 1935, ibid.

participation in financing foreign commerce had made considerable headway in many trading nations. During the 1920s, the British, German, French, Italian, and Japanese governments all established institutions to provide their exporters with credit. By sharing a portion of the financial risk and by supplying information on commercial conditions throughout the world, the institutions had been successful in assisting traders. Until the depression, these arrangements had not troubled U. S. exporters since the steady stream of dollars going abroad made marketing American goods easy. As funds dried up, however, United States export interests found themselves hard pressed to meet this form of competition. By 1931, American foreign traders were agitating for a bank that would enable them to sell manufactured goods on terms comparable to those offered by other countries. Exporters argued that such an organization was essential if the United States hoped to retain old markets and open new ones.[3]

In the fall of 1933, the movement accelerated when the executive heads of the American Manufacturers' Export Association, the National Foreign Trade Council, and the Council on Inter-American Relations, as well as representatives of several important industries, formed a committee to investigate the possibility of establishing a financial body designed to promote American overseas commerce. The committee intended to collaborate with interested government authorities, commercial bankers, exporters, and importers in pursuit of this objective.[4] During the following January, members of the committee met with the Assistant Secretary of State Francis B. Sayre to discuss the matter in greater detail. After the meeting, they sent Sayre a lengthy report outlinning their objectives.

Calculating that the decline in exports had resulted in the loss of 1.65 million jobs and that the existing banking system was

3. Stuart, speech to the National Foreign Trade Convention, November 19, 1935, General Correspondence File, Part 1, RG 234; Hawthorne Arey, "History of Operations and Policies of Export-Import Bank of Washington," mimeograph, pp. 12–13; *New York Times*, February 10, 1934, p. 22; press release by the National Foreign Trade Council, received February 12, 1934, File No. 600.1115 Financial Institute in Interest of American Trade/6, General Records of the Department of State, RG 59 (National Archives, Washington, D.C.); V. D. Seaman to F. L. Roberts, October 21, 1932, ibid.

4. Letter to William Phillips, November 23, 1933, File No. 600.1115 Financial Institute in Interest of American Trade/8, RG 59.

incapable of meeting the needs of the nation's foreign traders, the committee concluded that "an adequate credit structure for foreign trade can at this time be established only with the assistance of the Government by means of funds and credit available through the Reconstruction Finance Corporation." Besides providing intermediate length credits, the bank could aid in the liquidation of frozen foreign balances, handle government to government credits, and extend insurance. The institution also could assist in the solution of problems confronting American investors in foreign countries and help implement the provisions of commercial agreements. The report emphasized the need for an increased level of cooperation between private and governmental bodies. It did recommend, however, that, even though the government should supply most of the funds, private managers should direct the bank since they were better able to judge the quality of credits.[5]

The committee envisioned a modified Edge Law bank, which could receive funds from the Reconstruction Finance Corporation (R.F.C.). The plan called for an initial capitalization of $30 million with the R.F.C. providing $25 million and private sources supplying the remainder. The holders of the common stock, which excluded the government, would select twelve directors representing agricultural, industrial, and commercial interests. Realizing that the proposal was heavily weighted in behalf of private groups, Henry B. DuBois, a member of the committee, informed Sayre that the administration should view the plan as a basis for further consideration. The committee, he went on, was solely interested in cooperating with the government in bringing about the best possible program. "On the question of management," DuBois concluded, "the sponsors of the plan of course realize that, if the Government is going to be called upon to participate largely in providing capital and credit, it will also wish to determine the extent to which the institution is to be controlled and supervised by the Government."[6]

DuBois's observation proved prophetic. The first Export-

5. John Abbink and Henry DuBois to Francis B. Sayre, January 17, 1934, File No. 600.1115 Financial Institute in Interest of American Trade /1, RG 59.
6. Ibid.; DuBois to Sayre, January 22, 1934, File No. 600.1115 Financial Institute in Interest of American Trade/3, RG 59.

Import Bank, created on February 2, 1934, was a government body designed to finance trade with Russia. Working independently of the foreign trade interest groups, officials in Washington decided that the government should be the bank's only stockholder. They did not, therefore, use the Edge Law plan and established instead an institution over which they retained full control. Perhaps mirroring the hopes of its influential readers, the *Wall Street Journal* predicted that the government would eventually allow private capital to participate in the bank, but nothing of this nature occurred.[7] On March 9, Washington announced the formation of a second bank to handle certain financial arrangements with Cuba; as with the Russian bank, the government controlled the institution. In July, the Roosevelt administration expanded the services of the second bank to include the rest of the world except Russia. With this move, American foreign traders had the opportunity to receive governmental aid for trade with any country.[8]

The creation of the banks represented a significant departure in the nation's foreign commercial policy. Since the end of the war, government leaders had insisted that private capital underwrite the expansion of exports. During the 1920s, moreover, bankers had not tied foreign loans to the purchase of American products. The Export-Import Banks reversed these policies by relying on tax-supported dollars to finance the immediate sale of U. S. goods. The circumstances associated with the establishment of the banks, furthermore, reflected a duality of purpose that persisted throughout the decade. On the one hand, the banks were a response to the desire of American foreign trade groups for governmental support. To this degree, the needs of private interest groups defined the institutions' operations. On the other hand, the banks served as a vehicle through which the government could pursue its foreign policy objectives. For the most part, the two purposes were compatible with one another,

7. Officials in the State Department, Commerce Department, and the R.F.C. were involved in establishing the bank, Arey, "History of Operations and Policies of Export-Import Bank," pp. 4–5; *Wall Street Journal*, February 2, 1934, p. 6; ibid., February 10, 1934, p. 9.

8. Because the two institutions were staffed by the same personnel, operated under the same rules, and later were merged, they can be discussed as if they were one, Arey, "History of Operations and Policies of Export-Import Bank," pp. 5–7.

but the potential for discord did exist.[9] Finally, by helping American economic interests expand, the government committed itself to involvement in international affairs.[10]

Because Roosevelt created the Export-Import Banks as independent agencies under the authority granted him in the National Industrial Recovery Act, he did not have to secure immediate congressional approval for his actions.[11] A board of trustees consisting of members from the departments of state, commerce, agriculture, and the treasury, as well as from the R.F.C., and the banks themselves controlled the institutions. R. Walton Moore, an assistant secretary of state and later counselor of the department, became chairman of the board, serving in that capacity until 1941. Inasmuch as the Russian bank remained unused, the board decided in April 1935 to merge the two institutions, a process completed by the end of June. Early in 1936, the Roosevelt administration reorganized the bank, placing it under the supervision of an advisory committee of five men representing the bank, R.F.C., and the departments of

9. The bank's activities provide an example of the relationship existing between functional and cosmopolitan groups. Export-oriented interest groups played an important role in formulating bank policy but they did not dominate the decision-making process. In the final analysis, policy-makers on the highest level controlled the institution. The functional-cosmopolitan relationship is discussed by Thomas J. McCormick, "The State of American Diplomatic History," in *The State of American History*, ed. Herbert Bass, pp. 127–230; Samuel P. Hays, "Political Parties and the Community-Society Continuum," in *The American Party Systems*, ed. William Nisbet Chambers and Walter Dean Burnham, pp. 168–73.

10. James M. McHale has argued recently that the Export-Import Bank was an extension of N.R.A. concepts into foreign trade and posed an alternative to the State Department's hope of stimulating foreign commerce by reducing trade barriers. Even with the end of N.R.A., McHale believes that certain "planners" were able to implement many of their ideas through the bank. As will be clear, my interpretation of the bank, which places greater emphasis on the foreign policy context within which the institution functioned, is considerably different. The bank had more in common with the R.F.C. than N.R.A. See James M. McHale, "The New Deal and the Origins of Public Lending for Foreign Economic Development, 1933–1945" (Ph.D. dissertation, Univ. of Wisconsin, 1970), pp. 1–5 (his analysis of the war years is convincing); James M. McHale, "National Planning and Reciprocal Trade," *Prologue* 6 (Fall 1974): 189–90.

11. Roosevelt maintained that the bank was necessary to enable him to carry out the intention of Congress as stated in N.I.R.A., see Franklin D. Roosevelt, *The Public Papers and Addresses of Franklin D. Roosevelt*, ed. Samuel I. Rosenman, 1934:76–81.

state, commerce, and the treasury. Jesse H. Jones, chairman of R.F.C., headed the committee and accepted ultimate financial responsibility for the institution's operations. An executive council of the board of trustees, headed by the bank's president, administered the bank's routine operations.[12]

Operating under the laws of the District of Columbia, the bank could perform general banking business as well as buy and sell government securities, gold, and bullion. In addition, it could negotiate intergovernmental agreements. It would receive its working capital from the R.F.C.[13] The banking laws of the District of Columbia, however, proved to be too confining: they did not allow discounting, and they limited the size of a single borrower's loans to 10 percent of the bank's unimpaired capital and surplus. But foreign trade financing often required banks to discount notes and to extend large sums to individual traders. Consequently, in early 1935, when Congress extended the life of the bank for two years, it granted the institution immunity from the District's banking laws and authorized it to borrow an unlimited amount of funds, subject only to the approval of the secretary of the treasury. These provisions strengthened the bank by giving it additional flexibility.[14]

Foreign traders had mixed reactions to the establishment of the first Export-Import Bank. Although they desired governmental assistance, traders hoped the bank's activities would not

12. Arey, "History of Operations and Policies of Export-Import Bank," pp. 4–5, 8–9; Export-Import Bank, "Annual Report of the Export-Import Bank of Washington, 1936," mimeograph, pp. 9–10; Jesse Jones, *Fifty Billion Dollars*, p. 217; Export-Import Bank, "Annual Report of the Export-Import Bank of Washington, 1937," mimeograph, p. 7.

13. Feis to Hull, February 18, 1934, File No. 811.516 Export-Import Bank/9, RG 59.

14. Because the end of N.R.A. made legislative action necessary for the continued existence of the banks, the administration attached the necessary enabling provisions to a bill calling for the continuation of the R.F.C., which was passed with ease. Feis to Hull, January 24, 1935, File No. 811.516 Export-Import Bank/62, RG 59; U.S. Congress, Senate, Committee on Banking and Currency, Report no. 21, 74th Cong., 1st sess., *Extension of Functions of Reconstruction Finance Corporation*, p. 7; U.S. Congress, Senate, Committee on Banking and Currency, 74th Cong., 1st sess., *Hearings to Extend the Functions of the Reconstruction Finance Corporation*, p. 24; U.S. Congress, House, Committee on Banking and Currency, 74th Cong., 1st sess., *Hearings, A Bill to Extend the Functions of the Reconstruction Finance Corporation*, pp. 44, 61–62, 66–71.

be limited to Russia. More significantly, they worried that the government might overlook the wishes of private groups. To avoid this, the American Manufacturers' Export Association and the National Foreign Trade Council set up a committee to draft guidelines for the new institution. In explaining their motivation, committee members indicated an apprehension that the government would overlook many important details unless it gained the confidence of those active in foreign commerce. One of the initial tasks undertaken by the first president of the Export-Import Bank, George N. Peek, was to establish ties with groups in the private sector of the economy. Addressing the 1934 convention of the American Bankers' Association, Peek suggested that the bankers form a committee to cooperate with the bank. "I believe," he noted, "that if we cultivate that closer contact, we with you, and you with us, we may be able to render one another considerable service in the months ahead." [15]

The Bankers' Association complied with Peek's request by creating an advisory committee. After its first meeting, the committee offered to provide publicity for the institution and to promote cooperation with commercial banks. The committee members also recommended the formation of an executive committee to advise the bank on foreign transactions and act as a consultant on special projects. With regard to a lending policy, the bankers thought the Export-Import Bank should concentrate on those transactions that were of longer duration or of greater risk than commercial institutions could handle. The bank should assume a portion of the risk in approved deals and should try to solve the difficulties of obtaining foreign exchange. Finally, the com-

15. *New York Times*, February 10, 1934, p. 22; press release by National Foreign Trade Council, received February 12, 1934, File No. 600.115 Financial Institute in Interest of American Trade/6, RG 59; F. C. Engergart to Hull, February 16, 1934, File No. 800.516 Export-Import Bank/6, RG 59; M. R. Dormitzer to Hull, February 20, 1934, File No. 800.516 Export-Import Bank/8, RG 59; "RFC Aids Foreign Trade," *Business Week* (February 10, 1934): 6–7; Resolution by American Manufacturers' Export Association, February 7, 1934, File No. 600.1115 Financial Institute in Interest of American Trade/5, RG 59; *New York Times*, February 11, 1934, sec. 2, p. 6; Arey, "History of Operations and Policies of Export-Import Bank of Washington," p. 7; Speech before the American Bankers' Association Convention, October 22, 1934, File No. 1, Speeches and Statements of George N. Peek, Records of the Export-Import Bank °S.A.F.T., RG 20 (National Archives, Washington, D.C.).

mittee suggested that all requests for Export-Import Bank assistance be channeled initially through commercial banks, which would screen applications and reduce the possibility of the government bank supplanting private institutions.[16]

Having received the cooperation of the banking community, Peek next suggested that the influential National Foreign Trade Council also establish an advisory committee. Since its formation by many of the nation's most powerful business leaders in 1914, the council had worked to improve coordination among those involved in overseas economic activities. It sought to aid in the development of a sound foreign trade policy by holding meetings, issuing reports, and consulting with government officials. With a membership drawn primarily from commerce, industry, transportation, and banking (including individuals from such leading corporations as United States Steel, General Motors, Chrysler, General Electric, Westinghouse, Caterpillar Tractor, and Standard Oil of New Jersey and from such financial institutions as Chase National Bank, National City Bank of New York, Bankers Trust, and Guaranty Trust), the National Foreign Trade Council reflected the views of those members of the nation's industrial sector who had a significant stake in the international economy. Eugene P. Thomas, president of the council since 1932 and formerly a vice-president of United States Steel, lobbied persistently during the 1930s for governmental support for American exporters, especially those represented by his organization. Consequently, Thomas and the members of the National Foreign Trade Council responded enthusiastically to Peek's suggestion by forming an advisory committee to work with the Export-Import Bank and the committee of the Bankers' Association.[17]

16. "A Plan of Cooperation with the Export-Import Banks," December 3, 1934, General Correspondence File, Export-Import Bank, Part 1, RG 234; "Page One," *Banking: Journal of the American Bankers' Association* 27 (December 1934): 1.

17. Speech before the National Foreign Trade Convention, November 2, 1934, File No. 1, Speeches and Statements by George N. Peek, press releases 1, RG 20; Peek to Sayre, December 15, File No. 811.516 Export-Import Bank/60½, RG 59; "Joint Statement by Exporters' and Importers' Advisory Committee and Export-Import Bank," December 14, 1935, Office of the Secretary, General Correspondence 96227, Records of the Department of Commerce, RG 40 (National Archives, Washington, D.C.). For background on the origins of the N.F.T.C., see Burton I. Kaufman,

In March 1935, the two advisory committees along with representatives of agricultural interests and the government held a two-day meeting which produced a number of recommendations that provide a key to understanding the way private groups defined the role of the bank. One objective of the conferees was to ensure that bank officials would remain in close contact with those actively involved in foreign commerce. Business and financial leaders also were hopeful that the institution would provide American exporters with the same degree of aid other governments afforded their nationals. To accomplish this goal, the bank would have to assume a portion of the risk in approved deals and be willing to match foreign competition by extending credits in excess of the export value of the products. The foreign trade interests further recommended that the bank not withhold support from the sale of capital goods which could manufacture products that would compete with American exports. Other recommendations coming from the conference were that the bank cooperate in the liquidation of blocked balances, that it consider barter arrangements, and that, in general, it become the focal point for the nation's international commerce.[18]

By early 1935, foreign trade interests had made considerable progress in formulating their objectives and in transmitting them to the proper government officials. These private interests clearly wanted the Export-Import Bank to provide sufficient financial support so that American exporters could compete on an equal basis with exporters from other nations. If the bank had adopted their guidelines, foreign trade groups would have succeeded in obtaining maximum financial support with a minimal amount of government control. In other words, the Export-Import Bank would have functioned in the American tradition of public risk taking and private profit making.[19]

Efficiency and Expansion, pp. 82–84; for an idea of its membership, see the list of the Board of Directors in each annual report, for example, see *Report of the Twenty-fifth National Foreign Trade Convention* (New York, 1939), pp. ix–x; also see Eugene P. Thomas, "European Government Attitude toward Forward Trade," *Foreign Trade in 1931: Official Report of the Eighteenth National Foreign Trade Convention* (New York, 1931), pp. 400–411.

18. E. P. Thomas to Earl B. Schwulst, April 8, 1935, General Correspondence File, Ex-Im Bk., Part 1, RG 234.

19. For an interesting essay on the evolution on this tradition, see Rob-

Prior to the creation of the advisory committees, bank officials had issued a declaration of general policy. According to this statement, the Export-Import Bank existed to supplement, not supplant, the existing banking structure. It would, therefore, limit its actions primarily to transactions that regular financial institutions would not undertake. The bank would allow commercial banks to share in its loans if they desired to do so and would offer three types of credit: short-term of up to 180 days, intermediate of from 180 days to one year, and long-term of from one to five years. On the first two types, the bank charged ¾ percent interest over what it paid the R.F.C. for its funds. On the long-term credits, it increased the charge to 1 percent.

An important question was whether the bank would extend credit on a without-recourse basis. Under this arrangement, in case of default, the bank would not have recourse against the exporter but would have to deal directly with the foreign buyers. On the other hand, loans extended on a with-recourse basis would enable the Export-Import Bank to retain access to the exporter. This setup also meant that exporters would not receive a governmental guarantee since they would be responsible for repayment. Because of the guarantee aspect, the foreign trade community preferred without-recourse financing. Administration officials appreciated the need for measures allowing American exporters to match foreign competition, but they also understood that without recourse financing could lead to political involvement abroad, particularly if the buyer was a governmental agency. The bank's initial policy statement reflected this ambivalence, suggesting that it would not consider the guaranteeing of credit risks or the acceptance of paper on a without-recourse basis as its primary field of action. Nevertheless, the bank could undertake unusual transactions, which included terms and risks outside the ordinary business routine, provided it levied charges commensurate with the risk. In the case of fabricated articles, the bank would cover up to 75 percent of the total credit or net delivered cost, whichever was lower; it would treat nonfabricated articles on a case-by-case basis.[20]

ert A. Lively, "The American System," *Business History Review* 29 (March 1955): 81–96.

20. "Policy Statement of Export-Import Bank," July 20, 1934, General Correspondence File 96227, RG 40.

As the recommendations of the joint conference of advisory committees demonstrated, foreign trade leaders were anxious to have the bank broaden its use of without-recourse financing. Besides wanting the Export-Import Bank to adopt a general policy of assuming a portion of the trading risk, businessmen hoped the bank would do so for a client's entire export business, instead of limiting itself to individual deals. Of those exporters replying to a poll taken by the National Federation of Foreign Trade Associations, over 80 percent believed the bank's policy of extending credits on a with-recourse basis would not help them develop export sales and 65 percent favored a guarantee plan using without-recourse credits. Despite pressure for a more aggressive policy, the bank's new policy statement of May 1935 was virtually the same as the original one. Bank officials again indicated that they would use nonrecourse financing only in exceptional circumstances. At least on the level of official policy, therefore, foreign trade groups appeared unable to secure the degree of governmental support they desired.[21]

While exporters sought a liberalization of the credit policy, they also discussed the possibility of having the bank offer credit insurance. Various foreign governments, in particular the British, had programs that insured exporters against insolvency on the part of the purchasers. Although he did not believe the bank's powers were broad enough to accommodate this function, Peek was willing to ask Congress for the necessary legislation, provided the exporters and importers of the country supported him and were ready to pay the required premiums.[22] Nothing came of

21. Thomas to Schwulst, April 8, 1935, General Correspondence File, Ex-Im Bk., Part 1, RG 234; "Replies to Questionnaires Sent to Exporters by National Federation of Foreign Trade Associations," n.d. (probably December 1934), General Correspondence 9622, RG 40; also see *New York Times*, December 23, 1934, sec. 2, p. 15 for publication of some of the results; "New Policy Statement," May 21, 1935, press release No. 19, Office File No. 1, Speeches and Statements of George N. Peek, press releases, 1, RG 20. For the State Department's analysis of the statement, see Livesey to Sayre, July 19, 1935, File No. 811.50633/2, RG 59.

22. Thomas to Schwulst, April 8, 1935, General Correspondence File, Ex-Im Bk., Part 1, RG 234; Charles E. Stuart, "Governmental Export Credit Aids," contained in letter, Stuart to Col. M. McIntyre, September 6, 1935, OFF: File 971, Export-Import Bank, August 1935–1936, Franklin D. Roosevelt Papers (Franklin D. Roosevelt Library, Hyde Park, New York); Stuart to James B. Alley, September 4, 1935, General Corre-

the movement, however, even though foreign traders made intermittent appeals for credit insurance throughout the decade. Actually, without-recourse financing provided the same benefits as insurance and not only guarded against insolvency but also guaranteed payment regardless of what happened.[23] The extent to which the bank relied on without-recourse financing, therefore, became an index of the administration's commitment to aid exporters.

Although the Export-Import Bank's official position remained unaltered during 1935, by the middle of the year signs of change appeared. The day following the release of the new policy statement, Charles E. Stuart, executive vice-president of the bank, informed a group of foreign traders that "it has become obvious in many cases that the extension by the Bank of a percentage of non-recourse facilities is essential to the American shipper or manufacturer for consummating a particular deal." Later in the year, Stuart traveled through Europe to examine the governmental trade financing arrangements of several countries. Upon returning to the United States, he urged Roosevelt to liberalize the policy of the Export-Import Bank so that American exporters could more easily meet foreign competition.[24] What Stuart's recommendations suggest is that some Export-Import Bank officials were allying themselves with foreign traders to encourage an expansion of the bank's lending powers. As this alliance occurred, the Department of State became the leading opponent of attempts to alter the bank's policy, especially with regard to Latin American affairs. Thus, by the end of 1935, there emerged

spondence File, Ex-Im Bk., Part 2, RG 234; Peek, "Foreign Trade Credits," November 2, 1934, File No. 1, Speeches and Statements of George N. Peek, press releases 1, RG 20.

23. Grosvenor Jones to F. H. Rawls, December 10, 1938, General Correspondence 96227, RG 40; W. L. Pierson to Richard C. Patterson, Jr., March 28, 1939, File No. 610.1 Federal, 1936–1940, Federal Export-Import Bank, Records of the Bureau of Foreign and Domestic Commerce, RG 151 (National Archives, Washington, D.C.).

24. Charles E. Stuart, "The Export-Import Bank," May 22, 1935, File No. 1 Speeches and Statements of George N. Peek, press releases 1, RG 20; Stuart, "Governmental Export Credit Aids," contained in letter, Stuart to McIntyre, September 6, 1935, OFF: File 971, Export-Import Bank, August 1935–1936, Roosevelt papers; Stuart to Alley, September 4, 1935, General Correspondence File, Ex-Im Bk., Part 2, RG 234.

a tripartite configuration in which export-oriented groups and bank officials joined together to urge the State Department to accept liberalized lending rules.[25]

Another factor keeping the bank from acting consistently was the clash that erupted between the institution's first president, George N. Peek, and the State Department over foreign trade policy. A successful vice-president of John Deere and Company prior to his service on the War Industries Board, Peek had become president of the Moline Plow Company in 1919 only to preside over its bankruptcy a few years later. His concern about the economic difficulties confronting farmers and his apprehension about the dominant position of industrial corporations in America made him a leading spokesman for agricultural interests. During the 1920s, he had championed the McNary-Haugen concept of having the federal government protect domestic price levels by buying surplus crops and disposing of them abroad at lower world prices. Farmers would cover the resultant deficits by paying an equalization fee on each unit sold to processors. A bitter opponent of those who wanted to lower tariffs, he had no sympathy for the unconditional most-favored-nation principle on which the State Department planned to base its trade agreements program. He also did not approve of raising farm prices by reducing production, the approach ultimately adopted by the New Deal. Because of his aggressiveness, experience, and political appeal, however, Roosevelt appointed him head of the Agricultural Adjustment Administration. Peek's strong opposition to the domestic allotment scheme and his disagreements with those who wanted to use the Agricultural Administration as a vehicle for social and economic reforms eventually forced Roosevelt to remove him from the Agricultural Department late in 1933. After serving as head of a temporary committee to study trade policy, Peek became president of the Export-Import Bank and a special adviser on foreign trade. In the latter capacity, he had the authority to coordinate information dealing with inter-

25. The State Department was well represented on the bank's board of trustees and executive committee, and was in a position to veto any proposal, memorandum by Feis, August 9, 1935, File No. 811.50633/5, RG 59; Jones, *Fifty Billion Dollars*, p. 220. Rather than acting as "planners," the exporters and their governmental spokesmen that McHale focuses on functioned more like an interest group seeking special concessions. See McHale, "National Planning and Reciprocal Trade," pp. 189–99.

national commerce and to promote specific transactions. A stubborn and skillful fighter, Peek was in a position where he could influence decisively the character of America's foreign commercial policy.[26]

Peek's new appointments to the bank and as special adviser on foreign trade caused concern within the State Department. Officials in charge of the trade agreements program tried to curb Peek's influence by recommending that the responsibility for formulating commercial policies and negotiating trade agreements remain in the existing departments. These officers also requested that the Executive Committee on Commercial Policy, chaired by a member of the department, continue in operation. The issue was more than a bureaucratic squabble, however, because State Department leaders understood that only by restricting Peek's authority could they protect the unconditional most-favored-nation approach to international commercial relations. Characteristically, Roosevelt did not act on these recommendations for several months until concluding, in June 1934, that the executive committee would remain, and that the Department of State, not the special adviser, would oversee the trade agreements program.[27] Even so, the matter was not settled; because of the president's mercurial nature, Peek continued to have an opportunity to affect policy.

Along with members of the State Department, exporters of manufactured goods were uneasy about Peek. They feared his close association with agricultural interests would make him insensitive to their needs. The bank president's announcements that exporters had overestimated the necessity for credit assistance and that commercial banks should handle most of the foreign trade financing undoubtedly reinforced these apprehensions.[28] Although the tension between manufacturers and

26. For an overall assessment of Peek, see Gilbert Fite, *George N. Peek and the Fight for Farm Parity*, pp. 21–43, 244–66, passim; for Peek's defense of his objectives, see George N. Peek and Samuel Crowther, *Why Quit Our Own*, passim.

27. Memorandum by Sayre, March 2, 1934, File No. 103.99995/1, RG 59; Sayre to Roosevelt, April 5, 1934, OFF: File 971 Export-Import Bank, 1933–August 1934, Roosevelt Papers; Julius Pratt, *Cordell Hull*, 1:115–17.

28. *New York Times*, February 23, 1934, p. 33; ibid., February 27, 1934, pp. 27, 34; Peek and Crowther, *Why Quit Our Own*, p. 194; Peek, "America Must Choose," April 5, 1934, File No. 1, Speeches and Statements of George N. Peek, speeches, RG 20. He also insisted that the bank

Peek and the jurisdictional dispute over who had final authority on trade matters did retard the bank's development somewhat, the conflict between Peek and the State Department over commercial policy remained the biggest stumbling block in the path of the Export-Import Bank.

In a series of speeches and reports, Peek analyzed the economic ills facing the nation. Beginning with the premise that the depressed condition of agriculture, which had begun in the 1920s, was mainly responsible for the general economic decline, he concluded that the administration should look first to the restoration of agricultural prosperity. Because farmers depended heavily on exports, this approach placed a great deal of emphasis on finding new foreign markets. In a report to Roosevelt, Peek noted that from 1910 to 1932 17.86 percent of farm income came from exports, while the portion of industrial income attributable to exports was only 5.25 percent. Furthermore, the earlier policy of attempting to expand industrial exports regardless of the effect on agriculture had failed when the United States no longer could lend other nations the means to purchase American goods. The soundest course for the nation to adopt, Peek insisted, was to send abroad, preferably in manufactured form, "those products we can best produce, particularly those agricultural products which are the backbone of our foreign trade and our domestic prosperity." Although he believed the country would have to liquidate some of its industrial and agricultural overcapacity, Peek thought this could be done in an orderly manner so that production would more nearly balance domestic demand plus potential foreign markets.[29]

---

follow a cautious policy and not become a Santa Claus, *New York Times*, February 27, 1934, p. 27.

29. Extract from Hearings before Senate Committee on Finance, February 14, 1933, File No. 1, Speeches and Statements of George N. Peek, press releases, RG 20; testimony before Senate Agricultural Committee, February 1, 1935, ibid.; address to the Association of Land Grant Colleges and Universities, November 20, 1934, File No. 1, Speeches and Statements of George N. Peek, speeches, RG 20; Peek to Roosevelt, December 31, 1934, OFF: File 971 Export-Import Bank, September–December 1934, Roosevelt Papers; Exhibit 3 in Peek to Roosevelt, May 23, 1934, OFF: File 971, Export-Import Bank, 1933–August 1934, Roosevelt Papers; speech to Foreign Trade Conference, October 17, 1934, File No. 1, Speeches and Statements of George N. Peek, press releases, RG 20; Peek and Crowther, *Why Quit Our Own*, p. 17.

To understand more fully the status of the nation's international economic accounts, Peek studied America's balance of payments over the period 1896 to 1933. On the basis of his research, he decided that the heavy overseas investment during the 1920s had been of questionable value to the United States. Even though American nationals had sent approximately $7.14 billion abroad, foreigners had only spent $2.572 billion for U. S. goods and services. They had used the remainder to buy stocks and bonds as well as to build up short-term investments and bank deposits. By the end of the 1920s, these bank deposits totaled more than $3 billion; but they fell dramatically from 1930 to 1933 when foreigners withdrew $2.55 billion. This rapid decline diminished the country's gold stock which, by helping demoralize the banking system, produced a series of panics. Peek was further disturbed by his discovery that since the war, the movement of capital in international transactions nearly exceeded the movement of merchandise. In 1919, 7.6 percent of dollar settlements had been for investments, but by 1930, this portion had risen to 41.6 percent. At the same time, the share of dollar settlements used for commodity and service transactions fell from 70.7 percent to 41.8 percent.[30]

Besides signaling the bankruptcy of American policy, Peek believed the depression marked a major transition in international economic relations. As nations tried to become self-sufficient, they increased their control over foreign commerce to the point where they no longer relied on unconditional most-favored-nation trade policies. England's rejection of free trade and abandonment of the gold standard symbolized the end of the old order, an order Peek thought would never reappear. The emergence of bilateral trade patterns, characterized by preferential tariffs, quotas, and embargoes, meant that foreign commerce had become the affair of governments rather than of individuals. According to Peek, this transformation boded ill for the United States, since this country did not benefit from the special trade arrangements negotiated by others. He noted, as

30. George N. Peek, "Letter to the President on International Credits for Foreign Trade and Other Purposes—1896–1933" (Washington, D.C., 1934), pp. 5–6; also see his speech to the National Foreign Trade Conference, October 17, 1934, File No. 1, Speeches and Statements of George N. Peek, press releases, RG 20.

indicative of the trend, that for the first time in over a decade, exports from Great Britain exceeded those from America in 1933.[31]

Because of the current state of international economic relations, Peek believed the United States would have to adopt new trade tactics or face increased loss of foreign commerce. He recommended that the country follow the British example by establishing a board of trade to coordinate the numerous governmental bodies dealing with overseas trade. The board would compile accurate records of America's commercial and financial relations with each foreign nation, permitting the U. S. to follow a selective trade policy. The country would send abroad those goods it produced most competitively in exchange for necessary raw materials and other products that did least violence to the domestic economy. By working to unravel blocked exchanges, the board of trade could also ensure that American traders received payment for past exports.[32] With methods similar to those of other nations, Peek was convinced that the U. S. could return to the essence of trading, which he defined as an exchange of goods on a commodity basis. A reliance on monetary exchange was not necessarily beneficial, Peek believed, since the nation could find its assets diminished by the amount of the unpaid trade balance. The bank president, therefore, supported a two-price system whereby goods sold in the domestic market would receive higher prices than those sold in the world market. If the administration could persuade foreign governments to consent to this practice, there was little likelihood they would retaliate against United States goods.[33]

31. "Foreign Trade and Money," January 30, 1935, File No. 1, Speeches and Statements by George N. Peek, press releases, RG 20; Excerpts of Testimony before Senate Agricultural Committee, February 1, 1935, ibid.; "America Must Choose," April 4, 1935, File No. 1, Speeches and Statements of George N. Peek, speeches, RG 20; "Foreign Trade Under New Conditions," May 24, 1935, File No. 40, Office File, press releases, RG 20; Peek and Crowther, *Why Quit Our Own,* pp. 167–72.

32. Speech to the National Foreign Trade Conference, October 17, 1934, File No. 1, Speeches and Statements of George N. Peek, press releases, RG 20; "Foreign Trade Credits," November 2, 1934, ibid.

33. These ideas are contained in various speeches and articles by Peek, see "Foreign Trade and Money," January 30, 1935; "Foreign Trade and Yankee Trading," June 9, 1934; testimony at Hearing Before Senate Agricultural Committee, February 1, 1935, File No. 1, Speeches and Statements of George N. Peek, speeches, RG 20; "Foreign Trade Under New

Peek was insistent that the nation restructure its foreign trade policy because he assumed America could not attain permanent prosperity without the revival of foreign commerce. As he observed, "Everyone is agreed we should have foreign trade. The question is *what* we shall export—what shall import—and *how* it can be accomplished."[34] International commerce was "the alternative to the drastic economic and social readjustment which will be necessary if we lose our foreign trade." A key to Peek's approach was his belief that the expanded role of government in overseas commerce and finance would eliminate the need for regimentation in internal affairs.[35]

It is not surprising that Peek was critical of the Roosevelt administration's reciprocal trade agreements program, opposing the unconditional most-favored-nation principle on several counts. First, it could jeopardize the legitimate interest of American production for the home market. Second, the United States could encounter difficulties in bargaining, because nations would have no incentive to conclude trade agreements if they expected automatically to obtain the concessions America had granted to another country. Moreover, some countries might cancel concessions extended to the U.S. when they discovered that the gains they received did not accrue to their special advantage but applied to all. Peek also did not agree with the assertion that the limitation of concessions to principal suppliers of commodities would minimize the effects of automatic tariff generalization. Usually not one but several nations were major suppliers and often the main source of particular items shifted from year to year. This approach, furthermore, would virtually

Conditions," May 24, 1934, File No. 4, Office File, press releases, RG 20; "Our Foreign Trade Objectives," *Banking: Journal of the American Bankers' Association* 27 (January 1935): 23, 59.

34. Emphasis in original, "Foreign Trade and Money," January 30, 1935, File No. 1, Speeches and Statements of George N. Peek, speeches, RG 20; also see "America Must Choose," April 5, 1934, ibid.

35. "Foreign Trade Under New Conditions," May 24, 1934, File No. 4, Office File, press releases, RG 20; also see his address to the Association of Land Grant Colleges and Universities, November 20, 1934, File No. 1, Speeches and Statements of George N. Peek, speeches, RG 20; address to the National Foreign Trade Conference, October 17, 1934, File No. 1, Speeches and Statements of George N. Peek, press releases, RG 20. Peek's intense opposition to regulatory policies (particularly those involving any limitation of agricultural production) is a major theme of *Why Quit Our Own.*

rule out negotiations with small countries, which were not principal suppliers to the American markets. Peek's final criticism of the New Deal foreign trade policy was that its emphasis on triangular trade patterns was misdirected. Most of the world's commerce was bilateral, with a large part of the so-called triangular trade involving the transfer of nonmerchandise items. Peek reasoned that the wisest course was to negotiate accords on a conditional most-favored-nation basis, as the country had done prior to the Harding administration.[36]

The bank president did offer some penetrating criticisms of the American overseas economic policy. His insights into the changing nature of world trade and the problems associated with the principal supplier concept were worthy of greater consideration than they ultimately received.[37] Yet his proposals did contain crucial weaknesses. Peek's emphasis on the primacy of agriculture was out of place in an increasingly urban America. Farmers unquestionably needed assistance, but they probably stood to gain more from a healthy industrial sector than from a recovery program primarily attuned to agrarian problems. Furthermore, there is reason to doubt whether Peek's plan of regulating only foreign trade was practical, since this would not have remedied dislocations within the domestic economy and would have increased efforts to find new outlets for the ever-mounting surpluses. With the government playing the major role in the search for overseas markets, the likelihood of foreign entanglements would have grown. Finally, the probability that the government could regulate foreign commerce but not the domestic economy was very small.

36. Memorandum by Peek, December 4, 1934, contained in letter, Stephen Early to Roosevelt, December 5, 1934, OFF: File 971, Export-Import Bank, September–December 1934, Roosevelt Papers; Peek to Roosevelt, December 12, 1934, ibid.; also see address to the Association of Land Grant Colleges and Universities, November 20, 1934, File No. 1, Speeches and Statements of George N. Peek, speeches, RG 20; "Foreign Trade and Money," January 30, 1935, File No. 1, Speeches and Statements of George N. Peek, press releases, RG 20; Peek and Crowther, *Why Quit Our Own*, pp. 250–60.

37. See Lloyd C. Gardner, *Economic Aspects of New Deal Diplomacy*, pp. 43–44; while acknowledging the validity of Peek's contention that the changing nature of world trade necessitated a new commercial policy, Gardner has pointed out some of the weaknesses of the bank president's alternative.

The State Department's trade policy, of course, differed significantly from the one Peek advocated. Cordell Hull and Francis B. Sayre, the assistant secretary in charge of the trade agreements program, were the principal architects of the department's position. Hull, a professional politician from Tennessee, had served in both the House of Representatives and the Senate before becoming secretary of state, a position he held until late 1944. In all likelihood, his long tenure was attributable to his popularity with members of Congress, which made him a political asset for Roosevelt, and to his toughness as a bureaucratic fighter. As Raymond Moley, George Peek, and others discovered, Hull, while often slow moving and cautious, was a difficult person to best in a prolonged power struggle. He was also a devout believer in Wilsonian international principles, particularly economic affairs. Hull's primary objective as secretary of state was the removal of the many obstacles to world trade that had emerged since 1919. Although eager to aid American farmers, he believed that lower tariffs, not the McNary-Haugen concept, would solve their problems. Assistant Secretary Sayre was in complete agreement with Hull's approach to foreign policy. An international lawyer, Harvard University professor, and son-in-law of Woodrow Wilson, Sayre believed that America should strive to create an international economic system based on reduced tariff barriers and equal opportunity. Given these conditions, the nations of the world would enjoy peace and prosperity.[38]

Under the direction of Hull and Sayre, therefore, the State Department viewed world politics from a Wilsonian perspective. As disclosed in a series of speeches delivered from 1934 on, department officers argued that the Republican administrations

38. Cordell Hull, *The Memoirs of Cordell Hull*, 1:81–88, 106–7, 120–39; Pratt, *Cordell Hull*, 1:1–12, 17–18; William R. Allen, "The International Trade Philosophy of Cordell Hull, 1907–1933," *American Economic Review* 43 (March 1953): 101–16; William R. Allen, "Cordell Hull and the Defense of the Trade Agreements Program," in *Isolation and Security*, ed. Alexander DeConde, pp. 107–32; Arthur W. Schatz, "Cordell Hull and the Struggle for the Reciprocal Trade Agreements Program, 1932–1940" (Ph.D dissertation, Univ. of Oregon, 1965), pp. 28–37; Francis B. Sayre, *Woodrow Wilson and Economic Disarmament*, Department of State, Commercial Policy Series, no. 20, pp. 2–12; Sayre dedicated his book, *The Way Forward: The American Trade Agreements Program* (New York, 1939), to Hull.

had erred by failing to adjust the nation's tariff policy to reflect its new status as a world creditor.[39] Instead of reducing duty levels, the Republicans had relied on foreign lending to support the export trade. When the flow of loans stopped, debtor nations faced balance of payments deficits which they tried to close by restricting international commerce. Although it was not the sole cause of the depression, the resulting maze of trade restrictions posed one of the major barriers to the return of worldwide prosperity.[40]

State Department officials felt that the unconditional most-favored-nation policy offered the best method of removing these obstacles for three major reasons. The first was that, due to its make-up, the country's foreign trade required a world system based on triangular trade patterns. The U. S. shipped large quantities of raw materials, such as cotton, wheat, corn, and hog products, to Europe but did not import enough goods from that area to pay for the exports. America's commerce with tropical countries, to which it mainly sent manufactured products, also produced an adverse balance of payments. Meanwhile, the nation's trade with the British Dominions and Argentina, a third trading bloc, was favorable. "From this it must be clear," explained Sayre, "that any policy which proves destructive to triangular trade strikes at the very heart of American commercial interests." Because of the nation's favorable balance of payments, attempts to match trade on a bilateral basis would reduce the level of exports. Triangular trade patterns, thus, were in America's best interests, but these patterns depended on the unconditional most-favored-nation principle.[41]

39. The State Department's Commercial Policy Series provides scholars with a detailed description of New Deal foreign commercial policy.

40. Department officials also emphasized the need for domestic recovery programs, Sumner Welles, *The Trade-Agreements Program*, Department of State, Commercial Policy Series, no. 2, pp. 4–6; Cordell Hull, *International Trade and Domestic Prosperity*, Department of State, Commercial Policy Series, no. 3, pp. 2–9; Francis B. Sayre, *American Commercial Policy*, Department of State, Commercial Policy Series, no. 6, pp. 3–6; Cordell Hull, *Restoration of International Trade*, Department of State, Commercial Policy Series, no. 11 (Washington, 1935), p. 2; Sayre, *Woodrow Wilson and Economic Disarmament*, pp. 1–10.

41. Francis B. Sayre, *Most-Favored Nation vs. Preferential Bargaining*, Department of State, Commercial Policy Series, no. 15, pp. 6–9; Francis B. Sayre, *Trade Agreements and the Farmer*, Department of State, Com-

A second argument was that the State Department's policy could promote prosperity without imposing controls on either domestic or foreign commerce. Taking direct aim at one of the weak spots in Peek's program, Secretary Hull warned that the regulation of foreign trade "forces the country that pursues these policies into an extension of internal control over its domestic institutions."[42] The third justification for the unconditional most-favored-nation approach was that it eased international tensions, whereas discriminatory trade arrangements created jealousies and hardships. A commonly held assumption within the department was that nations would rather fight than tolerate a deterioration of living conditions. Hence, the closing of international trade and the emergence of competing economic blocs were among the leading causes of war. Accordingly, the unconditional most-favored-nation policy was "the principal instrument which is working for the maintenance of the peace of the world in a world in which that peace is so definitely threatened."[43] Speaking to the United States Chamber of Commerce in the spring of 1935, Cordell Hull stretched this analysis to its most extreme conclusion. After noting that the disruption of international trade had opened the door for political upheavals in various countries, he discussed the full significance of the depression:

> The dangerous political situations that exist throughout the world today, the international tension, the recrudescence of the military

mercial Policy Series, no. 25, pp. 7–9; Francis B. Sayre, *Building for Peace*, Department of State, Commercial Policy Series, no. 33, pp. 3–6.

42. Hull, *International Trade and Domestic Prosperity*, pp. 7–8; Sayre, *Most-Favored Nation vs. Preferential Bargaining*, p. 6.

43. George S. Messersmith, *Some Aspects of the Assistance Rendered by the Department of State and its Foreign Service to American Business*, Department of State, Commercial Policy Series, no. 40, p. 17; for a full development of this theme, see the following addresses by Francis B. Sayre: *Trade Policies and Peace*, Department of State, Commercial Policy Series, no. 21; *Building for Peace*; *The Hull Agreements and International Trade*, Department of State, Commercial Policy Series, no. 35; *The "Good Neighbor" Policy and Trade Agreements*, Department of State, Commercial Policy Series, no. 34; *Liberal Trade Policies the Basis for Peace*, Department of State, Commercial Policy Series, no. 37; *The Winning of the Peace*, Department of State, Commercial Policy Series, no. 38; *To World Peace through World Trade*, Department of State, Commercial Policy Series, no. 43; also see Cordell Hull, *Recent Developments in Foreign Trade*, Department of State, Commercial Policy Series, no. 51.

spirit, the expansion of standing armies, the enormously increased military budgets, the feverish efforts made to invent new instruments of warfare, new weapons for offense and defense—all these have emerged and developed in a world in which the international economic structure has been shattered, in which normal peaceful commercial intercourse has been broken and vast unemployment and human distress resulted. It is the collapse of the world structure, the development of isolated economies, that has let loose the fear which now grips every nation and which threatens the peace of the world. We cannot have a peaceful world, we cannot have a prosperous world, until we rebuild the international economic structure.[44]

The importance of the administration's foreign trade program, therefore, was not merely that it provided expanded markets. For, in the words of Secretary Hull: "What is fundamentally at stake today is no less than the very survival of the entire western civilization that has been laboriously built up through centuries. History offers abundant proof that the development of order under law and the growth of international commerce have been among the principal forces which have shaped and nourished the progress of that civilization." The chief tasks confronting mankind, therefore, were the reassertion of law in international relations and a reinvigoration of international trade. The creation of a sound world economic order, furthermore, was "essential to the attainment of those three great demands of men and women everywhere—freedom, security, and peace."[45]

The conflict between Peek and Hull came into the open in the latter part of 1934 when Peek proposed a cotton barter deal with Germany. Under the terms of the transaction, German textile interests would purchase 800,000 bales of cotton. They would buy 25 percent of it at the market price, paying in dollars, and would purchase the remaining 75 percent at the market price plus a fixed premium, but would pay in reichsmarks. The Export-Import Bank, acting as the agent for American brokers, would be in charge of selling the German currency. However, the bank could sell reichsmarks only for the purchase of German pro-

44. Cordell Hull, *The Foreign Commercial Policy of the United States*, Department of State, Commercial Policy Series, no. 9, pp. 7–8.

45. Hull, *Recent Developments in Foreign Trade*, p. 11; for the development of this theme, see Sumner Welles, *Post-War Commercial Policy*, Department of State, Commercial Policy Series, no. 71, p. 8.

ducts, and at a rate below the prevailing level but not less than the dollar value of reichsmarks prior to the devaluation of the dollar. Because of the premium price on 75 percent of the cotton, the bank could offer reichsmarks at a discount without absorbing a loss. In effect, the deal involved the subsidization of foreign trade as well as providing an advantage for German products.[46] In addition to violating the State Department's position on preferential trade arrangements and its opposition to barter deals, the proposal raised the issue of whether Germany would be dumping goods in the United States by selling them at a lower price than in Germany. If the attorney general so ruled, the law required the secretary of the treasury to impose countervailing duties against the offending products.

The forces opposed to the transaction moved quickly into action. On November 28, Hull forwarded three long memoranda to Roosevelt, indicating that with the exception of Peek there was complete acceptance of the unconditional most-favored-nation principle by those in charge of formulating foreign trade policy. Members of the Interdepartmental Trade Agreements Committee, the Tariff Commission, the Department of Commerce, and the Department of Agriculture agreed with the State Department's position that bilateral trade arrangements would destroy the natural course of trade.[47]

In early December, the Interdepartmental Trade Agreements Committee explained to the president why it opposed the cotton deal. One reason was that the plan was not economically sound. It would not necessarily lead to increased purchases of American cotton because the Germans might decide against paying a premium price to U.S. exporters. The subsidization of German imports, moreover, could have an adverse effect on the recovery program by forcing domestic prices to fall in order to match lower-priced imports. In addition, the proposal discriminated against American exporters of noncotton products. A second major objection was that the transaction jeopardized the trade

46. Memorandum from Interdepartmental Trade Agreements Committee to Henry A. Wallace, December 6, 1934, File No. 622.1115/108A, RG 59; Memorandum on German Cotton Deal, December 8, 1934, File No. 65A473,18,3246/1 Ex-Im Bk. of Wash., 1933–1935, Department of the Treasury (U.S. Department of the Treasury, Washington, D.C.).

47. Hull to Roosevelt, November 28, 1934, PSF: State Department 1933–35, Roosevelt Papers.

agreements program. If the United States gave special terms to Germany, other nations might be reluctant to enter into agreements with this country unless they too received individual concessions. The Brazilian ambassador had already expressed doubts about whether his country would conclude a proposed trade pact with the United States if the deal with Germany went through.[48]

In spite of this opposition, Peek moved steadily ahead. He obtained a preliminary ruling from the general counsel of the treasury that the proposal would not constitute dumping; and on December 12, he appeared to receive Roosevelt's sanction for the plan. Although, in principle, the president did not agree with Peek's recommendations for a new foreign trade policy, he was not as strongly opposed to them as were his advisers. Besides, Roosevelt was usually willing to bend a principle if he could gain something by doing so.[49] At the moment when Peek was about to consummate the deal however, Hull succeeded in marshaling sufficient support to persuade the president to reconsider. Consequently, the issue remained unresolved throughout the remainder of the winter.[50]

In March, Peek again contacted Roosevelt about the possibility of reopening conversations with those opposed to the cot-

48. Memorandum from Interdepartmental Trade Agreements Committee to Henry A. Wallace, December 6, 1934, File No. 622.1115/108A, RG 59; this memorandum was sent to Roosevelt on December 11, 1934, OFF: File 971, Export-Import Bank, September–December 1934, Roosevelt Papers.

49. Herman Oliphant to W. L. Pierson, December 10, 1934, File No. 662.1115/110, RG 59; W. Phillips to Hull, December 13, 1934, Correspondence II, Container 37, Folder 81, Cordell Hull Papers (Library of Congress, Washington, D.C.). Although he agreed with Hull's theories on foreign trade, the president did not rule out the possibility of negotiating some barter transactions. Nonetheless, he did not favor the McNary-Haugen approach of Peek, Roosevelt to Hull, November 19, 1934, in *Franklin D. Roosevelt and Foreign Affairs*, ed. Edgar B. Nixon, 2:274; press conference, November 23, 1934, ibid., pp. 282–86.

50. Hull, *Memoirs*, 1:373–74; for examples of the steps taken by various State Department officials to strengthen their position, see Green Hackworth to Sayre, February 4, 1935, File No. 662.1115/154½, RG 59; Feis to Hull, December 26, 1934, Subject File, Container 85, Folder 384, Hull Papers; excerpt of a letter from Sayre to G. E. Petty, contained in Peek to Roosevelt, March 11, 1935, File No. 662.116 Fruit/86, RG 59; Executive Committee Meeting, December 11, 1935, File No. 662.115/163, RG 59; Sayre to Roosevelt, April 6, 1935, OFF: File 971, Export-Import Bank, March–May 1935, Roosevelt Papers.

ton agreement with the Germans. This time the president decisively rejected Peek's request. "This transaction received very careful consideration and study last December," Roosevelt wrote. "In effect it involved a questionable modification of the anti-dumping laws; it ran into conflict with the foreign commercial policy of the United States; and the particular form of the proposal was open to very serious economic objections. For these reasons it was decided not to enter into the transaction. I do not feel that any new circumstances have arisen sufficient to alter that decision."[51] The president, thus, handed the State Department a major victory. By the end of the year, Peek had resigned because of Roosevelt's attitude toward international commercial matters; and the president was publicly identifying liberal trade policies, grounded in the unconditional most-favored-nation principle, as one of the most important factors working for world peace.[52]

To a great extent, the Export-Import Bank became a victim of the Hull-Peek controversy; as long as the outcome of that struggle remained in doubt, the bank's position in the overall foreign trade picture was cloudy. The fact that its president was one of the principals in the debate reinforced this uncertainty, particularly since Peek was more concerned about the nation's commercial policy than about the operation of the bank. Because of this uncertainty and because the newness of the institution necessitated a certain amount of experimentation, the bank functioned on a limited scale during 1934 and 1935.[53]

By 1936, however, changes were imminent. Warren L. Pierson, the bank's new president, thought the institution should play

51. Peek to Roosevelt, March 11, 1935, File No. 662.116 Fruit/86, RG 59; Peek to Roosevelt, March 9, 1935, OFF: File 971 Export-Import Bank, March–May 1935, Roosevelt Papers; Roosevelt to Peek, April 8, 1935, ibid.

52. Peek and Crowther, *Why Quit Our Own*, chap. 1; press conference, November 17, 1935, Nixon, *Roosevelt and Foreign Affairs*, 3:72–80; Roosevelt to Hull, February 6, 1936, ibid., pp. 186–87; Chautauqua speech, August 14, 1936, ibid., pp. 377–83; speech in St. Paul, October 9, 1936, ibid., pp. 452–54.

53. Export-Import Bank, "Annual Report of the Export-Import Bank of Washington, 1936," p. 5; Gardner Patterson, "The Export-Import Bank," *Quarterly Journal of Economics* 58 (November 1943): 68. For the argument that Hull viewed the bank with suspicion, see McHale, "New Deal and Origins of Public Lending," pp. 144–46; McHale, "National Planning and Reciprocal Trade," pp. 191–93, 197.

a more ambitious role than it had in the past. Pierson had been a successful Los Angeles lawyer before coming to Washington in 1933 to work in the R.F.C. He had been the bank's general counsel while Peek headed the institution and retained those duties when he took over the presidency. Pierson saw foreign trade as "probably the most interesting phase of modern business," and believed that the great movements of history were closely allied with man's desire to increase his material holdings. World trade was critical, but the increased complexity of international commerce caused by the depression had reduced the exchange of goods. National governments therefore, had become intimately involved in trade procedures, with the Export-Import Bank representing the U. S. government's growing involvement in commercial affairs. Pierson assumed that the bank could make a significant contribution to stimulating foreign trade by supporting sound business propositions.[54] The change in bank leadership also gave export-oriented groups an opportunity to repeat their requests for a liberalized lending policy. Fred I. Kent, the representative of both advisory committees, wrote Jesse Jones in January 1936, that it was "important to American foreign trade to put our exporters upon the same basis of operation as those of competitive foreign countries." The present moment, he continued, was propitious for a study designed "to develop the policies that shall prevail in the future."[55] Under Pierson's leadership, the bank began to press for many of the changes foreign trade groups desired.

Even though it operated at a low level during its first two years, the Export-Import Bank established routines that persisted throughout the remainder of the decade. In keeping with its earlier promise, the bank worked closely with commercial banks which handled most of the actual discounting, collection, and administrative details. The Export-Import Bank agreed to reimburse these institutions any time the need arose. This procedure, in conjunction with the small scale of its activities, al-

54. Warren L. Pierson, "Foreign Trade and the Export-Import Bank of Washington," May 29, 1935, File No. 1, Speeches and Statements of George N. Peek, press release, RG 20.

55. Fred I. Kent to Jesse Jones, January 10, 1936, General Correspondence File, Ex-Im Bk., Part 2, RG 234; also see Jones to Alexander Dye, February 24, 1936, File No. 610.1 Federal, 1936–1940, Federal Export-Import Bank, RG 151.

lowed the bank to function with a staff of no more than thirteen. Of equal significance, the procedure meant that the governmental institution did not replace the private foreign trade banking machinery.[56]

Bank officials also developed a loose set of guidelines for judging credit requests. They tried to determine the impact of prospective loans on the American economy as well as on the development of friendly relations with other countries. They were, moreover, interested in gaining access to new markets which would lead to permanent increases in U.S. trade. When dealing with nations in default on previous loans from American citizens, bank officers considered whether the credit would diminish the possibility of the bondholders being paid. In addition, they refused to finance the sale of munitions and insisted that each borrower comply with the N.R.A. provisions affecting its trade or industry.[57] To an extent, the bank placed a higher priority on expanding trade than it did on receiving payment on repudiated debts. The bank did not have to abide by the terms of the Johnson Act, which closed the U. S. money market to foreign governments in default on their obligations to the American government, and by dealing with United States exporters, the bank could avoid negotiating directly with groups that had stopped paying American bondholders.[58]

During its first three years of operation, the Export-Import

56. Warren L. Pierson, "Export-Import Bank Operations," *Annals of the American Academy of Political and Social Science* 211 (September 1940): 39; Charles R. Whittlesey, "Five Years of the Export-Import Bank," *American Economic Review* 29 (September 1939): 40. On the size of the bank's staff, see U.S. Congress, House, Committee on Appropriations, *Hearings, Legislative Establishment Appropriation Bill for 1938*, 75th Cong., 1st sess., p. 23; memorandum by Moore, June 15, 1935, OFF: File 971, Export-Import Bank, May–August 1935, Roosevelt Papers.

57. With the death of the N.R.A. in 1935, the last provision obviously no longer applied, Warren L. Pierson, "Export-Import Bank of Washington, 1938," mimeograph (Washington, D.C., 1939), p. 2; Charles E. Stuart, "The Export-Import Banks," August 21, 1934, General Correspondence File, Ex-Im Bk., Part 1, RG 234.

58. In 1934, at the urging of Senator Hiram Johnson, Congress passed a bill which forbade governments in default on their war debt payments to float loans in the United States. Because the Johnson Act applied only to intergovernmental debts, it did not have an adverse impact on hemispheric relations, see J. Chalmers Vinson, "War Debts and Peace Legislation," *Mid-America* 50 (July 1968): 211–17; also see *New York Times*, February 15, 1934, p. 27.

Bank performed a few special functions in addition to financing foreign trade. In several instances, the bank took control of obligations, held by other government agencies, that had arisen from earlier transactions. In 1936, it purchased from the R.F.C. and the Farm Credit Administration promisory notes of the Republic of China resulting from sales of cotton, wheat, and flour. The following year, bank officials collected notes issued by a German corporation in connection with the 1931 purchase of wheat from the Grain Stabilization Corporation. A second function, which will be discussed in greater detail in Chapter 5, was that the Export-Import Bank bought and minted silver bullion for the Cuban government. This transaction did not directly involve foreign commerce but it was related to United States-Cuban relations. A third function not immediately connected to the export of goods was the agreement to discount, with full recourse against American holders, the notes issued by the Banco do Brazil in payment for the blocked balances of American exporters in Brazil. By the end of 1936, these transactions accounted for approximately $65 million of the bank's total authorization of $112,728,013.[59]

The rest of the bank's business dealt with commercial transactions. At the beginning of 1937, it had committed $10,115,317 for the export of agricultural products and $37,650,808 for industrial exports. In each case, the amount disbursed was far below the commitments ($849,284 and $238,764 respectively). A combination of factors caused this discrepancy. American exporters occasionally were underbid or they were unable to raise the capital necessary to finance their share of the burden. Sometimes the foreign buyer decided against the transaction after the bank had made a commitment. In other cases, commercial banks undertook the entire financial burden once the bank committed itself.[60]

59. Export-Import Bank, "Annual Report, 1936," pp. 4–7; Export-Import Bank, "Annual Report, 1937," pp. 3–4; Patterson, "The Export-Import Bank," p. 68; Dye to Malcolm Kerlin, July 16, 1937, File No. 610.1 Federal, 1936–1940, Federal Export-Import Bank, RG 151; Dye's total for the three transactions seems excessive.

60. Dye to Kerlin, July 16, 1937, File No. 610.1 Federal, 1936–1940, Federal Export-Import Bank, RG 151; Arey, "History of Operations and Policies of Export-Import Bank," pp. 15–16; Whittlesey, "Five Years of the Export-Import Bank," p. 496.

The commercial activities of the Export-Import Bank reflected distinct geographic patterns. As its 1936 Annual Report noted: "Generally, proposals to finance the exportation of industrial products concern Mexico, South America, and the Far East, while those concerning agricultural exports relate to Europe, and to a lesser extent, China." In agriculture, the bank dealt primarily with cotton and tobacco interests who exported to Italy, Poland, Czechoslovakia, and Spain. Increasingly, however, the bank assisted American exporters competing for sales in Latin America and, on a more limited scale, Asia. In part, this was a continuation of the earlier trend produced by the nation's emergence as a leading exporter of industrial goods. It further indicated that American trade with non-European areas was growing faster than trade with Europe. By the middle of the 1930s, moreover, United States exporters needed government support to retain access to non-European markets.[61]

An appreciation of the bank's dual nature is essential in assessing its significance for American foreign policy, especially in non-European areas of the world.[62] Foreign trade groups exerted continual pressure on the government to liberalize the bank's lending policy; and during the late 1930s, exporters received greater support than they had earlier. American policymakers, nevertheless, were reacting only partially to business demands. They concluded that the bank should expand its activities in order to achieve objectives broader than the immediate goal of expanding trade. While responsive to commercial pressures, Washington officials were not dominated by them. In the case of proposed credits to the Soviet Union, for example, State Department officers subordinated economic considerations in hopes that they could extract political concessions from Soviet officials. The Russian episode, therefore, deserves close analysis because it dramatically discloses an important facet of the bank's operations.

61. Export-Import Bank, "Annual Report, 1936," p. 7; Whittlesey, "Five Years of the Export-Import Bank," pp. 491–92, 496; Pierson, "Export-Import Bank Operations," p. 37.

62. Virtually all the bank's dealings with European countries involved the sale of agricultural goods which required only short-term assistance; these actions did not raise the political issues associated with longer-term without-recourse financing.

4

A Missed Opportunity?
The Bank and Soviet-American Relations

The American response to the Bolshevik revolution combined elements of disdain and disbelief; and until Franklin Roosevelt became president, American policymakers steadfastly refused to recognize the legitimacy of the Soviet government. In August 1920, Bainbridge Colby, Woodrow Wilson's last secretary of state, laid down the basis for the United States position. America would not regularize relations with Russia unless Bolshevik leaders agreed to withdraw their support from revolutionary movements in other countries and to abide by principles of international relations that were in accord with those of the United States.[1] The Republican administrations of the 1920s continued Wilson's policy, although they did add refinements of their own. Replying to a Russian approach on recognition, Secretary of State Charles Evans Hughes insisted that the Soviets would have to restore confiscated property, honor their predecessors' international obligations, and halt foreign propaganda before Washington would consider opening formal diplomatic relations.[2]

1. Colby to Baron Camillo Avezzana, August 10, 1920, *Foreign Relations, 1920*, 3:463–68; for background, see Ronald Radosh, "John Spargo and Wilson's Russian Policy, 1920," *Journal of American History* 52 (December 1965): 548–65; the profound nature of the Lenin-Wilson confrontation is discussed by Henry Roberts, *Eastern Europe*, chap. 2; N. Gordon Levin, Jr., *Woodrow Wilson and World Politics*, Arno J. Mayer, *Political Origins of the New Diplomacy* (New York, 1950); George F. Kennan, *Soviet-American Relations, 1917–1920*, 2 vols. (Princeton, 1956–1958); and William A. Williams, "American Intervention in Russia," in *Containment and Revolution*, ed. David Horowitz, paperback ed. (Boston, 1968), pp. 26–75.
2. Hughes to Consul at Revel, December 18, 1923, *Foreign Relations, 1923*, 2:788; for more on the American view of the principles at issue, see Hughes, "Russia: Response to the Delegation of 'The Women's Committee

Herbert Hoover remained a firm advocate of nonrecognition. He maintained that the Soviets would have to respect Russia's international obligations not because the amount owed America was great, which it was not, but because of the principle involved. "This principle," Hoover explained, "is that unless foreign merchants and investors may enjoy property and security of contract under the terms of the institution by which they acquire them, then the whole fabric of international trade and commerce will disappear and the world will go up into chaos." Each country had a duty to observe property rights since the alternative to self-enforcement was "to force the test of war which America has always refused to do." The United States could not enter into political relationships with a nation until it acknowledged these rules, because "upon confidence in the good faith in these principles among nations rests the whole fabric of international life." For Hoover the axioms were absolute laws, not academic theories, which nations had to follow to achieve economic salvation. This ideological stance adopted by American officials reflected a realistic appraisal of the nation's interests. The country's new status as a world creditor and its rapid growth in international commercial affairs meant that the spread of Soviet principles, which emphasized confiscation and the repudiation of existing obligations, would create a hostile international environment. American policymakers, therefore, recognized that the Soviet example posed a legitimate long-run challenge to the United States.[3]

Notwithstanding the absence of diplomatic relations during

---

for Recognition of Russia'," Charles E. Hughes, *The Pathway of Peace*, pp. 60–64.

3. Herbert Hoover, "American Relations to Russia," May 15, 1922, Secretary of Commerce, Official File, Chamber of Commerce, International Chamber of Commerce, 1921–1922, Herbert Hoover Papers (Herbert Hoover Library, West Branch, Iowa). Joan Hoff Wilson's otherwise excellent analysis of U.S. business contacts with the Soviet Union during the 1920s is marred by her contention that Washington's ideological opposition to Soviet Russia was primarily the product of bureaucratic politics. Professor Wilson also maintains that American officials failed to coordinate economic and political foreign policy. See Joan Hoff Wilson, *Ideology and Economics*, passim; for a thoughtful analysis of her book, see Robert Freeman Smith, "Businessmen, Bureaucrats, Historians, and the Shaping of United States Foreign Policy," *Reviews in American History* 2 (December 1974): 575–81.

the 1920s, trade and other contacts between the two countries sprang up. State Department officials did not place formal restrictions on trade nor did they oppose the extension of commercial credits or even the sale of goods on a long-term basis, providing there was no public sale of securities.[4] In addition, Hoover encouraged the growth of direct economic ties with the Soviet Union, rejecting Hughes's proposal to use German agents to distribute American manufactured products. The secretary of commerce was eager to install American technology in Soviet factories and to place U. S. citizens in positions from which, when the proper moment arrived, they could undertake leadership in the reconstruction of Russia.[5]

Attracted by the possibility of quick profits, American businessmen and speculators launched several trade promotion schemes shortly after the Bolshevists assumed power.[6] When Lenin adopted the New Economic Policy in March 1921, the American business community was encouraged because it interpreted this shift as an admission of the unworkable nature of socialist principles. More importantly, business leaders recognized that the new policy opened Russia to outside economic penetration.[7] By the middle of the decade, the United States

4. Castle to Fred Eberhardt, March 3, 1933, Department of State, *Foreign Relations of the United States: The Soviet Union, 1933–1939* (Washington, D.C., 1952), pp. 3–5 (hereafter referred to as *Foreign Relations: Russia*); certain government officers, acting in an unofficial capacity, did try to enforce limited trade restrictions, Wilson, *Ideology and Economics*, pp. 29–30, 34–36, 43–50.

5. See the exchange, Hughes to Hoover, December 1, 1921; Hoover to Hughes, December 6, 1921, Secretary of Commerce, Official File, Russia, 1921, Hoover Papers.

6. Antony Sutton, *Western Technology and Soviet Economic Development 1917 to 1930*, pp. 287–90; Sutton notes that since the United States had a far smaller portion of the prerevolutionary debt than did France, Britain, or Germany, Americans who favored an expansion of trade with the Soviet Union encountered less pressure from disgruntled bondholders than did exporters in the other countries. Also see Edward M. Bennett, *Recognition of Russia*, pp. 62–67; William A. Williams, *American-Russian Relations, 1781–1947*, pp. 180–201.

7. The business community's reaction is thoroughly covered by Peter G. Filene, *Americans and the Soviet Experiment, 1917–1933*, chap. 4, esp. pp. 103–13; Filene demonstrates that many Americans perceived the Soviet Union as a challenge to the basic aspects (private property, free enterprise, the profit motive, individualism) of Western civilization, see pp. 63, 96, 103, 208–9, 243, 274, 283–84.

and the Soviet Union had made considerable progress toward institutionalizing trade connections. American manufacturing and commercial groups formed the American Commercial Association to Promote Trade with Russia, the American-Russian Chamber of Commerce, and the Allied American Corporation. Under the leadership of the Chase National Bank of New York, a number of banks tried to arrange a more satisfactory way of financing trade with the Soviet Union. In the meantime, the Russians organized the Amtorg Trading Corporation in New York to function as the agent for Soviet export and import bureaus as well as to seek credits. Soviet officials also provided foreign companies with opportunities to participate in Russian development programs.[8]

The efforts to expand Russo-American economic exchanges proved effective. After 1925, the United States was the largest exporter to the Soviet Union and the second leading source of foreign investment.[9] Symbolic of the increased American presence was the contract signed with Henry Ford: the Soviets agreed to purchase $30 million worth of automobiles and parts in return for which Ford would furnish the technical advice needed to construct an automobile manufacturing plant. Although he was the archetypal American capitalist, Ford admired the Soviet attempt to reconstruct a vast nation by relying on machines; he believed that ultimately machines would liberate men, irrespective of the political economy within which they functioned. By the end of the decade, the Soviets looked mainly to the U.S. for technical assistance, so much so that, during the last six months of 1929, the number of new technical agreements signed with American firms surpassed those concluded with German groups. A combination of reasons accounted for the growing Russian dependence on United States technical expertise, but a major element was the Soviet preference for American

8. Ibid., pp. 114–16; Sutton, *Western Technology and Soviet Economic Development*, pp. 6–11, 287–89; Williams, *American-Russian Relations*, p. 211; Louis Richard Batzler, "The Development of Soviet Foreign Relations with the United States, 1917–1939" (Ph.D. dissertation, Georgetown Univ., 1956), pp. 117–18 .

9. Filene argues that by the end of 1927, Americans viewed Russia as fertile ground for development, Filene, *Americans and the Soviet Experiment*, pp. 117–18; Batzler, "Development of Soviet Foreign Relations," p. 117, table 1 in appendix.

mass production techniques over the more conservative European methods.[10]

The rapid expansion of Soviet economic ties led some American businessmen to favor a reappraisal of the government's official nonrecognition policy, but the major stimulus did not come primarily from business interests. Under the leadership of Senator William E. Borah, Raymond Robins, and Alexander Gumberg, a cautious prorecognition force did emerge.[11] Its pressure was felt at the highest levels of government: both Warren G. Harding and Calvin Coolidge toyed with the possibility of recognizing the Soviets. Harding's untimely death and decisive action by Secretary Hughes, however, preserved the existing policy. But while the State Department was able to hold the line on the question of diplomatic recognition, it was unable to enforce the ban on long-term financing. In 1927 the department permitted the American Locomotive Company to extend long-term credits to Moscow. A far more serious blow to the department's stance came the following year when the Soviets paid Averill Harriman in bonds for the cancellation of his manganese concession. According to the agreement, Harriman promised to float a loan in the U. S. to assist in the development of the Russian manganese industry.[12]

10. Other factors favoring the United States were a decline in the availability of German credits and the concern of Soviet leaders about the great number of Germans who held key places in Russian industry, Sutton, *Western Technology and Soviet Economic Development*, pp. 246–49, 295, 346, 348; Filene, *Americans and the Soviet Experiment*, pp. 121–25.

11. Certain individuals, like Borah and Robins, were concerned about the destabilizing effect of nonrecognition on international relations. In addition, most business leaders were more interested in improving economic relations than in granting recognition. Finally, the growth of trade led some officials, like Julius Klein, to argue that recognition was not necessary to give an advantage to Americans in Russia; see Williams, *American-Russian Relations*, pp. 201–8; Filene, *Americans and the Soviet Experiment*, pp. 115, 88–99; Batzler, "Development of Soviet Foreign Relations," p. 121; Joan Hoff Wilson, "American Business and the Recognition of the Soviet Union," *Social Science Quarterly* 52 (September 1971): 358–60; Klein to Hoover, "Russian Affairs and the Geneva Conference," May 19, 1927, Secretary of Commerce, Official File, Conferences, Economic Geneva, 1927, Hoover Papers.

12. Given Hughes's reaction to the Coolidge bid for policy revision, it is questionable whether Harding could have reversed the nonrecognition

This relaxation of American policy toward the Soviet Union produced a counter-movement, particularly within the State Department, that was committed to nonrecognition and the withholding of long-term financial assistance.[13] Robert F. Kelley, head of the department's Division of East European Affairs from 1926 until its merger into a larger unit a decade later, played an important role in this process. As befit one who had studied at Harvard and the Sorbonne, Kelley approached matters from the perspective of a scholar. Under his direction, the East European Division accumulated an excellent library on Soviet affairs. In addition, the American legation at Riga, Latvia, became one of the world's best sources of information on the Soviet Union. Kelley also arranged a training program in which the department's Soviet specialists studied Russian linguistics, literature, and history. Altogether, the program involved approximately three years of post-graduate work at European universities. From this course of study came a group of diplomats, including George F. Kennan, Charles Bohlen, and Elbridge Durbrow, who were to play important roles in United States-Soviet relations. Although he joined the department too early to participate in Kelley's training program, Loy Henderson, another influential figure, became knowledgeable about the Soviet Union through his work at Riga and in the East European Division.[14]

policy since he gave the secretary of state a free hand in foreign affairs. Nonetheless, by the end of the 1920s, the commerce and treasury departments were favoring a more liberal trade policy with Russia and apparently received support from highly placed government officials, perhaps even at the presidential level; see Bennett, *Recognition of Russia*, pp. 60–69; Robert Maddox, "Keeping Cool with Coolidge," *Journal of American History* 53 (March 1967): 774–75; Wilson, *Ideology and Economics*, pp. 31–32, 39–47; Sutton, *Western Technology and Soviet Economic Development*, pp. 89–91, 290–91, 297–99.

13. Those business groups which would have been harmed by Soviet imports opposed altering the policy, Wilson, "American Business and Recognition of Russia," pp. 356–58.

14. George Kennan describes the training routine formulated by Kelley, George F. Kennan, *Memoirs (1925–1950)*, paperback ed. (New York, 1969), pp. 29–50; Kennan notes that the Russian section of the American legation at Riga became so proficient that, by 1933, there were only three areas in the non-Soviet world from which the section could learn things, pp. 49–50. Also see Williams, *American-Russian Relations*, pp. 209–10; Robert E. Bowers, "Hull, Russian Subversion in Cuba, and Recognition of the U.S.S.R.," *Journal of American History* 53 (December 1966): 543–

Kelley and his subordinates believed that the Soviet Union provided a profound ideological challenge to the United States. The Soviet emphasis on class rule, combined with its commitment to world revolution, meant that Marxist philosophy was at odds with the principles of western civilization. The American Soviet experts, however, assumed that the communist system was "unnatural" and would prove incapable of governing Russia for an extended period of time. The inherent instability of bolshevism would ultimately work to the advantage of the West by forcing changes in the nature of the Russian government.[15] The major differences between Soviet Russia and the United States, therefore, were over fundamental principles. As late as 1969, Charles Bohlen argued that the two countries had virtually no conflicts of interest: The "tension between us is, in my opinion," he contended, "caused by the ideological factor."[16]

Throughout the 1920s, Kelley maintained that the United States should not deal in an official capacity with the Soviet Union until it accepted Western principles of international behavior. By definition, Russia's acceptance of these rules would entail important internal modifications. One of the chief weapons that the State Department had to force Russian acceptance of the West's position, Kelley argued, was the control of American capital. For the most part, the department followed Kelley's recommendations by refusing to recognize the Bolshevik government and opposing projects that necessitated floating bonds in

47; Betty Crump Hanson, "American Diplomatic Reporting from the Soviet Union 1934–1941" (Ph.D dissertation, Columbia Univ., 1966), pp. 13–22.

15. Kennan, *Memoirs*, pp. 58–59, 64–65, 71–73; George F. Kennan, *Russia and the West under Lenin and Stalin*, p. 313; an interesting critique of Kennan's position is contained in William Welch, *American Images of Soviet Foreign Policy*, pp. 105–111. A famous exposition on the inherent instability of the Soviet government is Kennan's "Mr. X" article, "Sources of Soviet Conduct," *Foreign Affairs* 25 (July 1947): 566–82; also see Charles E. Bohlen, *The Transformation of American Foreign Policy*, pp. 121–22.

16. Bohlen, *Transformation of American Foreign Policy*, pp. 51, 106, 112–13; descriptions of the American diplomatic community's assessment of the role played by ideology in Soviet foreign policy are provided by Richard Ullman, "The Davies Mission and United States-Soviet Relations, 1937–1941," *World Politics* 9 (January 1957): 233, 237–38; Hanson, "American Diplomatic Reporting from the Soviet Union," pp. 48, 66–68, 161–99.

the United States. Recognition and loans, therefore, were the levers by which America hoped to moderate the Soviets.[17]

From 1929 to 1933, American policymakers reappraised their stance toward Russia. With the initiation of the first Five Year Plan in 1928, the Soviet need for machinery and equipment increased tremendously. This enlarged demand occurred at virtually the same moment that American industry was seeking new markets to offset the impact of the depression. Not only did the Russian market keep some industries from collapsing, but its potential seemed limited only by the extent to which American exporters could arrange satisfactory credit terms.[18] After 1930, however, the Soviets reduced imports from the United States. Although this reduction was part of an overall curtailment of imports, Amtorg officials hinted that the absence of recognition had caused the decline. By the spring of 1933, many businessmen had decided that trade with the Soviet Union offered a way out of the depression but that American policy stood in the path.[19]

In addition to trade considerations, the international uncertainties associated with the Japanese invasion of Manchuria and Hitler's rise to power forced a reassessment of Russo-American relations. Even though both of these events endangered the Soviets more directly than the Americans, U. S. leaders recognized that the normalization of ties between the two nations

17. Williams, *American-Russian Relations*, pp. 209–10; Sutton, *Western Technology in Soviet Economic Development*, pp. 297–98; Bennett, *Recognition of Russia*, p. 58.

18. American exports to Russia increased steadily from 1928 to 1930, by which point 98 percent of the goods shipped consisted of metals, manufactures, machinery, and vehicles, Department of Commerce, *Foreign Commerce and Navigation of the United States for the Calendar Year of 1930*, p. LXVI; Charles D. Martin, *Foreign Markets for Tractors*, Department of Commerce, Trade Information Bulletin, no. 502 (Washington, 1927), p. 31; Charles D. Martin, *Foreign Markets for Agricultural Implements*, Department of Commerce, Trade Information Bulletin, no. 488, p. 15; "What Business with Russia," *Fortune* 31 (January 1945): 156; *New York Times*, September 5, 1932, p. 24.

19. Williams, *American-Russian Relations*, pp. 218, 236; Robert P. Browder, *The Origins of Soviet-American Diplomacy*, pp. 37–39; Donald G. Bishop, *The Roosevelt-Litvinov Agreements*, pp. 2–4; Filene, *Americans and the Soviet Experience*, chap. 8; *New York Times* for the following dates, April 24, 1932, p. 7; April 30, 1932, p. 15; July 3, 1932, sec. IV, p. 17; June 25, 1933, p. 2; July 3, 1933, p. 3.

could have a stabilizing effect on world affairs.[20] For both political and economic reasons, therefore, the American policy of nonrecognition seemed open to question; by 1932, these doubts had crept into the higher echelons of the State Department. Secretary of State Henry Stimson considered the possibility of recognizing the Soviets; but in part because of opposition from Hoover and Kelley, he decided against the move.[21] Nonetheless, supporters of the existing policy were clearly on the defensive.

Hoover's defeat in 1932 removed the most important defender of nonrecognition. Shortly after taking office, Roosevelt confided to colleagues that he intended to resume relations with Russia, provided he could obtain a satisfactory agreement with Soviet leaders and could avoid arousing domestic opposition. Accordingly, the president kept close tabs on public attitudes and initiated steps to allay the fears of those who opposed recognition. By the fall of 1933, Roosevelt decided that public opinion, as expressed through newspaper editorials, the sentiments of religious leaders, and the results of unofficial polls, viewed the renewal of ties with favor.[22] The president believed current events made nonrecognition an outmoded policy. He viewed the resumption of relations in terms of its stabilizing impact on international politics rather than from the commercial standpoint of opening new markets for American exporters (although he considered the two to be closely related).[23] The president re-

20. Browder, *Origins of Soviet-American Diplomacy*, pp. 49–79; Bishop, *Roosevelt-Litvinov Agreements*, pp. 4–5, 7; Wilson, "American Business and the Recognition of the Soviet Union," pp. 364–65, 368; Williams, *American-Russian Relations*, p. 237.

21. Historians disagree about Stimson's willingness to end nonrecognition, see Williams, *American-Russian Relations*, pp. 222, 228; Browder, *Origins of Soviet-American Diplomacy*, pp. 66–69; Bennett, *Recognition of Russia*, pp. 77–78.

22. Herbert Feis, *1933: Characters in Crisis*, p. 307; Browder, *Origins of Soviet-American Diplomacy*, p. 100; Robert F. Bowers, "Senator Arthur Robinson of Indiana Vindicated," *Indiana Magazine of History* 61 (September 1965): 189–204; Beatrice Farnsworth, *William C. Bullitt and the Soviet Union*, pp. 76–78. For a description of the ways in which Roosevelt created support for recognition, see Bennett, *Recognition of Russia*, pp. 89–104; Filene, *Americans and the Soviet Experiment*, pp. 261–67; Batzler, "Development of Soviet Foreign Relations," pp. 129–30.

23. In line with her thesis on the division between American economic and political policies, Wilson argues that Roosevelt was concerned with international political factors, Wilson, *Ideology and Economics*, pp. 113–21; also see Thomas R. Maddux, "American Relations with the Soviet

ceived support from some members of the Brains Trust (especially Raymond Moley) and could always count on Henry Morgenthau, Jr. Nonetheless, among high governmental officials, Roosevelt stood out clearly as the chief proponent of recognition.[24]

State Department officers exhibited attitudes on recognition ranging from a stubborn defense of the status quo to a begrudging acceptance of the need for change.[25] In a memorandum to Roosevelt in late July 1933, Kelley warned that increased contacts between the two nations would produce additional friction unless the Soviets agreed to alter their policies as a prelude to a normalization of relations. Until the Bolshevists acknowledged their international obligations and promised to cease propaganda and related activities within the United States, nonrecognition was a sound policy. The Russian government's monopoly of foreign trade, furthermore, meant that the administration would have to obtain a guarantee of the most-favored-nation principle. The question of repudiated debts and confiscated property was especially critical, Kelley argued, because it signified that Moscow "had rejected international obligations which the experience of mankind has demonstrated are vital to the satisfactory development and maintenance of commerce and friendly intercourse between nations." In a later memorandum, Kelley pointed out that the principle of a new government honoring debts contracted by a previous one was important for the United States because as a creditor nation, its citizens were engaged in worldwide financial activities.[26]

Union, 1933–1941," (Ph. D. dissertation, Univ. of Michigan, 1969), pp. 18–31; Browder, *Origins of Soviet-American Relations*, pp. 108–112; entry for October 23, 1933, FCA Diaries, Henry Morgenthau, Jr. Papers (Franklin D. Roosevelt Library, Hyde Park, New York).

24. Bennett, *Recognition of Russia*, p. 101; William P. Gerberding, "Franklin D. Roosevelt's Conception of the Soviet Union in World Politics," (Ph.D. dissertation, Univ. of Chicago, 1959), p. 11.

25. As Bowers notes, the problem is not finding who in the department opposed recognition but discovering who favored it, Bowers, "Hull, Russian Subversion in Cuba, and Recognition of the U.S.S.R.," p. 543.

26. Kelley, "Problems Pertaining to Russian-American Relations Which, in the Interests of Friendly Relations Between the United States and Russia, Should Be Settled Prior to Recognition of the Soviet Government," July 27, 1933, *Foreign Relations: Russia*, pp. 6–11; Kelley, "Recommendations and Considerations in Connection with Question of Russian Gov-

Secretary of State Hull agreed, advising the president not to resume relations or to extend financial assistance before the Russians accepted the American terms. The Soviet desire for credits or loans and recognition, he argued, provided the United States with two powerful weapons to achieve its objectives. "I am convinced from the experience of other countries," the secretary warned, "that, unless we utilize every available means of exerting pressure on the Soviet government in order to obtain a settlement of outstanding problems, there is little likelihood that such problems can be satisfactorily solved." Because the Russians seemed to prefer credits to recognition, Hull believed the control of financial aid could become America's most effective means for extracting concessions. A short time after Hull's letter went to the president, Kelley reiterated the secretary's point on the use of financial leverage, calling it "one of the most effective weapons we have to obtain from the Soviet Government some measure of conciliation in reaching a solution of outstanding problems." Kelley urged the administration not to offer credits or loans until the two nations reached a definite agreement.[27]

Along with Kelley, William C. Bullitt was another important figure in Soviet-American relations. In 1919, Bullitt had tried to arrange a rapprochement between Lenin and the West, but had been bitterly disappointed when Woodrow Wilson ignored his advice. After falling out with Wilson and other Democratic party leaders, Bullitt remained out of public service for over a decade before Roosevelt appointed him special assistant to the secretary of state in 1933. Even though he was virtually the only member of the department who favored opening relations with the Soviets, Bullitt agreed with Hull and Kelley on the way to handle negotiations. He recommended that the administration withhold recognition and financial assistance until the Soviets accepted the American principles of international relations. "Before recognition and before loans," Bullitt commented, "we shall

ernmental Indebtedness to the Government of the United States," October 25, 1933, ibid., pp. 23–24.

27. Hull to Roosevelt, September 21, 1933, ibid., pp. 12–13; Feis maintains that Bullitt and Kelley actually wrote the letter, Feis, *1933*, p. 312; Kelley admitted that he had urged Hull to acquaint Roosevelt with the possibility of using loans and recognition as levers, Kelley to Phillips, September 25, 1933, *Foreign Relations: Russia*, p. 14.

find the Soviet Government relatively amenable. After recognition or loans, we should find the Soviet Government adamant."[28]

In the period immediately preceding the initiation of recognition talks with Soviet representatives, Bullitt, Kelley, Undersecretary of State Ray Walton Moore, and Assistant Secretary of State William Phillips shared a common concern that the president might either extend credits or grant recognition before obtaining satisfactory agreements on the points troubling United States-Soviet relations. Most of the memoranda written during this time represent an attempt by these officials to keep Roosevelt in line with the State Department's position. Thus, while department officers disagreed on some issues, they were united in the belief that the government should use diplomatic recognition and control of capital to force concessions from Moscow. It is somewhat ironic that the movement for a reappraisal of the nation's Russian policy provided the State Department with an opportunity to regain some of the power it had lost during the late 1920s.[29]

Implicit in the State Department's position was the assumption that the only stumbling blocks to smooth relations were of Soviet origin; responsibility for the future lay with Moscow. That attitude, no doubt, explains why it was Roosevelt who took the lead in initiating negotiations and ultimately dominated the discussions. With the exception of Bullitt, department officers did not learn of the recognition invitation to the Soviets until

28. For a discussion of Bullitt's earlier years, see Farnsworth, *Bullitt and the Soviet Union*, pp. 1–95; Lloyd C. Gardner, *Architects of Illusion*, pp. 3–21. Bullitt's comments on the anti-Soviet sentiment within the State Department are contained in the entry for September 27, 1933, FCA Diaries, Morgenthau Papers; Bullitt to Hull, October 4, 1933, *Foreign Relations: Russia*, pp. 16–17. Gerberding correctly observes that in light of the October 4 memorandum, it is hard to believe that Bullitt was as strongly in favor of recognition as Morgenthau contended, Gerberding, "Roosevelt's Conception of the Soviet Union," p. 17.

29. Feis, *1933*, pp. 312–14; Maddux, "American Relations with the Soviet Union," pp. 59–60. Undersecretary Moore also recommended the adoption of a rigid negotiating position, memorandum by Moore, October 4, 1933, *Foreign Relations: Russia*, pp. 15–16. Bowers argues that Kelley went as far as he could, without resorting to insubordination, to block recognition; Bowers also makes a convincing case that Hull considered the possibility of spiking United States-Soviet negotiations by insisting that Moscow-directed agents were trying to subvert the revolution in Cuba, Bowers, "Hull, Russian Subversion in Cuba, and Recognition of the U.S.S.R.," pp. 547–53.

shortly before the president made the news public. Furthermore, Roosevelt timed the negotiations to coincide with Hull's departure for the Pan-American Conference in Montevideo, Uruguay. And, when the talks threatened to bog down, the president stepped in, wrapping things up in a series of confidential discussions with Maxim Litvinov, the Soviet commissar for foreign affairs.[30]

The final terms of the recognition agreement were reasonably close to those worked out by the Division of East European Affairs. Litvinov signed pledges on propaganda and subversive activities that were more extensive than any others to which the Soviets had agreed. The foreign commissar also promised religious and legal safeguards for American citizens in Russia that were as far-reaching as the United States could expect in lieu of a consular treaty. The fact that Litvinov agreed to these conditions emphasizes the importance Moscow attached to recognition.[31] Notwithstanding agreement on these issues, however, negotiators could not arrive at a debt settlement because of a disagreement over the amount Russia should pay. After extended talks, Morgenthau, Bullitt, Roosevelt, and Litvinov signed a gentleman's accord: the Soviet government consented to pay between $75 million and $150 million, the exact amount to be worked out in later negotiations. The agreement stated that the Soviet Union would repay the debt by making additional interest payments on loans granted to it by the government of the United States or its nationals. Following diplomatic recognition, Litvinov remained in Washington for discussions on the debt question. When these negotiations proved fruitless, he left for Moscow in late November 1933.[32]

30. Bowers, "Hull, Russian Subversion in Cuba, and Recognition of the U.S.S.R.," pp. 553–54; Gerberding, "Roosevelt's Conception of the Soviet Union," pp. 19–20; extract of radio address by Moore, November 22, 1933, *Foreign Relations: Russia*, pp. 42–43.

31. Cordell Hull, *The Memoirs of Cordell Hull*, 1:297–98; Browder, *Origins of Soviet-American Diplomacy*, pp. 128, 148; for copies of the letters, see *Foreign Relations: Russia*, pp. 28–36.

32. During the debt settlement talks, Bullitt made one of his first attempts to exert financial leverage by warning Litvinov that if the Soviets made an absurdly low offer, they would not receive any loans from the United States government or its nationals, Bullitt to Roosevelt, November 15, 1933, *Foreign Relations: Russia*, pp. 25–26. For the terms of the agreement, see memorandum by Roosevelt and Litvinov, November 15, 1933,

Throughout the talks preceding recognition, American diplomats assumed they were dealing from a position of strength. Although Roosevelt had ignored his advisers' suggestion by normalizing relations before settling the debt question, he did tie the provision of financial aid to a satisfactory resolution of that issue. Since Hull and Kelley had indicated that the control of credit and loans gave the United States leverage over the Soviet Union, State Department officers could make Moscow's willingness to accept a debt settlement determined by the Americans the acid test of Soviet good faith. Aside from this reservation, however, both sides had reason to be pleased with recent events. The Soviet Union felt more secure in the Far East and expected American help in strengthening its economy and defenses.[33] The United States, in the meantime, could anticipate a revival of trade with Russia as well as a growing degree of stability in international relations.[34]

Following Litvinov's departure from the United States, Bullitt, the newly designated ambassador to Russia, visited Moscow for a series of talks with Soviet leaders. By his own admission,

ibid., pp. 26–27. Maddux faults Roosevelt and Bullitt for the imprecise nature of the gentleman's agreement and suggests that prolonged negotiations at that point would have clarified issues and perhaps avoided later problems. However, it was not the wording of the agreement that caused the ultimate failure of the debt settlement negotiations. Without an imprecise statement, moreover, the Washington talks themselves might have broken down, Maddux, "American Relations with the Soviet Union," pp. 69–70.

33. For more on the Russian reaction, see Chargé in Latvia to Phillips, November 23, 1933, *Foreign Relations: Russia*, pp. 43–46; Browder, *Origins of Soviet-American Diplomacy*, pp. 157–60; Maddux, "American Relations with the Soviet Union," pp. 76–78, 101–2; Adam Ulam maintains that Stalin had a great admiration for American efficiency and technology and that the Soviets thought formal relations with America would aid them in the new Five Year Plan and in erecting defenses against possible Japanese expansion, Adam B. Ulam, *Expansion and Coexistence*, pp. 211–13; Xenia Eudin and Robert Slusser contend that the Soviets' most important diplomatic achievement in 1933 was the establishment of relations with the United States, Xenia J. Eudin and Robert M. Slusser, eds., *Soviet Foreign Policy 1928–1934*, 2:369.

34. For more on the American reaction, see Browder, *Origins of Soviet-American Diplomacy*, pp. 169–75; Feis, *1933*, pp. 325–326; Bullitt to Roosevelt, July 8, 1933, in *Franklin D. Roosevelt and Foreign Affairs*, ed. Edgar B. Nixon, 1: 289–94; Joseph C. Grew, *Ten Years in Japan*, p. 108; Maddux, "American Relations with the Soviet Union," pp. 76–78, 101–2.

he received a very warm reception, including an assurance from Stalin that he would be willing to see the American diplomat whenever Bullitt desired. The Russian fear of an imminent attack in the Far East, which if prolonged for two or three years could invite a joint attack by Poland and Germany, dominated the discussion. The Soviets wanted a series of nonaggression pacts with the United States, China, and Japan, but were willing to settle for American moral support or for any signal which would make Japan believe that the United States would cooperate with Russia. Bullitt rejected each Soviet request for joint action in the Pacific, but he remained deeply impressed by the cordiality of his hosts.[35]

Following recognition, officials in Washington considered the question of providing Russia with financial assistance. After rejecting the possibility of transferring private American credits in Germany to Russia in exchange for long-term obligations of the Soviet government, Robert Kelley concluded that the U.S. government should advance the credits necessary for the development of trade. By placing American business interests on an equal footing with the Russian monopoly of foreign commerce, a governmental institution would eliminate the Soviet practice of playing off one group against another. Equally important, the creation of a governmental bank would enable the administration to withhold financial assistance until the Soviets signed a satisfactory debt settlement. Participation by the American government would also have a moderating influence on Japanese aggression in the Far East. With the formation of the first Export-Import Bank in February 1934, Washington had an institution which could achieve the objectives laid out by Kelley.[36]

35. Theodore Marriner to Phillips, December 24, 1933, *Foreign Relations: Russia*, pp. 53–54; Bullitt to Phillips, January 4, 1934, ibid., pp. 55–62; Phillips to Roosevelt, December 26, 1933, Nixon, *Roosevelt and Foreign Affairs*, 1:551–52; by the spring of 1934, Soviet leaders appear to have given up hope of obtaining a nonaggression pact with the United States, Robert F. Browder, "Soviet Far Eastern Policy and American Recognition, 1932–1934," *Pacific Historical Review* 21 (August 1952): 263–73.

36. Kelley to Moore, January 16, 1934, File No. 800.51W89USSU/21 3/4, General Records of the Department of State, RG 59 (National Archives, Washington, D.C.); memorandum by Kelley, "Primary Purposes of Export-Import Bank," February 23, 1934, attached to Moore to Hull,

Debt negotiations quickly became the thorniest element in Soviet-American relations. Although other irritants—the Soviet desire for a nonaggression pact, the selection of a site for the American embassy in Moscow, and the Russians' unwillingness to provide proper ruble exchange for the American diplomatic corps—did produce disagreements, they were not of sufficient magnitude to jeopardize the overall relationship between the two nations. It is significant that, although Roosevelt had been the predominant figure in the events leading to recognition, he left the debt discussions in the hands of Hull, Kelley, Phillips (all of whom were in Washington), and Bullitt (who was in Moscow). With the exception of Bullitt, these men were skeptical about the wisdom of dealing with the Soviets; they all believed the United States had sufficient economic leverage to compel Russian leaders to honor their international obligations.[37]

The debt negotiations began on February 20, 1934, when the Americans presented the Soviet ambassador, Alexander Troyanovsky, with a proposal that established the debt at $150 million and created a twenty-year repayment period. The debt would carry a 5 percent interest charge; to pay the principal and interest, the American government would charge 10 percent additional interest on loans or credits from itself or any of its nationals. At the same time that the State Department made this proposal, officials of the Export-Import Bank began negotiating with Amtorg. In accordance with the department's policy, however, bank officers refused to provide credits until the two nations settled the claims question.[38] The initial Soviet response was strongly negative. Litvinov complained, with some justification, that the "gentleman's agreement" had not mentioned anything about interest accruing on the debt and had referred only

February 23, 1934, Export-Import Bank folder, Ray Walton Moore Papers (Franklin D. Roosevelt Library, Hyde Park, New York); also see a memorandum dealing with the need for a government bank to finance trade with Russia, January 1, 1934, General Correspondence File, Export-Import Bank of Washington, Part 1, General Records of the Reconstruction Finance Corporation, RG 234 (National Archives, Washington, D.C.).

37. See Farnsworth, *Bullitt and the Soviet Union*, pp. 118–19; Gardner, *Architects of Illusion*, pp. 14–15.

38. For a copy of the American draft, see Hull to Bullitt, April 7, 1934, *Foreign Relations: Russia*, pp. 78–79; Kelley to American Embassy, Warsaw, March 2, 1934, PSF: Russia, 1933–36, Franklin D. Roosevelt Papers (Franklin D. Roosevelt Library, Hyde Park, New York).

to loans which the Soviets could use for purchases anywhere.[39]

As the talks threatened to reach an early stalemate, American officials moved to strengthen their position. The day after Bullitt reported Litvinov's complaints, the board of trustees of the Export-Import Bank passed a resolution forbidding the bank to engage in transactions prior to a satisfactory settlement of the debt question. The resolution had Roosevelt's approval. This decree negated a clause in the proposed Johnson Act which would have allowed government agencies to extend credits to foreign governments even if those governments were in default to the American government. As Hull wired Bullitt, the passage of the Johnson Act "coupled with failure to reach [debt] agreement would prevent the Soviet Government and its agent Amtorg from making any purchases in the United States otherwise than for cash certainly where the sellers expect to dispose of the obligations."[40]

At this point, Bullitt and Hull began applying economic pressure. Bullitt threatened to cable Roosevelt to disband the bank if Litvinov did not change his position. The American ambassador explained to Marshall Kliment Voroshilov, people's commissar for defense (who desperately wanted 200,000 tons of rails to assist in the double-tracking of the Trans-Siberian Railway), that the United States would not extend credits unless the Russians settled their debts. In his discussions with Ambassador Troyanovsky, Hull suggested that the two nations halt all talk of commercial and financial assistance until there was a resolution of the debt issue. Despite the initial complications, Bullitt remained optimistic; he thought Soviet lack of understanding, not bad faith, had caused the difficulties.[41]

39. Bullitt to Hull, March 15, 1934, *Foreign Relations: Russia*, pp. 66–67; Troyanovsky also opposed paying interest on the debt, memorandum by Kelley, February 21, 1934, ibid., pp. 65–66; Litvinov had a point—the gentleman's agreement did not refer to interest on the debt and did use the word "loan."

40. Hawthorn Arey, "History of the Operations and Policies of Export-Import Bank of Washington," mimeograph, p. 5. Bullitt received word of this decision on March 17, see Hull to Bullitt, March 17 and 19, 1934, *Foreign Relations: Russia*, p. 67, 68.

41. Bullitt to Hull, March 21, 23, and 28, 1934, *Foreign Relations: Russia*, pp. 69, 70, 71–75; memorandum of conversation between Hull and Troyanovsky, March 26, 1934, ibid., pp. 70–71.

During the following months, the talks revealed disagreements over the size of the debt Moscow owed, the role of the Export-Import Bank in overseeing Soviet purchases in the United States, and the level of interest rates. Nevertheless, by August both sides admitted that they could reach agreement on these points; the main problem to be settled was the number of years which the Soviet Union would have to repay the new obligations owed the Export-Import Bank.[42] On August 24, Troyanovsky presented the Russian point of view. Moscow wanted total assistance of $200 million, an amount double the commonly accepted debt figure. Half of the aid could be in the form of short-term commercial credits, but the other half had to be a twenty-year financial credit which the Soviets would use for the purchase of goods in the United States. Russia offered to pay 7 percent interest on both credits and to allow the Export-Import Bank to handle the financial arrangements.[43]

Russian diplomats insisted on long-term aid for two principal reasons. They wanted to purchase large quantities of machinery and industrial equipment and could not do so unless the repayment period was substantially longer than the five year term being offered by America.[44] But more importantly, they were reluctant to enter into an agreement that might jeopardize Russia's relations with other nations. Litvinov first raised this issue in July when he noted that England, France, Germany, and others had larger debt claims against the Soviet Union than did the United States. Because these countries might demand equal treatment once the Soviets signed an American accord, the Russians and Americans had to arrive at a settlement that no other nation could match. Since the other creditors could not lend the Soviet Union double the amount of their claims, the United States should accept this arrangement. The Soviets, Litvinov argued, could not make additional interest payments on private credits inasmuch as they would be obliged to make

---

42. Memoranda by Kelley, August 10, 15, and September 5, 1934, ibid., pp. 129–32, 134–35, 140–41; Hull to Bullitt, September 27, 1934, ibid., p. 152.

43. Memorandum by Kelley, August 24, 1934, ibid., pp. 135–37.

44. Memoranda by Kelley, August 3 and 10, 1934, ibid., pp. 127–28, 129–32.

a similar agreement on private credits obtained elsewhere. Consequently, long-term financial assistance from the American government was the only satisfactory basis for an accord. Bullitt learned, furthermore, that Stalin would not approve any arrangement unless he could offer it to France and England with the certainty they would reject it. The American ambassador accepted the accuracy of the Soviet position, suggesting that the State Department try to work out a formula to meet the difficulty.[45]

American officials, however, demonstrated little flexibility on this point. With the passage of the Johnson Act and the decision of the attorney general that the Soviets had defaulted on their obligations to the United States government, the Soviet Union could not gain access to private long-term American capital.[46] Because Hull contended that twenty-year credits were actually loans, and that public opinion and Congress would not tolerate the extension of governmental loans to other countries (especially if those nations had not repaid their earlier debts), he argued that the United States government would have to limit itself to the extension of credits of up to five years in duration. In certain cases, Washington would consider stretching the terms to seven years.[47]

During the period in which the disputed points crystalized, the State Department's firm approach to the negotiations followed logically from its belief that the Soviets would ultimately accept the American terms. As Bullitt noted, following Litvinov's negative reaction to the first proposal: "I derived the impression that if we maintain our position energetically and forcibly we shall be able to arrive at a solution in large measure satisfactory to us." The American ambassador later reported telling a Russian official that "if the Soviet Government wanted the collaboration of the United States in any field of world affairs it would be necessary to clean the air of distrust by settlement of the indebtedness." He remained convinced Moscow understood that

45. Bullitt to Hull, July 9 and September 15, 1934, ibid., pp. 115–16, 147–48; for more on the Soviet position, see memorandum by Kelley, September 5, 1934, ibid., pp. 144–45.

46. Press release, May 5, 1934, File No. 800.51W89USSR/47, RG 59; Hull to Bullitt, May 7, 1934, *Foreign Relations: Russia*, p. 89.

47. Memoranda by Kelley, August 24, August 15, and September 5, 1934, *Foreign Relations: Russia*, pp. 135–37, 134–35, 140–41.

"the cooperation of the United States is not a thing to throw away lightly."[48]

In an attempt to carry out their position both "energetically and forcibly," American officials periodically warned the Soviets that failure to accept the United States position would rule out any possibility of economic assistance. After the Soviets had made an unacceptable offer in the first part of April 1934, Hull informed Troyanovsky that, in view of the Russian attitude, the United States would suspend all commercial and financial relations pending a clarification of the situation. In Moscow, Bullitt mentioned that unless the Soviets changed their minds, "it might become necessary for the Government of the United States to announce that no credits of any kind would be permitted for Soviet trade." The ambassador further indicated that the U. S. would not alter its position; any change would have to come from the Soviet Union. Bullitt then wired Hull that American diplomats should not enter into additional discussions until Litvinov had time "to be impressed by an attitude of complete negation on our part."[49]

Following Troyanovsky's August 24 proposal of a $200 million credit, United States negotiators again warned the Soviets that a continued refusal to accept American terms was not in their best interests. Secretary of State Hull cautioned the Russian ambassador that if there was no hope of reaching a settlement, "it would be better to dissolve the Bank and drop the matter entirely, accepting the consequences which such action would entail." After rejecting the new offer, the State Department issued a press release stating that in light of the Russian overture, "It is not possible to be optimistic that any settlement will be reached." In a press conference held shortly thereafter, Undersecretary Moore noted that the United States had gone the limit in making concessions. To go further would be "an unthinkable sacrifice of the public interest."[50] Meanwhile in

48. Bullitt to Hull, March 15 and June 15, 1934, ibid., pp. 66–67, 107–8.
49. Hull to Bullitt, April 5, 1934, ibid., pp. 76–77; Bullitt to Hull, April 8, 1934, ibid., pp. 79–81.
50. Memorandum by Kelley, August 10, 1934, ibid., pp. 129–32; Phillips statement read at press conference, August 24, 1934, ibid., p. 137; Moore, statement for the press, September 6, 1934, File No. 800.51W89-USSR/120, RG 59.

Moscow, Bullitt kept up the pressure, reminding Russian officials of the consequences of prolonging a settlement. In late September, he suggested that failure of present negotiations "might well be a death blow to the development of really friendly and intimate relations between our countries." When talking with the Soviet foreign minister, Bullitt emphasized the serious effect a failure of negotiations would have on Russian-American affairs. In general, the ambassador tried to produce in Litvinov "as complete a state of gloom as possible with regard to the future of Soviet-American relations if no settlement should be made." During a visit to Washington in late January 1935, Bullitt also warned Troyanovsky that the Soviet attitude toward the debt question could easily end all possibility of fruitful cooperation between the two countries.[51]

The United States ambassador added a new element to the American bargaining position when he began complaining about Comintern, the Communist International. He informed Litvinov that if the Soviet Union combined a negative attitude on debts and claims with the resumption of Comintern activities against the United States, the two nations would never reach an accord. Angered by this remark, Litvinov replied that no country ever started talking about the activities of Comintern unless it wished to have as bad relations as possible with Russia. Mention of this subject, he continued, was merely an excuse for breaking diplomatic relations. Bullitt may well have been deliberately provoking the Soviets: only five days earlier, he had wired Hull that the Soviet foreign minister was trying to prevent the Communist International from violating Russian pledges to the American government. Moreover, a reliable source had notified Bullitt that the Soviet government was holding a tight rein on Comintern to keep it from jeopardizing relations with America.[52]

A further characteristic of the American approach to the negotiations was a tendency to believe that pressure from Japan

51. The American ambassador noted that Soviet officials "seemed to be somewhat disturbed by my remarks." Bullitt to Hull, September 27, 1934, *Foreign Relations: Russia,* 149–50; Bullitt to Hull, October 5, 1934, ibid., pp. 155–56; memorandum by Bullitt, January 30, 1935, ibid., pp. 168–69.

52. Bullitt to Hull, October 5 and 10, 1934, ibid., pp. 156–59; Bullitt to Hull, October 2, 1934, PSF: Russia, 1934, Roosevelt Papers.

and Germany would persuade Russian leaders to accept United States terms. Ambassador Bullitt, in particular, analyzed Soviet behavior from this perspective. In an Easter Day letter to Roosevelt, he noted that the Japanese had let the United States down badly since the Russians no longer feared an attack in the spring or summer. Because the Soviets did not believe they needed America's immediate help, "their underlying hostility to all capitalist countries now shows through the veneer of immediate friendship. We shall have to deal with them according to Claudel's formula of the donkey, the carrot, and the club." As an example of the club, Bullitt intended to give Litvinov the impression that if the Soviets did not wish to take advantage of the Export-Import Bank, the Japanese government would be eager to use it to finance large purchases from certain American heavy industries. Late in May, Bullitt again explained Moscow's refusal to reach an agreement in terms of the absence of Japanese pressure. "The nub of the matter," he reasoned, "is this: if the Soviet government should again become convinced that an attack by Japan was likely or imminent we should probably find Litvinov willing to reach agreement on the basis of our proposals. So long as the Soviet Union feels completely secure, I believe that no agreement acceptable to us will be acceptable to the authorities in Moscow." The ambassador later cabled Hull that if the Soviets remained adamant, the United States "should await a turn in world events which might make the Soviet Government more malleable."[53]

With the negotiations still deadlocked in September 1934, Bullitt's analysis remained unchanged. "The answer," he wrote Roosevelt, "I think, is that the Russians have had so much success lately that they are feeling exceedingly cocky." A favorable harvest and improved relations with France had caused the Soviets to feel more secure in the event of a war with Japan and, according to Bullitt, had led them to believe that friendly relations with America were less important than they previously had been. If a Japanese attack again seemed likely or if the United States began to develop any sort of understanding with Japan, "it would not take the Soviet government very long to discover

53. Bullitt to Roosevelt, April 1, 1934, Nixon, *Roosevelt and Foreign Affairs*, 2:47–48; Bullitt to Hull, May 21 and June 9, 1934, *Foreign Relations: Russia*, pp. 99–100, 104–5.

that our demands with regards to debts and claims were most reasonable." Even when the debt-loan talks ended unsuccessfully, the American embassy in Moscow hinted that the growing Soviet fear of Germany could make Russia regret "its intransigent attitude towards the United States."[54]

During these talks, American diplomats assumed they were bargaining from a position of strength, but the Soviets did not enjoy the same degree of confidence. In the period from 1932 to 1934, Stalin not only had to contend with the emergence of a potentially hostile Japan and Germany but also faced internal problems caused by the collectivization of agriculture, unforeseen difficulties in the execution of the five year plans, and renewed signs of secret political opposition. The conjunction of these events led to the Kremlin's decision in late 1933 to alter the objectives of Soviet foreign policy. Stalin and the Commissariat for Foreign Affairs hoped to work out an arrangement with Western nations which would preserve the peace or, if war broke out, at least would provide the Soviet Union with allies. Signing nonaggression pacts with east European nations, France, and Italy, attaining recognition by the United States, and reappraising of the League of Nations were all part of this policy. Despite the new approach, however, Soviet leaders did not abandon their vision about the hostile nature of the capitalist world, nor did they discount the possibility of arriving at an understanding with Germany. Instead, they reacted in a highly pragmatic fashion to an international situation that was potentially disastrous for the Soviet Union.[55]

54. Bullitt to Roosevelt, September 8, 1934, Nixon, *Roosevelt and Foreign Affairs*, 2:210–11. Earlier, after intimating that America's relations with Japan had improved, Bullitt had asked Litvinov if the Soviets could say the same thing. The foreign minister replied that the only improvement was that the two nations were not yet at war, Bullitt to Hull, July 9, 1934, *Foreign Relations: Russia*, p. 116; John Wiley to Hull, March 25, 1935, ibid., pp. 186–87.

55. Eudin and Slusser, *Soviet Foreign Policy*, 2:357–62, 369–73, 399–408; also see Karl Radek's comments on the Soviet desire for peace, ibid., pp. 587–90. Ulam argues that by 1933, Soviet leaders realized that the main premise of their policy since 1921—that future wars would be fought among imperial powers and would benefit Russia—no longer was valid. Consequently, they were in the process of reappraising their entire policy, Ulam, *Expansion and Coexistence*, pp. 194–219. Litvinov's statement to the Central Executive Committee on December 29, 1933, provided a preview on the new phase. Arguing that capitalist nations could become

The Soviets, therefore, had to guard against the possibility of an American accord undermining other aspects of their foreign policy. Nonetheless, Russian leaders had been eager to open contacts with the United States and had given Bullitt a cordial welcome. Because they believed that political rapprochement required a solid economic base, the Soviets realized that a satisfactory debt-loan agreement was essential. They understood that an immediate cooling in the relationship between the two nations would encourage Japanese aggression, as well as deny Russia important American economic assistance. Because they stood to gain from an agreement and could lose considerably if relations foundered, Soviet officials had every reason to favor closer ties with the United States.[56]

Moscow's desire for an agreement did not appear to lessen when the discussions of the debt-loan issue encountered obstacles. In May, Ambassador Bullitt informed Hull of his impression "that the Soviet Government is most anxious to arrive at agreement and that this desire will not diminish as time goes on." The following month, the secretary reported that well-informed sources had the strong impression that the Soviets were "most eager to engage in trade transactions which [the Export-Import] Bank was created to carry on and that any official statements to the contrary are pure bluff." Over the next two months, Bullitt reported that Russian leaders, on the orders of Stalin, were congenial to American diplomats. Bullitt also noted that the Soviet military thought a Japanese attack was inevitable and sought intimate relations with the United States. These impressions led the American ambassador to the view that the Soviets desired the cooperation of the United States and only

---

pacifist at a certain point, the foreign minister suggested that the Soviets might be able to ally with them in the short run, Jane Degras, ed., *Soviet Documents on Foreign Policy*, 3 vols. (London, 1953), 3:48–61.

56. Ulam notes that the reception Stalin gave Bullitt during his first visit to Moscow was unparalleled—even Ribbentrop did not receive similar treatment when he arrived in 1939, Ulam, *Expansion and Coexistence*, p. 213. Litvinov feared that the United States would not remain on friendly terms with the Soviet Union without mutual trade, Bullitt to Hull, March 21, 1934, *Foreign Relations: Russia*, p. 69; also see Bullitt to Hull, April 10, 1934, ibid., p. 83; Lindsay Parrott to Roosevelt, April 28, 1934, PSF: Russia, 1934, Roosevelt Papers; memorandum by Kelley, May 5, 1934, Moore Papers; Bullitt to Hull, May 15, 1934, File No. 800.51W89USSR/56, RG 59.

Litvinov's stubbornness stood in the way.[57] This attitude persisted following the decisive American rejection of Troyanovsky's offer in late August; Bullitt still found the Russians desirous of reaching an accord.[58] After his return to Moscow for talks, Troyanovsky insisted that Stalin retained friendly sentiments toward the United States and wanted to reach a financial settlement. In December, Louis Fischer, an American writer living in Moscow, informed the American embassy that Stalin had given Troyanovsky an oral message for delivery to Washington which conveyed great friendliness, explained why Russia could not accept the American proposal, and asked the United States government to formulate a new offer.[59]

When negotiations resumed in Washington late in January 1935, the Soviet position appeared anything but truculent. During his first meeting with Hull, Troyanovsky avoided mentioning the debt issue, talking primarily about his recent trip through Japan. The Russian ambassador believed that Japanese army and navy elements were in control of the country and that recent troop movements threatened Soviet Russia. Troyanovsky suggested that if the United States, Great Britain, and Russia could speak or act simultaneously along similar lines, they might be able to restrain the militarist elements in Japan. Only after making these observations did the ambassador indicate that he would discuss the debt-loan question at a later date.[60]

57. Bullitt to Hull, May 9, 1934, Foreign Relations: Russia, pp. 91–93; Hull to Bullitt, June 15, 1934, ibid., p. 108; Bullitt to Hull, June 15, July 22, and July 27, 1934, ibid., pp. 107–8, 121–22, 123–24; Bullitt to Hull, February 23, 1934, File No. 800.51W89USSR/99, RG 59; Bullitt to Roosevelt, August 5, 1934, PSF: Russia, 1934, Roosevelt Papers.

58. The ambassador wrote: "I was somewhat surprised by the vehemence with which Skvirsky [Boris Skvirsky, counselor of the Soviet Embassy, who was then in Moscow] insisted that the Soviet Government was even more anxious to reach a settlement than it had been when Litvinov was in Washington." Bullitt to Hull, September 13, 1934, Foreign Relations: Russia, pp. 144–45.

59. Wiley to Hull, November 28, 1934, ibid., pp. 164–65. The embassy was not certain of the precise nature of Stalin's message for, as Wiley noted: "Fischer was so impressed by the confidential nature of the foregoing as to be almost inarticulate. I was therefore unable to elicit any further clarification of what he was attempting to convey." Wiley to Hull, December 15, 1934, File No. 800.51W89USSR/162, RG 59.

60. Following Troyanovsky's remarks on the Far East, Hull insisted that the U.S. had gone to the outside limit in its last proposal; nonetheless, he would make one further offer which the Soviets should not refuse if

During an extended luncheon with Bullitt in Washington on January 30, 1935, Troyanovsky asked if he could talk over the debt settlement with the American ambassador rather than Hull; Troyanovsky feared that negotiations with the secretary of state might end disastrously. Not surprisingly, Bullitt did not go along with the offer, a decision which left Troyanovsky "most depressed."[61] Talks the following day proved anticlimatic. The Soviet ambassador repeated earlier Russian complaints that the American credit terms were so short that acceptance of them would make Russia's relations with other countries more difficult. The Soviets had to receive $100 million on a long-term basis. The United States, however, again refused to extend a credit of this duration. In light of the impasse, both sides agreed that the negotiations had come to an end.[62]

Nonetheless, some discussions did continue through the spring of 1935. Soviet officials soft-pedaled the significance of the unsatisfactory conclusion of the talks and avoided antagonizing the United States. Litvinov insisted that, even though a debt settlement had eluded them, the two countries were "confronted with more serious general objects for which it is possible to work without injuring the material claims of this or that state."[63] In contrast to the Russian attitude, the Americans acted as if there was little hope for the future. Hull's recommendations that the United States withdraw naval and air attachés from Moscow, abolish the Consulate General, and reduce the personnel of the embassy suggest he thought an accord was unlikely. The phasing out of the unused first Export-Import Bank, as well as Bullitt's and Hull's belief that the presence of an American delegation at the Seventh World Congress of Comintern violated the terms of the recognition agreement, gave further evidence of the deterioration of relations from the American standpoint. By the

---

they were at all interested in reaching a settlement, memorandum by Hull, January 28, 1935. *Foreign Relations: Russia*, pp. 166–68.

61. Extract from memorandum by Bullitt, January 30, 1935, ibid., pp. 168–69.

62. Memorandum by Kelley, January 31, 1935, ibid., pp. 170–71.

63. Browder makes this point, *Origins of Soviet-American Diplomacy*, p. 189; Litvinov's statement was printed in the *Moscow Daily News*, see Wiley to Hull, February 3, 1935, *Foreign Relations: Russia*, pp. 174–75; also see Wiley to Hull, February 5, 11, and 14, 1935, ibid., pp. 176–77, 181–82, 182–84.

time of the Comintern Congress, Hull thought relations between the two nations were back where they had been prior to recognition.[64]

Soviet-American relations during the years 1933–1935 did come nearly full circle. A perilous international situation and serious domestic difficulties caused Stalin to adopt tactics designed to keep the country out of war. The bid for American support was one aspect of a general shift in Russian foreign policy.[65] After achieving recognition, but failing to obtain backing for a collective security pact, Soviet leaders hoped they could cement relations with the United States by material ties. The Soviets clearly understood that the diplomatic significance of normalized relations would dwindle without the substantive bond provided by economic links. Since Moscow sought large quantities of machine tools, road building machinery, and railway equipment for its defense program and Five Year Plan, Russian officials had additional incentives to bargain with Washington. Although American policymakers thought the Japanese had reduced their pressure on Russia, Moscow continued to prepare for trouble throughout 1934. Moveover, Soviet diplomatic successes in Europe made the Far East the area of the Kremlin's deepest concern.[66] To argue, therefore, that the Russians sought

64. Hull to Wiley, January 31, 1935, *Foreign Relations: Russia*, p. 171. Bullitt and Hull interpreted the appearance of an American delegation at Moscow as a flagarant violation of the recognition agreement. Interestingly, Bullitt chose to ignore the Comintern's call for a united front against fascism, which was the main purpose of the meeting, Farnsworth, *Bullitt and the Soviet Union*, pp. 143–49; Gardner, *Architects of Illusion*, p. 18; Williams, *American-Russian Relations*, pp. 240–41; Browder, *Origins of Soviet-American Diplomacy*, pp. 204–12; Bishop, *Roosevelt-Litvinov Agreements*, pp. 45–52.

65. Adam Ulam argues convincingly that Stalin adopted a highly pragmatic foreign policy during the 1930s: the Soviets tried to improve relations with the West but did not write off the possibility of reaching an accommodation with Hitler. Ulam does not believe there is any reason to assume that Stalin knew in advance which way he eventually would go or that he thought he would have to select one path over the other, Ulam, *Expansion and Coexistence*, pp. 207–8, 217–30, 270–78. Roberts makes a somewhat similar case, Roberts, *Eastern Europe*, pp. 118–69.

66. See note 56 for the Soviet attitude on the need to establish mutually profitable trade; for Bullitt's analysis of Russia's major requirements, see Bullitt to Hull, October 2, 1934, PSF: Russia, 1934, Roosevelt Papers; Eudin and Slusser, *Soviet Foreign Policy*, 2:410–11, 656–58, 670–82;

only recognition because this act itself provided them with the time necessary to construct a secure position in the Pacific is to fall wide of the mark. Recognition without follow-up actions would prove relatively meaningless, and both Russian and American negotiators realized it.[67] The Soviets could profit greatly from the satisfactory conclusion of the debt-loan negotiations, provided the settlement did not endanger their relations with other nations.[68] In their deliberations with the United States, therefore, Russian officials had little room in which to maneuver.[69]

On the surface, American diplomats did not seem to be in a much more flexible position. Hull argued that Congress and public opinion would not tolerate the extension of credits to foreign governments of much over five years in duration. Others have commented that isolationist sentiment was so strong as to

---

Ulam, *Expansion and Coexistence*, pp. 233–34; Degras, *Soviet Documents on Foreign Policy*, 3:147–49.

67. Hull was the first to argue that the Soviets merely wanted recognition, a reversal of his earlier view that the Soviets were primarily interested in credits or loans, Hull to Bullitt, September 15, 1934, *Foreign Relations: Russia*, p. 145–46; Bishop and Farnsworth agree with Hull, Bishop, *Roosevelt-Litvinov Agreements*, pp. 163–65; Farnsworth, *Bullitt and the Soviet Union*, pp. 125–26; other historians incorrectly believe that the Soviets no longer sought American support after mid-1934 because they were not under pressure in the Far East, see Maddux, "American Relations with the Soviet Union," pp. 107–8, 113; Browder, *Origins of Soviet-American Diplomacy*, p. 193; Batzler, "Development of Soviet Foreign Relations," pp. 164–65; Edward M. Bennett, "Franklin D. Roosevelt and Russian-American Relations 1933–1939," (Ph.D. dissertation, Univ. of Illinois, 1961), pp. 185–86. Bennett later indicated, however, that the Soviets were greatly concerned in 1935 about the possibility of an attack by Germany and Japan and sought closer ties with the United States, Bennett, *Recognition of Russia*, pp. 209–12.

68. The Russians reported that debt negotiations with the United States were awakening British and French creditors, Bullitt to Hull, September 13, 1934, *Foreign Relations: Russia*, pp. 144–45; Wiley to Hull, November 28, 1934, ibid., pp. 164–65; extracts from memorandum by Bullitt, January 30, 1934, ibid., pp. 168–69. Soviet leaders feared that by antagonizing European creditors they would strengthen the hand of those within Great Britain and France who, if able to gain office, would make an agreement with Hitler, Ulam, *Expansion and Coexistence*, pp. 218–21, 227–33.

69. To the degree that Soviet officials believed American business interests could force Washington to extend credits without a debt settlement, however, they were not inclined to bargain, Wiley to Hull, February 3, 1935, *Foreign Relations: Russia*, pp. 174–75.

preclude closer ties with foreign countries.[70] United States leaders, however, may have had more maneuverability than a superficial view suggests. In May 1935, the Export-Import Bank approved in principle granting a fifteen-to-twenty year credit to the Portuguese government for the construction of a bridge. The secretaries of state, commerce, and the treasury concluded that the proposed transaction would not violate national policy. In this instance, administration officials decided that the bank could extend a credit far in excess of a five year term and that an agency of the United States government could engage in financial transactions with another government.[71]

Furthermore, segments within the American business community favored the extension of credits to Russia and became impatient as negotiations stalled. Had the two nations reached an agreement that included a sizeable increase in exports to the Soviet Union, the State Department could have counted on these business groups for support. (Instead, the State Department regarded many of the petitions supporting trade with the Soviet Union as the product of communist propaganda and ignored them.) By presenting the opening of credits solely as a commercial transaction, the Roosevelt administration could have begun the economic steps necessary to solidify relations without risking a political backlash.[72] As will be discussed later, in 1938

70. Memoranda by Kelley, August 15 and 24, 1934, ibid., pp. 134–35, 135–36; Browder, *Origins of Soviet-American Diplomacy*, pp. 199, 216; Farnsworth, *Bullitt and the Soviet Union*, pp. 137–39. Bennett comments on the isolationist sentiment but notes that even without this attitude, the Roosevelt administration did not give much evidence of desiring a positive course of action, Bennett, *Recognition of Russia*, pp. 193–96.

71. Memorandum on national economic policy, May 9, 1935, File No. 800.516 Export-Import Bank/79, RG 59. The transactions did not go through; commercial considerations, not concern over national policy, proved to be the stumbling block.

72. For examples of business opinion in favor of Soviet-American trade, see Maddux, "American Relations with the Soviet Union," pp. 96–99, 108–9; Wilson, *Ideology and Economics*, pp. 129–30; and the following file numbers, 661.115/627, 800.51W89USSR/96, 800.51W89USSR/117, 800.51W89USSR/130, 800.51W89USSR/159, RG 59; on the petitions issue, see Moore to Louis Howe, July 17, 1934, OFF File 971, Export-Import Bank, 1933–August 1934, Roosevelt Papers. Not surprisingly, Russian bondholders opposed a debt settlement which did not cover the entire debt, Albert Coyle to Kelley, May 5, 1934, File No. 800.51W89USSR/53, RG 59; Coyle to Kelley, August 22, 1934, File No. 800.51W89USSR/106, RG 59.

when the administration chose to support Chiang Kai-shek against Japan, it did so without arousing public opposition by using the resources of the Export-Import Bank and portraying the deal in strictly commercial terms. Hull's arguments, therefore, about the adverse nature of public opinion and the bank's inability to offer long-term financial assistance do not fully explain U. S. policy.

Throughout the negotiations American diplomats assumed the United States had sufficient leverage to obtain Soviet compliance with its terms. Before November 1933, the Russian experts argued that Moscow's desire for recognition and capital would give America its bargaining advantage; after November 1933, the experts relied solely on the control of capital. Rather than being naive or unable to cope with the wily Soviets, State Department officers were simply cautious negotiators who believed that Russia needed America more than America needed Russia. Specifically, they thought the Russians' need for foreign economic assistance as well as the dangerous international scene facing the Soviets would make them malleable.[73] Furthermore, these experts realized that the debt settlement involved a principle of international economic relations vital to the expanding commercial and financial interests of their own nation.[74] The

73. This argument runs counter to that of historians who stress either the naivete of American statesmen (whom one historian describes as "quixotic figures" jousting at aggressive forces "with the rubber lance of world opinion") or who claim an agreement was nearly impossible because of the way Roosevelt handled the recognition negotiations. See Bishop, *Roosevelt-Litvinov Agreements*, p. 163; Bennett, *Recognition of Russia*, pp. 136–38; Browder, *Origins of Soviet-American Diplomacy*, p. 216; Maddux, "American Relations with the Soviet Union," pp. 70, 127; Williams does point out the rigid negotiating stance adopted by Washington, Williams, *American-Russian Relations*, pp. 244–47. To a surprising degree, the American approach to the Soviet Union during the period 1933 to 1935 anticipated the United States posture at the end of World War II when, once again, American policymakers thought Russia needed America more than America needed Russia, see Harry S. Truman, *Memoirs*, 2 vols. (Garden City, N.Y., 1955), 1:70–72. Thomas G. Paterson has described how the Truman administration tried to use economic leverage as a diplomatic tool prior to negotiations, rather than as a bargaining instrument, in an episode similar to the 1934 debt-loan negotiations, see Thomas G. Paterson, "The Abortive American Loan to Russia and the Origins of the Cold War, 1943–1946," *Journal of American History* 56 (June 1969): 70–92.

74. Smith, "Businessmen, Bureaucrats, Historians," p. 579.

Russian episode, therefore, discloses how foreign policy considerations could dictate the circumstances under which the Export-Import Bank would act. Despite the certainty that United States exporters would benefit from credits, State Department officers were primarily concerned with the noncommercial aspect of the bank's operations.

5

Behaving like a Good Neighbor
The Bank and Latin America, 1934-1937

A more complex set of factors guided the bank's activities in Latin America than had been the case with Russia, although in both instances American policymakers remained keenly aware of the noncommercial implications involved. The large U. S. economic stake in Latin America produced groups eager to have the Export-Import Bank safeguard and promote their own interests. In analyzing the requests for financial assistance, moreover, State Department officials were careful to see that the bank did not violate the nation's overall approach to international commercial relations or hemispheric affairs. Thus, the bank's Latin American policy comprised elements of immediate financial gain, long-run commercial relations, and noncommercial considerations.

In the years after the outbreak of World War I, United States economic involvement in Latin America grew at an astounding rate.[1] Not only did the countries of the Southern Hemisphere provide growing markets for manufactured products and valuable sources of raw materials, they also absorbed increasing amounts of long-term capital. By 1930, U. S. long-term investment in Latin America was slightly larger than in Europe, with nearly two-thirds of it consisting of direct investments. Since the flow of capital from Britain and other western European countries to Latin America did not return to its prewar level, United States investment increased absolutely and relatively. America's growing presence in Latin America, however, pro-

1. For a discussion of America's economic activities in Latin America during and shortly after World War I, see Burton I. Kaufman, "United States Trade with Latin America," *Journal of American History* 57 (September 1971): 342–63; Joseph S. Tulchin, *The Aftermath of War*, passim.

duced increasing ill will.[2] By 1924, American nationals virtually controlled the financial policies of eleven of the twenty Latin American republics, and in six of these, United States military forces helped maintain political stability. During 1925, the resurgence of economic nationalism in Mexico challenged both extensive American investments in that country and the principles upon which the U. S. based its growing stake in the world economy. The American intervention in Nicaragua in late 1926 and a war scare with Mexico the following year further strained hemispheric bonds. The nadir of inter-American relations was reached at the Havana Conference in 1928 when several Latin American countries tried to pass a resolution outlawing intervention by one nation in the internal affairs of another.[3] Even though the conference did not adopt the proposal, Washington understood the warning that its policies needed drastic overhauling.

During his last two years in office, Calvin Coolidge tried to lessen the anti-American sentiment. To deal with the growing dispute between the Mexican government and U. S. oil companies over subsoil rights, Coolidge sent Dwight Morrow, a leading Wall Street banker, to Mexico City to arrange a satisfactory settlement. The American government, in addition, assumed the lead in negotiating a series of arbitration and conciliation treaties, broadening the range of disputes that could

2. United Nations Department of Economic and Social Affairs, "The Growth of Foreign Investments in Latin America," in *Foreign Investments in Latin America*, ed. Marvin Bernstein, pp. 35, 41–43; William O. Scroggs, "The American Investment in Latin America," *Foreign Affairs* 10 (April 1932): 502. Also see Paul T. Ellsworth, "An Economic Policy for America," *American Economic Review* 30 (February 1941): 309; Alvin T. Hansen, "Hemispheric Solidarity," *Foreign Affairs* 19 (October 1940): 15–18; and Percy Bidwell, *Economic Defense of Latin America*, pp. 10–12.

3. Samuel Guy Inman, "Imperialistic America," *The Atlantic Monthly* 134 (July 1924): 108–9; Sumner Welles, "Is America Imperialistic?" ibid. 134 (September 1924): 412–13; Kenneth F. Woods, " 'Imperialistic America'," *Inter-American Economic Affairs* 21 (Winter 1967): 55–72; Robert Freeman Smith, *The United States and Revolutionary Nationalism in Mexico, 1916–1932*, pp. 229–38; William Kamman, *A Search for Stability*, especially pp. 69–96; Bryce Wood, *The Making of the Good Neighbor Policy*, pp. 5–6, 13–47. At the Havana Conference, Charles Evans Hughes, head of the American delegation, received the support of only four countries (Peru, Nicaragua, Cuba, and Panama) all of which were responsive to pressure from the United States, see Laurence Duggan, *The Americas*, p. 52.

be arbitrated and speeding up the conciliation machinery. As a final move, Reuben J. Clark, the undersecretary of state, concluded that the Monroe Doctrine did not condone United States intervention in the affairs of Latin American states. Clark supported preventive intervention, nevertheless, based on the principles of security and self-preservation.[4]

The Hoover administration continued efforts to promote better pan-American relations. Following his victory in 1928, Hoover embarked on a ten-week good-will tour through Latin America. Shortly after assuming office, the new president announced that the United States would not intervene by force to uphold contracts between American citizens and Latin American governments or nationals. Such an assurance, Hoover maintained, was the only basis on which other countries would welcome the economic cooperation of United States subjects. To encourage better relations, he arranged for the publication of Clark's findings, presided over the withdrawal of American troops from Nicaragua, and planned for the ultimate removal of U.S. marines from Haiti.[5] In a significant reversal of earlier policy, Secretary of State Henry Stimson announced that the Hoover administration would return to Thomas Jefferson's practice of granting recognition on a de facto basis instead of insisting that new governments establish institutions acceptable to this country.[6]

Despite Hoover's steps, many problems remained by 1933. The United States had not renounced the principle of intervention nor had it modified the sections of treaties with Cuba, Haiti,

4. Duggan, *The Americas*, p. 55; Robert Freeman Smith, "The Morrow Mission and the International Committee of Bankers on Mexico," *Journal of Latin American Studies* 1, part 2 (November 1969): 149–66; Smith, *United States and Revolutionary Nationalism in Mexico*, pp. 238–65; a portion of Clark's decision is reprinted in *The Evolution of Our Latin American Policy*, ed. James W. Gantenbein, pp. 401–7.

5. Alexander DeConde, *Herbert Hoover's Latin American Policy*, passim; Herbert Hoover, *The Memoirs of Herbert Hoover*, 2:33; Robert Ferrell, "Repudiation of a Repudiation," *Journal of American History* 51 (March 1965): 669–73; Kamman, *Search for Stability*, pp. 169–217; Dana G. Munro, "The American Withdrawal from Haiti, 1929–1934," *Hispanic American Historical Review* 49 (February 1969): 5–23.

6. The new policy did not apply to the five Central American republics, which had agreed not to recognize revolutionary governments until they held elections; Henry L. Stimson, *The United States and the Other American Republics*, Department of State, Latin American Series, no. 4, pp. 7–15.

Panama, and Mexico which gave it the right to intervene. The American tariff policy, moreover, caused considerable resentment in Latin America; and passage of the Smoot-Hawley tariff heightened this feeling. Although many Latin American raw materials continued to have easy access to U. S. markets, the new duties did injure the Cuban sugar industry, the Chilean, Mexican, and Peruvian copper industries, and the Venezuelan, Mexican, and Colombian oil industries.[7] The depression, of course, further strained hemispheric relations. Most Latin American nations depended on the export of a few primary products, and many countries also relied heavily on the continuous supply of foreign funds to finance their public works program and to fund earlier debts. After 1929, the price of primary products fell drastically (in 1930/31, the prices of Latin America's chief exports decreased by 50 to 75 percent), new foreign loans virtually ceased, and many nations no longer could service their foreign obligations. Several countries introduced exchange controls in an effort to alleviate pressure on their balance of payments, and these measures threatened to disrupt the multilateral trade patterns which had characterized Latin American trade.[8]

Largely in response to the depression conditions, a number of revolutions broke out throughout the southern continent in 1930/31, and these disturbances frequently produced governments that had little regard for the rights and privileges of American interests. To a certain extent, the revolutions represented the heightened sense of nationalism which arose in Latin America about 1930. Growing numbers of Latin Americans were concluding they would have to exercise greater control over their societies if they hoped to achieve balanced and stable economic

7. Duggan, *The Americas*, pp. 57–58; the strong anti-United States sentiment at the Havana Conference of 1928 was primarily a reaction to the American intervention and tariff policies, DeConde, *Herbert Hoover's Latin American Policy*, pp. 10–11; Donald Dozer, *Are We Good Neighbors?*, p. 15; Wood, *The Making of the Good Neighbor Policy*, p. 128.

8. Scroggs, "The American Investment in Latin America," pp. 502–4; A. E. George, "Foreign Loans and Politics in Latin America," *Journal of the American Bankers' Association* 23 (November 1930): 417–18, 463; United Nations Department of Economic and Social Affairs, "The Growth of Foreign Investments in Latin America," pp. 50–51; League of Nations, *The Course and Phases of the World Economic Depression*, pp. 190–91.

growth.[9] The combination of long-term ills and depression-spawned policies, therefore, forced U. S. policymakers to consider new ways of preserving the American stake in Latin America.

Since he had been a prominent critic of the Republicans' handling of hemispheric relations, President Roosevelt naturally was inclined toward revising the old policies. Along with Norman Davis and Sumner Welles, both of whom would play an instrumental role in the formation of New Deal foreign policy, Roosevelt had denounced U. S. armed interference in the affairs of its Latin American neighbors. Although reluctant to forego completely the right of intervention, these men sought to restrict its use to emergency cases, for instance, when a foreign government no longer could ensure the safety of American lives and property. At all costs, the United States should avoid the old dollar diplomacy tactic of interfering to force payment of debts. The Democratic leaders further sought to turn the Monroe Doctrine into a multilateral document by impressing upon the Latin American republics that the independence and integrity of each one of them was of interest to the others and not merely to the U. S. By consulting with other nations and by advocating joint action if the circumstances required it, the United States could continue to promote hemispheric stability but would no longer appear as the sole policeman. "Single-handed intervention by us in the internal affairs of other nations must end," wrote Roosevelt in 1928, "with the cooperation of others we shall have more order in this hemisphere and less dislike." The Democratic critics also recommended lowering trade barriers to encourage greater commerce and more cordial relations. "There is no more effective means of enhancing friendships between nations," Welles informed Roosevelt in early 1933, "than in promoting commerce between them. We cannot expect to

9. Norman H. Davis, "Wanted: A Consistent Latin American Policy," *Foreign Affairs* 9 (April 1931): 547–48, 561–67; Max Winkler, "Does It Pay to Lend Abroad?" *Journal of the American Bankers' Association* 23 (June 1931): 963; George, "Foreign Loans and Politics in Latin America," p. 417; William A. Williams, "Latin America," *Inter-American Economic Affairs* 11 (Autumn 1957): 25–26; Arthur P. Whitaker and David C. Jordan, *Nationalism in Contemporary Latin America*, p. vii; David Green, *The Containment of Latin America*, pp. 11–12.

preserve the sincere friendship of our neighbors on this Continent if we close our markets to them. We cannot enjoy the markets of the American Continent, which have as vast a potentiality for development as any in the world, unless we permit the citizens of our sister nations to trade with us."[10]

The principles of nonintervention and the expansion of international commerce formed the basis of what later became known as the good neighbor policy. In speaking of this program, Roosevelt reiterated his opposition to armed interference and his desire that the nations of the Western Hemisphere cooperate to uphold the Monroe Doctrine. In addition, he urged the governments of the Americas to "abolish all unnecessary and artificial barriers and restrictions which now hamper the healthy flow of trade between the peoples of the American republics." The Roosevelt administration quickly put the good neighbor policy into practice: Hull signed a nonintervention pledge at the Montevideo conference in late 1933 (although America did reserve the right to use force for the protection of lives and property), and the following June, Congress passed the Reciprocal Trade Agreements bill. To further demonstrate the new approach, the administration hastened the withdrawal of American military forces from Haiti and reduced the degree of U. S. influence in the island republic's internal affairs.[11] Roosevelt, moreover, opposed attempts to create an official or semiofficial body to oversee the collection of defaulted foreign loans owed American citizens. Realizing that other nations would view even a semiofficial organization with suspicion, New Deal policy-

10. Franklin D. Roosevelt, "Our Foreign Policy," *Foreign Affairs* 4 (July 1928): 576, 583–86; Davis, "Wanted," pp. 548–67; Sumner Welles, statement of February 21, 1933, in *Franklin D. Roosevelt and Foreign Affairs*, ed. Edgar B. Nixon, 1:18–19; the memorandum is reprinted in Charles Griffin, "Welles to Roosevelt," *Hispanic American Historical Review* 34 (May 1954): 190–92.

11. Pan American Day Address, April 13, 1933, *New York Times*, p. 4; address to the Woodrow Wilson Foundation, December 28, 1933, Nixon, *Roosevelt and Foreign Affairs*, 1:558–63; also see the annual address of January 3, 1934, partially reprinted in ibid., p. 573; for a general discussion of the American acceptance of nonintervention, see Edward O. Guerrant, *Roosevelt's Good Neighbor Policy*, chap. 1; Munro notes the eagerness of the United States to withdraw from Haiti, Munro, "American Withdrawal from Haiti," pp. 24–25.

makers did not wish to complicate foreign relations, especially in Latin America, by raising the specter of dollar diplomacy. Consequently, they supported the formation in October 1933 of the Foreign Bondholders' Security Corporation which, although in close contact with Washington officials, was a private institution.[12]

As described in a series of official speeches, the good neighbor policy became a blend of three interrelated elements: economic, political, and cultural. American policymakers were in general agreement that if the United States had any intention of retaining, much less expanding, exports to its southern neighbors, the nation had to lower its tariff levels. For, as Sumner Welles put it, "No nation can refuse to buy the products of its neighbors and expect for any length of time to continue to sell them its own products." The country had more at stake than attaining new markets, however, since the decline of trade throughout Latin America endangered political and social stability there and made the people willing, in the words of Francis B. Sayre, "to listen to leaders preaching 'anti-foreign' and nationalistic programs." The growth of commerce would undercut domestic unrest and promote good-will. Accompanying the attempts to improve trade relations was a decision to avoid interfering in the domestic affairs of Latin American nations. This political phase of the good neighbor policy would assure Latin Americans that they had nothing to fear from the expansion of United States economic interests. Finally, State Department officials believed that interhemispheric relations would improve, and commerce expand,

12. The Roosevelt papers contain a considerable amount of correspondence dealing with the debt collection issue, Roosevelt to Sam Rayburn, May 20, 1934, enclosed in a letter to Hiram Johnson, May 20, 1934, Nixon, *Roosevelt and Foreign Affairs*, 1:152; Raymond Stevens to Roosevelt, July 28, 1933, ibid., 1:334–36; Roosevelt to Hiram Johnson, July 31, 1933, ibid., 1:338; Stevens to Roosevelt, August 5, 1933, ibid., 1:348–49; Roosevelt to Hull, August 31, 1933, ibid., 1:382; Roosevelt to Frederick Steiver, November 6, 1933, ibid., 1:462–63. Herbert Feis favored a private collection agency instead of a government one; because creditors would not receive immediate payment, a government body would lay itself open to embarrassment, as had happened with the war debts. In addition, a private body would not complicate foreign relations, Feis to Hull, September 15, 1933, ibid., 1:396–98; also see Green, *The Containment of Latin America*, p. 21.

if the peoples of the two continents had a fuller appreciation of the cultures existing in the different republics.[13] As originally conceived, the new policy went a long way toward meeting the grievances expressed at the Havana Conference. Whether the United States could succeed in implementing the policy, especially in the face of concerted trade drives by nonhemispheric nations, and whether even a smoothly executed policy could placate growing Latin American nationalism remained to be seen.[14]

An example of the difficulties facing American policymakers emerged in 1933, when the Roosevelt administration had to deal with the increasing social and political unrest in Cuba. Throughout the 1920s, American financial interests had expanded their control over the Cuban economy while U. S. tariffs diminished the volume of Cuba's sugar exports to this country. This combination of events produced a sharp decline in American exports to Cuba (from $160 million in 1926 to $27 million in 1932) and a growing Cuban nationalist movement which was critical of American dominance. Even though Cuban president Gerardo Machado, who was closely linked with U. S. business interests, preserved a semblance of order throughout most of the period from 1928 to 1932, he did so by relying on increasingly repressive measures. By the time Roosevelt assumed office, Machado's ability to control events seemed open to question. State Department officials followed events in Cuba closely but were uncertain as to what to do. For a short period, Washington appeared to be waiting for an upswing in the world economy to solve the

13. Sumner Wells, *The Roosevelt Administration and its Dealings with the Republics of the Western Hemisphere*, Department of State, Latin American Series, no. 9, pp. 2–16; Sumner Welles, *Pan American Cooperation*, Department of State, Latin American Series, no. 10, pp. 1–73; Sumner Welles, *Inter-American Relations*, Department of State, Latin American Series, no. 8, pp. 1–7, 10–11; Sumner Welles, *The Way to Peace on the American Continent*, Department of State, Latin American Series, no. 13, pp. 9–10; Francis B. Sayre, *Our Relations with Latin America*, Department of State, Latin American Series, no. 14, pp. 6–8.

14. Welles believed that inter-American relations should be the cornerstone of U.S. foreign policy, Welles, *Relations Between the United States and Cuba*, Department of State, Latin American Series, no. 7, pp. 1–2; Welles, *Pan American Cooperation*, p. 1; Welles, *The Way to Peace on the American Continent*, p. 10; Welles's statement of February 21, 1933, Nixon, *Roosevelt and Foreign Affairs*, 1:18–19; also see Lloyd C. Gardner, *Economic Aspects of New Deal Diplomacy*, p. 63.

problem, but as the depression persisted, the State Department began to consider various other ways of keeping the Cuban pot from boiling over.[15]

As they struggled with this situation, American policymakers found themselves becoming uncomfortably immersed in Cuban affairs. Initially, the State Department had hoped to persuade Machado to institute a series of reforms in return for expanded trade with the United States; and Sumner Welles, who temporarily dropped his duties as assistant secretary of state to become an ambassador, went to Havana to work with the Cuban president. But because Machado refused to cooperate, Welles made little headway. In August 1933, the leaders of the Cuban army seized control, and the American ambassador, incorrectly assuming his troubles were nearly over, threw his support to the new government. In spite of Welles's backing, the government soon collapsed in the face of a coalition, made up of students, young professionals, and the lower echelons of the army, that was committed to far-reaching economic and social reforms, as well as to the end of the United States protectorate. Ramón Grau San Martín, a physician and university professor, became president, but he was dependent on the support of Sergeant Fulgencio Batista and uncommissioned army officers. Suspecting the new regime of communist leanings, Welles repeatedly asked Roosevelt and Hull to intervene militarily. Despite sharing the ambassador's distaste for a radical government in Cuba, the president and secretary of state hesitated to accept his advice. U. S. intervention in Cuba in late 1933 would have wrecked the Montevideo conference, besides indicating to the remaining Latin American nations that American policy had changed very little. Roosevelt and Hull, therefore, refrained from direct military interference, but they did send additional warships into Cuban waters and withheld recognition from the new government. Because nonrecognition meant that Cuba could not receive economic assistance or negotiate a new trade agreement with America, the policy made it virtually impossible for Grau

15. Robert Freeman Smith, *The United States and Cuba*, pp. 29–33, 103–42; Sumner Welles, *"Good Neighbor" Policy in the Caribbean*, Department of State, Latin American Series, no. 12, p. 8; Sumner Welles, *Two Years of the "Good Neighbor" Policy*, Department of State, Latin American Series, no. 11, pp. 5–6.

San Martín to stabilize the country. Welles continued to work with groups opposed to the existing government and helped organize the coalition which gathered behind Batista to take control of the country in January 1934.[16]

The Roosevelt administration supported the new regime by granting recognition and negotiating a new treaty in which the United States relinquished the right to intervene militarily in Cuban affairs. Roosevelt also extended economic assistance by guaranteeing Cuban sugar easier access to American markets through a lower tariff and a larger quota of the nation's total sugar imports. As a further step to help promote prosperity, the president created the Second Export-Import Bank. American policymakers believed that a healthy Cuban economy would safeguard U. S. interests by alleviating social and political turmoil. A prosperous Cuba would have the additional advantage of reducing the need for future American interference in Cuba's affairs.[17]

The first action taken by the new Export-Import Bank involved helping the Cuban government increase the volume of money in circulation by initiating public works programs and paying the salaries owed public employees. The bank assisted in minting pesos by buying silver bullion, minting it, and then

16. The events leading up to the overthrow of Grau San Martín are described in Smith, *The United States and Cuba*, pp. 144–56; Lester D. Langley, *The Cuban Policy of the United States*, pp. 153–60; E. David Cronon, "Interpreting the Good Neighbor Policy," *Hispanic American Historical Review* 39 (November 1959): 538–67; Wood, *The Making of the Good Neighbor Policy*, pp. 48–106; Green, *The Containment of Latin America*, pp. 13–15; Irwin F. Gellman has graphically described the extent of American involvement in Cuban affairs during these months and has outlined the social and economic reforms initiated by the Grau regime, Irwin F. Gellman, *Roosevelt and Batista*, pp. 11–83; for the State Department's concern about the role which communists played in the Cuban revolution, see Robert E. Bowers, "Hull, Russian Subversion in Cuba, and Recognition of the U.S.S.R.," *Journal of American History* 53 (December 1966): 547–54.

17. U.S. policy ensured that Cuba's pre-1930 social and economic class structure remained intact; consequently, foreign-owned enterprises retained their important position within the Cuban economy, Smith, *The United States and Cuba*, pp. 153–64; Langley, *The Cuban Policy of the United States*, pp. 161–62; Green, *The Containment of Latin America*, pp. 15–18; Wood, *The Making of the Good Neighbor Policy*, p. 109; Gellman, *Roosevelt and Batista*, pp. 84–121.

turning it over to the Cuban government.[18] These silver transactions were more significant than they appeared on the surface. Not only did they enable the Cuban government to increase the amount of currency in circulation, they also provided a considerable amount of seigniorage. At the end of 1936, the bank had assisted in coining nearly 50 million pesos, resulting in seigniorage of about 32.5 million pesos. (As a comparison, this sum amounted to roughly 15.6 percent of the revenue collected by the Cuban government from fiscal year 1934/35 through fiscal year 1936/37.) The seigniorage, therefore, provided the government with crucial assistance in its attempts to improve economic conditions. In turn, this benefited the United States by fostering Cuban stability and increasing Cuba's purchasing power for American products. During the period from 1934 to 1937, U. S. exports to Cuba rose sharply, from $45,323,000 to $92,263,000. This expansion represented a growth of 104 percent compared to a 57.5 percent increase in U. S. exports to the entire world and a 72.8 percent increase in U. S. exports to Latin America as a whole.[19]

When Roosevelt expanded the Export-Import Bank's range of operations to include all areas of the world, the State Department officials concerned with inter-American relations wanted to guard against the possibility of having the bank work at cross-

18. Dr. J. Martinez Saenz to Welles, March 9, 1934, File No. 811.516 Second Export-Import Bank/1, General Records of the Department of State, RG 59 (National Archives, Washington, D.C.); also see Welles to Roosevelt, March 12, 1934, OFF 159; Cuba 1934, Franklin D. Roosevelt Papers (Franklin D. Roosevelt Library, Hyde Park, New York). Although the Treasury Department had earlier performed similar services for Cuba, the State Department supported the formation of a government bank so that it could stimulate Cuban-American trade as well as provide monetary assistance to the Cuban government; for examples of proposed projects see Saenz to Welles, March 9, 1934, File No. 811.516 Second Export-Import Bank/1, RG 59; Hull to Jefferson Caffrey, March 30, 1934, File No. 811.516 Second Export-Import Bank/4A, RG 59.

19. Duggan to Welles, July 23, 1938, File No. 837.51/2152, RG 59. The Cuban government collected the following sums for each fiscal year; 1934/35: 64,702,000 pesos, 1935/36: 65,336,000 pesos, 1936/37: 78,084,000 pesos, Department of Commerce, *Foreign Commerce Yearbook*, 1937, p. 232; also see Hull to Peek, March 27, 1935, File No. 811.516 Second Export-Import Bank/3A, RG 59; Department of Commerce, *Foreign Commerce and Navigation of the United States for the Calendar Year of 1937*, pp. 785–86.

purposes with official policy. Donald R. Heath of the Division of Latin American Affairs was among the first to devote attention to this issue. Since the countries to the south offered a good market for United States capital goods, he presumed that a large portion of the bank's intermediate and long-term credits would involve trade of this nature. The major problem was that the bank's operations could result in political misunderstandings inasmuch as the American government "would become a creditor of foreign commercial and probably semi-governmental enterprises." Other difficulties could be pressure from United States exporters to undertake loans on unattractive risks, the possibility that the moderate financial costs would encourage foreign interests to make unnecessary purchases, the problem of obtaining accurate banking reports on prospective customers, and the chance of graft. Heath suggested that the State Department remain in close contact with the bank's operations 'in order to study its possible political and economic effects and determine the Department's policy and relationship to the program."[20]

Requests by American exporters for assistance in liquidating blocked balances precipitated a discussion about one of the most perplexing commercial conditions of the 1930s. Severe balance of payments difficulties had forced most Latin American nations to resort to some form of exchange restriction. In turn, certain European nations, which had bought more from a particular Latin American country than they had sold to it, established compensation agreements requiring the Latin American nation to draw on the proceeds from its favorable balance of trade and, thus, to free the exchange of the European country. Not only did this practice favor the European nation, it destroyed triangular trade patterns by steering commerce along bilateral lines. By the middle of the decade, therefore, American policymakers concluded that the compensation agreements restricted trade far more than did protective tariffs, and that they were a prime cause of the prolongation of the depression. Although State Department officials still advocated multilateral trade, they realized that the continued refusal of other nations to accept the American approach could force them to alter their position.[21]

20. Division of Latin American Affairs to Edwin C. Wilson and Welles, March 21, 1935, File No. 811.516 Export-Import Bank/73, RG 59.
21. For an analysis of the exchange situation in Latin America and its

The European method of handling blocked accounts appealed to some American foreign traders, and these exporters found a firm ally in George N. Peek, the Export-Import Bank president. In May 1935, Peek contacted State Department officials to determine their attitude on providing credits to thaw frozen exchanges. While it was unwilling to adopt a general position at that time, the department did agree to consider each of the bank's proposals on its own merits.[22] Nevertheless, Heath and A. P. Upgren, of the Trade Agreements Division, argued in favor of a broad policy decision. They did not agree with Peek's assessment that the expansion of American exports hinged on the bank's willingness to liquidate blocked funds by without-recourse purchases of foreign governments' obligations. The two State Department men pointed out that this approach could lead to political entanglements because the United States government would become the creditor of a foreign government. Even if the likelihood of political difficulties was minimal, favorable action by the bank in the case of one nation would "create bad feeling toward the United States in countries whose obligations the banks would refuse to discount." Since large corporations held a major portion of the frozen credits, Heath and Upgren thought these concerns could handle the problem without governmental aid. They also feared that the administration would be vulnerable to criticism for bailing out big businesses that had continued to export with full knowledge of the exchange risks involved. Furthermore, American bondholders might complain if the government guaranteed the payment of frozen balances but not of defaulted bonds. Finally, Heath and Upgren questioned whether the State Department should support a policy that would increase exports but would not provide

---

implications for the United States, see a report by John H. Williams, September 4, 1934, *Foreign Relations, 1934*, 4:392–422; after examining conditions in Brazil, Uruguay, Argentina, and Chile, Williams recommended that the administration not alter its commercial policy but concentrate on persuading European governments to avoid compensation arrangements; also see Welles to McIntyre, October 26, 1934, Nixon, *Roosevelt and Foreign Affairs*, 2:244–47.

22. At this point, Peek had proposals dealing with Nicaragua and Brazil, see Report of Executive Committee Meeting, May 15, 1935, File No. 811.516 Export-Import Bank/83, RG 59; memorandum by Donald R. Heath, May 23, 1935, File No. 811.516 Export-Import Bank/99, RG 59.

any means of expanding imports. The two officials believed many of these objections would disappear if the bank was to discount paper on a full-recourse basis, but they noted that officers of the National Foreign Trade Council and the bank did not favor this approach. Rather than rely on with-recourse financing, American exporters preferred to handle the notes themselves or to obtain their money through free or bootleg exchange channels. "If this is true," Heath and Upgren argued, "it would seem that either the firms are not in essential need of the capital tied up in their blocked accounts or the credit risk of the notes is quite unsatisfactory."[23]

After deciding against a general policy statement, the State Department considered the Export-Import Bank's proposal to purchase the obligations of the Bank of Nicaragua on a without-recourse basis. Because Nicaragua was a poor credit risk and was already in default on debts owed the United States government, and since there was opposition to the U. S. government becoming financially involved in Nicaragua, the State Department vetoed the proposal.[24] Once again, it was officials on the divisional level who offered the strongest opposition to the bank's proposal. Willard L. Beaulac, an assistant chief in the Latin American Division, argued that irrespective of the attractiveness of the deal, it was undesirable for the United States government "to become the creditor of a Central American Government, or to allow itself to become involved in the exchange situation in any of those countries." Such a step would mark a return to the dollar diplomacy of Secretary of State Philander Knox and might be even worse, since Knox had relied on private banks to float loans: "He did not go so far as to arrange for direct loans by this Government or its agencies to the Governments of those countries or their agencies." Since dollar diplomacy had led to intervention, there was "no reason to suppose that, if the Export-Import Bank became the creditor of a Central American Government, or acquired a direct interest

23. If the bank accepted the paper of one country, moreover, it would have to do likewise for all countries to avoid hard feelings, Donald R. Heath and Arthur R. Upgren, "Assistance of Export-Import Bank in Liquidating American Blocked Credits in Foreign Countries," May 18, 1935, File No. 811.516 Export-Import Bank/99, RG 59.
24. Memorandum by Donald R. Heath, May 23, 1935, ibid.

in the exchange situation in Central American countries, there would not exist the same tendency for us to become involved in Central America." Inasmuch as Peek's proposal would result in the United States assuming an interest in the exchange conditions of Nicaragua, America would inevitably exert some influence on Nicaraguan politics. "Our entire hands off policy," Beaulac warned, "would be dissipated as far as Central America is concerned. Instead of being a good neighbor, we would again be regarded as an international Shylock." He concluded by suggesting that there was "no greater threat to our relations with the countries of Central America than the possibility that this Government will attempt another venture into the realm of 'dollar diplomacy' by permitting the Export-Import Bank to become involved in the exchange situation in those countries."[25]

Peek's additional recommendation that the Export-Import Bank assist in unblocking American balances in Brazil provoked extended debate because it involved more complex issues than had been at stake in the Nicaraguan proposal. Part of this complexity stemmed from the internal changes which the depression had produced in Brazil. Prior to the revolution in 1930, Brazil had been dominated by an oligarchy which drew its strength from an economy geared to the export of a few primary products (largely coffee and cotton) and to foreign investment. When Getulio Vargas seized power in 1930, Brazil began moving toward a policy of economic nationalism.[26] This process, how-

25. Willard Beaulac, "Proposed Credit of $1,500,000 from the Export-Import Bank to the National Bank of Nicaragua," May 15, 1935, ibid. In a note attached to the memorandum, Beaulac also commented: "One can readily imagine the situation which would result, however, should the Export-Import Bank, as agency of this Government, be obliged to take over the assets of the National Bank of Nicaragua, the property of the Nicaraguan Government, on account of the failure of the Bank to redeem its notes. The political effects of such action not only in Nicaragua but in other Latin American countries would be so great that it would be far preferable that this Government never try to utilize the guarantee indicated. A guarantee under such conditions is of little worth."

26. Donald W. Griffin, "The Normal Years: Brazilian-American Relations 1930–1939" (Ph.D. dissertation, Vanderbilt Univ., 1962), p. 2; John D. Wirth, *The Politics of Brazilian Development 1930–1945*, pp. 7–13 (I have accepted Wirth's definition of economic nationalism as the determination to obtain sufficient economic power to ensure political independence, ibid., p. 7); Whitaker and Jordan, *Nationalism in Contemporary*

ever, was a gradual one (as well as ultimately incomplete), and throughout the decade, supporters of differing economic policies vied for political influence. Roberto Simonsen, president of the São Paulo Industrial Federation, led those who advocated industrial development and a nationalist trade policy based on bilateral patterns and barter agreements. Oswaldo Aranha, who was, in succession, finance minister, ambassador to the United States, and foreign minister, preferred the older economic framework and stressed the need for a resurgence of liberal foreign trade policies under American leadership. The existence of these widely divergent economic views helps explain why Vargas pursued an unsteady economic course during the decade.[27]

Economic competition between the U. S. and Germany for Brazil's allegiance further complicated American-Brazilian relations. In the fall of 1934, Germany instituted a series of commercial controls designed to secure needed supplies of raw materials and to increase exports. Brazil was important to Nazi trade officials because her dependence on cotton and coffee exports left the country vulnerable to economic pressure. Nazi leaders relied heavily on compensation agreements, which at times approximated pure barter, to force Brazil to use the proceeds derived from export sales in Germany to purchase German goods. Although this process provided Brazilians with an expanding market during a difficult period, it forced their trade into a bilateral pattern since exporters could not obtain exchange from sales to Germany for use elsewhere. Brazilian authorities, moreover, discovered that the Germans were reselling cotton and coffee below cost in the Scandanavian countries in order to acquire free exchange; and when they tried to retaliate by suspending further compensation deals, the reaction from agricultural and commercial groups in Brazil was strong enough to force a resumption of the German trade. Brazilian officials found themselves in an awkward position; they could not trade with Germany except on the Germans' terms, and they could not afford to halt the trade altogether. Consequently, Germany's

---

Latin America, pp. 79–81; Frank D. McCann, Jr., *The Brazilian-American Alliance, 1937–1945,* pp. 12–31.

27. Aranha became an intimate of Sumner Welles and also worked his way into the good graces of Washington society, Wirth, *Politics of Brazilian Development,* pp. 17–19, 24–25.

position in Brazil's trade improved throughout the decade; after 1935, she replaced the United States as Brazil's leading trading partner. This growth of German influence in Brazil posed a direct threat to American material interests and to the U. S. conviction that world trade should proceed along multilateral lines.[28]

The activities of American exporters with frozen balances in Brazil added a final complexity to United States-Brazilian relations. Since Brazil's exports to America exceeded her imports by approximately three times, United States businessmen believed they had sufficient leverage to force favorable exchange treatment if they could receive governmental support. In the spring of 1933, American traders began to complain that the Brazilian government was endangering future commercial relations between the two countries by reducing exchange allotments for United States exports. "American companies and exporters," the American Chamber of Commerce for Brazil cabled Roosevelt, "are being compelled to discontinue shipments which will soon result [in the] closing [of] American branch houses and [will] practically annihilate already diminished American exports."[29] The National Foreign Trade Council, under the direction of Eugene P. Thomas, the Council of Inter-American Relations, and Fred I. Kent, then the supervisor of exchange for the Federal Reserve Bank of New York, took the lead in trying to secure State Department support for a plan to guarantee payment of frozen credits. They had in mind an arrangement whereby the Reconstruction Finance Corporation would purchase

28. The American decline in Brazil's trade was relative, however, since Germany's gains came primarily at the expense of Great Britain. The various German trade schemes are outlined by Cleona Lewis, assisted by John C. McClelland, *Nazi Europe and World Trade*, pp. 139–44; for a discussion of German-Brazilian trade ties, see Bidwell, *Economic Defense of Latin America*, pp. 38–43; also see the excellent analysis by Stanley Hilton, "Brazil and Great Power Trade Rivalry in South America, 1934–1939" (Ph.D. dissertation, Univ. of Texas, 1969), pp. 12–35, 47–50, 58–59, 62–74, 134–53. Hilton notes that the demand of the Brazilian military for new equipment reinforced the drive for trade ties with Germany, ibid., pp. 75–89. While hoping to avoid becoming too closely aligned with either Germany or the United States, Vargas seemed to move closer to the former until war broke out in 1939, Wirth, *Politics of Brazilian Development*, pp. 17–68; also see Griffin, "The Normal Years," pp. 70–75, 258–311.

29. American Chamber of Commerce for Brazil to Roosevelt, May 12, 1933, *Foreign Relations*, 1933, 5:43–44.

notes issued by the Bank of Brazil and guaranteed by the allotment of a percentage of the dollars Brazil received from exports to the United States.[30]

State Department officials, however, responded coolly to these requests, restricting their support to obtaining a pledge from the Brazilian government to provide American interests with equal treatment in the allocation of exchange. The department believed that private interests should arrange a settlement on their own and had difficulty understanding why American bankers were unwilling to provide the same degree of financial support for liquidation agreements as did English bankers. The New York commercial banks, however, remained uninterested in deals of this nature.[31] After failing to obtain government support, the National Foreign Trade Council and the Council on Inter-American Relations concluded an agreement with Brazilian authorities in June 1933: Brazil agreed to repay the United States firms that held balances of up to $50,000 within ninety days and to issue monthly notes over the next six years to pay off those firms with blocked balances in excess of this amount. Although they were able initially to resist the pressure from business and financial groups, State Department officers suffered no delusions about the strength of their position. They informed Brazil that if American interests did not receive equitable treatment in the long run, the United States would be obliged "to put into effect an arrangement under which it would retain in this country a certain percentage of the dollar exchange arising from its purchases abroad."[32]

By the latter part of 1934, American exporters again faced the problem of blocked balances in Brazil. As in the earlier case,

30. Memorandum by Edwin C. Wilson, May 26, 1933, ibid., pp. 51–52; Hull to Kent, May 26, 1933, ibid., pp. 50–51; Kent to Hull, May 27, 1933, ibid., pp. 53–54; Griffin, "The Normal Years," pp. 96–97.
31. Memorandum by Edwin C. Wilson, May 26, 1933, Foreign Relations, 1933, 5:51–52; Hull to Kent, May 26, 1933, ibid., pp. 50–51; Griffin, "The Normal Years," pp. 96–97.
32. E. P. Thomas to William Phillips, June 15, 1933, Foreign Relations, 1933, 5:56–59; Phillips to Roosevelt, June 27, 1933, ibid., pp. 60–61; Griffin, "The Normal Years," pp. 97–98; Taylor to Alley, August 8, 1935, Ex-Im Bank of Wash., Part 2, RFC General Correspondence File, Records of the Reconstruction Finance Corporation, RG 234 (National Archives, Washington, D.C.); memorandum by W. R. Manning, May 20, 1933, Foreign Relations, 1933, 5:46–48.

they hoped to involve the government in the liquidation process, this time by utilizing the Export-Import Bank. Not only was Peek receptive to their arguments, he believed he could use this incident to gain a wider acceptance for his views on international commercial policy.[33] The bank president proposed a funding program in which the Brazilian government would issue long-term bonds to the American holders of deferred balances and would support the certificates by a lien on the proceeds of coffee sales in the United States. By purchasing these bonds at face value, the Export-Import Bank would provide American exporters with immediate liquidity. When Peek presented his proposal to the bank's executive committee on commercial policy, the other members unanimously opposed it on several points. They maintained that the proposition did not provide for the expansion of Brazilian exports to the United States. In addition, because the plan would leave Brazil with fewer dollars to make purchases elsewhere, it would jeopardize the multilateral payments system. More importantly, the deal could easily have an adverse effect on America's international economic relations by establishing a precedent that other nations could use against the United States: nations that had refrained from entering into discriminatory trade pacts for fear of antagonizing Washington would no longer be under the same constraint.[34]

Hull, Welles, and Sayre made repeated attempts to persuade Roosevelt not to accept Peek's suggestions. They pointed out that a diversion of trade from established channels would endanger international good-will and that, from the perspective of self-interest, triangular trade operations were "necessary in order to maintain the position of American commerce in many

33. As discussed in chap. 3, Peek was also sponsoring the German cotton deal in late 1934. Brazilian officials informed the State Department that if the United States went ahead with its cotton transaction, they would conclude a bilateral trade agreement with Germany. American commercial policy was clearly at a crossroads. A move toward bilateralism could have produced a snowballing effect, accelerating the destruction of existing trade systems. For Brazil's perspective, see Wirth, *Politics of Brazilian Economic Development*, pp. 36–40; Hilton, "Brazil and Great Power Trade Rivalry," pp. 101–3.

34. Memorandum from the Office of the Economic Adviser, December 18, 1934, File No. 611.0031 Executive Committee/339, RG 59; Griffin, "The Normal Years," pp. 120–21.

countries which now buy more from us than we buy from them, particularly the chief European trading countries." Hull, in particular, warned that an attempt to force an exchange deal with Brazil could "be used to justify many of our best customers, including Great Britain, Japan, France, Italy, and Canada, in applying the same principle to our trade since the trade relations between ourselves and these countries are the reverse of those in Brazil." He urged the president to resist the pressure from those groups who sought exceptional terms in the few cases where the country could do so. "Those who press them upon us," the secretary argued, "are all too often inadequately informed of all American interests, with the exception of their own."[35]

For the moment, the State Department's position again triumphed. As part of a new trade agreement signed between Brazil and the United States, American exporters received a pledge from the Brazilian government to furnish exchange for future transactions and to work off the arrears.[36] Foreign traders, however, did not give up hope of receiving governmental financial assistance. Eugene P. Thomas took the initiative for export interests, periodically contacting members of the State Department in early 1935 to see if they would agree to use the Export-Import Bank to purchase Brazilian funding notes.[37] In the middle of May, the bank's credit committee supported Thomas, recommending that the bank purchase from American foreign traders the dollar notes issued by the Bank of Brazil on a without-recourse basis in settlement of commercial indebtedness. (Unlike the earlier proposal, however, Brazil would not guarantee the notes with a lien on coffee exports to America.) The bank's executive committee also expressed interest in the proposal,

35. Welles to McIntyre, October 26, 1934, Nixon, *Roosevelt and Foreign Affairs*, 2:244–47; Henry Kannee to McIntyre (which contained a message from Sayre), November 23, 1934, ibid., pp. 287–88; Hull to Roosevelt, February 15, 1935, ibid., pp. 410–11.

36. Taylor to Alley, August 8, 1935, Ex-Im Bk. of Wash., Part 2, RG 234; Griffin, "The Normal Years," pp. 122–25; for a discussion of the negotiations leading up to the trade agreement, see Hilton, "Brazil and Great Power Trade Rivalry," pp. 91–111.

37. Memorandum by Edwin C. Wilson, February 1, 1935, File No. 611.3231/787, RG 59; E. P. Thomas to Hull, February 20, 1935, File No. 811.516 Export-Import Bank/153½, RG 59; memorandum by R. F. Kelley, May 15, 1935, File No. 811.516 Export-Import Bank/83 RG 59.

provided the terms of the agreement were satisfactory to the State Department.[38]

The department did not turn to the recommendation until July, and as had been the case with the Nicaraguan proposal, officers on the divisional levels voiced the strongest opposition. Repeating many of his earlier objections, Heath indicated that the transaction would make the United States government the direct creditor of the Brazilian government and could produce ill-will from other nations with whom the bank refused to take similar action. Besides not giving any promise of expanding trade, the proposal would primarily assist large corporations, who were capable of carrying notes without distress. Finally, Heath warned that if the Brazilian government had to default on its dollar bonds in order to pay off the new notes, something he assumed probably would happen, American bondholders could legitimately claim they had been sacrificed in favor of the export interests.[39]

A. H. Hansen, of the Trade Agreements Division, also had strong reservations about the recommendation, especially since it would produce a creditor-debtor relationship between the two governments. In place of the credit committee's proposal, Hansen suggested that Brazil pay the smaller exporters immediately and issue bonds to the larger exporters, who could then use the notes as collateral for Export-Import Bank credits to help finance new trade opportunities. Hansen believed that the solvency of the larger firms together with such security as they could offer would minimize the risk of the bank becoming the creditor of the Brazilian government. Even from a strictly business standpoint, however, Hansen thought it unjustifiable for the bank to discount the notes on a without-recourse basis. Therefore, when

38. Credit committee to executive committee, May 14, 1935, Export-Import Bank Credit Files, Project No. 80, National Foreign Trade Council, Records of the Export-Import Bank of Washington, RG 275 (National Archives, Washington, D.C.); memorandum by R. F. Kelley, May 15, 1935, File No. 811.516 Export-Import Bank/83, RG 59.

39. The arguments in favor of the move were that important export interests would be pleased (whereas a refusal could produce ill-will toward the department), and that the release of new funds could stimulate exports. Heath did note that the impetus for the proposal came from exporters and not the Brazilian government, Heath to Joseph McGurk and Welles, July 13, 1935, File No. 811–516 Export-Import Bank/153½, RG 59.

Robert Kelley, the State Department's chief spokesman on the bank's executive committee, called a meeting to work out a departmental position, the consensus was not to oppose the transaction as long as it was conducted on a with-recourse basis. Department officials based their decision on the belief that it was inadvisable, "from considerations of foreign policy, for an agency of the Government of the United States to be placed in a position where it may become a direct creditor of the Brazilian Government." After listening to Kelley's arguments, the executive committee informed Thomas that the bank would consider the Brazilian transaction only on a with-recourse basis.[40]

The issue did not end here. In late August, Thomas again asked the bank to purchase Brazilian notes, without recourse to American exporters. This request gave Peek another opportunity to arrange an exchange agreement under which Brazil would use the proceeds of its coffee sales as collateral for the notes. Despite its earlier opposition to similar proposals, the bank's executive committee did not immediately reject the plan. At Kelley's suggestion, the committee agreed to inform Thomas that the bank would not make any commitment until the recently signed trade agreement became effective: "After the Agreement had gone into effect, the Bank, for the purpose of facilitating new foreign business, would give consideration to the making of loans against the notes received from Brazil in settlement of blocked balances."[41]

Wayne Taylor, a vice-president of the Export-Import Bank, came away from the meeting believing that the executive committee would support without-recourse financing when the time was ripe for action; and in early October, he made Thomas an

40. A. H. Hansen to R. F. Kelley, July 17, 1935, File No. 811.516 Export-Import Bank/153½, RG 59; circular by Kelley, July 20, 1935, ibid. Peek agreed with Kelley but for different reasons. The bank president persisted in his hope of arranging a compensation agreement, memorandum of executive committee meeting, July 24, 1935, File No. 811.516 Export-Import Bank/100, RG 59.

41. Peek to Jones, August 22, 1935, Ex-Im Bk. of Wash., Part 2, RG 234; meeting of executive committee of Export-Import Bank, August 23, 1935, File No. 611.3231/1022, RG 59; meeting of executive committee, August 23, 1935, Project No. 80, National Foreign Trade Council, RG 275.

offer which incorporated this principle.[42] This news must have buoyed Thomas's spirits since he was still attempting to secure government financial support.[43] Thomas believed that American exporters did not want the bank to accept Brazilian obligations as collateral for loans to finance new business and hoped the institution would purchase the notes outright. He informed Heath that, at the request of American export interests, he had deliberately suspended negotiations with Brazilian authorities until the exporters could receive the assurances they wanted from the State Department.[44]

In the middle of October 1935, the National Foreign Trade Council asked the bank to reconsider its earlier position.[45] On

42. The accounts of the meeting are not clear on whether the committee approved a nonrecourse agreement. Only a month earlier, State Department officials had opposed a transaction of this nature, and there is no indication that they changed their views. At the meeting, Taylor did support without-recourse lending, and he could have been reading his own views into the committee's decision, Taylor to Thomas, October 3, 1935, File No. 811.516 Export-Import Bank/153½, RG 59.

43. In early September, the State Department caught wind of an attempt by Thomas to obtain a liquidation agreement of the type Peek supported, Hull to Hugh Gibson, September 4, 1935, File No. 611.3231/995, RG 59; the American Chamber of Commerce in Brazil also supported some form of coercive exchange control which would take advantage of Brazil's favorable balance of trade with the United States, Carol Foster to Hull, October 2, 1935, File No. 832.5151/729, RG 59; Thomas complained that the department was too zealous in supporting small exporters and too lax in assisting large ones: "It is the large business of the major exporters," he asserted, "that makes possible the facilities of carriage enjoyed in kind by even the smallest American foreign trader." Thomas to Moore, September 30, 1935, File No. 832.5151/714, RG 59.

44. Thomas to Taylor, October 15, 1938, File No. 811.516 Export-Import Bank/153½, RG 59. Thomas's comment caused Heath to note: "Mr. Thomas' statement that he had deliberately held up conclusion of the Frozen Credit Agreement which he is negotiating until he could persuade the Export-Import Bank to bail out the American exporters is interesting in view of the fact that within the last two weeks the Department has had a dozen letters protesting the delay in settlement of American frozen credits in Brazil." Memorandum by Heath, October 19, 1935, File No. 832.5151/733½, RG 59.

45. The department learned in early October that the National Foreign Trade Council had reached an agreement on the terms for a settlement of the frozen balances but that final signature would await ratification of the trade agreement, Wilson to American Exporters' and Importers' Assoc., October 10, 1935, File No. 832.5151/712, RG 59.

the heels of this request, the credit committee issued a proposal favorable to export interests. The committee recommended that the bank open lines of credit for exporters and accept as collateral, in lieu of ultimate recourse, the dollar notes issued by the government of Brazil to settle blocked balances under the agreements of 1933 and 1935. The credit committee further recommended that in export transactions where the bank had agreed to purchase a specified percentage of obligations on a without-recourse basis, it buy all or part of the remaining notes on a similar basis if the exporter pledged Brazilian liquidation obligations as security. Finally, the committee proposed that the bank purchase Brazilian notes up to a total of $25,000 for each holder upon proof of export business to that amount, and buy one-half of each holder's remaining obligations upon an indication of future export business amounting to four times the value of the notes offered for purchase. The credit committee's suggestions, however, encountered opposition within the bank itself. Warren L. Pierson, the legal counsel, rejected the first two recommendations because they were economically unsound and could lead to diplomatic complications in the case of a default. Since it did not involve without-recourse financing, however, Pierson believed that the third proposal had merit.[46]

Thus, American exporters failed to receive the type of financial assistance they sought. After the ratification of the United States-Brazil trade agreement in February 1936, the National Foreign Trade Council worked out a limited funding arrangement. The exporters initially wanted to include exchange arrears arising out of the shipment of goods from places other than the United States, but Jesse Jones would not allow it. This practice, he argued, would primarily benefit large corporations. After being defeated on this proposal, the council did sign an accord in which the bank would purchase, on a full-recourse basis, up to $27.75 million of the notes issued by the Bank of Brazil in payment for blocked accounts. Significantly, members of the export community used only $1,716,977 of the commitment.[47]

46. Credit committee to executive committee, October 22, 1935, File No. 811.516 Export-Import Bank/153½, RG 59; Pierson to credit committee, October 23, 1935, ibid.
47. Hull to Gibson, February 8, 1936, *Foreign Relations, 1936*, 5:293–94; Hawthorne Arey, "History of Operations and Policies of Export-Import

Although by the spring of 1936 the State Department had come out on top in the debate over the funding of Brazil's exchange arrears, the future remained unclear.[48] The beginnings of economic nationalism within Brazil could result in the adoption of policies that would discriminate against American interests. The growth of German trade also could prove troublesome because the methods used by Germany threatened to pull Brazil into her economic orbit. Finally, the department found itself under strong domestic pressure to support plans that either could lead to the adoption of policies similar to the German ones or that risked unfortunate political developments which might violate the good neighbor policy.

To direct the bank's general operations in Latin America, the State Department ended up with an imprecise set of guidelines. Nearly all officers agreed that the Export-Import Bank could prejudice the good neighbor policy by making the United States government the creditor of a national, provincial, or municipal government in another American republic. Hence, the department vetoed several proposals because without-recourse financing would have produced this relationship. If rigorously adhered to, this attitude meant that the bank could discount notes guaranteed by an agency of a Latin American government only on a with-recourse basis. And even so, some officials believed that the bank should not purchase the notes of governments that re-

Bank of Washington," mimeograph, p. 12. Under the terms of the accord, exporters with claims of $18,000 or less received immediate payment and those with larger claims obtained notes from the Brazilian government over a fifty-six month period, Gibson to Hull, June 11, 1936, *Foreign Relations, 1936*, 5:295–98.

48. For the argument that exporters triumphed in this episode since they received assurances from Jesse Jones that the Export-Import Bank would undertake without-recourse financing in the future, see James M. McHale, "The New Deal and the Origins of Public Lending for Foreign Economic Development, 1933–1945," (Ph.D. dissertation, Univ. of Wisconsin, 1970), pp. 108–33; James M. McHale, "National Planning and Reciprocal Trade," *Prologue* 6 (Fall 1974): 196–99. I am not, however, convinced by this argument: first, the limited use exporters made of the commitment does not suggest that they believed they had won an important victory; second, Jones's promise was largely a reiteration of the bank's 1935 policy statement which exporters had thought inadequate; and third, the bank did not begin extending nonrecourse loans on a consistent basis until late 1937, and it did so then because of a number of contemporary events rather than to fulfill a prior commitment.

mained in default to American bondholders, on the theory that if these nations could obtain additional credits, they would not have any incentive to repay outstanding debts. In certain cases, department officers considered two other factors: they opposed a transaction involving an agency of the Peruvian government because that government had not treated American interests on a most-favored-nation basis; and they vetoed proposals concerning Costa Rica and Nicaragua because political instability within these countries made the transactions too risky. Barring these restrictions, the bank could support deals involving Latin American governments on a with-recourse basis and could purchase paper without recourse to the exporter if the debtor was a private concern.[49]

Despite these general guidelines, however, the bank did participate in some transactions that made it the creditor of an agency of a Latin American government. In May 1935, it agreed to buy, on a without-recourse basis, the obligations of the Mexican state of Chihuahua after the Latin American Division concluded that these notes had adequate security.[50] Five months later, the bank considered a proposal for a nonrecourse purchase of the obligations of Vera Cruz, Mexico, in order to help finance

49. Executive committee meeting, June 10, 1935, File No. 811.516 Export-Import Bank/43, RG 59; Welles to Moore, October 8, 1935, File No. 812.151/106, RG 59; Duggan to Kelley, January 14, 1936, File No. 811.516 Export-Import Bank/153½, RG 59; memorandum by W. L. Beaulac, December 22, 1936, File No. 65A473, 18,3246/1, Ex-Im. Bk. of Wash./1 1936–1937, Department of the Treasury, (U.S. Department of the Treasury, Washington, D.C.); G. Jones to Draper, April 23, 1937, Office of the Secretary, General Correspondence 96227, General Records of the Department of Commerce, RG 40 (National Archives, Washington, D.C.); Duggan to Kelley, May 3, 1937, File No. 811.516 Export-Import Bank/153½, RG 59; Heath to Duggan and Earl Packer, November 4, 1935, ibid., Heath to Kelley, November 11, 1936, ibid.; memoranda of executive committee meetings of April 14, 22, and May 4, 1937, File No. 811.516 Export-Import Bank/126, RG 59; G. Jones to Draper, December 11, 1936, Office of the Secretary, General Correspondence 96227, RG 40; the question of which transactions were acceptable became quite complex, see Heath to Duggan, April 1, 1936, File No. 811.516 Export-Import Bank/153½, RG 59.

50. The bank agreed to finance up to 67 percent of the Armco International Corporation's costs on a nonrecourse basis, see agreement of May 31, 1935, Project No. 77, Armco International Corporation, RG 275; also see George Muller to Pierson, June 18, 1936, File No. 811.516 Export-Import Bank/153½, RG 59.

the sale of American pipes, meters, and other water works equipment. Because the federal government would provide part of the revenue to secure the notes, the undertaking would make the bank the creditor of the Mexican government, as well as of the Vera Cruz government. The proposal ran into opposition within the State Department as Sumner Welles argued that its acceptance would cause the bank to pursue "a course counter to the policy which we all agreed upon last summer."[51] Although other members of the department not only supported him but voiced their disapproval of the Chihuahua transaction, Welles found himself overruled by Assistant Secretary Moore. Moore suggested that a way around Welles's opposition was to have the bank's board of trustees write the State Department a letter indicating that the proposal was solely a commercial transaction; Moore believed this step would remove any political obligations or connotations. Despite Welles's continued reservations, the executive committee accepted Moore's view.[52] During the period from 1935 to 1937, the bank participated on a without-recourse basis in several ventures that made it the creditor of agencies of the Mexican government. Other than Moore's comments in the fall of 1935, there is no evidence to indicate how the department justified this departure from its earlier position. Perhaps the department's belief that the Mexican government was strong enough to ensure the collection of tax revenues led American policymakers to conclude that a default was unlikely. After 1937, the bank did refuse to finance sales to Mexico because of the controversy over the confiscation of American oil properties, yet the Mexican authorities continued to make good on all previous Export-Import Bank credits.[53]

51. Reed to Packer, October 4, 1935, File No. 812.151/106, RG 59; Welles to Moore, October 8, 1935, ibid.; Reed to Welles, October 5, 1935, ibid.
52. Memorandum by Duggan, October 11, 1935, File No. 812.151/107, RG 59. Because of a breakdown in negotiations, the two parties did not sign an agreement until early 1937. At this point, the bank participated on a 50 percent without-recourse basis, see Fairbanks Morse and Co. to Pierson, December 22 and 24, 1936, Project No. 152, Fairbanks Morse and Co., RG 275; agreement signed on January 7, 1937, ibid.
53. Altogether, the bank participated in six transactions involving the sale of railroad equipment, water works equipment, and machinery to Mexico; there is no indication that the Mexicans defaulted on their obligations, see the material contained in Project No. 157, American Car and

In practice, therefore, the bank's Latin American policy was ambivalent. While the State Department succeeded in working out a set of guidelines to prevent the bank from jeopardizing the good neighbor policy, the transactions with Mexico indicated that deviations did occur. A combination of reasons explain this situation. The commitment of upper level State Department officers to avoid an intergovernmental creditor-debtor relationship was not as strong as that of division level officials. Assistant Secretary Moore's attitude during the discussion of the Mexican proposal in the fall of 1935 was a case in point. While Welles opposed the deal with Mexico, moreover, he supported a proposal to have the bank assist in liquidating blocked balances in Nicaragua, even though it meant the risk of making the U. S. government a creditor of an agency of the Nicaraguan government. Welles defended his position by insisting that the possibility of political difficulties there was remote because any government in Nicaragua would respect the obligations in order to ensure American friendship. Even Laurence Duggan, head of the Latin American Division and an opponent of the Nicaraguan proposal, at one time wanted to help the Bank of Venezuela establish a stabilization fund primarily because he believed the Export-Import Bank should do business in that country. The fact that his proposal would have made the bank a creditor of the Venezuelan government apparently did not concern Duggan.[54]

Officers of the Export-Import Bank favored a liberalization of the institution's lending policy as did American exporters, who were primarily interested in shifting the financial risk to the government, not in the broader political implications involved. In the cases discussed above, the bank's credit committee, an internal body, supported exporters' requests for financial assistance. The executive committee, however, on which the State Department had representatives, vetoed many of the proposals.

Foundry Co., National Railways of Mexico, and Project No. 171, Harnischfeger Corporation, Mexico, RG 275; and "Activities of the Export-Import Bank of Washington and the Second Export-Import Bank of Washington, February 12, 1934–December 31, 1939," Ex-Im Bk., RG 234.

54. Memorandum by Duggan, October 11, 1935, File No. 812.151/107, RG 59; memorandum by Beaulac, December 22, 1936, 65A473, 18, 3246/1, Ex-Im Bk. of Wash./1 1936–1937, Treasury Department; Pierson to Taylor, December 29, 1936, ibid.

Assuming that the credit committee's recommendations reflected the attitude of most bank officials, it seems that the Export-Import Bank became an advocate of exporters' interests. For example, during the discussion over the Mexican proposal in the fall of 1935, an official of the bank criticized the opposition of Edward L. Reed, of the Division of Mexican Affairs, arguing that the Roosevelt administration had created the Export-Import Bank to assist American manufacturers finance exports in situations where ordinary banking facilities were not available. The bank officer maintained that it frequently was a question of helping U. S. traders or of allowing foreign competitors to gain the trade. Even though Reed still opposed the deal, he realized that he faced a delicate situation: "Business is business, and, in the absence of evidence that a general political upheaval in Mexico is imminent, it may be difficult for this Department reasonably to oppose the deals in question." Similarly, Donald Heath opposed a particular transaction because it could lead to political problems, but he understood that if the American corporation did not obtain financial support, foreign firms would receive the order.[55]

The major opposition to a more aggressive bank policy existed at the desk level of the State Department. Although he did backslide on the Bank of Venezuela proposal, Duggan opposed the Nicaraguan transaction because he believed the deal would violate "the policy which the Department adopted of declining to recommend any operation of the Export-Import Bank which might involve the Bank in the exchange situation in any of the Central American countries. The political risks to the Government are so great that they far outweigh any possible advantages which might accrue from the operations of the Export-Import Bank." This policy, Duggan concluded, applied with greatest emphasis "in Nicaragua, the country involved in the present proposal."[56] Edward Reed and Donald Heath also opposed spe-

55. Reed to Welles, October 5, 1935, File No. 812.151/106, RG 59; Heath to Duggan and Packer, November 4, 1935, File No. 811.516 Export-Import Bank/153½, RG 59.

56. Memorandum by Duggan, October 11, 1935, File No. 812.151/107, RG 59; Duggan to Kelley, January 14, 1936, with attached note Duggan to Welles, January 16, 1936, File No. 811.516 Export-Import Bank/153½, RG 59; Duggan explained his reasons for opposing a deal with Peru in Duggan to Kelley, May 3, 1937, ibid.

cific proposals because they were concerned about the deals' implications for U. S. policy in Latin America. Willard Beaulac offered the best explanation of why the bank's participation in a Venezuelan stabilization fund would be unwise: the transaction would create an intergovernmental debt and would give the American government "a natural and direct interest in whatever step the Government of Venezuela might take during the life of the credit with reference to that situation [the exchange situation]. That interest might become known in Venezuela, and, if so, would be variously interpreted."[57]

The opinions at the divisional level of the department, coupled with a general appreciation by American policymakers that the nation's overall approach to Latin America had to be one of repairing past harm, helped account for the bank's initially conservative loan policy. The early years of the good neighbor policy were ones in which the United States tried to convince the other American republics that they had nothing to fear from their northern neighbor. The renunciation of the principle of intervention, the avoidance of intergovernmental creditor-debtor relationships, and the negotiation of trade agreements were all steps Washington took to smooth hemispheric ties. Although the Export-Import Bank played only a minor role, there was an increase in United States exports to Latin America: they went from $340 million in 1934 to $639 million in 1937; and the share of American exports going south rose, during the same period, from 15.9 percent to 19.1 percent.[58]

In spite of the growing volume of commerce, however, American traders continued to encounter many obstacles in Latin America. By late 1937, Warren L. Pierson recommended an expansion of the bank's lending operations, particularly to assist in the sale of heavy machinery and railroad equipment. "Me-

57. Reed to Packer, October 4, 1935, File No. 812.151/106, RG 59; Reed to Welles, October 5, 1935, ibid.; Duggan to Packer, November 4, 1935, File No. 811.516 Export-Import Bank/153½, RG 59; memorandum by Beaulac, December 22, 1936, 65A473, 18, 3246/1 Ex-Im Bk. of Wash./1 1936–1937, Treasury Department.

58. "Export-Import Bank Loans to Latin America," *Foreign Policy Reports* 17 (June 15, 1941): 83; Edward Orr Elsasser, "The Export-Import Bank and Latin America, 1934–1945" (Ph.D. dissertation, Univ. of Chicago, 1954), pp. 93–94; Department of Commerce, *Foreign Commerce and Navigation*, 1937, pp. 785, 789.

dium credits for this type of business, including the risk of exchange," he contended, "are provided by other industrial countries without or with but limited recourse to the exporters. Germany, through various currency devices and barter arrangements, and long-term credits, and Great Britain, through insuring credit and exchange risks, are seriously encroaching upon our trade in all parts of the world." Pierson believed that the Export-Import Bank represented "this Government's efforts to enable Americans doing business abroad, to meet new conditions, and to place them upon a more nearly equal basis with their foreign competitors. With conservative direction it can carry out the purposes for which it was created without risk of serious loss to the Government."[59] Pierson's suggestions reflected exporters' sentiments for greater governmental support which, in conjunction with the growth of German and British competition in the Western Hemisphere and the emergence of economic nationalist movements in many Latin American countries, meant that the future course of American policy remained unsettled. The coincidence of these three forces placed Washington under great pressure to become more aggressive in the hemisphere.[60]

59. Pierson also suggested that the bank assist in exporting cotton and tobacco surpluses and in discounting the securities (on a full-recourse basis) issued by foreign governments in settlement of blocked dollar balances, see Pierson to members of the advisory committee, October 15, 1937, Office of the Secretary, General Correspondence, 96227, RG 40.
60. Cordell Hull, *The Memoirs of Cordell Hull*, 1:496–98; Dozer, *Are We Good Neighbors?*, p. 49; Gardner, *Economic Aspects of New Deal Diplomacy*, pp. 49–60; Elsasser, "Export-Import Bank and Latin America," pp. 100–102.

6

New Opportunities in a Familiar Area
The Bank and China, 1934-1937

The conditions governing the Export-Import Bank's role in the Far East were nearly as complex as those in Latin America. From the time of its creation until the middle of 1937, despite being involved in only one Far Eastern transaction, the bank became an integral part of the drive by American interests to participate in the Chinese Nationalists' program of economic modernization. As in other cases, the bank's action represented something more than a desire to achieve short-run economic benefits, although this was one obvious consideration. United States officials recommended action by the bank because they believed that Chinese economic growth would promote stability throughout the Far East and would accommodate future American commercial expansion in China.[1] Through the bank's actions, therefore, Washington had become involved in the broader question of the ultimate destiny of Asia by mid-1937. By so doing, the United States had altered its previously passive approach to Far Eastern affairs.

Following World War I, American policymakers took the lead in establishing a new pattern of international relations in the Far East. The second consortium, in which banking groups from Great Britain, France, Japan, and the United States agreed to share administrative and industrial loans to the Chinese government, and the Washington Conference provided the framework of the new order.[2] The system's chief weaknesses were, first, the exclusion of Russia and Germany and, second, an incomplete

1. Some comments by C. F. Remer are relevant to this issue, C. F. Remer, *Foreign Investments in China*, pp. 317, 334–35.
2. The best analysis of these events is provided in Akira Iriye, *After Imperialism*, pp. 2–22; also see Akira Iriye, *Across the Pacific*, pp. 138–39, 143; Remer, *Foreign Investment in China*, pp. 329–31.

acceptance of China's demand for total national sovereignty. Chinese leaders regarded the consortium as an attempt to monopolize governmental borrowing which carried with it the threat of external control over the country's finances. For the Far Eastern order to succeed, the nations that signed agreements in Washington would have to cooperate in meeting the challenges provided by Chinese nationalism and the Soviet Union.[3]

During the 1920s, the primary difficulties facing American policymakers arose from the unsettled conditions within China. Not only was the country racked by civil strife but also strong antiforeign sentiments were spreading among virtually all segments of the Chinese population. Furthermore, the alliance between the Soviet Union and the Kuomintang in 1924 raised the prospect that hostility to foreign interests would become the keynote of emerging Chinese nationalism.[4] In response to this situation, Secretary of State Hughes chose to protect American interests by cooperating as closely as possible with Japan and relying on armed intervention along China's coast.[5] The Kuomintang's consolidation of power after 1927, however, brought this policy into question and caused Hughes's successor, Frank Kel-

3. China's two major grievances were the continuation of extra-territoriality and the control of tariff levels by outside nations, Iriye, *After Imperialism*, pp. 20–21; Iriye, *Across the Pacific*, pp. 144–45; after 1931, Chinese officials refused to deal with the consortium because of Japanese participation, memorandum by Hornbeck, March 31, 1936, *Foreign Relations, 1936*, 4:472–73; also see Remer, *Foreign Investments in China*, p. 331; the last point is made by Iriye, *After Imperialism*, p. 22.

4. William L. Neumann has pointed out that during the interwar years, United States officials faced two major problems in China: how to protect American interests from depredations by the Chinese; and how to safeguard American interests, and China herself, from Japanese expansion. The first issue dominated the 1920s and the second emerged in the 1930s; both, however, were the result of the rise of Chinese nationalism. See William L. Neumann, "Ambiguity and Ambivalence in Ideas of National Interest in Asia," in *Isolation and Security*, ed. Alexander DeConde, pp. 140–41.

5. Ibid., p. 143; William L. Neumann, *America Encounters Japan*, pp. 179–80; also see William A. Williams, "China and Japan," *Pacific Historical Review* 26 (August 1957): 259–79; Franklin D. Roosevelt, "Shall We Trust Japan?" Asia (July 1923): 475–78, 526, 528 (he concludes that the U.S. could trust Japan); William L. Neumann, "Franklin D. Roosevelt and Japan, 1913–1933," *Pacific Historical Review* 22 (May 1953): 143–53; Iriye, *Across the Pacific*, pp. 150–55.

logg, to revise the American position. Believing it fruitless to oppose the rising tide of Chinese nationalism, Kellogg granted the principle of tariff autonomy to the Nationalists in July 1928, thereby making the United States the first Washington Conference power to extend de facto recognition to the new government. By trying to meet the Chinese reform efforts halfway, American officials hoped to reduce the actual sacrifices that U. S. interests would have to make. To a degree, Kellogg's policy paid off: In the aftermath of the treaty, American investment flowed into China and United States technical and economic advisers assisted in Chinese development.[6]

The Sino-Soviet dispute of 1929 and the Japanese invasion of Manchuria two years later destroyed this seemingly favorable trend and represented the parameters which bounded American Far Eastern policy. Besides producing a confrontation with Russia, Chiang Kai-shek's seizure of the Chinese Eastern Railway in northern Manchuria raised the broader question of whether the unification of China would result in the expulsion of all foreigners. Despite championing the rights of a nation his country refused to recognize, Secretary of State Henry L. Stimson tried repeatedly to use the newly proclaimed Kellogg-Briand Pact to resolve the incident in Russia's favor, before it erupted into a major war. Stimson's efforts were not responsible for the peaceful settlement of the dispute, but his actions did reflect U. S. policymakers' concern that Chinese nationalism could endanger American interests. These officials remained hesitant to support Chiang's forces until they were positive the revolution was moving in an acceptable direction.[7]

6. American policymakers were divided on the proper way to respond to the Chinese revolution: John MacMurray, the American minister in China, opposed Kellogg's steps which he thought would only increase antiforeign sentiment; Nelson T. Johnson, an assistant secretary of state, leading adviser on Far Eastern affairs, and later ambassador to China, supported the secretary because he feared that the nation's interests would suffer far greater losses if the United States did not react positively to many of the changes occurring within China. See Russell D. Buhite, *Nelson T. Johnson and American Policy Toward China, 1925–1941*, pp. 22–39; Warren I. Cohen, *America's Response to China*, pp. 113–23; Iriye, *After Imperialism*, pp. 154, 231; Arthur N. Young, *China and the Helping Hand, 1937–1945*, p. 4.

7. For a description of the Sino-Soviet dispute of 1929, see Robert Ferrell, *American Diplomacy in the Great Depression*, chap. 4; also of in-

The second incident, which represented a reversion to the pre-World War I form of imperialism, overshadowed the first in immediate significance, although its long-run importance may have been no greater. As the growing strength of the Kuomintang forced Japanese civilian leaders to seek a united front with Western nations, the depression undercut their strength by providing mass support for Japan's military clique, who favored an aggressive posture in Manchuria. The civilian elite, under attack for pursuing a weak foreign policy and for being unable to restore prosperity at home, could not muster enough strength to check the fighting which spread throughout Manchuria in late 1931 and early 1932.[8]

America's response to the new crisis was consistent with its earlier actions; since 1922 Washington had assumed it could arrive at an accommodation with Japan. In addition, many American officials viewed the Manchurian incident in the context of the issues raised earlier by the Sino-Soviet dispute, concluding that, within limits, the Chinese had unnecessarily provoked the Japanese. Eventually, the crisis did cause some people (especially Stimson) to reconsider their views; but because the British, mainly interested in not antagonizing the Japanese, refused to cooperate with Stimson, and because the State Department remained uncertain about conditions in China as well as Japan's ultimate objectives, the most realistic response was one of caution. American policymakers, therefore, announced their continued support for the principles which historically had been the basis of the country's Far Eastern policy, and then waited to see what would happen next.[9]

terest is Richard Current, *Secretary Stimson*, pp. 43–49; Johnson's analysis of the incident was similar to Stimson's, Buhite, *Nelson T. Johnson*, pp. 55–60.

8. Iriye argues persuasively that the depression sabotaged Foreign Minister Shidehara's attempt to establish closer ties with Western nations; Japan's later militant policy, therefore, was a response to the economic decline, Iriye, *After Imperialism*, pp. 242–95.

9. For the American reaction to the Manchurian invasion, see Armin Rappaport, *Henry L. Stimson and Japan, 1931–1933*, passim; Ferrell, *American Diplomacy in the Great Depression*, pp. 120–93; Current, *Secretary Stimson*, pp. 66–113; Dorothy Borg, *The United States and the Far Eastern Crisis of 1933–1938*, pp. 1–45; for the British reaction, see Christopher Thorne, "The Shanghai Crisis of 1932," *American Historical Review* 75 (October 1970): 1616–39.

Under the circumstances, the State Department's policy was reasonable; it is hardly surprising that U. S. statesmen were primarily concerned about protecting their own nation's interests and not in aiding China.[10] Moreover, the tendency of American officials to respond to Japanese aggression merely by restating, generally in moral tones, certain principles of international conduct should not obscure the recognition that these principles symbolized the type of world order most compatible with American material considerations.[11] The fact that American policy frequently was passive does not mean that U. S. policymakers thought the nation's interests were too inconsequential to warrant concern; passivity resulted from the decision that, all things considered, a course of inaction was the best way to safeguard these interests.[12]

In assessing America's Far Eastern policy during the 1930s, the views of Stanley K. Hornbeck, chief of the State Department's Division of Far Eastern Affairs from 1928 to 1937, are useful. Before joining the Department, Hornbeck had taught at several colleges in China (from 1909 to 1913) and in the U. S.; he was well acquainted with America's interests in the Orient and with conditions in that area of the world.[13] When discussing

10. Iriye and Cohen emphasize this point, Iriye, *Across the Pacific*, pp. 179–80, 197–98; Cohen, *America's Response to China*, pp. 134–35, 161–63. Stanley K. Hornbeck neatly summarized the United States position: "Just as Chiang Kai-shek and other Chinese leaders have foremost in their minds the interests of China, so we have foremost in our minds the interests of the United States. We are fortunately situated in that our interests and those of China usually run along parallel lines; at least they do not conflict." Memorandum by Hornbeck, March 13, 1937, *Foreign Relations, 1937*, 3:44–46.

11. The moral aspect is noted by Borg, *The United States and the Far Eastern Crisis*, pp. 95–99; Cohen, *America's Response to China*, pp. 131, 134–35; Iriye, *Across the Pacific*, pp. 179, 197. To paraphrase Barrington Moore's comments on the relationship of economic factors to the moral issues surrounding slavery in ante-bellum America, it should be obvious that economic factors created the United States world view and that one cannot fully understand the significance of the moral pronouncements without being aware of the material basis from which they emerged.

12. Borg's description of America's passive policy is very good, Borg, *The United States and the Far Eastern Crisis*, pp. 89–99, 155–56, 165–71; also see Iriye, *Across the Pacific*, pp. 180–81.

13. *New York Times*, December 12, 1966; James C. Thomson, Jr., "The Role of the Department of State," in *Pearl Harbor as History*, ed. Dorothy Borg and Shumpei Okamoto, p. 82.

America's approach to international relations, Hornbeck distinguished between a policy and a plan of action. A nation based its policy on deep-rooted principles which grew out of the country's past and were more or less constant. For the United States, the leading principles were the preservation of national security and the attainment of equal opportunity and fair treatment for American nationals and trade. While these principles remained fixed, the country's plan of action—Hornbeck's phrase for the strategy and tactics by which officials tried to implement policy —could fluctuate, depending on who held office and the circumstances under which they had to labor. One had to be careful, Hornbeck maintained, not to interpret shifts in plans of action as alterations of fundamental principles. He did acknowledge, nevertheless, that the violation of a major principle for an extended period could modify a policy.[14]

Assuming relatively fixed principles, then, American day-to-day actions in the Far East would vary according to a number of factors. If the Japanese followed an expansionist policy which explicitly challenged the Washington treaty system, U. S. policymakers would face a situation that jeopardized the basic premises of their policy. Yet if there was a chance that the moderate elements within Japan could return to power and if the Japanese continued to express agreement with American principles (even though their actions often belied their words), some hope of maintaining the treaty structure would exist.[15] In any event, America's ability either to persuade or to compel Japan to alter her policy was dependent on certain contingencies. Since Wash-

14. Hornbeck, *Principles of American Policy in Relation to the Far East*, address to the Ninth Conference on the Cause and Cure of War, January 18, 1934, pp. 2–11; "A Letter to the Editor," *Amerasia* 1 (March 1937): 16–19; Hornbeck's memorandum on the Washington Conference, November 12, 1934, Correspondence, II, July 1934–March 1935, Container 37, Folder 80, Cordell Hull Papers (Library of Congress, Washington, D.C.); Thomson, "Role of Department of State," pp. 89–91; also see memorandum by Hornbeck, May 9, 1933, attached to Phillips to Roosevelt, May 9, 1933, in *Franklin D. Roosevelt and World Affairs*, ed. Edgar B. Nixon, 1:103–7.

15. Joseph Grew, the American ambassador in Japan during the 1930s, was one of the leading proponents of this view, but even he became increasingly pessimistic as the decade wore on; see Waldo Heinrichs, *American Ambassador*, pp. 201–8; although the Japanese wanted to modify the Washington treaty structure, they did not unilaterally renounce it until the fall of 1938.

ington officials had neither the power nor the inclination to act unilaterally, they would have to cooperate with other nations who had parallel interests. The Soviet Union was one possibility but the State Department was unwilling to work with Moscow. Although American policymakers feared being left alone in the Far East, as had happened in 1931 at the time of the Manchurian incident and wanted to coordinate their actions with Great Britain, they were unwilling to give the explicit political guarantees which the British probably would have demanded.[16] Conditions within China, furthermore, limited the steps the United States could take. Obviously a Chinese capitulation to Japan would doom any American move. A group capable of unifying China, and doing so in a manner that did not endanger foreign interests, had to appear before the United States could seriously consider adopting an active China policy.

This context helps make comprehensible the Roosevelt administration's response to the events of 1933–1936. In April 1934, Eiji Amau, spokesman for the Japanese Foreign Office, announced that Japan would maintain the stability of East Asia and would oppose joint operations by foreign powers in China, directly challenging the Washington treaty system.[17] While unwilling to provoke an incident, Cordell Hull informed Tokyo of the American position that no nation could "make conclusive its will in situations where there involved the rights, obligations and the legitimate interests of other sovereign states" without

16. Even though cooperation with Great Britain was a definite feature of United States Far Eastern policy (for example, see Hornbeck to Hull, May 14, 1936, *Foreign Relations, 1936*, 4:480–81), American officials were concerned about the course of British policy, see Roosevelt to Davis, November 9, 1934, Nixon, *Roosevelt and Foreign Affairs*, 2:263; Davis to Roosevelt, December 14, 1934, ibid., pp. 315–18; Borg, *The United States and the Far Eastern Crisis*, p. 79. Thorne argues that following the Shanghai crisis, the British Foreign Office concluded that England could not count on future American support; presumably only a firm commitment by the United States could have reversed this opinion, Thorne, "The Shanghai Crisis of 1932," pp. 1637–38.

17. For a detailed analysis of the events leading up to the statement and of the American reaction, see Borg, *The United States and the Far Eastern Crisis*, chap. 2; for a copy of the statement itself, see Grew to Hull, April 20, 1934, Department of State, *Foreign Relations of the United States: Japan, 1931–1941* (2 vols., Washington, D.C., 1943), 1:223–25 (hereafter referred to as *Foreign Relations: Japan*), and see Saito to Phillips, including two enclosures, April 25, 1934, ibid., pp. 228–30.

the consent of those countries. The following month, the Japanese ambassador, Hirosi Saito, suggested to Hull that the two countries divide the Pacific into eastern and western spheres. Not surprisingly, the American secretary of state rejected the offer. He also expressed doubt that equality of trade would continue if Japan became dominant in East Asia, and intimated that stability would return to the Far East when the Japanese ceased actions that endangered the security and interests of others. Because the American navy remained below the levels authorized by the Washington conference, because the Japanese challenge was limited for the present to rhetoric, and because of the uncertain situation in China, the United States understandably restricted its opposition to words.[18]

Throughout most of 1935 and the first half of 1936, the Japanese attempted to increase their influence in portions of China. American policymakers followed these events closely but could do little to affect their outcome. Until the administration increased its naval strength and unless Chiang Kai-shek, or another leader acceptable to the United States, could create some semblance of unity with China and stand up to Japan, American prospects were dim. The passivity of United States policy, therefore, was a logical response to existing conditions but not necessarily a long-run commitment to inaction.[19]

Beginning in the last half of 1936, a series of events took place within China which promised to alter the overall situation in the Far East. Under the leadership of Chiang Kai-shek, the Nation-

18. Hull to Grew, April 28, 1934, *Foreign Relations: Japan*, 1:231–32; Saito's memorandum to Hull, May 16, 1934, ibid., pp. 232–33; Hull's memorandum, May 19, 1934, ibid., pp. 233–36; Phillips to Grew, June 18, 1934, ibid., pp. 237–39; Cordell Hull, *The Memoirs of Cordell Hull*, 1:279, 281–84. Largely in response to the Far Eastern situation, Roosevelt decided to build up the navy to treaty limits, Neumann, "Franklin D. Roosevelt and Japan," pp. 152–53; Roosevelt to Malcolm Peabody, August 19, 1933, Nixon, *Roosevelt and Foreign Affairs*, 1:370; also see Joseph C. Grew, *Ten Years in Japan*, pp. 145–52; Thomson, "Role of Department of State," pp. 94–97; Akira Iriye, "The Role of the United States Embassy in Tokyo," Borg and Okamoto, *Pearl Harbor as History*, pp. 108–14.

19. Japan's actions in 1935 did force American officials to speculate on whether they would have to revise their policy to reflect the vast changes occurring in the Far East, see Borg, *The United States and the Far Eastern Crisis*, chap. 5, pp. 176–88; Borg also notes that if China successfully opposed Japan, the United States would face an entirely new situation, see pp.193–94.

alists extended their control over some provinces that earlier had remained beyond their grasp. The success of the central government in repelling an attack on Suiyan by Japanese-directed and -supported Mongol troops, moreover, produced a wave of nationalist sentiment. This feeling was reinforced by the Sian incident in which certain warlords forcefully detained Chiang for a few days before releasing him on Christmas day. During these months, the Nationalists also were successful in reducing the amount of brigandry in the countryside. With these achievements, the Nanking regime secured greater influence than at any time since 1928.[20]

The Nationalists made similar economic gains. Because of the prolonged pressure caused by America's silver purchase program, the Chinese switched from a silver standard to a managed currency system in November 1935. With the assistance of the American and British governments, the monetary reform was successful: it provided the central government with a financial mechanism to aid in unification, and it promoted stable exchange rates which eased the country's balance of payments problem. In addition, the improving financial condition enabled the Nanking government to make significant strides toward settling defaulted debts. By June 1937, the Nationalists had funded approximately 80 percent of the principal amount due Western creditors and had made progress as well in repaying internal obligations. Besides these actions, the Kuomintang drew up a number of plans to foster growth in industry, transportation, and agriculture.[21] Although it is now clear that these steps fell far short of the measures needed to modernize Chinese society, to those Western observers who based their analyses on activities

20. Johnson to Hull, January 12, 1937, *Foreign Relations, 1936*, 4:453–58; "China Annual Economic Report for 1937," File No. 128–X Peiping, General Correspondence, Reports of Commercial Attaché, Shanghai, Records of the Bureau of Foreign and Domestic Commerce, RG 151 (National Archives, Washington) Borg, *The United States and Far Eastern Crisis*, pp. 187–88; also see *New York Times*, January 4, 1937, p. 35; Roosevelt's comments at a press conference, September 25, 1936, Nixon, *Roosevelt and Foreign Affairs*, 3:439–41.

21. Young, *China and the Helping Hand*, pp. 3–11; Arthur N. Young, *China's Wartime Finance and Inflation, 1937–1945*, pp. 3–8, 67–74, 131–37; John King Fairbank, *The United States and China*, pp. 223, 228–29; Albert Feuerwerker, *The Chinese Economy, 1912–1949*, Michigan Papers in Chinese Studies, no. 1, pp. 51–52.

in treaty port cities (the most modern segment of the country), and on reports by Kuomintang officials, China could well have taken on the appearance of a nation on the threshold of modernization. When the Chinese government began negotiating foreign contracts to purchase railroad and industrial equipment in late 1936 and early 1937, these views undoubtedly received reinforcement.[22]

This activity had considerable significance for the United States. Since the early part of the decade, America had been China's leading trading partner. To symbolize their continued interest in East Asia, the National Foreign Trade Council and the Pacific Foreign Trade Council held their annual convention in Honolulu, Hawaii, in 1932. Three years later, the National Foreign Trade Council's economic mission to the Far East was favorably impressed with what it observed in China and recommended that the American government cooperate with U. S. businesses in competition with foreign firms. Given this assistance, the members of the mission believed that China would become a promising field for future trade. American investments, however, remained small, and according to a recent estimate, they never amounted to more than 7 percent of total foreign investment in China before 1937.[23] Nevertheless, the Chinese eco-

22. Recent studies of the nationalist period have demonstrated the superficial nature of the modernization programs: since these projects left most of the country untouched, the stagnant peasant economy persisted. In addition, the Kuomintang used from 70 to 75 percent of its revenue for military expenses and debt servicing, failed to reform the tax structure, and did not try to deal with the fundamental problem of agricultural and industrial growth. Its fiscal policies, moreover, had the net result of taxing the consumption goods of the poor to finance interest payments to rich bondholders. As a whole, the Kuomintang's actions discouraged productive investment, Feuerwerker, *The Chinese Economy*, pp. 1–4, 47–58. 73–75; Fairbank, *The United States and China*, pp. 219–39; Hou Chiming, *Foreign Investment and Economic Development in China, 1840–1937*, pp. 27, 155–88. Both Feuerwerker and Fairbank comment on the tendency of Western observers to overstate the significance of the Kuomintang's modernization program; Young seems to share this unfortunate tendency.

23. Charles K. Moser, *Where China Buys and Sells*, Department of Commerce, Trade Information Bulletin, no. 827, pp. iv, 53–54; National Foreign Trade Council, *Foreign Trade in 1932*, passim, National Foreign Trade Council, *Report of the American Economic Mission to the Far East*, pp. 17–60; Hou, *Foreign Investment and Economic Development in China*, p. 21. Remer has estimated that U.S. interests had invested nearly $240

nomic development programs did provide new opportunities for American commercial and financial interests. Of equal importance, the successful conclusion of these economic plans would provide a check on Japanese expansion by promoting political stability in China.[24]

Notwithstanding the potential benefits for the United States, it was the Europeans who took the lead in responding to the possibilities provided by the Nationalists' programs.[25] As early as 1930, British officials had worked out a scheme whereby their government remitted the unpaid balance of its share of the Boxer Indemnity Fund for expenditure on public works, principally the rehabilitation and construction of Chinese railways. Under this arrangement, British manufacturers received a preference in all undertakings. With the improvement of conditions in China, other European governments began to offer assistance for their exporters. By the fall of 1936, Julean Arnold, the American commercial attaché in Shanghai, reported that the Italian government was using its portion of the Boxer fund in the same fashion as the British. The German government also had established machinery to provide long-term credits and had arranged several barter transactions. Because German concerns could extend credit of up to ten years duration and since some German businesses could erect industrial plants with the understanding that the Chinese would repay the loans from the new industries' earnings, Germany's activities in China grew steadily. Manufacturers in Czechoslovakia and Belgium, moreover, made offers similar to the Germans. These nations became leaders in the sale

---

million in China by 1930; about $155 million of this amount consisted of direct investments with the remainder being divided approximately evenly between government securities and philanthropic societies, Remer, *Foreign Investments in China*, p. 317.

24. As Chiang's strength grew, members of the Japanese general staff concluded that the unification of China under the Kuomintang was inevitable. Consequently, they suggested that Japan cooperate with Chiang in the formation of an East Asian league, Akira Iriye, "Japan's Foreign Policies between World Wars," reprinted in *The Origins of the Second World War*, ed. Esmonde M. Robertson, pp. 264–67.

25. Even though dependent on foreign capital, Kuomintang leaders continued to oppose the consortium and were concerned about the political significance of foreign investment, Fairbank, *The United States and China*, p. 223.

of capital equipment to China precisely because of their ability to furnish long-term credits.[26]

Throughout most of 1936, the majority of U. S. foreign trade groups were apathetic about the Far East. This attitude seems to have been particularly prevalent within the financial community; Thomas Lamont of J. P. Morgan & Co. reported in April that large American banking houses were indifferent if not skeptical about China. Furthermore, the recent securities legislation barred most leading banks from floating long-term obligations. Even though Lamont thought someone could organize a group of "first class Houses that might be interested in future Chinese business," he was unwilling to take this step immediately.[27] The timidity of American financial interests forced manufacturers desirous of expanding into China to seek governmental assistance. As in Latin America, however, exporters discovered that Washington would not provide the financial guarantees they sought. Secretary of Commerce Daniel Roper complained that the firms interested in China generally assumed that because private commercial institutions would not accept the risks, Washington "should assume such risks in line with reports of what other governments were doing."[28]

Ironically, the Kuomintang's policy of refunding external obligations initially caused uneasiness in the United States. Although Americans did not hold a large volume of Chinese securities, the State Department was worried that United States interests might not receive settlements comparable to those offered other

26. Charles K. Moser to E. P. Thomas, November 1, 1935, File No. 640, China, Boxer Indemnity, 1935–1940, RG 151; Arnold's views were contained in a letter from W. L. Painter to Moser, October 27, 1936, File No. 640, China, General, 1932–1939, RG 151.

27. Memoranda by Hornbeck, March 26 and December 29, 1936, *Foreign Relations, 1936*, 4:469–72, 502–3; Thomas Lamont to Sir Charles Addiss, May 5, 1937, *Foreign Relations, 1937*, 4:591–92.

28. Daniel Roper to John Boettinger, February 24, 1937, File No. 640, China, Foreign Loans, Folder 1932–1939, RG 151. In his reply to Painter, Moser also noted: "Personally, I have not been impressed with such proposals (for government guarantees) as providing the bases of a sound public or business policy. I am convinced rather to the contrary, that business houses which are able to finance their commercial ventures privately and are to derive the benefits themselves, should not expect relief from acceptance of at least a part of the responsibilities that must be incurred." Moser to Painter, November 6, 1936, ibid.

nationals.[29] American policymakers repeatedly cautioned the Nationalist leaders against trying to drive a hard bargain or negotiating agreements that diluted the rights of creditors. The uncertainty surrounding the repayment of old debts reinforced the skepticism of financial groups, and made it difficult for Washington to promise the diplomatic and financial support desired by private U. S. interests.[30]

The nature of the Chinese Nationalists' economic development program created a further problem. To spur the growth of manufacturing and to provide additional government revenue, Kuomintang leaders decided to monopolize leading segments of the economy, an indication that China would follow the world trend toward statism. In early 1937, the central executive committee of the Kuomintang issued a manifesto attributing the nation's poverty to the impact of foreign encroachments and to the backwardness of domestic productivity. These conditions compelled China to adopt a policy of modified state capitalism. Nelson T. Johnson, the United States ambassador, learned that the Nationalists intended to monopolize heavy industries but to leave light industries to private initiative.[31]

State Department officers were concerned about this news since they believed the monopolies might violate existing Sino-American treaties. Secretary Hull also feared that the Kuomintang was heading in a direction incompatible with American

29. Americans held the following obligations of the Chinese government or its institutions: 1. one-fourth of the Hukuang Railway Loan of 1911; 2. Chicago Bank loan (negotiated in 1916 but not extended until 1919); 3. Pacific Development loan of 1919; 4. Grand Canal Conservancy loan, 1918–1921; 5. certain miscellaneous loans, Remer, *Foreign Investment in China*, pp. 295–301.

30. Hull to Johnson, March 7, 1936, *Foreign Relations, 1936*, 4:579; Hull to Clarence Gauss, April 22, 1936, ibid., pp. 590–91; memorandum by Hornbeck, April 1, 1936, ibid. pp. 583–84; Hull to Robert Bingham, April 5, 1936, ibid., pp. 584–86; memorandum by Hornbeck, May 19, 1936, ibid., p. 593; Hull to Johnson, April 28, 1937, *Foreign Relations, 1937*, 4:672–73. Washington was more concerned about the Nationalists' attitude toward private investment than were most European capitals. The British, however, did share some of the American nervousness, see comments by Sir Frederick Leith-Ross, June 25, 1936, *Foreign Relations, 1936*, 4:490–94.

31. Johnson to Hull, January 27, February 27, and June 10, 1936, ibid., pp. 600–603, 606–8; Johnson to Hull, February 23, 1937, *Foreign Relations, 1937*, 3:27–29; Johnson to Hull, April 23, 1937, *Foreign Relations, 1937*, 4:583–84.

and world prosperity. "The policy of the Chinese Government to which you refer," the secretary telegraphed Johnson, "does not differ materially from policies of economic nationalism in some other countries and runs counter to the trade policy of this Government." Responding to these events, American officials took steps to protect U. S. interests by lodging several protests with the Chinese Ministry of Foreign Affairs.[32]

The events of early 1937, however, reduced many of the American apprehensions. By May, the Chinese government had worked out satisfactory refunding arrangements with U. S. financial interests for the Hukuang Railway loan, the Chicago Bank loan, and the Pacific Development Corporation loan.[33] Furthermore, the American attitude toward the Nationalists' development program had always been ambivalent; many officials were resigned to some form of state capitalism and now looked for ways to ensure a place for the United States in the new framework. Ambassador Johnson was a leading proponent of this view. Noting that governmental regulation of the economy had become a widespread phenomenon, even within the United States, the ambassador suggested that the Chinese actions would not necessarily be detrimental to the U. S. since China lacked the capital and modern technical skills necessary to achieve modernization. Americans could have some leverage over development programs as long as the State Department did not alienate the Nationalist leaders by adopting a strict bargaining position. The best approach, Johnson advised, was for United States officials "to introduce a certain elasticity into our discussions with the Chinese authorities concerning economic relations."[34]

32. For the official American position on the question of monopolies, see Moore to Johnson, September 4, 1935, *Foreign Relations, 1935*, 3:786–88; Hull to Johnson, April 1, 1937, *Foreign Relations, 1937*, 4:651–52; Johnson to Hull, May 19, June 10, and June 18, 1934, *Foreign Relations, 1936*, 4:603–4, 606–9; Phillips to Johnson, June 24, 1936, ibid., p. 609; George Merrell to Hull, July 1, 1936, ibid., pp. 609–10; Johnson to Hull, September 20, 1936, ibid., pp. 617–19.

33. H. H. Kung to Johnson, March 31, 1937, *Foreign Relations, 1937*, 4:670; Johnson to Hull, May 17 and 21, 1937, ibid., p. 673. Hornbeck urged the vice-president of the Continental Illinois National Bank and Trust Company of Chicago to accept a Chinese offer rather than run the risk that the Nationalists would drop the matter because of quibbling over details, memorandum by Hornbeck, March 11, 1937, ibid., pp. 665–66.

34. To a degree, the note of September 4, 1935, anticipated this position. Realizing that the United States was powerless to reverse the trend

The continuation of favorable economic trends in China further lessened American doubts. The growth of governmental revenue enabled Kuomintang officials to stabilize domestic finances and to carry on with the funding of external debts; the resulting improvement in the nation's credit status made it easier to attract the capital necessary for development programs. Even though the government still spent too large a portion of its income for military purposes, faced heavy smuggling in North China (which jeopardized the balance of payments), and was heavily dependent on outside financial support, a sense of progress began to spread throughout the country.[35]

The Nationalists, furthermore, were eager to obtain American economic assistance. In February, Ambassador Johnson forwarded a request from the Chinese Ministry of Railways to Warren Pierson for Export-Import Bank aid in the sale of railroad equipment. The following month, A. Bland Calder, the assistant commercial attaché in Shanghai, reported that one reason China had agreed to American terms in settling the Hukuang loan was "the desire of the Chinese Government to make a gesture of good will by way of encouraging the re-entry of America into Chinese financing." Administration officials found that some

---

toward monopolies, the State Department wanted to ensure that other interests did not receive exclusive or preferential positions and that the Chinese did not impose "unreasonable restraints" on international trade, Moore to Johnson, September 4, 1935, *Foreign Relations, 1935*, 3:786–88. Johnson did point out that the trend toward state capitalism would force the American government into a closer alliance with those firms dealing with monopolized industries, Johnson to Hull, September 4, 1936, *Foreign Relations, 1936*, 4:613–14; Johnson to Hull, March 9 and May 12, 1937, *Foreign Relations, 1937*, 4:573–76, 595–98.

35. For comments on the events of early 1937, see August 15, 1937, File No. 128-X Peiping, Reports of Commercial Attaché, RG 151; Julean Arnold, *China Annual Economic Report of 1937*, ibid.; A. Bland Calder, "Special Weekly Financial Report," S–105, March 3, 1937, File No. 600, China, Finance and Investments, 1937–1938, RG 151; Calder, "Special Weekly Financial Report," S–113, March 11, 1937, ibid.; Calder, "Special Weekly Financial Report," S–120, March 24, 1937, ibid. This period also witnessed an intensified German trade drive in China, W. E. Dodd to Roosevelt, June 12, 1937, PSF: (Germany) Dodd, 1936–1938, Franklin D. Roosevelt Papers (Franklin D. Roosevelt Library, Hyde Park, New York); advance copy of an article for the *Christian Science Monitor*, Arnold to Foreign Service Division, February 10, 1937, File No. 400, US-China, 1937–1938, RG 151.

American interests were willing to go into China if Washington would share the financial risks.[36]

The announcement that the president of the Export-Import Bank would tour China in the spring of 1937 sparked a lively debate among U. S. officials in China over America's future economic stake there. Leading officers in the commercial attaché's office argued strenuously in support of a major effort to expand American commerce. Both Arnold and Calder had had extensive experience in the Far East; Arnold had worked in China almost steadily since 1902 and Calder had been in the Shanghai office since 1918.[37] Arnold believed that the Nationalists' modernization program would shift the makeup of China's imports from consumer items to capital goods. This transition held unfortunate implications for United States trade, which consisted primarily of cotton, leaf tobacco, wheat, flour, petroleum, and lumber products. To protect its share of the China market, America would have to adjust to the altered conditions. Arnold maintained that the United States could meet China's growing demand for capital goods by establishing adequate means for extending credit. He recommended that Washington examine the European financial mechanisms as a model.[38]

Calder developed this theme more fully in two important reports in April, 1937. He insisted that the chief handicap facing

36. Johnson to Hull, February 1, 1937, File No. 893.51/6318, General Records of the Department of State, RG 59 (National Archives, Washington, D.C.); Calder, "Special Weekly Financial Report," S–115, March 13, 1937, File No. 600, China, Finance and Investments, 1937–1938, RG 151; Hornbeck to Lamont, March 24, 1937, *Foreign Relations, 1937,* 4:579–80; Ernest Draper to Moore, February 13, 1937, Office of the Secretary, General Correspondence, 96227, General Records of the Department of Commerce, RG 40 (National Archives, Washington, D.C.); John Chevalier to Johnson, March 15, 1937, Personal Correspondence, 1937, Nelson T. Johnson Papers (Library of Congress, Washington, D.C.); Oursler to Roosevelt, June 5, 1937, PPF 2993, Fulton Oursler, Roosevelt Papers; An American Businessman in China, "For Government Support of U.S. Enterprise," *Amerasia* 1 (July 1937): 199–202.

37. Department of State, *Register of the Department of State,* October 1, 1938 (Washington, 1938), pp. 49, 66.

38. Arnold to Bureau of Foreign and Domestic Commerce, November 19, 1936, File No. 400, US-China, 1936, RG 151; Arnold, "Chinese-American Trade," SR No. S–66, December 1, 1936, ibid.; officials in Washington did not always share Arnold's enthusiasm, see Moser to James Dunn, November 23, 1936, ibid.

American interests was inadequate organization. British exporters and financiers, on the other hand, cooperated closely with one another and received strong support from their government. The English had established a special set of offices in Shanghai to house the commercial counselor, the financial adviser to the embassy, and the representative of the Export Credits Guarantee Department. Largely due to this arrangement, British traders and bankers had been able to obtain first-class credit risks. The lack of proper coordination further hindered American commercial groups because they could not bargain effectively with the growing number of Chinese monopolies. To correct this situation, Calder recommended the formation of a commission under the auspices of the Export-Import Bank and with the collaboration of officers from the departments of state, commerce, treasury, and agriculture. These officials would work in close association with the business advisory committee of the Shanghai branch of the American Chamber of Commerce. By creating a united front of American interests and by developing a sound loan policy, the commission would go a long way toward controlling the terms of proposed transactions. "We must bear in mind," Calder observed, "that the securing of American credits at this time, officially, that is as extended by a U. S. Government agency, is so momentous in the plans of the Chinese Government that it will stretch itself to satisfy our demands BEFORE we start, but would do far less for us AFTER we get started, and AFTER the full publicity value of the inauguration of credits has been exploited."[39]

Ambassador Johnson, however, disagreed with Arnold and Calder, arguing that the United States did not have to participate in the railroad development programs in order to promote exports. "Personally," he wrote Thomas Lamont, "it seems to me that the more railways the Chinese are able to build, no matter who builds them, the more markets there will be for some of our products." Furthermore, he continued, "because of the size of our railway facilities and the equipment shops necessary to their maintenance, we will always be in a position more quickly

39. Emphasis in original, Calder, SR No. S–127, April 9, 1937, File No. 128-X Peiping, Reports of Commercial Attaché RG 151; Calder, SR No. S–137 April 23, 1937, ibid.

to supply the needs of Chinese railways than anyone else."[40] In addition, Johnson disapproved of Calder's proposal for a credit commission because he doubted that American financial and manufacturing groups were sufficiently attracted to the China market to warrant such an undertaking. "It may be conceded," he noted, "that American manufacturers are always on the lookout for opportunities to sell their products, but it has seemed to me not quite so evident that the need to sell to foreign countries is so strong that the American Government or American bankers would be willing to extend unusually favorable credit terms to bring this about." The ambassador believed that U. S. industries could concentrate on "replenishing the void caused by the four years of depression" for the time being. Until the urge to sell American products in China was compelling enough to justify a commission, he saw no need for one.[41]

Arnold and Calder quickly countered the ambassador's recommendation. Arnold claimed that Johnson had failed to note that capital goods had become an important segment of China's imports. For America to obtain a position of consequence in this market, the commercial attaché noted, "it must be prepared to participate in this aspect of China's trade." The failure of the United States to act would mean that the Chinese would become accustomed to the goods of other nations. If this occurred, Americans would have "no prospect of inducing the Chinese to purchase our products to any considerable extent." Arnold further insisted that American export interests were sufficiently eager for new business that they would support efforts to construct a strong foundation for the future.[42] In general agreement with Arnold's analysis, Calder argued that a coordinated ap-

40. Johnson to Lamont, May 11, 1937, Personal Correspondence, Johnson Papers.

41. Johnson to Hull, May 7, 1937, *Foreign Relations, 1937,* 4:592–95; Johnson agreed that there was need for greater coordination of information even though he realized that this could lead to other developments, including the credit plan, which seemed "at present of doubtful utility." Johnson also insisted that the government give equal assistance to all American businessmen and not favor one group over another, memorandum by Johnson, May 10, 1937, contained in Frank Lockhardt to Hull, May 21, 1937, File No. 893.51/6394, RG 59.

42. Arnold to Dye, May 11, 1937, File No. 640, China, Foreign Loans, 1932–1939, RG 151.

proach was essential to create "a leverage which would enormously strengthen the Ambassador's hand (fill it with aces is the term we used in Nanking) in the representations he is obliged to make from time to time when vexatious problems arise adversely affecting American business." Would it not be better, Calder asked, for official U. S. agencies to use the lever of credit to obtain those conditions which would make American business in China more secure and permanent? The Nationalist government was not so set on its course of action that it would not listen "to reason or collaborate with us if it is going to be worth its while to do so."[43]

The Export-Import Bank provided American officials with a readily available means for controlling credit. By 1936, the bank began receiving applications for assistance in the sale of equipment to Chinese railways. While Pierson thought that some exporters exaggerated the importance of China, he assumed the market had potential. "Since the Open Door policy of John Hay," he observed, "the United States has looked to China as a valuable market, and has done much to cultivate it. I do not believe that we should abandon it to the Japanese or anyone else."[44] Nonetheless, the bank had been largely inactive in that region of the world. In March 1936, it did extend a $500,000 commitment to the Wah Trading Corporation for the sale of trucks to China, but the corporation did not use the funds because a commercial bank agreed to finance the transaction at a lower rate of interest. Eleven months later the bank participated in a minor undertaking involving the sale of sulphur.[45]

In early 1937, Pierson's interest in China grew. Writing to an

43. Calder further argued that the money spent to promote exports to China would produce a beneficial effect on domestic employment; he calculated that every dollar the government spent would produce $7.61 worth of labor over a ten-year period. For this reason alone, he favored the extension of governmental credits, memorandum by Calder, May 10, 1937, enclosed in Arnold's letter to Dye of May 11, 1937, ibid.

44. Memorandum by Pierson, March 30, 1936, File No. 65A473,18, 3246/1, Department of the Treasury (U.S. Department of the Treasury, Washington, D.C.).

45. W. K. Lecount to Pierson, February 8, 1937, File No. 65A473,28, 3246/1 Ex-Im Bk. of Wash., 1936–1937, Department of the Treasury; also see Project No. 159, Wah Trading Corporation, China, General Records of the Export-Import Bank of Washington, RG 275 (National Archives, Washington, D.C.).

official of the American Locomotive Sales Corporation, he noted that it was "an excellent time for American firms to gain a foothold in China. I hope you will keep me informed regarding any developments." In response to a growing number of requests for financial assistance from American firms and an inquiry from the Chinese Ministry of Railways, Pierson decided in March to go to China so he could obtain first-hand knowledge of economic conditions there. The bank president occupied a desk within the State Department for several weeks prior to his departure in order to familiarize himself with the department's handling of Far Eastern affairs. Upon arrival in China, he traveled extensively for two months, holding numerous talks with leading Chinese governmental and business officials, members of the American and British economic communities, and officers of the American foreign service. Impressed by the rising strength of the Nationalist government, Pierson concluded that "Chiang's policy of avoiding an open break with Japan in spite of frequent irritating incidents, and at the same time refusing stubbornly to make further substantial concessions to the Japanese militarists, has impressed the latter." As a result, he thought Japan and China would be able to settle their difficulties peacefully.[46] Pierson also believed American interests could benefit by selective participation in the Chinese economic development programs. He therefore recommended that the Export-Import Bank assist in financing the sale of approximately forty American locomotives to the Chinese Ministry of Railways. On May 4, the bank's executive committee authorized the institution to make without-recourse purchases from American corporations of up to $1.6 million of promissory notes issued by the Ministry of Railways.[47]

46. Pierson to Maxwell Hamilton, March 6, 1937, Project No. 159, American Locomotive Sales Corp., RG 275; Minister of Railways to Pierson, December 21, 1936, Project No. 166, Andersen, Meyer & Co., Ltd., RG 275; Hamilton to Pierson, March 19, 1937, ibid.; Hull to Gauss, April 3, 1937, *Foreign Relations, 1937,* 4:580–81; Hornbeck to Grew, March 22, 1937, Personal Correspondence, 1937, Johnson Papers; Pierson, "Summary of Report of Warren Lee Pierson," June 28, 1937, File No. 033.1190 Pierson, Warren Lee/24, RG 59; he sent a copy of the summary to Roosevelt, Pierson to McIntyre, July 17, 1937, OFF: File 971, Export-Import Bank, 1933–45, Roosevelt Papers.

47. The executive committee's commitment was one of principle only: that is, it did not involve an immediate contract. American corporations

Calder and Arnold hoped to take advantage of Pierson's arrival to gain support for their views, but on certain points, Pierson agreed with Johnson.[48] He did not believe a credit commission was necessary nor did he think the bank should station a representative in China. Moreover, he concurred in the view that since American manufacturers relied primarily on domestic demand, they were not as export conscious as manufacturers in other nations. Finally, he discovered that many American businessmen did not appreciate the practical implications of the recent changes in China. Pierson parted company with Johnson at this point, however, and remained cautiously optimistic about America's opportunities. Despite various difficulties, he was convinced that China was "a land of potential resources of great magnitude, not the least of which consists of a tremendous, intelligent, and industrious population." Perhaps having the American ambassador in mind, he noted that "some of our people [in China], in both official and private life, have been too close to the events which have been and are now in progress in that country to be able fully to evaluate their economic significance to the United States." Like Arnold, he was convinced that China was altering the character of her imports and that she was "constantly increasing her purchases of heavy machinery, railroad and electrical equipment, all products which we are

---

did not sign a contract until near the end of the following month and this only involved half of the committed funds, Pierson to Jones, Project No. 166, Andersen, Meyer & Co., Ltd., RG 275; executive committee meeting, May 4, 1937, ibid.; Gauss to Hull, May 1, 1937, *Foreign Relations, 1937*, 4:585–86; summary of executive meetings held April 14, April 22, and May 4, 1937, File No. 811.516, Export-Import Bank/126, RG 59. Baldwin Locomotive Works and the American Locomotive Corporation agreed to divide future orders equally rather than compete with one another; American export groups had frequently favored such action because they believed intra-American competition gave advantages to foreign corporations, Gauss to Hull, May 1, 1937, *Foreign Relations, 1937*, 4:585–86; Johnson to Hull, May 8, 1937, File No. 893.51/6383, RG 59. Eager to gain U.S. financial assistance, the Chinese Ministry of Railways informed Pierson that each new railroad would establish the influence of the country supplying the money, Johnson to Hull, April 26, 1937, *Foreign Relations, 1937*, 4:584–85.

48. Lockhardt to Hull, April 23, 1937, File No. 033.1190 Pierson, Warren Lee/11, RG 59; Ambassador Johnson was worried that Pierson's trip could result in the United States undertaking some financial ventures of dubious worth, Johnson to Hornbeck, April 19, 1937, Personal Correspondence, 1937, Johnson Papers.

particularly well qualified to supply."[49] Thus, in assessing the opportunities which new conditions in China had opened up for the United States, Pierson arrived at a conclusion close to Calder's and Arnold's.

To facilitate economic expansion, Pierson suggested that American bankers and manufacturers study the Chinese situation carefully and possibly send senior officers abroad on information-gathering missions. But the key to this new market, Pierson realized, lay in arranging proper credit terms, for the Chinese preferred American goods even though they were often more expensive than products from other nations. Ultimately, Pierson thought, private financiers would recognize the vast potential of China; until then, however, the Export-Import Bank could fill the void by participating in various transactions. Not only would this involvement foster the immediate sale of American goods, it would, as he pointed out in a summary report of his journey, "arrest the impression widespread throughout the world that we are prepared to abandon our proper share in the commerce of the Far East." Timely action by the bank could serve the nation's long-term economic interests by signaling continued, and official, United States concern with Chinese affairs.[50]

Pierson envisioned the bank serving as a catalyst for the private sector of the economy; if this segment did not respond positively, neither he nor other leading policymakers thought the government should assume a significant role in Chinese development programs. By the spring of 1937, the American business community in China, centered in Shanghai, seemed optimistic. Following the lead of the commercial attaché's office, business leaders organized a foreign trade week in May. The celebrations, timed to coincide with similar activities in the United States,

49. Calder to Jones, June 8, 1937, File No. 600, China, Finance and Investment, 1937, RG 151; Pierson, "Summary of Report of Warren Lee Pierson," File No. 033.1190 Pierson, Warren Lee/24, RG 59.

50. "Summary of Report of Warren Lee Pierson," File No. 033.1190 Pierson, Warren Lee/24, RG 59; Pierson made some of these points in a speech to the Los Angeles Chamber of Commerce after his return from the Far East. Following his talk, he held a confidential meeting with a number of bankers to discuss the problems of financing trade with China, see the clippings from the Los Angeles Times and Herald-Express sent to Walter Measday, June 24, 1937, File No. 640, Foreign Loans, China General 1932–1939, RG 151.

concentrated on the theme that China was embarking on a new era of industrial growth which held great promise for foreign trade. Symbolic of this transformation was the completion of a trans-Pacific radio-telephone service which began operation on May 19 with Madame Chiang Kai-shek and Eleanor Roosevelt exchanging greetings. This communications network, in conjunction with the recently opened air transport system, represented closer ties between the East and West.[51]

Members of the economic community in China were eager to move ahead, but the distance they could go depended on the attitude of powerful financial and business elements within the United States. If these groups remained indifferent (as Johnson had predicted), the American presence in China would continue on a limited level. Largely in response to this situation, Calder prepared a lengthy study of China's financial status. The study's original intention had been to provide Pierson with information, but Calder realized it could serve a larger purpose if Washington officials made it available to selected exporters and bankers, especially Thomas Lamont, whom he thought was "pretty much the key to the situation so far as Wall Street is concerned." Despite Lamont's deep-seated prejudices, Calder thought there was room for optimism since the Morgan partner was "also very much interested in China developments as a world financier." The assistant commercial attaché urged immediate action because he feared that, at this strategic moment in Chinese history, American interests were "in some degree at least 'asleep at the switch.' " In his report, Calder pointed out that the growing political and economic stability of the Nationalist government created a good environment for foreign investment. Loans for railroad development were particularly attractive because the risk was low and an improvement in the transportation sys-

51. Arnold played a major role in the festivities of foreign trade week, even arranging to have leading administrators send messages of support, see Arnold to Dye, February 17, 1937, File No. 400, US-China, 1937–1938, RG 151; Arnold to Foreign Trade Week Committee, April 21, 1937, ibid.; for copies of the messages sent by Daniel Roper, George Davis (president of the United States Chamber of Commerce), and Alexander Dye (head of the Bureau of Foreign and Domestic Commerce), see ibid.; for newspaper coverage of the week-long celebration, including accounts of business attitudes and of the opening of radio-telephone links, see Arnold to Dye, May 26, 1937, ibid.

tem would enable the Chinese to use their resources to better advantage. As the process of modernization progressed, the country would become "a greater consumer of foreign commodities, despite efforts toward self-sufficiency."[52]

Officials of the Bureau of Foreign and Domestic Commerce in Washington did not believe they should personally deliver the reports, but they had no objections to sending copies through the mail. Before the bureau could act, however, it received a request from J. P. Morgan & Co. for a copy of Calder's findings on the financial situation in China. On July 2, the bureau complied with this request and six days later it sent copies to the National City Bank, Guaranty Trust Co., Chase National Bank, and Irving Trust Co. At the same time, the bureau contacted leading officials of Andersen, Meyer & Co., U. S. Steel Products Co., and American Locomotive Co. to notify them of the availability of the report. By early July 1937, therefore, Commerce Department officials had taken steps to acquaint important segments of the business and financial communities with the expanding opportunities in China.[53]

The movement to enlarge the American stake in China picked up additional momentum in late June with the arrival in the United States of H. H. Kung, the Chinese minister of finance. Kung was head of a special mission to study economic and industrial developments in Europe and America as well as to arrange financial assistance for the Chinese development programs. While in London, the finance minister concluded an agreement for a railroad loan and made tentative arrangements for a currency stabilization loan in the neighborhood of

52. Calder suggested that the Bureau of Foreign and Domestic Commerce contact J. P. Morgan & Co., Irving Trust, Bankers Trust, Chase National Bank, National City Bank, Moody's Investor Trust, U.S. Steel Products Co., American Locomotive Company, and Andersen, Meyer & Co., Ltd., Calder to Jones, June 8, 1937, File No. 600, China 1937, RG 151; Calder, "A Study of China's Financial Situation," SR No. S–155, June 5, 1937, ibid.

53. Dye to Jones, July 7, 1937, ibid.; J. P. Morgan & Co. to the Bureau of Foreign and Domestic Commerce, June 22, 1937, ibid.; Jones to J. P. Morgan & Co., July 2, 1937, ibid; on July 8, the bureau mailed copies of the report to the other banks mentioned in note 52, above, and notified its New York office to contact officials of the above-mentioned corporations about the availability of the report, Jones to New York office, July 8, 1937, ibid.

£10,000,000 ($50 million). Since Kung had originally been interested in a much larger loan (from $500 million to $1 billion) to enable the Nationalists to refinance existing debts, Washington anticipated that he would broach this subject with American financial groups.[54]

Shortly after Kung's arrival in New York on June 21, two events took place that suggest an attempt to generate greater enthusiasm for American involvement in China. On June 26, the Chinese Ministry of Communications signed a contract with RCA Victor Company to purchase $408,000 worth of radio, telephone, and telegraph equipment. More important than the contract itself were the follow-up actions of the minister of communications: he invited the leading members of the American diplomatic community for a celebration dinner during which he observed that the coincidence of the conclusion of the negotiations with Kung's visit to the United States was especially fortuitous. The Chinese apparently hoped news of the signing would facilitate Kung's efforts in New York and Washington.[55] On June 29, the day after publication of the RCA deal, Jesse Jones mentioned publicly for the first time the Export-Import Bank commitment of May 4 when he announced that the bank would assist two American corporations in the sale of 20 locomotives to the Chinese Ministry of Railways. In his statement, issued after talking with Kung, Jones noted that the Chinese

54. For a notice of Kung's arrival, see *New York Times*, June 22, 1937, p. 15; State Department officials followed Kung's activities in England with a great deal of concern, Bullitt to Hull, May 30 and June 3, 1937, *Foreign Relations, 1937*, 4:599–601, 602–3; Hull to Bullitt, June 1, 1937, ibid., pp. 601–2. Kung believed that if the Nationalists could pay off the existing debt with a new loan at a lower rate of interest, they could balance the budget. Since the British could not float a loan of that size by themselves, Kung hoped he could interest American bankers in the project, Bullitt to Hull, June 3, 1937, ibid., pp. 603–4; also see memorandum by Hornbeck, "China and Possible Impending Overtures on the Subject of Financial Assistance," June 4, 1937, File No. 893.51/6397, RG 59; Bingham to Hull, June 21, 1937, *Foreign Relations, 1937*, 4:605–7; memorandum by Hornbeck, June 25, 1937, ibid., pp. 608–9.

55. Willis Peck to Hull, June 28, 1937, *Foreign Relations, 1937*, 4:609–10. A member of the Division of Far Eastern Affairs thought the order could "lay the ground for a further and sustained demand for American materials for replacements and extensions." John Vincent to Hornbeck and Hamilton, July 2, 1937, File No. 893.51/6405, RG 59.

were interested in additional credits for the purchase of American products.[56]

Kung himself took steps to attract American investment. In an interview with reporters in his suite at the Waldorf-Astoria hotel, the finance minister maintained that the Chinese badly needed scientific and technical assistance as well as foreign capital; if United States interests wished to help, he could guarantee them security. A few days later, speaking at a dinner held in his honor by prominent American companies and individuals, Kung again promised full governmental protection for foreign investors. Because China currently provided the world's largest market for capital goods, Kung explained that immense benefits awaited U. S. industries. At the same dinner, E. P. Thomas, who thought Kung's visit augured well for future Chinese-American trade, agreed to cooperate with the finance minister. Finally, Warren L. Pierson hinted that the recent railroad transaction could be the first of several deals if American manufacturers collaborated with the Export-Import Bank.[57]

Besides sounding out private sources, Kung held a series of talks with administration officials, including the president. He conferred with Henry Morgenthau, Jr., about the possibility of receiving assistance for the Chinese currency program. In the wake of Roosevelt's request to "go the limit" in helping China, Morgenthau arranged to purchase 62 million ounces of Chinese silver at 45¢/ounce on the condition that Kung buy gold with the proceeds. The Chinese would hold the gold at the Federal Reserve Bank of New York and could only use it to stabilize the yuan. Treasury Department officials also agreed to loan the Nationalists up to $50 million in dollar exchange as long as they secured the loan with an equivalent amount of gold. Morgenthau and Kung believed this arrangement would greatly

56. This transaction utilized approximately one-half the May 4 commitment, *New York Times*, June 31, 1937, p. 33.

57. Ibid., June 27, 1937, section 2, pp. 1–2; W. Cameron Forbes, who had headed the American Economic Mission to China in 1935, also spoke at the dinner; other concerns represented were the National City Bank, Standard Vacuum Oil Company, Chase National Bank, Bank of China, Andersen, Meyer & Co., General Motors Export Division, California Texas Oil Company, American Foreign Power Company, and United Aircraft Export Corporation, see *New York Times*, July 7, 1937, p. 16.

strengthen China and, by so doing, would benefit United States trade.[58]

After completing negotiations at the Treasury Department, Kung met with Jones and Pierson to discuss the possibility of Export-Import Bank credits. On July 9 the finance minister offered to purchase $50 million of miscellaneous capital goods from the United States during the next two years provided the bank bought, on a without-recourse basis, 50 percent of the notes issued to the American suppliers. United States exporters and Chinese banking institutions would divide the remainder of the financing. Three days later, Kung presented a detailed list of China's intended purchases.[59] At a meeting on July 26, the bank's board of directors agreed in principle to Kung's offer but decided to hold off on specific arrangements because of a resumption of fighting in North China. On August 2, American policymakers concluded that the present moment was an inauspicious one for action, but "We might undertake to examine an initial transaction with the idea of going through with it if conditions begin to look better."[60]

Although it was not evident at the time, the fighting which followed the Marco Polo Bridge incident brought an end to hopes for closer Sino-American economic ties. Despite the failure of this movement, however, many American interests were beginning to shed their indifference to China and, with the support of governmental agencies (in some cases led by the agencies) they were laying plans to tap China's rich potential.[61]

58. Morgenthau Diaries, Book 75, pp. 46–48, Book 77, pp. 171–72, 239–43, Book 78, pp. 12–31. Henry Morgenthau, Jr. Papers (Franklin D. Roosevelt Library, Hyde Park, New York). Also see memorandum by Feis, July 8, 1937, *Foreign Relations, 1937*, 4:610–11; press release by Depart- of Treasury, July 9, 1937, ibid., pp. 611–12.

59. Part of this memorandum is reprinted in a memorandum by Pierson, July 12, 1937, *Foreign Relations, 1937*, 4:612–13; the full memorandum, including the itemized list, can be found in Pierson to Hornbeck, July 12, 1937, File No. 893.51/6418, RG 59. Kung suggested the following purchases: railway equipment, $18 million; trucks and cars, $5 million; textile machinery and equipment, $7.5 million; mining machinery, $5.5 million; chemical plant equipment, $4 million; power plant equipment, $6.5 million; equipment for docks and wharves, $3.5 million.

60. Feis to Welles, July 27, 1937, File No. 893.51/6422, RG 59; memorandum by Feis, July 27, 1937, *Foreign Relations, 1937*, 4:616; Pierson to Hornbeck, August 2, 1937, ibid., pp. 616–17.

61. Although Borg maintains that during 1937 there was no sign that

Besides indicating a desire for material benefits, the actions of the Treasury Department and the Export-Import Bank had important political ramifications: U. S. officials realized that any measures which strengthened the Nationalists would help them withstand Japanese pressure. In his talks with Treasury Department officials, Finance Minister Kung frequently commented that a strong China was the best guarantee for peace in the Far East. American support for China's currency, he continued, would help achieve this objective. Morgenthau concurred with Kung's assessment, arguing at one point that "fifty years from now the fact that China was not gobbled up by Japan and again became a strong nation may be the most important thing we did here."[62] By the middle of 1937, therefore, American policymakers thought they had discovered the one piece of the Far Eastern puzzle which previously had been absent: a Chinese government that would unify the country without endangering the rights of foreign nations. The resumption of fighting did raise the question of the Nationalist government's ability to survive; but if it could create the impression of being able to do so, U. S. officials would no longer fear that steps taken to support the Kuomintang would threaten American interests.

American bankers were inclined to act in China, the evidence suggests a shift in attitude was under way. Pierson's trip to China, the Export-Import Bank credit, the RCA deal, and the response to Kung's visit in the United States all substantiate this interpretation. For Borg's position, see *The United States and the Far Eastern Crisis*, p. 274; for more on the shift of bankers' attitudes see Arnold, "China Annual Economic Report for 1937," File No. 128-X Peiping, Reports of Commercial Attaché, RG 151; John Chevalier, secretary of the American Asiatic Association, wrote Johnson that "the NY financial crowd are [*sic*] much less afraid of the China picture than they were a year ago." Chevalier to Johnson, March 15, 1937, Personal Correspondence, 1937, Johnson Papers.

62. Kung made this point in his dinner address, *New York Times*, July 7, 1937, p. 17; for his discussion with Morgenthau see Morgenthau Diaries, Book 78, pp. 17–31, Morgenthau Papers.

7

World Crisis in the Late 1930s
The Bank and Latin America, 1937-1939

The Japanese attack in North China was just one of an increasing number of domestic and foreign problems that the Roosevelt administration faced by the second half of 1937. The court packing scheme and the growing number of sit-down strikes helped spark a congressional reaction to the president's leadership; the sharp economic tailspin which began in September 1937 reinforced this opposition. Because the post-1933 recovery had been partial at best, the new tremors sent the economic indices tumbling downward. Industrial production fell 33 percent, profits were down 35 percent, and individual stock averages declined by over 45 percent. Altogether, income and production fell more abruptly from September 1937 to June 1938 than they had from 1929 to 1933. The economic contraction was among the sharpest ever recorded, and it marked one of the few times the economy experienced two major downturns without an intervening upswing. These mounting internal difficulties indicated that Roosevelt would have to take steps to promote stability, but they also limited his freedom of action by feeding the opposition forces.[1]

When the president shifted his view to international affairs, he witnessed a scene that was even more gloomy than the one

1. Kenneth D. Roose, *The Economics of Recession and Revival*, pp. 3, 235; Milton Friedman and Anna J. Schwartz, *A Monetary History of the United States, 1867–1960*, pp. 493–99. The recession had little impact outside the United States with the exception of Latin America, where the decline in the price of primary products and a drop in the level of American exports caused hard times, see Department of Commerce, *The United States in the World Economy*, Economic Series no. 23, pp. 196, 199. For information on the emergence of congressional opposition, see James T. Patterson, *Congressional Conservatism and the New Deal* (Lexington, 1967), passim.

at home. In the Far East, the Japanese offensive threatened to close off China to Western interests. In Latin America, the Germans and, to a lesser extent, the Japanese and Italians stepped up attempts to increase their economic and political influence. During 1938, moreover, Hitler expanded his pressure within Europe, thereby raising the prospect that the world would soon find Germany dominating the entire continent. Thus, New Deal policymakers had to contend with foreign difficulties which threatened to fragment the world into regional blocs.

The conjunction of domestic and international crises posed a severe challenge to American leadership. Because Axis expansion could limit America's access to foreign markets and endanger her security, the United States stood to benefit from any restraining measures. Since the New Deal policymakers did not intend to use force or to create an effective alliance system, they had to cast about for other means of achieving their goals. One approach was to rely on economic tools. In the fall of 1938, Secretary of the Treasury Henry Morgenthau, Jr., wrote the president recommending this course of action. The secretary believed that the United States could safeguard the peace and make the good neighbor policy "really effective" by utilizing the nation's financial strength in the Far East and in Latin America. "In these two areas," he argued, "we can move most effectively and with the least complications."[2]

The spread of economic nationalism throughout Latin America during the latter part of the 1930s complicated Washington's handling of hemispheric affairs. On March 13, 1937, Bolivian President David Toro authorized the seizure of properties owned by the Standard Oil Company of Bolivia. State Department officers quickly became involved in the incident, primarily because of their concern that the Bolivian government acknowledge the principle of adequate compensation. Unless Washington could uphold this principle, the extensive U. S. property holdings in Latin America might be endangered.[3] The Mexican

2. John Morton Blum, *From the Morgenthau Diaries,* 2:524–27.

3. The wide popular acclaim which greeted Toro's move was further cause for concern since it suggested that anti-United States actions could pay handsome political dividends, Herbert S. Klein, "American Oil Companies in Latin America," *Inter-American Economic Affairs* (Autumn 1964): 47–62; Cole Blaiser, "The United States, Germany and the Bolivian Revolutionaries (1941–1946)," *Hispanic American Historical Re-*

expropriation of foreign oil properties a year later caused even greater alarm both because the American economic stake was larger and because the action indicated that the ongoing Mexican revolution was again entering a radical phase. At no point since 1917 had Washington reconciled itself to the Mexican definition of subsoil rights or to Mexican land ownership laws, but the two nations had avoided a major confrontation largely because Mexican leaders had backed away from a determined policy of economic nationalism. By 1936, however, President Lázaro Cárdenas began laying the groundwork for a new wave of social and economic reforms, the implementation of which would lead to disagreements with foreign investors. The expropriation of foreign oil properties grew out of this movement.[4] Besides violating American principles of international behavior, the Bolivian and Mexican incidents prompted conservative elements within the United States to urge the administration to be firm in protecting property rights. At a time when the country needed a flexible policy, American statesmen operated under pressures that hindered their maneuverability.

A further problem was that Cordell Hull's reciprocal trade agreements program, one of the pillars of the administration's good neighbor policy, was far from being an unqualified success. In the case of Cuba, the trade agreement had ended Cuban hopes for economic diversification, by enabling American manufacturers to drive out domestic producers, and had linked the island's economy ever more tightly to sugar and tobacco production. Even more troublesome was the fact that Cubans did not have a guaranteed access to American markets for these

---

view 52 (February 1972): 26–30. Also see David Green, *The Containment of Latin America*, pp. 24–27; Bryce Wood, *The Making of the Good Neighbor Policy*, pp. 168–202.

4. For the American response to economic nationalism in Mexico after 1917, see Walter V. Scholes, "Reaction to Revolution: Hughes' Mexican Policy," in *United States Diplomatic History*, ed. Walter V. Scholes (Boston, 1973), 2:79–87; N. Stephen Kane, "Bankers and Diplomats: The Diplomacy of the Dollar in Mexico, 1921–1924," *Business History Review* 48 (Autumn 1973): 335–352; and the excellent account by Robert Freeman Smith, *The United States and Revolutionary Nationalism in Mexico, 1916–1932*. For a discussion of the Cardenas period, see Howard F. Cline, *The United States and Mexico*, pp. 215–51; Green, *Containment of Latin America*, pp. 27–34; Wood, *Making of the Good Neighbor Policy*, pp. 202–59.

items because the U. S. Congress could control the volume of imports by altering domestic agricultural programs. By the late 1930s, Cuba again experienced economic and political unrest.[5] Brazilian-American economic relations also were not developing the way Washington had hoped. Brazilian President Getulio Vargas wanted to alter his nation's dependent position within the world economy by encouraging the growth of manufacturing and the domestic consumption of native natural resources. Brazilian manufacturers, not eager to face heavy foreign competition, had opposed the United States-Brazil trade agreement of 1935. A rapid increase in trade with Germany, moreover, created powerful groups in Brazil who wished to retain the compensation mark trade system. Another group favoring close economic ties with Germany was the Brazilian military, who desperately sought foreign aid in order to rebuild. Realizing that the country faced a shortage of foreign exchange, military leaders saw the compensation system as an answer to their problems. For all these reasons, Vargas remained unwilling to lift the controls on foreign exchange and the United States-Brazil trade agreement did not have the results Hull had intended. Consequently, the secretary encountered continued frustrations in his dealings with the country that he thought was the key to all of Latin America. By the latter part of the 1930s, after Vargas had staged a successful coup, the question of whether Brazil would follow America's lead in international economic relations remained unanswered.[6]

The combined impact of these events strengthened the position of the Export-Import Bank officials who advocated a liberalized Latin American lending policy. In October 1937, Pierson succeeded in gaining the executive committee's authorization for a credit of up to $600,000 to assist the Westinghouse Electric International Company in the sale of locomotives to the Chilean States Railways. The commitment was for five years

5. Irwin F. Gellman, *Roosevelt and Batista*, pp. 114–21, 164–76.
6. Frank D. McCann, Jr., *The Brazilian-American Alliance, 1937–1945*, pp. 25–26, 148–75; Stanley Hilton, "Brazil and Great Power Trade Rivalry in South America, 1934–1939" (Ph.D. dissertation, Univ. of Texas, 1969), pp. 1–14, 37–60, 62–133, 224–84. Hilton notes that the July 1937 accord was not a victory for Hull; Brazil merely made a public pledge to uphold liberal trading practices and continued the compensation deals with Germany, ibid., pp. 314–20.

and included 50 percent financing, on a without-recourse basis. Initially the State Department had opposed the transaction; its Division of American Republics (formerly the Latin American division) cited several reasons: the United States government would become the creditor of the Chilean government; the Chilean government had not made satisfactory arrangements to fund debts owed American investors; and the deal would discriminate against some American exporters because repayment of the credit would accentuate Chile's dollar exchange shortage. But Pierson persuaded the department to withdraw its objections with the understanding that he would not regard the transaction as setting a precedent.[7] In early 1938, the executive committee expanded the authorization to include other American locomotive manufacturers and later amended the offer again by lengthening the term of the credit.[8]

Following this success, Pierson recommended in December that the bank participate in the sale of locomotives and other railway equipment to the Central Railways of Brazil. The bank president believed that the credit was sound and that Brazil's favorable balance of trade with the United States would enable her to repay the debt easily. The proposition had additional advantages. "Although South America represents a natural export market for the United States," he informed Herbert Feis, "we have been losing our position steadily during the past two years to European countries—especially Germany." The prompt placing of orders would curb this unfavorable trend and spur

7. Executive committee meeting, October 20, 1937, Project No. 174, The Westinghouse Electric International Co. (Chile), Records of the Export-Import Bank of Washington, RG 275 (National Archives, Washington, D.C.). As will become clear, the department did not believe that this deal altered the existing policy, Gantenbein to Heath, October 19, 1937, File No. 825.77/331, General Records of the Department of State, RG 59 (National Archives, Washington, D.C.); Gantenbein to Duggan, February 11, 1938, File No. 65A473,18,3246/1, Records of the Department of the Treasury (U.S. Department of the Treasury, Washington, D.C.); Pierson to Taylor, March 11, 1938, ibid.

8. Executive committee resolutions of February 24 and March 7, 1938, Project No. 174, The Westinghouse Electric International Co. (Chile), RG 275. Even at this point, the evidence suggests that State Department officers were not enthusiastic about the transaction, see Gantenbein to Duggan, February 11, 1938, File No. 65A473,18,3246/1, Treasury Department; Duggan to Feis, February 15, 1938, ibid.; Feis to Pierson, February 16, 1938, ibid.

domestic recovery as well by producing "a very perceptible and favorable effect in ten or more localities." Pierson also noted that manufacturing the rails would enable steel plants in Maryland and Chicago to open while "filling the locomotive and tool orders will maintain organizations that are rapidly disintegrating through the lack of new business."[9] In line with its earlier position, however, the State Department would not approve the proposal until the Brazilian government took steps to conclude an equitable agreement with American bondholders. Even though he accepted the department's objections, Pierson was disappointed about losing the business. He explained to Hull that he had supported the proposition because of his desire "to stimulate our heavy goods industries—which are currently greatly depressed—and to accomplish this desirable end by what appears to be sound medium-term financing." The department's decision, he went on, could "result in the business being directed elsewhere." During the first part of 1938, the Division of American Republics again rejected a bank proposal for assisting trade with Brazil because Brazil had not lived up to an earlier agreement to supply exchange promptly for imports from the United States.[10]

These episodes brought to the surface the tensions that existed between bank officers and various members of the State Department over the bank's role in Latin America. James Gantenbein, of the Division of American Republics, presented the case for those who wished to restrain the institution. After reviewing the period from 1934 to 1937, he recommended that the department adopt a consistent policy based on two principles: avoiding actions that could result in the American government becoming a creditor of a foreign government; and refusing credits

9. Pierson to Feis, December 3, 1937, File No. 811.516 Export-Import Bank/153½, RG 59; memorandum (and attached note) by Pierson, December 3, 1937, Project No. 200, Central Railways of Brazil, RG 275.

10. Pierson to Aranha, December 10, 1937, Project No. 200, Central Railways of Brazil, RG 275; for more on the reasons for the department's decision and for a partial reprint of Pierson's letter to Hull of December 9, 1937, see Gantenbein to Duggan, December 20, 1937, File No. 811.516 Export-Import Bank/146, RG 59; memorandum by Livesey, January 31, 1938, with attached memorandum from the Division of American Republics, February 1, 1938, File No. 832.5151/1004, RG 59; memorandum by Livesey, February 2, 1938, File No. 811.516 Export-Import Bank/147, RG 59.

to a government that was not making proper efforts to service its defaulted dollar bonds or was not negotiating for a settlement in good faith. Gantenbein also suggested that the bank avoid transactions that involved the sale of munitions or that involved foreign governments who treated American investors inequitably. A uniform policy would allow the administration to avoid embarrassment and charges of discrimination which could occur if the bank acted inconsistently.[11]

Pierson disagreed. Writing to Hull, he complained that the department's attitude was hamstringing the Export-Import Bank in Latin America. In no case had a refusal to extend credits caused a debtor government to settle its accounts with American bondholders. The department's guidelines, moreover, did not make any sense. "I do not wish to be understood as advocating unsound credits in South America or elsewhere," he continued, "but, assuming the business risk involved in a particular case is one the Bank is willing to accept, I submit that the existence of a default in the payment of bond interest or the creation of an inter-governmental debtor-creditor relationship should not *automatically* prevent the consummation of a transaction otherwise desirable." Not only did the department's current policy prevent the bank from adequately assisting American exporters, it facilitated "the efforts of aggressive European nations, particularly Germany, to supplant the United States in Latin American markets."[12]

Pierson's position found some support within the State Department. Frederick Livesey, a member of the office of International Economic Affairs, feared a formalized policy would force American business to forego sound transactions, thereby creating additional opportunities for German suppliers. He further argued that the department's concern about the Export-Import Bank becoming the creditor of a Latin American government ran counter to the intent of Congress. Livesey insisted that

11. Duggan had requested the study, Gantenbein to Duggan, December 20, 1938, File No. 811.516 Export-Import Bank/146, RG 59; the members of the Division of American Republics appear to have been in general agreement with Gantenbein, see the memoranda of January 12 and 31, 1938, File No. 811.516 Export-Import Bank/145, RG 59.
12. Emphasis in original, Pierson to Hull, February 17, 1938, File No. 811.516 Export-Import Bank/144, RG 59.

creditors were not always at a disadvantage if their debtors borrowed new funds for purposes for which they might otherwise have to pay cash. In any event, withholding credit as a coercive measure had failed because debtor nations could turn elsewhere for aid, with the result that debts remained unpaid and American exporters lost business. At the present time, Livesey believed, many government officials were more interested in promoting industrial exports than in seeing a resumption of payment on foreign bonds. Those private interests most directly involved in exports, like the National Foreign Trade Council, had little concern for investors because they realized that a conflict over the priority of payments could exist between themselves and the bondholders. Inasmuch as the bank afforded the government an opportunity to use credit "to influence our relations, economic and other, with foreign countries," Livesey opposed steps to restrict its activities.[13]

For the time being, the controversy ended in a compromise: Herbert Feis worked out a settlement whereby the department accepted the sentiment of Gantenbein's recommendations but did not formulate a set of rules. Instead of a rigid policy, officials would consider each case on its merits. Under some circumstances they might wish to have the bank extend credits to nations in default on outstanding obligations. Washington would also remain flexible on the question of the bank becoming a direct creditor of a Latin American government, even though ventures of this nature would entail political risks. Above all, the department should follow a course that would "avoid putting the Government again in a possible position where it must either fail to use reasonable vigor to try to secure payment for debts due the Bank, or lay itself open to charges of pressure." Feis thought that the bank was doing an adequate job of aiding American commerce; the chief difficulty was that "Mr. Pierson is distinctly ambitious for the Bank, and his general desire is to push out vigorously for business." The bank president, in Feis's

13. Livesey thought that the conflict between exporters and creditors "had long since been decided in favor of the industrial corporations and against the bondholders." He was a little hasty, however, in dismissing the influence of bondholders, see memorandum by Livesey, January 25, 1938, File No. 811.516 Export-Import Bank/145, RG 59.

opinion, lacked an appropriate awareness of the political and economic background against which his institution operated.[14]

In practice, the compromise resulted in an expansion of the bank's operations in Latin America. This point can be seen clearly in the department's reaction to a proposal involving the sale of five hundred steel cars to the Sorocabana Railway of Brazil. Laurence Duggan, chief of the Division of American Republics, opposed the deal because it could result in the U. S. becoming the direct creditor of the state of São Paulo; Feis objected to the transaction because the Brazilian government had not abided by its agreement to make exchange available for American imports. Undersecretary of State Welles, however, overrode his subordinates. He countered Duggan by insisting that, on the basis of his knowledge of the Sorocabana Railway, he did not believe the credit would produce an intergovernmental creditor-debtor relationship; he dismissed Feis's argument as being irrelevant. While he agreed that the bank should avoid becoming the creditor of a Latin American government, Welles supported the idea of considering each case on its merits. In this instance, the undersecretary did not think that the department had grounds for opposing the proposal.[15] Similarly in May 1938, the department agreed to the bank's financing the sale of locomotives and rolling stock to the Central Railways of Brazil. Because the department had taken exception to an identical proposal the previous December, this decision suggests a shift in policy. As in the case of the Sorocabana Railway, members of the Division of American Republics opposed the deal only to find that Welles rejected their advice. Additional indications of an expanded bank role were, first, the decision to discount, on

14. Note attached to Livesey's memorandum of January 25, 1938, ibid.; draft of intended letter from Feis to Pierson which Feis did not send, although Moore did confer with Pierson about the bank's lending policy, Moore to Feis, March 18, 1938, File No. 811.516 Export-Import Bank/144, RG 59; Feis to Welles, March 9, 1938, ibid.

15. Pierson endorsed the proposal both because he believed the Sorocabana Railway represented the best risk in Latin America and because the American railway car industry needed the business (at that point, only one company had any orders); Pierson further noted that everyone on the executive committee (presumably with the exception of the State Department's representative) approved of the deal, memorandum by Livesey, March 14, 1938, File No. 811.516 Export-Import Bank/153½, RG 59.

a with-recourse basis, notes from a commission house of the Colombian government, even though Colombia had not refunded its defaulted debts, and second, the decision to initiate in March 1939 revolving lines of credit (of from $2,000 to $20,000) to help smaller exporters finance the shipment of goods.[16]

Since 1934, American policymakers had watched carefully the growth of Nazi Germany's trade in Latin America, and they were deeply concerned about the intensified German trade drive in 1938. By relying on various forms of barter transactions, the Nazis appealed to those Latin American nations suffering from foreign exchange shortages. Since most did have exchange difficulties, the swapping arrangements allowed them to receive essential imports without straining their balance of payments. This practice had the further effect of enabling Germany to increase her share of trade with several Latin American nations over the period from 1934 to 1937: Germany's portion of Brazil's imports rose from 14 to 24 percent (in dollar value), her share of Chile's imports increased from 10.2 to 25 percent, of Mexico's imports from 9 to 19.7 percent, and of Argentina's imports from 9.7 to 10.4 percent. U. S. officials concluded that Germany had taken over a good deal of the business that American exporters could have handled if they had been able to offer more attractive terms.[17] In addition to worrying about the loss of valuable

16. Executive committee resolution, May 20, 1938, Project No. 200, Central Railways of Brazil, RG 275; memorandum to Welles, May 25, 1935, File No. 832.77/514, RG 59; Livesey to Welles, March 28, 1938, File No. 811.516 Export-Import Bank/153½, RG 59; Export-Import Bank, "Statement of Loans and Commitments, December 31, 1940" mimeograph, p. 6; Edward O. Elsasser, "The Export-Import Bank and Latin America, 1934–1945" (Ph.D. dissertation, Univ. of Chicago, 1954), p. 126.

17. Warren L. Pierson, "A Report to the American People," *Foreign Commerce Weekly* 4 (August 30, 1941): 33; T.R.B. "Washington Notes," *New Republic* 97 (December 28, 1938): 228. Figures taken from the appropriate sections of Department of Commerce, *Foreign Commerce Yearbook, 1937* and *Foreign Commerce Yearbook, 1939*. Pierson had tried to convince Hull of the last point in his letter of February 17, 1938, File No. 811.516 Export-Import Bank/144, RG 59; also see Pierson to members of the advisory committee of the Export-Import Bank, October 15, 1937, Office of the Secretary, General Correspondence, 96227, General Records of the Department of Commerce, RG 40 (National Archives, Washington, D.C.); Moore to Feis, March 18, 1938, File No. 811.516 Export-Import Bank/144, RG 59.

trade, Washington was troubled by the spread of German political influence, which frequently accompanied the expansion of commerce.[18]

In the late spring of 1938, a situation emerged in Haiti which fed on the administration's fear of German expansion; the result was an unprecedented move by the Export-Import Bank. The bank's involvement with the Republic of Haiti, therefore, requires careful analysis because the episode anticipated the future direction of American policy and demonstrated the implications that course held for the nation's relations with Latin America.

Economic difficulties, which began in mid-1937, had played havoc with Haiti's already weak economy. Brazil's decision to dump surplus coffee on the world market reduced the price of Haitian coffee exports by 50 percent. Because coffee normally accounted, in value, for 75 percent of the island republic's exports, the lower price had a general depressing effect. A boll-weevil attack, moreover, nearly wiped out the current cotton crop, Haiti's second leading export item. The banana industry, which had not lived up to earlier predictions, was not strong enough to fill the void created by the faltering coffee and cotton enterprises. To make matters worse, the repatriation of Haitian laborers from Cuba and Santo Domingo coupled with the possibility of military attacks by the Dominicans further strained the economy.[19]

The economic deterioration soon led to other difficulties. The recession threatened political stability by increasing the number of jobless and homeless and by weakening the position of the middle class—shopkeepers, professionals, and government employees. Because Haitian officials had to use all available funds to maintain the essential services of the government, they were

18. Percy W. Bidwell, "Latin America, Germany and the Hull Program," *Foreign Affairs* 17 (January 1939): 382; Alton Frye, *Nazi Germany and the American Hemisphere, 1933–1941*, pp. 72–76, 104–13.

19. Welles to Hull, June 4, 1938, File No. 838.51/3614a, RG 59; W. D. Whittemore to Pierson, June 16, 1938, Project No. 201, J. G. White Engineering Corp., RG 275; copy of Pierson's report on Haiti, July 14, 1938, Pierson to McIntyre, July 27, 1938, OFF 971, Export-Import Bank, 1937–45, Box 7, Franklin D. Roosevelt Papers (Franklin D. Roosevelt Library, Hyde Park, New York); memorandum by Sydney de la Rue, June 15, 1939, File No. 838.6156/101, RG 59.

forced to default on the two remaining series of a loan the country had floated in the United States in 1922. With the moratorium on loan payments, the State Department became interested in seeing that American bondholders received fair treatment. Of greater importance, the Haitian government required outside financial assistance to restore stability. The need for a new foreign loan concerned the United States because American representatives continued to cooperate in the administration of Haiti's finances, and because the State Department did not want some other country to use financial aid to gain influence in the republic.[20]

When the question of a loan did arise, Haitian authorities contacted U. S. officers for advice. At first, the American response was reserved. Duggan informed the Haitian minister that the department "would be glad to do whatever it could to help Haiti to secure funds within the limits of its present policy." The chief limitations were that, unlike its predecessors, the Roosevelt administration would not become the patron for a loan and that the State Department's assistance could "not involve interference in Haiti's internal affairs." As a clarification, the Division of American Republics recommended that the government "refuse to take the responsibility or to allow its own employees even when loaned to a foreign government to take the responsibility of determining in the last analysis what public works should be undertaken by a foreign government."[21]

The State Department quickly changed its attitude, however, upon learning that the financial interests (known as the Dahlberg group) who were going to handle Haiti's refunding loan

20. Ferdinand Mayer to Hull, December 22, 1937, *Foreign Relations, 1938*, 5:573–74; copy of Pierson's report on Haiti, July 14, 1938, Pierson to McIntyre, July 27, 1938, OFF 971, Export-Import Bank, 1937–45, Box 7, Roosevelt Papers; after gaining the State Department's approval, Haiti took this step in December 1937, Welles to Mayer, December 30, 1937, *Foreign Relations, 1938*, 5:576–78; Welles to Roosevelt, June 4, 1938, File No. 838.51/3614a, RG 59; memorandum by Selden Chapin, June 8, 1938, File No. 838.51/3637, RG 59; also see Dana G. Munro, "The American Withdrawal from Haiti, 1929–1934," *Hispanic American Historical Review* 49 (February 1969), 24–25.

21. While understanding the department's position, the Haitian minister feared the consequences this policy would have for his country, memorandum by Duggan, May 9, 1938, File No. 838.51/3605, RG 59; memorandum to Welles and Feis, April 28, 1938, File No. 838.51/3612, RG 59.

intended to employ a German engineering firm to carry out a public works program. The department also discovered that many groups in Haiti counted on American assistance as part of the good neighbor policy. An unfavorable response by the United States in all likelihood would lead these elements to look elsewhere for aid.[22] In responding to these events, Washington officials moved along several fronts. They explored the possibility of interesting a reputable American financial house in making the loan. Even though the department believed a U. S. firm would be able to obtain any form of security arrangement it desired, Wall Street was uninterested. By the end of May, Thomas Lamont told Adolph Berle, an assistant secretary of state, that while he was sympathetic with the idea of not letting Haiti fall into the hands of outside groups, he could not recommend the loan to American investors.[23]

The department also tried to persuade the Dahlberg group to make some changes. Selden Chapin, an officer in the Division of American Republics, talked at length with Ellery C. Huntington, Jr., several of whose clients had been approached by the Dahlberg group for an advance of from $1 million to $1.5 million. Chapin noted that the United States did not wish to see Haiti placed under too onerous a burden or one that would establish foreign influence in the country. It had been "a source of surprise to many of us," he continued, "that a venture which was said to be entirely American should find it necessary to use foreign engineers and possible foreign engineering equipment." Sharing Chapin's surprise, Huntington noted that his clients would not consider the proposal except on an all-American basis. In a conversation with some members of the Dahlberg group, Chapin repeated many of the points he had made to Huntington.[24]

22. Swedish-born Brer Gustave Dahlberg headed the financial group, Duggan to Berle, May 16, 1938, File No. 838.51/3613, RG 59; Mayer to Hull, May 27, 1938, File No. 838.51/3618, RG 59.

23. Chapin to Hull, May 25, 1938, File No. 838.51/3623, RG 59; Berle to Welles and Duggan, May 27, 1938, File No. 838.51/3626, RG 59; Roosevelt's attempt to interest Lehman Brothers in the operation likewise failed, see Welles to Roosevelt, June 4, 1938, File No. 838.51/3614a, RG 59.

24. Memorandum by Chapin, May 31, 1938, File No. 838.51/3638, RG 59; Chapin told the members of the group that the department "would be sorry to see Haiti fall into the hands of an irresponsible group or see any

The poor credit status of Haiti was in the department's favor because any extension of the moratorium on the 1922 loan would make it nearly impossible for the country to float a new issue. When the Dahlberg associates asked the State Department to try to prevent a prolongation of the moratorium, Chapin replied that he was powerless to act, that only the Haitian government could make such a decision. In early June, Washington learned that the Haitian financial representative would soon begin negotiations with the Foreign Bondholders' Protective Council to see about continuing the moratorium. The following day, during a phone conversation with the American minister in Haiti, Duggan indicated that the department was "anxious to go ahead and get this question of the moratorium out of the way in order that there won't be any further dilly-dallying around with entrepreneurs." The evidence, therefore, suggests that the State Department, if not actually promoting an extension, was not disappointed at the prospect of one occurring.[25]

Although American policymakers hoped they could block the proposed Dahlberg transaction, they did have to provide Haiti with financial relief. Failing to gain the support of private capital, the department looked to the Export-Import Bank; and after a brief period of negotiations, the bank agreed to finance a public works program. An analysis by W. D. Whittemore, a vice-president of the bank, explained the reasoning behind the decision. Despite a belief that the financial risks were greater than prudent banking would dictate, Whittemore thought these risks were "dwarfed into insignificance" by political considerations. "It has been represented to us," he explained, "that if the 'Good Neighbor' does not come to her rescue in her hour of need, distress will force Haiti to appeal to Europe (probably Continental) and one Power at least would welcome such an appeal." Because the interests of the United States would not be enhanced by having "another European power acquire a political and economic (if not military) base right in our front yard," the only

substantial foreign interests established in this country," memorandum by Chapin, June 8, 1938, File No. 838.51/3637, RG 59.

25. Memorandum by Chapin, June 8, 1938, File No. 838.51/3637, RG 59; Mayer to Hull, May 21, 1938, File No. 838.51/3611, RG 59; Mayer to Hull, June 8, 1938, *Foreign Relations, 1938*, 5:595; transcript of phone conversation, June 9, 1938, File No. 838.51/3633, RG 59.

course was to have the Export-Import Bank extend appropriate financial assistance. For the project to be a success, nonetheless, Haiti would need stable and "enlightened foreign supervision." After examining the proposal, Warren Pierson also favored action by the bank lest Haiti make concessions to European nations which would sacrifice "valuable rights to the ultimate disadvantage of Haiti and very likely of the United States."[26]

In the middle of June, the episode came to a quick conclusion. On June 14, the department discovered that the Dahlberg group was still active and hoped to sign a contract on the fifteenth or the seventeenth. On the fifteenth Haiti requested a renewal of the moratorium.[27] Three days later, the executive committee of the Export-Import Bank agreed to purchase from the J. G. White Engineering Corporation, on a without-recourse basis, up to $5 million in notes issued by the government of Haiti. Acting as an agent of the Haitian government, the White Corporation would prepare a detailed public works program which, when accepted by the government, it would direct and administer. Operating as part of the Haitian Department of Public Works, the company's engineers would approve all expenditures. The departments of public works and finance, however, could audit and approve the engineers' actions. In addition, the company would function as a purchasing agent for all supplies and equipment not produced in Haiti. The terms of the agreement reflected Pierson's concern that the bank be in a position to veto those projects it did not regard as sound.[28] Consequently, the bank

26. Whittemore to Pierson, June 16, 1938, Project No. 201, J. G. White Engineering Corp., RG 275; while agreeing in principle to the proposal, Pierson insisted that a bank official inspect the intended projects to see if they would improve Haiti's economy and if they would promote United States-Haiti commerce. After his visit, Pierson concluded that the proposals met these conditions, see copy of Pierson's report on Haiti, July 14, 1938, Pierson to McIntyre, July 27, 1938, OFF 971, Export-Import Bank, 1937–45, Box 7, Roosevelt Papers.

27. Mayer to Hull, June 14, 1938, File No. 838.51/3628, RG 59; Mayer to Hull, June 17, 1938, including enclosure, *Foreign Relations, 1938,* 5:596–97.

28. The resolution provides a concise summary of the reasoning behind the U.S. decision to act. After outlining Haiti's economic problems, it reads (in part): "WHEREAS, such unemployment has seriously interfered with trade between the United States of America and the Republic of Haiti; has given rise to grave concern for the well-being of the Haitian people; and unless alleviated, threatens to jeopardize important interests of the

would exercise a controlling influence over the Haitian public works programs.

This transaction marked an important change in the bank's policy. By discounting the notes of the Haitian government, the institution became the direct creditor of the government of a Caribbean republic and indulged in what amounted to an intergovernmental loan. Furthermore, this was the first time Washington did not insist that all the credit be spent in the United States and permitted some of it to be used for local labor and materials. It was a development of great consequence for the future that the bank became involved in an entire development project and not merely in financing the sale of individual items.[29]

The project also had transcendent foreign policy ramifications. Since the early part of the twentieth century, American officials had assumed they could reduce European influence in the Western Hemisphere by replacing European capital with American. In the case of Haiti in 1938, Washington policymakers moved one step further, concluding that the best way to retain U. S. dominance was to deny Germany the opportunity to gain an economic foothold. This decision produced side effects that contradicted some principles of Roosevelt's Latin American policy. As part of the attempt to become a good neighbor, State Department officials had decided that the U. S. government should not become involved in the internal affairs of other countries. In Haiti, the department initially resolved not to serve as a patron for the loan or to have any responsibility for the public works program. As the situation became more complex, however, the department brushed aside these reservations and followed a

---

people of the United States and their Government in strategic locations in the West Indies; . . ." Resolution of Executive Committee, June 18, 1938, Project No. 201, J. G. White Engineering Corp. RG 275; also see de la Rue to Chapin, June 23, 1938, File No. 838.51/3641, RG 59; and copy of Pierson's report on Haiti, Pierson to McIntyre, July 27, 1938, OFF 971, Export-Import Bank, 1937–45, Box 7, Roosevelt Papers.

29. Memorandum by Welles, June 14, 1938, Project No. 201, J. G. White, Engineering Corp., RG 275; Elsasser, "The Export-Import Bank and Latin America," pp. 128–30; Hawthorne Arey, "History of Operations and Policies of Export-Import Bank of Washington," mimeograph, pp. 17–18; for a different interpretation of the Haiti deal, see James M. McHale, "The New Deal and the Origins of Public Lending for Foreign Economic Development, 1933–1945" (Ph.D. dissertation, Univ. of Wisconsin, 1970), pp. 183–92.

course that entailed significant political involvement. This episode suggests that a more aggressive bank policy could achieve
certain American objectives, but only at the expense of others.
Furthermore it implied that United States policymakers had a
series of priorities in which the protection of American dominance took precedence over all else.

The loan to Haiti was warmly received by export interests.
"We have been impressed over the possibility of the great expansion of your Bank," E. P. Thomas wrote Pierson, "if the
Haitian contract may be considered a precedent." Thomas and
other exporters believed they could obtain a large volume of
business in Latin America if they received adequate governmental support.[30] Partially in response to this pressure but also
to gain a better understanding of the conditions confronting
American commerce in the hemisphere, Pierson spent two
months in the late summer and early fall of 1938 visiting Venezuela, Brazil, Argentina, Uruguay, Chile, Peru, Ecuador, and
Haiti.

His investigation of economic conditions in several countries
convinced Pierson that a major problem facing U. S. traders in
Latin America was a shortage of foreign exchange. The recession had produced unfavorable trade balances, causing some
nations to rely on restrictive trade practices. As had been the
case in the early years of the decade, these practices primarily
benefited those nations willing to adopt bilateral trade patterns.
Although reluctant to do so, Pierson did recommend that the
Export-Import Bank open credits to government banks in Uruguay, Brazil, and perhaps Argentina, so that these institutions
would have sufficient dollar exchange to pay for imports from
the United States. The Uruguayan and Argentine proposals included a proviso authorizing each government to secure the
credits by setting aside a percentage of the exchange created by
exports to the United States. The bank president assumed that
the arrangements would ensure a smooth flow of trade as well
as provide "the best possible method to prevent further loss of
business to European countries."[31] These recommendations ob-

30. Thomas to Pierson, August 16, 1938, included in a memorandum
from Whittemore to Board of Trustees of Export-Import Bank, August 22,
1938, General Correspondence, 96227, RG 40.
31. Davis to Hull, September 14, 1938, File No. 033.1120 Pierson,

viously indicated a willingness to reverse the bank's long standing policy of avoiding exchange transactions.

Pierson dealt with other matters besides the problem of dollar exchange shortage. He talked at length with Latin American leaders about the possibility of the bank assisting in the sale of heavy industrial goods. In Venezuela, he promised to help with the purchase of American materials needed for a development program and hinted that the Venezuelans might be able to use a portion of the credit to defray local labor costs. Pierson aided U. S. interests in Argentina with their efforts to obtain contracts for various government projects including sales to the Argentine State Railways. During his stay in Chile, he expressed a willingness to help the government build a copper smelting plant and to supply aid for the construction of a mechanical nitrate plant.[32] The bank president's only immediate success, however, came in Brazil where he persuaded American manufacturers to ease up on their credit terms in return for the bank's carrying 65 percent of the risk on a without-recourse basis. As a result of his efforts, Americans finally were able to conclude a deal with the Sorocabana Railway. Following Pierson's return to Washington, the bank participated on a without-recourse basis in the sale of railway equipment to the Central Railways of Brazil.[33]

Warren Lee/14, RG 59; Reed to Hull, September 21, 1938, File No. 033.1120 Pierson, Warren Lee/23, RG 59; Allen Dawson to Hull, September 21, 1938, File No. 833.51 Bank of Uruguay/1, RG 59; Caffrey to Hull, September 21, 1938, *Foreign Relations, 1938,* 5:356–57; memorandum from the office of the Economic Adviser, September 23, 1938, File No. 033.1120 Pierson, Warren Lee/23½, RG 59; Pierson to Welles, October 9, 1938, File No. 832.51 Bank of Brazil/6, RG 59.

32. Meredith Nicholson to Hull, September 13, 1938, File No. 033.1120 Pierson, Warren Lee/15, RG 59; Norman Armour to Hull, October 1, 1938, File No. 033.1120 Pierson, Warren Lee/26, RG 59.

33. Robert Scotton to Hull, September 23, 1938, File No. 832.77/524, RG 59; Caffrey to Hull, November 5, 1938, File No. 832.77/525, RG 59; A. M. Hamilton to H. Press, October 7, 1938, Project No. 210, American Locomotive Sales Corporation, RG 275; Export-Import Bank resolution, October 12, 1938, ibid. In the case of Argentina, the American corporations did not receive the bid, memorandum of executive committee meeting, December 1, 1938, File No. 811.516 Export-Import Bank/184, RG 59; in the deal with the Sorocabana Railway, the bank expanded its share of the participation from 50 to 65 percent and lengthened the terms from twenty months to five years, memorandum of executive committee meeting, December 8, 1938, Project No. 200, Central Railways of Brazil, RG 275.

Pierson's suggestion that the bank provide certain Latin American central banks with dollar exchange produced a divided response in Washington. The Commerce Department and the Trade Agreements Division of the State Department were highly critical. Officers in these agencies feared that the proposals would mean a return to the trade policy of the 1920s, when the United States financed exports through loans in lieu of tariff reductions. By relying on public funds instead of private capital, Pierson's recommendation went one step beyond the earlier policy. An additional disadvantage, and one which harked back to the old conflict between Cordell Hull and George Peek, was that the proposal amounted to a bilateral arrangement, even approximating a barter system. Nevertheless, some members of the State Department were willing to consider Pierson's request despite its apparent violation of principles underlying the U. S. approach to international trade.[34]

Perhaps sensing the split between policymakers, officials of the National Foreign Trade Council supported a position close to Pierson's. In a conversation with State Department officers, they complained that the administration's trade agreement program no longer guaranteed American interests equal treatment. The bilateral approach of Germany and Great Britain, on the other hand, was paying off for their nationals. The exporters wanted the department to become more aggressive in aiding American interests. Specifically, they supported an exchange agreement with Brazil that was similar to proposals the department had rejected in 1934/35. Although under pressure from several sources, Assistant Secretary of State Francis B. Sayre spurned the exporters' demand and lectured them on the importance of the principles at stake. They had to realize, Sayre insisted, that two social systems were at war with one another; if the foreign traders opted for the German approach, they would

34. "Possible Credit from the Export-Import Bank to the Bank of Brazil," Dye to Roper, September 26, 1938, File No. 832.51 Bank of Brazil/3, RG 59; Roper agreed with Dye's position, Roper to Hull, September 29, 1938, ibid.; memorandum of meeting, September 23, 1938, File No. 611.0031 Executive Committee/689, RG 59; memorandum to Sayre, September 23, 1938, File No. 833.51 Bank of Uruguay/3, RG 59; George Butler to Welles, October 15, 1938, File No. 832.51 Bank of Brazil/6, RG 59.

have to be prepared to accept the complete regimentation of all aspects of economic life. Sayre did indicate, however, that the department would consider E. P. Thomas's proposal for an Export-Import Bank credit to help release accounts in Brazil as long as the deal did not create a preferential position for Americans.[35]

The European crisis in the fall of 1938 further complicated the bank's activities in Latin America. Following the settlement at Munich, U. S. policymakers concluded that they would face increased competition in the Western Hemisphere. Secretary of the Treasury Morgenthau warned Roosevelt that the Axis powers would become bolder in their attempts to establish economic and political support in South America. The president himself believed that the recent display of German power completely reoriented America's international relations. For the first time since the Holy Alliance in 1818, the United States faced the prospect of an attack in its own hemisphere. While Roosevelt wanted to build up the air force, Morgenthau argued that the country could keep Germany and Italy out of Latin America "by an intelligent use of a small portion of our enormous gold and silver holdings."[36] Eventually, the United States would move along both these paths as it stepped up its efforts to prevent the spread of Axis influence.

At the Eighth International Conference of American States held during December in Lima, Peru, Secretary Hull took an additional step to protect American interests by trying to gain acceptance for a firm resolution of hemispheric solidarity against penetration by non-American states. Argentina and, to a lesser extent, Uruguay and Chile were reluctant to follow Hull's lead because they feared that a strong declaration would antagonize Germany and endanger important trade links. The delegates finally reached a compromise agreement under which the American republics affirmed their intention to help one another in case of a foreign attack. The resolution provided for joint action against underground infiltration and in response to a military assault. Even though he was a little disappointed with the results

35. Memorandum by Leroy D. Stinebower, October 24, 1938, *Foreign Relations, 1938*, 5:359–61.
36. Blum, *From the Morgenthau Diaries*, 1:526, 2:48, 50.

of the conference, Hull was satisfied that the declaration made a clear distinction between American and non-American states.[37]

The troubled condition of world affairs led to highly significant changes in the actions of the Export-Import Bank. In late 1938, the bank undertook an unusual commitment when it extended a $10 million credit to the International Telephone and Telegraph Corporation (I.T. & T.). The corporation needed funds to liquidate certain debentures and commercial bank loans, which fell due on January 1, 1939, and to expand its South American subsidiaries. Under ordinary circumstances, I.T. & T. could have drawn on private capital for the necessary financing, but the business recession and the war scare in Europe had dried up these sources. Failure by the corporation to refinance its obligations would have forced it into a partial reorganization, thereby providing foreign interests with an opportunity to acquire many of its properities. To avoid this, I.T. & T. officials contacted the government for assistance.[38]

Both Feis and Pierson were receptive to the corporation's request. Pierson noted that I.T. & T. furnished the only completely American-owned telegraph service between this country and Latin America. In the past, the corporation had been diligent in seeing that its South American properties did not fall into the hands of Europeans; and it had modernized and expanded its services in the leading Latin American countries. Because communications played an important role in international commerce, the bank president believed the government should ensure that a United States owned and operated company continued to function. Feis, agreeing with Pierson, recommended that the State Department approve action by the Export-Import Bank. Thus, in early December, the bank granted I.T. & T. a $10 million loan.[39]

37. Memorandum of a meeting held in Dr. Mello Franco's apartment, December 19, 1938, Folder 336, Lima Conference, Container 76, Cordell Hull Papers (Library of Congress, Washington, D.C.); also see, Cordell Hull, *The Memoirs of Cordell Hull*, 1:601–9.

38. Export-Import Bank resolution, December 8, 1938, Project No. 215, International Telephone and Telegraph Corporation, RG 275; also see the resolution of December 1, 1938, ibid.; memorandum by Pierson, March 24, 1938, ibid.; memorandum by Feis, March 31, 1938, File No. 811.43 International Telephone and Telegraph Corporation/9, RG 59.

39. Memoranda by Pierson, March 24 and June 10, 1938, Project No. 215, International Telephone and Telegraph Corporation, RG 275; mem-

Over all, the year 1938 witnessed several important alterations in the bank's approach to Latin America. The deal with
Haiti, the provision of more liberal terms to finance the sale of
heavy industrial goods (especially railroad equipment), and the
I.T. & T. transaction all indicated that the bank would become
more aggressive in expanding United States interests in the
hemisphere. Pierson's continued support for exchange deals and
the dissatisfaction of some export groups with the degree of governmental support they had received suggested that pressure to
expand the bank's activities would persist.[40] Washington's concern about the spread of non-American influences in Latin America complemented these forces. One final element was that the
State Department itself was no longer as impervious to the
arguments of bank officials and exporters as it once had been.

The status of American private capital in the hemisphere,
however, worked against this trend. The Foreign Bondholders'
Protective Council kept in contact with State Department officers to see that they did not overlook defaulted debts when
considering proposals for Export-Import Bank action.[41] The department, moreover, did continue to follow its earlier guidelines
on this issue, withholding approval of deals with Ecuador and
Colombia because of the unsatisfactory records of these governments in servicing foreign obligations.[42] Similarly, the department refused to consider a proposition involving a public
works project in Cuba until the Batista government began payments on existing public works debts and revised the nation's
tax system. Welles informed the Cuban president that if his

orandum by Feis, April 11, 1938, File No. 811.43 International Telephone
and Telegraph Corporation/10, RG 59; memorandum by Feis, November
21, 1938, File No. 811.516 Export-Import Bank/183, RG 59; Samuel Sabin
to Pierson, April 15, 1938, Project No. 215, International Telephone and
Telegraph Corporation, RG 275.

40. For example, see the unsigned and undated memorandum handed
to Roosevelt on December 8, 1938, OFF 971, Export-Import Bank, 1937–
45, Box 7, Roosevelt Papers.

41. Francis White to Livesey, August 29, 1938, File No. 832.77/519,
RG 59; Livesey to White, August 12, 1938, ibid.; Welles to Pierson, File
No. 821.51/2264, RG 59.

42. Notwithstanding Pierson's support for the proposal, Welles opposed
the bank's participation in a transaction with Colombia, Pierson to Duggan, August 6, 1938, File No. 822.151/17, RG 59; Duggan to Pierson,
November 13, 1938, ibid.; Pierson to Welles, November 9, 1938, File No.
821.51/2264, RG 59; Welles to Pierson, November 15, 1938, ibid.

people desired the cooperation of the United States government, they would have to "create the conditions which will make such cooperation possible." Despite the arguments of Pierson and Morgenthau that this attitude amounted to using a government agency as a lever to collect private debts, the department did not shift its position.[43]

The Bolivian and Mexican expropriations undoubtedly made the State Department more sensitive about the rights of foreign investors. Feis opposed having the bank deal with private groups in Mexico because of an unstable exchange situation "and the seriousness of questions in dispute between this Government and various American interests in regard to which the Mexican Government up to the present has made no satisfactory move toward settlement."[44] Thus, while the recession and growing world crisis produced pressures for more aggressive actions by the Export-Import Bank, the spread of expropriation caused U. S. officials to become protective of American property rights. To a degree, therefore, the interests of exporters and investors remained in conflict. Furthermore, a potential clash existed between several of the administration's foreign policy principles. The concept of reducing the influence of non-American states within the hemisphere could collide with the objective of non-interference in the internal affairs of another American republic. Concern about the growing prestige of a nonhemispheric power could also result in actions by Washington that undercut the commitment to a multilateral trade system based on equal opportunity for all nations. Until American policymakers could either harmonize these views or establish priorities, the future course of U. S. policy in Latin America would remain uncertain.

Nineteen thirty-nine loomed as a critical year for the nations of the Western Hemisphere. In January, Sumner Welles commented that the coming twelve months would be the most important "in the history of the State Department, and the Treasury, as far as South America goes."[45] Administration officials

43. Duggan to Welles, July 23, 1938, File No. 837.51/2152, RG 59; meeting of December 14, 1938, Morgenthau Diaries, Book 156, pp. 118–120, Henry Morgenthau, Jr. Papers (Franklin D. Roosevelt Library, Hyde Park, New York); J. Butler Wright to Welles, December 29, 1938, File No. 711.37/299, RG 59; Welles to Wright, January 4, 1939, ibid.
44. Feis to Pierson, July 12, 1938, File No. 812.6511/9, RG 59.
45. Quoted in Blum, *From the Morgenthau Diaries*, 2:51.

decided they would need to expand the powers of the bank so that it could handle the increasingly complex situation in Latin America. Accordingly, they asked Congress to extend the bank's life for five years and to establish provisions permitting the institution to obtain additional funds easily. They further recommended that the bank cooperate with other American republics in financing the sale in the United States of imported products which did not compete with domestic industry or agriculture. The proposals ran into difficulty. Congress did extend the life of the bank, but for only two years and placed a ceiling of $100 million on the amount it could have outstanding at one time.[46] Although this ceiling did not have an immediate effect, it became an important barrier as the year progressed. There was an additional question of whether the administration would be able to increase significantly imports from Latin America without antagonizing domestic producers.

Worldwide events did cause Ellis O. Briggs, an assistant chief of the Division of American Republics, to reappraise the department's attitude on the role of the bank in Latin America. Because the issue had become "the preservation and strengthening of a system of international relations in the American continent that will make for peace, economic stability, and equality of commercial opportunity," Briggs believed the department could no longer omit any action that would sustain that system. Since Washington's refusal to help the American republics solve their economic problems would enable others to do so, inaction would jeopardize U. S. trade and investment interests. "Many of those investments and part of that trade," he explained, "relate to industries and materials in which continued American control or participation is of great importance to our own national interest." Assistance by this country could both protect the

---

46. Statement drawn up by the executive committee of the Export-Import Bank in cooperation with the Division of American Republics, November 5, 1938, File No. 811.516 Export-Import Bank/178, RG 59; also see Welles's "Report of the Interdepartmental Committee on Cooperation with the American Republics, together with the Program of Cooperation Enclosed by the Committee," Welles to Roosevelt, November 10, 1938, OFF 3505, Roosevelt Papers. Welles's report was the outgrowth of a broad-ranged study lasting from May to November and involving thirteen departments and agencies. *New York Times*, February 22, 1939, p. 3; *New York Times*, February 24, 1939, p. 27.

nation's stake and "check the growing tendency toward expropriation of foreign (largely American) property in those countries."[47]

Strained economic relations with Brazil provided American policymakers with an opportunity to implement some of Briggs's recommendations. In response to the disturbances of 1937/38, Brazilian leaders had reestablished exchange controls and stopped payment on foreign loans. The shortage of exchange made barter transactions more appealing, with the result that Brazil's trade with Germany increased. The American ambassador in Rio de Janiero warned that this trend would continue unless the United States helped thaw Brazil's frozen exchanges.[48] Besides these issues, Brazilian authorities had been in contact with U. S. officials since late 1937 in hopes of receiving assistance for economic development programs. Roosevelt was anxious to reach a comprehensive accord with Brazil and invited Oswaldo Aranha, the minister of foreign affairs, to come to Washington in February for talks. The ensuing discussions focused on ways in which the American government could aid Brazil in clearing up exchange arrears owed United States exporters, forming a central bank that would regularize exchange fluctuations, and implementing a broad plan to increase the nation's productive capacity. Export-Import Bank officers handled the issue of payments due exporters and the financial considerations of the economic development plan.[49]

Bank officials continued to support an exchange agreement. W. D. Whittemore recommended action of this nature provided Brazil resumed debt payments and made a strong commitment

47. Briggs to Feis and Welles, February 17, 1939, File No. 811.516 Export-Import Bank/217, RG 59.

48. Hilton, "Brazil and Great Power Trade Rivalry," pp. 285–341; McCann, *Brazilian-American Alliance*, pp. 67–69, 111, 125–27, 154–67; Donald W. Griffin, "The Normal Years: Brazilian-American Relations 1930–1939" (Ph.D. dissertation, Vanderbilt Univ., 1962), pp. 152–57, 210–18, 310–18, 401–6; Caffrey to Hull, January 7, March 5, May 6, 1938, *Foreign Relations, 1938*, 5:332–33, 336–37, 344–47.

49. John D. Wirth, *The Politics of Brazilian Development, 1930–1945*, pp. 92–107; also see Souza Costa to Morgenthau, December 2, 1938, *Foreign Relations, 1938*, 5:363–67; memorandum by Briggs, February 21, 1939, *Foreign Relations, 1939*, 5:351; also see Government of Brazil to Export-Import Bank, February 28, 1939, File No. 223, Banco do Brazil, RG 275.

to earmark, or otherwise hold, sufficient surplus dollars to meet the payments due American exporters. Realizing that this approach might run counter to the nation's policy on bilateral trading, Whittemore contended that the administration would have to "fight fire with fire!" For political and economic reasons, the country had to retain its trade with Brazil. "Loss of it," he warned, "is likely to have unfavorable and expensive repercussions on our internal economy and its transfer to some other nation may be followed by unpleasant political repercussions."[50]

Rather than risk these developments, Washington officials signed an accord on March 8 under which the bank would purchase notes issued by the Bank of Brazil for the liquidation of American blocked balances. The bank agreed to buy $19.2 million of the obligations on a without-recourse basis. Although the accord did not commit Brazil to earmark dollar exchange, Aranha promised that his government would insure the acquisition by the Bank of Brazil of sufficient dollar exchange to cover U. S. imports. Besides the exchange agreement, bank officers agreed to cooperate with American manufacturers and exporters in supplying materials that Brazil needed to develop transportation, and Treasury Department officials promised to give Brazilians advice on the creation of a central bank and, if necessary, to ask Congress to place $50 million in gold at Brazil's disposal for stabilization purposes. In return for the American assistance, Aranha pledged that Brazil would free the exchange market, resume payment on defaulted external dollar debts, and stimulate the production of noncompetitive agricultural goods which would find a market in the United States. As a final measure, the foreign minister emphasized that his government would "observe a general policy which will inspire the confidence of United States investors giving them no more restrictions than those to which Brazilian investors may be subjected."[51]

Like the transaction with Haiti, the agreement worked out

50. Whittemore to Welles, January 23, 1939, File No. 223, Banco do Brazil, RG 275.

51. Pierson to Aranha, March 8, 1939, ibid.; Aranha to Pierson, March 9, 1939, ibid. The exchange of letters from Aranha to Morgenthau, March 8, 1939; Aranha to Hull, March 8, 1939; Morgenthau to Aranha, March 9, 1939; Hull to Aranha, March 9, 1939 are found in File No. 832.51/1406, RG 59. The Hull-Aranha exchange appears in Foreign Relations, 1939, 5:352–56.

with Brazil marked an important transition in the Export-Import Bank's policy. Between 1934 and 1938, the State Department had rejected exchange accords that would create an intergovernmental creditor-debtor relationship and might violate the most-favored-nation principle of the trade agreements program. By the spring of 1939, American officials no longer seemed concerned about the former and were willing to modify the latter rather than risk losing the Brazilian trade.[52] The bank's commitment to support an economic development program, furthermore, indicated that the administration would continue the pattern established in Haiti. The agreements had other significant aspects as well. By linking American financial assistance to Brazil's resumption of payments on past debts and to her promise to create a hospitable environment for future investment, the administration hoped to placate conservative elements at home and to promote an international economic system based on private enterprise. The reaction within Brazil to the accords provided the final significant element. Not only were many Brazilians convinced that Aranha had not received enough foreign aid, they also opposed the resumption of payment on foreign bonds. Throughout the rest of 1939, Brazilian leaders refused to make debt payments and remained reluctant to line up with the United States.[53]

After signing agreements with Brazil, the Export-Import Bank received a large number of other requests for assistance. By May, bank officials were considering major proposals involving nine Latin American republics. Because the total of these requests exceeded the institution's available funds, and since Welles believed that the remaining Latin American nations would make

52. By the time of this transaction, the State Department officials who opposed the bank's becoming a direct creditor of a Latin American government were so much on the defensive that I have found no signs of their dissenting from the decision. Because the terms of the agreement did not entail Brazil using the proceeds from exports to the United States to clear exchanges, American officials could argue that they were not creating a bilateral trade arrangement; thus, they could differentiate between the American and German approach to international commerce.

53. Hilton argues that Vargas's trade policy was a defeat for the New Deal. Consequently, Hull's program failed in the country he considered the key to South America, Hilton, "Brazil and Great Power Trade Rivalry," pp. 343–44; also see McCann, *Brazilian-American Alliance*, pp. 129–32; Griffin, "The Normal Years," pp. 165–70, 224–29, 407–33.

overtures in the months ahead, Washington officials had to screen each proposition carefully. They also realized they would have to ask Congress for an increase in the bank's lending capacity.[54]

Two of the projects which the Export-Import Bank undertook followed the Brazilian pattern. In May and June, United States officials signed agreements with the leaders of Nicaragua and Paraguay to assist those countries with their foreign exchange problems and development programs. Both Nicaragua and Paraguay needed outside support since they were among the weakest nations in Latin America.[55] Because Nicaragua contained a possible canal site, Washington was unwilling to see economic hardships make the country dependent on non-American financial sources. As for Paraguay, Roosevelt learned that U. S. aid could help the Paraguayans retain their independence from a bloc of nations (Argentina, Uruguay, and Boliva) under strong German influence. Timely American action might produce a friendly attitude throughout the entire bloc. In both cases, the State Department feared that European interests would act if the Export-Import Bank did not.[56]

Given these considerations, the bank opened lines of credit of $500,000 each to the Bank of the Republic of Paraguay and the National Bank of Nicaragua. The bank also agreed to loan $3 million to Paraguay and $2 million to Nicaragua to defray the cost of American equipment, materials, and technical services needed for development programs. As their part of the bargain, the leaders of Paraguay and Nicaragua promised to abide by a set of conditions similar to those contained in the United States-Brazil accord. The two countries would provide

54. The amount involved ranged from $117 million to $224 million, memorandum to Welles, March 27, 1939, File No. 810.51/1644a, RG 59.

55. Pierson believed that Nicaragua's difficulties resulted from inept economic leadership, Pierson to Jones, May 3, 1939, File No. 227, Republic of Nicaragua, Banco Nacional de Nicaragua, RG 275; Duggan likewise thought that no country could match Nicaragua's record of political irresponsibility and economic mismanagement, Duggan to Welles, April 27, 1937, File No. 817.001 Somoza, A./151, RG 59; Paraguay's plight stemmed primarily from the drain caused by the Chaco war, memorandum by Andrew Donovan, April 20, 1939, *Foreign Relations, 1939*, 5:758–59.

56. Welles to Pierson, November 28, 1938, File No. 834.154/51a, RG 59; see the unsigned memorandum handed to Roosevelt, June 1, 1939, OFF 338, Paraguay, Roosevelt Papers.

dollar exchange promptly to cover American imports, encourage the growth of noncompetitive agricultural products for export to the United States, and guarantee the security necessary to attract foreign investment and technical aid. Nicaraguan officials, furthermore, consented to resume paying American holders of a 1918 bond.[57]

American financial assistance, however, had other strings attached. The chaotic state of Nicaragua's fiscal affairs had meant that earlier attempts to flatten out exchange fluctuations had succeeded only when foreign interests controlled the nation's finances. Convinced that similar control was again necessary, Export-Import Bank officials insisted that an American financial expert oversee the National Bank of Nicaragua's operations and send Washington periodic reports of its international dealings. The presence of an American financial adviser touched a sensitive spot. Many Nicaraguans were resentful that the United States had only recently terminated a long domination of their country's finances. Consequently, American policymakers had to move cautiously; and they did not act until Anastasio Somoza, the Nicaraguan president, assured them that a foreign financial expert could come to his country without causing undue excitement.[58] The credit to the Bank of the Republic of Paraguay also increased U. S. involvement in the internal affairs of a Latin American republic. Because Export-Import Bank officers wanted to be acquainted with all matters affecting the nation's international financial position, they required the Paraguayan bank to employ, subject to their approval, a technical expert on inter-

57. Somoza to Roosevelt, May 22, 1939, *Foreign Relations, 1939,* 5:725–27; Roosevelt to Somoza, May 22, 1939, ibid., pp. 728–30; Pierson to Somoza, May 22, 1939; ibid., pp. 730–31; Resolution of Executive Committee, May 17, 1939, File No. 227, Republic of Nicaragua, Banco Nacional de Nicaragua, RG 275; José Estigarribia to Hull, June 13, 1939, *Foreign Relations, 1939,* 5:759–61; Hull to Estigarribia, June 13, 1939, ibid., pp. 761–63; Resolution of Executive Committee, June 1, 1939, File No. 228, Paraguayan Credits, RG 275.

58. Duggan to Welles, April 27, 1939, File No. 817.001 Somoza, A./151, RG 59; Pierson to Jones, May 3 and 10, 1939, File No. 227, Republic of Nicaragua, Banco Nacional de Nicaragua, RG 275; undated and unsigned memorandum, "Bases upon Which the Export-Import Bank of Washington Might Consider the Extension of Financial Assistance to the Republic of Nicaragua," ibid.; Resolution of Executive Committee, May 17, 1939, ibid.; Nicholson to Hull, File No. 817.51/2631, RG 59.

national financial affairs. It is hardly surprising that an American filled the position; but since this marked the first time Paraguay had employed a foreigner in such a capacity, it produced a difficult situation.[59]

The bank's commitment to support Paraguayan and Nicaraguan development plans resulted in a further extension of American influence. Before allowing individual expenditures, the bank and the government involved had to examine the utility of every proposal: in effect, an agency of the U. S. government had a decisive voice in shaping the programs. Furthermore, each government appointed a chief engineer (someone acceptable to the bank) to provide technical supervision for the projects. This official had to approve all purchases of American materials, and he could hire as many assistants as he required. In both countries, U. S. citizens became the chief engineers in addition to filling most of the other positions. Besides these controls, the Public Roads Administration in Washington assigned consulting engineers who could reject any aspect of the development plans. These officials had access to all pertinent records, received as many aides as they needed, and furnished an additional check on the recipient nation's use of the bank credit.[60]

By these measures, the United States secured an important position in the financial operations of Nicaragua and Paraguay and a decisive voice in the construction programs. The scope of the American involvement opened the way to attempts to interfere in internal matters; in Paraguay, Pierson instructed the bank's financial representative to do what he could to expedite the passage of enabling legislation for certain projects. As in Haiti, Americans assumed important positions in the Paraguayan and Nicaraguan programs; and in nearly every case they received substantially larger salaries than their fellow local work-

59. Undated and unsigned memorandum, "Conditions of Credit to the Banco de la Republica del Paraguay," File No. 228, Paraguayan Credits, RG 275; Resolution of Executive Committee, June 1, 1939, ibid.; Findley Howard to Hull, November 28, 1939, File No. 834.01A/12, RG 59.

60. Resolution of Executive Committee, June 1, 1939, File No. 227, Republic of Nicaragua, Banco Nacional de Nicaragua, RG 275; Agreement between Export-Import Bank and T. A. Jones, November 15, 1939, ibid.; Resolution of Executive Committee, June 1, 1939, File No. 228, Paraguayan Credits, RG 275; Agreement between Export-Import Bank and R. W. Hebard and Company, Inc., November 9, 1939, ibid.

ers. Because the situation in Haiti had led to a long series of complaints, State Department officials tried to keep the number of U. S. employees at a minimum, especially in Paraguay which historically had been an isolated country. The limited number of skilled Latin Americans, however, made this rule difficult to abide by, and the use of American nationals continued. "Rather terrifying sum total of gringos in little Paraguay," one State Department official bleakly concluded. "A few more at this time might be the straw which etc."[61]

Despite these difficulties, throughout the summer of 1939, American policymakers negotiated similar arrangements with a number of other Latin American republics. While these talks proceeded, the bank made commitments to assist exporters in the sale of railroad equipment and industrial machinery to concerns in Argentina, Brazil, Chile, and Colombia.[62] The increased activity of the institution, coupled with the likelihood that it would be busier in the future, made the $100 million loan ceiling imposed by Congress once again an object of concern. When Roosevelt asked Congress for a $3.86 billion appropriation in June 1939, he recommended that $500 million of the funds be used for loans to foreign governments and hinted that the Export-Import Bank would handle this program. Congress, nevertheless, proved to be too economy-minded and neutrality-

61. Howard to Hull, November 28, 1939, File No. 834.01A/12, RG 59; Duggan to Donovan, Josephus Daniels, and Collado, December 22, 1939, ibid.; Briggs to Donovan (undated), ibid.; Leap to Briggs, December 18, 1939, ibid.; note to Melvin Leap and Briggs (undated), ibid.; for the situation in Nicaragua, see Nicholson to Hull, August 19, 1939, 817.51/2624, RG 59; Chargé in Managua to Hull, October 24, 1939, File No. 817.51/2647, RG 59.

62. Memorandum to Duggan, Feis, and Welles, July 6, 1939, File No. 832.51/1508½, RG 59. The bank did offer to extend a credit of $5 million to the Banco de la Republica O. del Uruguay in August but the deal fell through, memorandum to Briggs, Feis, and Welles, February 6, 1939, File No. 833.51 Bank of Uruguay/8, RG 59; memorandum to Duggan, Feis, and Welles, June 7, 1939, File No. 833.51 Bank of Uruguay/10 RG 59; American Consul, Montevideo to Hull, August 9, 1939, File No. 833.51 Bank of Uruguay/11, RG 59; memorandum by Duggan, September 5, 1939, File No. 833.51 Bank of Uruguay/17, RG 59; "Activities of Export-Import Bank of Washington and Second Export-Import Bank of Washington, February 12, 1934 through December 31, 1939," General Correspondence File, Export-Import Bank, Part 3, Records of the Reconstruction Finance Corporation, RG 234 (National Archives, Washington, D.C.).

conscious to pass the president's bill. The bank continued to operate under the existing limitations until March 1940, when Congress raised the ceiling by another $100 million.[63]

By late summer, Washington officials feared that fighting would soon erupt in Europe. In anticipation of this event, Emilio Collado, a member of the Division of American Republics, prepared a study on the economic effects which a war would have on Latin America. Collado based his study on a number of assumptions; first, that there would be a general European war of more than six months duration; second, that western European nations would control the seas, so that England and France would continue to trade with Latin America while Germany's trade would decline sharply; and third, that England and France would be able to purchase supplies for at least two years. Although Latin America would lose most of the German trade, which in 1938 accounted for 10.5 percent of the region's exports and 17.1 percent of its imports, many of the nations would find their losses countered by an increased wartime demand for raw materials and foodstuffs. Because of their heavy dependence on German purchases of cotton and coffee, however, Brazil and most of the Central American countries would be hard hit. Collado contended that the Export-Import Bank could help ease the strain in Latin America by continuing its recent policies. The bank could ensure that the American republics had sufficient dollar exchange to maintain foreign commerce; and, even more important, the bank could expand its support for development projects. Furthermore, the war undoubtedly would accelerate the pace of industrialization on the southern continent. Although private capital could underwrite much of this process, there was, Collado reasoned, "a real role for this Government to cooperate with the governments of the other American republics and with American interests in such industrial development and investment." Consequently, the bank's current policy should be "intensified and redirected with a special view to the problems arising out of a European war." The projected economic dislocations caused by fighting in Europe, therefore, would necessi-

63. Press conference, June 22, 1939, PPF 1–P, Press Conferences, Vol. 13, January–June 1939, Roosevelt Papers; also see Blum, *From the Morgenthau Diaries*, 2:40–41. The attitude of Congress toward the bank is discussed more fully in chap. 9.

tate an expanded flow of governmental loans from the United States which "would make it more than ever desirable to obtain increased lending powers for the Export-Import Bank."[64]

Following the onset of fighting in September, the bank did enlarge its Latin American activities. Toward the end of the month, it allocated $5 million for discounting notes received by American exporters from the Chilean Fomento Corporation. The Chilean government had created the corporation to handle the reconstruction efforts needed after a disastrous earthquake. When the war began, the government used the corporation to ameliorate the difficulties caused by the loss of the German market and then made it the central institution to guide the expansion of national production. Inasmuch as the success of the economic plans depended on outside capital, which, by the fall of 1939, only the United States could supply, Washington officials were in a position to exercise some degree of control over the projects. By requiring the Export-Import Bank to approve each request and by obtaining assurances from Chilean leaders to respect American interests, the Roosevelt administration established safeguards for the nation's economic stake in Chile. The bank also extended a credit of $2.5 million to the government of Panama for use in rebuilding a highway to a strategically important airport at Rio Hato. Besides providing assistance for construction projects, the Export-Import Bank opened a $1 million credit for the National Bank of Costa Rica and resumed negotiations with the Bank of Uruguay.[65] As a final measure, it helped finance the sale of used ships to a government-owned steamship line in Brazil.[66]

64. Collado, "Economic Effects of a European War upon the Other American Republics," August 28, 1939, File No. 810.51/1656, RG 59.

65. Hull to Claude Bowers, September 19, 1939, *Foreign Relations, 1939*, 5:452; for a discussion of the *fomentos*, see George H. Soule, David Efran, and Norman T. Ness, *Latin America in the Future of the World*, pp. 169–70, 273–85; Hull to Dawson, September 19, 1939, File No. 819.51/105a, RG 59; Arey, "History of Operations and Policies of Export-Import Bank of Washington," p. 25; memorandum by Duggan, September 5, 1939, File No. 833.51 Bank of Uruguay/17, RG 59.

66. This transaction had several important ramifications: it excluded the possibility of Germany providing ships; it enabled the American firm to purchase new merchant ships under construction in the United States; and it provided American shipping lines with an opportunity to crack the Brazilian government's near-monopoly of the United States-Brazilian carry-

Even with the growing number of new commitments, the bank continued to abide by many of its old guidelines. Exporters and Pierson cooperated with members of the Treasury Department to urge the State Department to drop its opposition to deals with governments that had defaulted on foreign obligations. Secretary Morgenthau, in strong support of those who wished to revise the existing policy, argued that the treasury would like to see the administration "be as aggressive as possible in getting business for our American manufacturers and helping them through the Export-Import Bank." Would the president prefer, he wondered, to try for new business or to withhold action until the debtor nations settled their accounts.[67] Although Welles occasionally agreed with the secretary of the treasury, the State Department refused to approve transactions with the governments of Colombia, Peru, Cuba, and Ecuador because they had not resumed payment to American bondholders.[68] The outbreak of war caused

---

ing trade. See Resolution of Export-Import Bank, September 27, 1939, File No. 247, Moore-McCormack Lines, RG 275; Feis to Duggan and Welles, File No. 832.802 Lloyd Brasiliero/122, RG 59, Walter J. Donnelly, "Lloyd Brasiliero Orders Four Steamships from German Shipyards," E & T Notes, No. 195, January 23, 1939, File 128–X Rio de Janeiro, Reports of Commercial Attachés, Records of the Bureau of Foreign and Domestic Commerce, RG 151 (National Archives, Washington, D.C.); Arey, "History of Operations and Policies of Export-Import Bank of Washington," pp. 24–25.

67. Pierson to Feis, February 4, 1939, File No. 823.12/19, RG 59; Spruille Braden to Hull, May 15, 1939, *Foreign Relations, 1939*, 5:469–81; Braden to Hull, April 17, 1939, File No. 821.51/2315, RG 59; Duggan to Feis, Welles, and Hull, June 19, 1939, File No. 821.51/2352, RG 59; Blum, *From the Morgenthau Diaries*, 2:55–56; Collado to Duggan, Feis and Welles, December 13, 1939, File No. 823.51/1313, RG 59.

68. For Welles's position, see Blum, *From the Morgenthau Diaries*, 2:55–56; and the two telegrams, Welles to Hull, September 26, 1939, *Foreign Relations, 1939*, 5:504–8. For the department's position, see note to Duggan attached to Braden to Hull, April 17, 1939, File No. 821.51/2315, RG 59; Braden to Hull, November 2, 1939, File No. 821.51/2400, RG 59; Feis to Pierson, February 7, 1939, File No. 823.12/19, RG 59; memorandum by Collado, December 13, 1939, File No. 823.51/1313, RG 59. With respect to Cuba, Welles supported the decision to withhold credits pending satisfactory action on debts, memorandum by Duggan, June 16, 1939, File No. 837.515/470, RG 59; Welles (for Hull) to Wright, July 19, 1939, *Foreign Relations, 1939*, 5:530–34; memorandum by Welles, July 29, 1939, File No. 711.37/306, RG 59; Wright to Hull, September 13, 1939, File No. 837.61351/2173, RG 59; memorandum to Duggan, Feis, and Welles, June 5, 1939, File No. 822.51/818, RG 59.

the department to reexamine its position, but Hull still insisted that "where a country is in a position to conclude a reasonable transitional arrangement, this Government would not be justified in extending credits unless this operation was preceded by or accompanied by a satisfactory debt arrangement." If a nation was unable to make any payment, the department could approve emergency credits to pave the way for a future settlement. In addition to concern over defaulted debts, however, the State Department hesitated to support exchange transactions with Argentina and Uruguay unless these nations agreed to terminate their participation in bilateral trade agreements.[69]

The quickening pace of economic nationalism in Latin America placed another obstacle in the path of the bank. American policymakers refused to extend credits to Bolivia and Mexico until these countries reached a settlement that satisfied U. S. oil interests.[70] The emergence of a popular front government in Chile in early 1939 increased Washington's concern. When an officer of the new government inquired about the possibility of receiving economic assistance, the United States ambassador warned that "drastic action against American companies would make it very difficult, if not impossible, for our Government or for one of its agencies, e.g., the Export-Import Bank" to act favorably on the request.[71] Not only did U. S. officials believe they

69. Hull to Welles, September 29, 1939, *Foreign Relations, 1939,* 5:508–511; memorandum to Duggan and Feis, March 28, 1939, File No. 833.51 Bank of Uruguay/12, RG 59; memoranda by Harry Hawkins, March 28, 1939 and April 7, 1939; memoranda by Collado, March 31, and April 14, 1939, ibid.; File No. 835.5151/1039, RG 59; memorandum by Hawkins, April 7, 1939, ibid.; memorandum by Collado, April 14, 1939, ibid.

70. Memorandum by Duggan, August 7, 1939, *Foreign Relations, 1939,* 5:313; Dawson to Hull, September 27, 1939, ibid., pp. 318–319; Duggan to Hull and Welles, July 13, 1939, File No. 812.77/1304, RG 59; Duggan to Pierson, June 7, 1939, File No. 812.75/94, RG 59; memorandum to Duggan, Welles, and Feis, October 31, 1939, File No. 812.51/2406, RG 59.

71. Armour to Hull, February 24, 1939, *Foreign Relations, 1939,* 5:439–43; Welles to Armour, March 11, 1939, ibid., pp. 443–45. Following the extension of credit to the Chilean Fomento Corporation, American officials found that, contrary to an earlier promise, the Chilean government might use a portion of the funds to construct a copper smelter which could jeopardize United States interests, memorandum by Collado, October 21, 1939, File No. 825.6352/105, RG 59; Pierson to Duggan, December 26,

had to preserve a vital principle of international relations, they had to contend with adverse congressional and public reactions to the confiscations. In deference to these sentiments, Warren Pierson and Jesse Jones assured members of a Senate committee that the bank would not make loans to any country that had illegally seized American property.[72]

Despite these perplexing issues, by the end of the year, American officials had made important strides toward reformulating the Export-Import Bank's Latin American policy. Under the impact of the recession and the growing international crisis, the State Department acceded to the repeated requests of bank officers and exporters for a liberalized attitude on lending. The department's new position was not due solely to pressure from export-oriented groups; foreign traders received a substantial assist from officials concerned about increased German influence in Latin America. These two positions blended together easily in the assertion that the United States government should act to protect traditional markets and to curb the growing prestige of a non-American nation in the Western Hemisphere. As a consequence, the bank assumed larger portions of the risks than it had before and entered into agreements making it the direct creditor of foreign governments or their agencies. The other element shaping bank policy was the emergence of economic nationalism, especially after the Mexican oil expropriation in early 1938. Initially, this movement caused American policymakers to withhold credits, but eventually, it led them to link the extension of financial assistance with promises to repay debts and to provide a hospitable climate for U. S. economic interests. In the agreements with Brazil, Nicaragua, Paraguay, and Chile, State Department officers insisted that the recipient nation abide by the American definition of international economic relations.

1939, including a letter from C. E. Calder (president of American and Foreign Power Co., Inc.) to Pierson, December 20, 1939, File No. 825.51/1175½, RG 59.

72. Hull to Welles, September 30, 1939, *Foreign Relations, 1939,* 5:320–21; as the bank approached its loan ceiling, American policymakers had to be even more considerate of congressional opinion if they hoped to obtain additional appropriations, Welles to Armour, March 11, 1939, ibid., pp. 443–45; memorandum by Feis, March 28, 1939, File No. 832.6363/225, RG 59.

The department apparently hoped to resolve the conflict between exporters and investors through the use of financial and diplomatic leverage.

The bank's new activities were a microcosm of broader changes in the nation's foreign policy. Many Americans became reluctant to give up the advantages afforded the United States by the bilateral actions of the Export-Import Bank. At the Panama conference held in the fall of 1939, the delegates created the framework for a multilateral approach to hemispheric economic relations by proposing the Inter-American Bank, a multinational institution designed to underwrite development programs. Although Roosevelt initiated some actions in this direction, private American financial and industrial groups cooperated with conservative politicians to emasculate the plan. The failure of the Inter-American Bank severely undercut the multilateral approach because it meant that development projects had to rely for funds on private capital or the Export-Import Bank.[73] The bank's actions in 1938 and 1939 also changed the character of the good neighbor policy. By placing financial advisers in various Latin American countries, American policymakers resorted to many of the controls traditionally associated with dollar diplomacy. This time, however, the United States government replaced private banks as the provider of funds. The conditions attached to the extension of credits for development programs produced additional American interference in the internal affairs of neighboring states. Although the United States government no longer intervened to force payment of debts, it relied on other means to exert its influence.[74]

73. Green, *The Containment of Latin America*, pp. 59–83.
74. Bryce Wood's concentration on cases involving the expropriation of American oil properties caused him to miss the broader aspects of U.S. policy. Although American policymakers avoided direct intervention to settle the disputes in Bolivia and Mexico, they did apply economic pressure. More important, these episodes spurred the development of a new policy in which the United States exchanged financial assistance for a guarantee of American interests. In other words, Washington hoped to lock the barn door before the horses escaped instead of the other way around, as happened in the cases of Bolivia and Mexico. See Wood, *The Making of the Good Neighbor Policy*, esp. chaps. 6–10. Wood's thesis that national security came to exceed the interests of private corporations (see pp. 167, 193–94, 280–82, 310–14, 332–59) also is misleading because he defines the issues too narrowly. The fact that American policymakers de-

Unquestionably some of the bank's activities benefited Latin American countries. In many cases, moreover, these countries had solicited financial assistance. Nonetheless, the tactics adopted by the bank during 1938 and 1939 produced a fundamental change in American policy.[75] By linking bank credits to Latin America's acceptance of a dollar exchange system, which allowed private capital to move freely, and by advocating the creation of noncompetitive agricultural and industrial enterprises, the United States was promoting an improved version of the old order; it was not sponsoring a new definition of hemispheric relations. The tendency of American policymakers to opt for credits in the place of tariff reductions also raised a question in the minds of some Latin Americans about where they would find new markets. At the end of the 1930s, Latin America found itself in the familiar role of being a pawn in a game of international economics dominated by the industrial nations.[76] As New Deal officials moved to safeguard their nation's stake in the Western Hemisphere, they resorted to measures that decisively altered the nature of the good neighbor policy.

------

cided that broader issues outweighed the immediate demands of petroleum companies does not tell us much unless we know how these officials defined national interest. As I have tried to demonstrate, they maintained that the nation could achieve peace and prosperity within an international system built on Wilsonian principles. Even though the State Department opposed the petroleum industry in specific cases, one should not conclude that the department was uninterested in creating an international setting compatible with the American economic system as a whole. As U.S. officials saw it, the interests of the system outweighed those of any one member.

75. David Green's emphasis on Roosevelt's idea of giving the Latin Americans their share of economic opportunity is well taken; as he demonstrates, however, the president was unable to achieve his objective, *The Containment of Latin America*, pp. 47–83, passim.

76. See the complaints of Uruguay, Reed to Hull, November 2, 1938, File No. 833.51 Bank of Uruguay/6, RG 59; American Consul in Montevideo to Hull, August 9, 1939, File No. 833.51 Bank of Uruguay/11, RG 59; and of Chile, Wesley Frost to Hull, July 21, 1939, File No. 825.51/1123, RG 59. Of the leading industrial nations, Great Britain was the big loser during the 1930s. In April 1936, the *London Financial News* interpreted the recent United States-Brazil agreement as the beginning of an American attempt to dominate the hemisphere by exaggerating the dangers of German commercial and political aggression, see summary of "United States Trade Drive in South America," *London Financial News*, April 26, 1939, contained in a memorandum from Solomon Adler to White, May 9, 1939, Morgenthau Diaries, Book 208, p. 352, Morgenthau Papers.

8

World Crisis of the Late 1930s
The Bank and the Far Eastern War
1937-1939

The Japanese invasion of North China in July 1937 posed
a more difficult problem for American policymakers than did
the situation in Latin America. The attack, which occurred just
as United States and Chinese officials were meeting in Washington to discuss economic relations, caused the State Department to suspend temporarily a proposed Export-Import Bank
credit. In August, as the fighting spread, the department postponed consideration of extending any financial assistance.[1] Besides undercutting American support for China's modernization
program, Japan's actions endangered the peace of the Far East
and created the possibility that Tokyo would establish an exclusive economic sphere in China. In short, the invasion not only
challenged the open door policy, it threatened the entire United
States position in the western Pacific.

Confronted by this sudden turn of events, American officials
had two choices. One was to remain aloof from the struggle
and thereby allow Japan to gain control of much of China. This
choice implied either that U. S. interests in China could prosper
under Japanese suzerainty, that these interests were not worth
protecting, or that Japan could not maintain effective control
over China for a long period of time. The other choice was for
the United States to oppose Japanese expansion by assisting
China and by putting pressure on Japan. The United States had
sufficient economic resources and technical expertise to be of
assistance to China and could exert economic leverage against
Japan. In 1938, the U. S. supplied nearly 44 percent of Japan's
imports and purchased 27.9 percent of Japan's exports. America,

1. For the details of the United States-Chinese talks, see chap. 6.

moreover, shipped Japan a large volume of potential war materials, including copper, automobiles and parts, machinery, engines, oil, iron, and steel. These materials accounted for 58.8 percent of all American exports to Japan in 1937; in 1938, the proportion rose to 66.3 percent. Thus, the United States could reduce significantly the flow of vital goods into Japan.[2]

In the first months following the Japanese attack, Washington officials issued various statements suggesting that America's policy was in a state of flux. Although they expressed a general disapproval of Japan's actions, these officials could not decide what steps the United States should take. While most leaders did not want to become involved in the dispute, they insisted on protecting American lives and rights in China. Gradually, these two objectives came into conflict; policymakers had to choose between noninvolvement and the protection of American interests.[3] When they reached this point, they began to alter their views on noninvolvement.

Secretary of State Hull, presenting the initial American position in a press release on July 16, 1937, announced that the existence of serious hostilities anywhere in the world affected the interests, rights, and obligations of the United States. America, Hull said, advocated peace and self-restraint, respected the rights of others, and recommended that all nations adopt these principles as well as those relating to the equality of commercial opportunity and the equality of treatment in international relations.[4] Hull's statement, largely a reiteration of traditional foreign policy objectives, merely expressed America's displeasure with the use of force to solve international disputes. It did not establish any guidelines for future actions.

During the remainder of 1937, several actions by American

2. Ethel B. Dietrich, *Far Eastern Trade of the United States*, pp. 18, 22; Roosevelt apparently believed that America could rely on its economic power, in lieu of military force, to control Japanese expansion. In a conversation with Vice-President James N. Garner, the president argued that economic sanctions (quarantines) could be made effective and would not lead to war. John Morton Blum, *From the Morgenthau Diaries*, 1:489.

3. This dilemma is discussed in a message from Joseph C. Grew to Cordell Hull, September 15, 1937, *Foreign Relations, 1937*, 3:525–30; see also the report by Nelson Trusler Johnson to Hull, September 6, 1937, ibid., pp. 513–14.

4. Press release by Hull, July 16, 1937, *Foreign Relations: Japan*, 1:325–26.

leaders implied that the U. S. would not offer major opposition to the Japanese. On August 13 and again on September 5, Roosevelt indicated that American residents in China should leave and that those who remained would do so at their own risk. While sending a small contingent of marines to help safeguard the lives of American nationals in China, the administration asked Congress for a $500,000 appropriation to cover emergency relief and evacuation expenses. By the middle of September, the president announced that Washington would not allow government-owned vessels to carry munitions to either belligerent; private vessels could continue to do so, but only at their own risk.[5] During the Brussels conference in October and November, the U. S. refusal to approve the use of economic sanctions gave additional support to the view that America would pursue a passive policy with respect to Japan. This interpretation was in no way challenged by the swift and peaceful settlement of the *Panay* incident in the last month of the year.

But the United States, meanwhile, continued to express verbal disapproval of the Japanese assault. At a press conference in the latter part of August, Hull specifically applied the principles of his July 16 announcement to the Far Eastern conflict. He asked that both sides reach a peace settlement based on the ideals contained in the Washington Conference treaties and the Kellogg-Briand Pact. Roosevelt gave further indication that American policy might harden; by refusing to invoke the Neutrality Act, he enabled the Chinese, who could not meet the cash-and-carry provisions of the act, to continue their trade with America.[6] Perhaps more significant was the step the president took in October when, after toying with the idea of placing a trade embargo on Japan, he delivered the famous "quarantine" speech in which he recommended that peace-loving nations isolate aggressor states.[7]

5. Harold L. Ickes, *The Secret Diary of Harold L. Ickes*, 2:193; *New York Times*, September 6, 1937, p. 1; press release by the State Department, September 14, 1937, *Foreign Relations: Japan*, 2:201.

6. Press release by Hull, August 23, 1937, *Foreign Relations: Japan*, 1:355–57; press release by the State Department, September 14, 1937, *Foreign Relations: Japan*, 2:201; Roosevelt also indicated that American policy on the application of the Neutrality Act was on a twenty-four-hour basis.

7. *New York Times*, October 6, 1937; Roosevelt's plan for a trade em-

Roosevelt also considered the possibility of establishing an Anglo-American naval blockade of Japan, a plan he believed would bring the Japanese to their knees without risking a war. Roosevelt initiated secret naval discussions with the British in early 1938 and wanted to gain their support for a world conference to settle outstanding issues. Prime Minister Neville Chamberlain's rejection of the U. S. offer, however, ended any immediate hope for Anglo-American cooperation.[8] Despite being frustrated on this front, the administration provided China with a limited amount of financial assistance in the closing months of 1937. Secretary Morgenthau persuaded Roosevelt to allow the treasury to continue its purchase of silver from China and to permit the Chinese to borrow foreign exchange against gold held on deposit in America. These measures helped stabilize China's currency, thereby enabling the country to avoid severe monetary fluctuation and associated political disturbances.[9]

During the first months following the resumption of fighting in north China, therefore, American policymakers were undecided about what actions to take. No one was eager to challenge Japan, nor was anybody willing to see Japan dominate China. Two important factors helped condition any decision which the American government might make. The first was the effect of Japanese domination on American interests in China. The second, which was closely related to the first, was Japan's ability to carry out an extended campaign and to consolidate her control over large areas of China. If Japan needed massive outside as-

---

bargo is discussed in Sumner Welles, *Seven Decisions That Shaped History*, pp. 71–72. Welles thought that this plan was of interest since it illuminated the background of the "quarantine" speech. For a complete discussion of the quarantine speech episode, see Dorothy Borg, *The United States and the Far Eastern Crisis of 1933–1938*, pp. 369–98.

8. Roosevelt thought that Japan's dependence on American and British markets made the country vulnerable to a blockade. He appears to have hoped that the "quarantine" speech and the Brussels conference would educate public opinion to accept a more aggressive policy, see John McVickar Haight, Jr., "Franklin D. Roosevelt and a Naval Quarantine of Japan," *Pacific Historical Review* 40 (May 1971): 203–26. The president also startled the British by proposing a distant blockade of Japan; the Chamberlain government, however, quickly rejected the suggestion, Lawrence Pratt, "The Anglo-American Naval Conversations on the Far East of January 1938," *International Affairs* 47 (October 1971): 745–63.

9. Blum, *From the Morgenthau Diaries*, 1:483–84; see also Allan Seymour Everest, *Morgenthau, the New Deal and Silver*, p. 120.

sistance to implement her policies, the United States could expect to have a certain amount of influence. But if Japan could get by with minimal foreign assistance, China and the American interests therein would be left at the mercy of the victorious Japanese.

Those Americans who were cognizant of Japan's recent actions in the Far East had few illusions about the meaning of a Japanese-dominated China for the United States. During November 1937, Julean Arnold sent Washington a copy of an article written by a Chinese economist, D. K. Lieu, which explained how Japan hoped to achieve economic self-sufficiency by exploiting China and Manchuria. Japan would control all China's basic industries in order to ensure herself a steady supply of raw materials. The captive Chinese market would also allow Japan to mass produce many items which she currently could not turn out. Lieu predicted that America's trade in both China and Japan would decline as the Japanese established a closed economic system. In a note accompanying the article, Arnold commented that Japan's plan to use North China both as a possible source of raw materials and as a monopolistic market was of special interest. For those who believed that Japanese control would benefit American trade, Arnold warned:

> The situation in Manchuria, which many anticipated would be developed under Japanese auspices in a manner to offer increased markets for their products, has resulted in quite the reverse as Manchuria today is far less of a market for American goods than prior to Japanese occupation, although Japan has invested hundreds of millions of dollars in development enterprise in that territory. It can only be expected that should other sections of China fall under Japan's control, our trade will suffer accordingly.

During the following months, American officials often referred to the Manchurian experience as an example of what to expect when Japan took control of an area.[10]

10. Memorandum from Julean Arnold to Far Eastern Section, November 22, 1937, Division of Regional Information, File No. 442.1 General, 1933–1944, Records of the Bureau of Foreign and Domestic Commerce, RG 151 (National Archives, Washington, D.C.); D. K. Lieu's article was entitled "The Economic Significance of the Sino-Japanese Conflict." He noted that since 1932 Japan's trade with Manchuria had tripled while that of the United States had risen by only 30 percent; he believed that what had happened in Manchuria would be repeated in China if Japan came

Immediately after the outbreak of hostilities, Frank S. Williams, the commercial attaché in Tokyo, reported that Japan had sufficient resources and stockpiles to enable her to conduct an extensive military campaign against China. Three weeks later, however, he disclosed that Japan's financial situation was reaching a serious stage. If faced with a long war, Japan would need to import large volumes of raw materials. Because the extra military expenditures would impair Japan's credit abroad, the Japanese would not be able to receive foreign loans to help cover the costs of these goods. Instead, they would have to pay for the imports with foreign exchange and gold, both of which were in short supply. Williams believed that the financial pressures would be such that Japan would have to declare a moratorium for three or four months on all foreign currency commitments.[11]

During the next few months, Williams again changed his opinion about Japan's financial condition. In the fall, he reported that the war had produced very little interruption in the normal business routine of most Japanese and that the success of their forces in China had created an optimistic mood within leading financial circles. By December, Williams concluded that his earlier prediction about a moratorium had been in error; he now thought Japan could weather the Chinese crisis unless a long, drawn-out guerilla war developed. He was convinced that Japan's financial authorities had calculated their expenditures in such a way as to conserve financial resources. He did believe, nevertheless, that there would be room for considerable amounts of foreign capital in North China once peace was established.[12] From the perspective of the American commercial attaché in Tokyo, Japan appeared to possess sufficient resources to carry

---

into control. For an analysis of the problems facing American interests in Japanese-dominated Manchuria, see Errol MacGregor Clauss, "The Roosevelt Administration and Manchukuo, 1933–1941," *The Historian* 32 (August 1970): 595–611, especially pp. 602–9.

11. Frank S. Williams, "Special Report for the Week Ended July 10, 1937," File No. 600, Japan, 1937, RG 151; Frank S. Williams, "Special Financial Report for the Week Ended July 31, 1937," ibid.

12. Frank S. Williams, "Special Financial Report for the Week Ended December 10, 1937," ibid.; also see a memorandum by Maxwell Hamilton, September 20, 1937, *Foreign Relations, 1937*, 3:533–34 for confirmation of the view that Japan, although undergoing economic stresses, would not be forced to abandon the military venture in China.

out a successful campaign, but would be dependent on foreign capital for the development of the subdued territories. Based on this analysis, the United States could not be certain that the Japanese would be able to seriously interfere with the open door in China.

Japanese actions in early 1938 soon undercut this line of reasoning. In the middle of January, Japan's decision to sever relations with China ended any hope of a negotiated settlement.[13] The Japanese armed forces, moreover, continued their offensive which, by the beginning of June, placed them in control of the key seaboard and railway communications that stretched from the Amur River on the Siberian border to the Yangtze River in Central China. As the Japanese extended their control over these areas, they erected puppet governments in North and Central China and initiated aggressive economic programs.[14] In North China, they established a Reserve Bank which began to issue its own notes in an attempt to displace the Chinese legal tender. Japan's primary objective was to replace the Chinese yuan with a currency tied to the yen, which would then provide the monetary basis for an economic bloc. Japanese officials exchanged Reserve Bank notes for yuan which they then took to the Shanghai exchange market to use for the purchase of foreign currency. This process served both to provide backing for the new notes and to weaken the Chinese currency. The latter accentuated inflation within China and provided a convenient excuse for Chinese officials to adopt a system of foreign exchange rationing in the spring of 1938.[15]

13. For a lengthy discussion of the Japanese attempts to achieve a settlement, see Borg, *The United States and the Far Eastern Crisis of 1933–1938*, pp. 442–85.

14. A. Viola Smith, "Present Trends of Japanese Economic Penetration in China," June 29, 1938, Reports of Commercial Attaché, Peiping, File No. 128–X Peiping, RG 151.

15. A. Bland Calder, SR No. S–37, "Finance, Currency and Banking in China in 1938," February 6, 1939, File No. 128–X Peiping, RG 151; A. Bland Calder, SR No. S–7, "The Currency Phase of Sino-Japanese Hostilities," September 12, 1938, File No. 600, China, 1938, ibid.; A. Bland Calder, SR No. S–20, "Comments on the Japanese Reply of November 18 to the American Note of October 6, with Regard to the Currency and Exchange Features," November 26, 1938, ibid. For a discussion of monetary conditions within China during the early part of 1938 and the reasons behind the adoption of foreign exchange rationing, see Arthur N. Young, *China and the Helping Hand, 1937–1945*, pp. 63–65.

Japan hoped to make North China into a virtual domestic market by creating a currency bloc in which the new Reserve Bank notes and the yen would be nearly equal in value. By controlling the exchange rates, the Japanese depreciated the value of the yuan with respect to foreign currencies other than the yen. The Chinese in North China consequently had to pay more yuan for all imports except from Japan. By November 1938, there was a 44 percent price differential in favor of Japanese goods. Japanese control of the exchange rates allowed them to purchase goods from North China without having to provide foreign exchange at a fixed (and unfavorable) rate. The objective of this currency manipulation and trade control apparently was the exclusion of all non-Japanese traders from the occupied areas.[16]

The Japanese also revised tariff levels to favor their commerce; and, in a move which held ominous overtones for Western interests, they created two large development companies to monopolize the basic industries in North and Central China. By means of subsidiaries, the development companies would control the railroads, communications, utilities, mines, and heavy industries in each area. According to A. Viola Smith, the American trade commissioner in Shanghai, although foreigners would be allowed to purchase stock in these companies, the Japanese would exert every influence to manipulate foreign capital so that Japan remained dominant in China. As Smith noted, with the creation of these monopolies, the open door was in danger of being "banged, barred, and bolted."[17]

Throughout the summer and fall of 1938, concern about these and other Japanese actions caused American statesmen to respond in several ways. Because the Japanese repeatedly bombed

16. A. Bland Calder, SR No. S–20, "Comments on the Japanese Reply of November 18," November 26, 1938, File No. 600, China, 1938, RG 151; Arthur Young outlines some of the difficulties that handicapped the Japanese currency scheme but agrees that by the end of 1938, the Japanese-supported notes were circulating in North China, see Young, *China and the Helping Hand*, pp. 66–69; A Bland Calder, SR No. S–26, "China Annual Economic Report for 1938," January 30, 1938, File No. 128–S Peiping, RG 151.

17. A. Viola Smith, "Present Trends of Japanese Economic Penetration in China," June 29, 1938, File No. 128–X Peiping, Reports of the Commercial Attaché, Peiping, ibid.

civilian areas in China, Hull announced in June that the American government would discourage the sale of aircraft and aircraft parts to countries which persisted in this practice. The State Department quickly received the cooperation of American business groups and by July, this "moral embargo" was about 95 percent effective. In conjunction with the effort to halt the sale of aircraft, the Department of Commerce began to discourage exporters and manufacturers from extending private credits to Japan.[18] No matter how effective these moves were, they lacked legal sanction and consequently did not make the American government an active participant in an attempt to contain Japan.

The continued interference by Japanese authorities with American property and rights, however, led the U. S. government to lodge a formal complaint against Japan. On October 6, 1938, the American ambassador to Japan, Joseph C. Grew, delivered a note to the Japanese Prime Minister and Minister for Foreign Affairs, Prince Fumimaro Konoye, in which he criticized Japan for violating the principles of the open door policy. Grew stated at the time of the occupation of Manchuria, Japan had promised to maintain the open door. Instead, the Japanese had taken over the principal economic activities in the area and had forced a large part of American enterprise to withdraw. Through the use of exchange control, Japan had allowed goods to move freely between Manchuria and itself, but had restricted trade between Manchuria and other areas. In light of this situation, the U. S. government had become apprehensive, "less there develop in other areas of China which have been occupied by Japanese military forces since the beginning of the present hostilities a situation similar in its adverse effect upon the competitive position of American business to that which now exists in Manchuria." To prevent this, the American government asked Japan to discontinue its discriminatory exchange control and its creation of monopolies or preferential bodies. The United States

18. Hull to Grew, June 11, 1938, *Foreign Relations, 1938*, 3:617; see also a copy of a letter sent to those companies involved in the sale of aircraft, July 1, 1938, *Foreign Relations: Japan*, 2:201–2; memorandum of conversation between Leighton Rogers, president of the Aeronautical Chamber of Commerce, and Charles Yost, July 26, 1938, *Foreign Relations, 1938*, 3:621–22; Aide-Mémoire, Department of State to British Embassy, November 9, 1938, ibid., pp. 625–26.

further requested that the Japanese stop interfering with the property and rights of its nationals in China.[19]

Although the "moral embargo" and the note of October 6 did alert Japan to America's uneasiness about the course of events in the Far East, they were not as important as the steps Washington took to strengthen China. Secretary Morgenthau had continued his purchases of Chinese silver, buying 50 million ounces in March and April 1938. For the first time, the U. S. allowed China to use the proceeds from silver purchases for purposes other than currency stabilization. As a result, the Chinese were able to acquire enough American exchange to pay for their military purchases. This program in itself, however, proved to be inadequate; China's silver supply was dwindling, and the Chinese government needed large credits to buy strategic materials.[20]

By July, several American officials had concluded that it would be in the general interest of the United States to provide extensive assistance to China. Warren Pierson held this opinion and thought that the Export-Import Bank could be of service. He met with Stanley Hornbeck, who was then serving as the State Department's political adviser, to discuss the feasibility of some bank action along these lines. Both men believed that the United States was justified in helping China attain objectives that also would be to America's advantage. If U. S. aid could keep China from collapsing, American interests, as well as those of the Chinese, would benefit. Pierson and Hornbeck realized that if the United States chose to act in this manner, the political aspects of any financial transaction would be more important than the commercial ones.[21] In other words, the Export-Import Bank could participate in transactions of questionable economic value provided the advantages for American foreign policy were great enough.

19. Grew to Konoye, October 6, 1938, *Foreign Relations: Japan*, 1:785–90. The note dealt with the problems the two men had discussed three days earlier; see Oral Statement, Grew to Fumimaro Konoye, October 3, 1938, ibid., pp. 782–85.

20. Blum, *From the Morgenthau Diaries*, 1:508–9, 2:58; also see Everest, *Morgenthau, the New Deal and Silver*, p. 121; Young, *China and the Helping Hand*, p. 61.

21. Memorandum by Hornbeck, July 15, 1938, *Foreign Relations, 1938*, 3:538–40.

In part at the urging of William Bullitt, who was then ambassador to France, Roosevelt decided that the United States should do everything possible to assist in the sale of flour and grey goods to the Chinese government. In early August, he ordered the Treasury Department to pursue the matter with the departments of state and agriculture and, if necessary, the Reconstruction Finance Corporation, the Commodity Credit Corporation, and the Export-Import Bank. Morgenthau and Secretary of Agriculture Henry Wallace had favored a similar plan two months earlier, but Hull had then opposed it unless the administration made an identical offer to Japan. In August, however, the secretary of state agreed to give the matter full consideration. Nevertheless, the American government postponed a final decision until the arrival of a group of Chinese financiers who had been invited to confer with officials in the Treasury Department.[22]

Morgenthau was extremely eager to do something to help the Chinese and thought that this mission represented the last opportunity to keep Japan from completely dominating the western Pacific. In a conversation with Herbert Feis and Maxwell Hamilton, chief of the State Department's Division of Far Eastern Affairs, Morgenthau learned that these officials would try to persuade Hull to approve any promising proposal. The Chinese delegation, headed by K. P. Chen, a prominent Shanghai banker, arrived near the end of September. Chen quicked informed Morgenthau that China no longer sought what were essentially relief loans (that is, money to be used for cotton and wheat) but wanted more substantive assistance.[23]

Japan's military successes undoubtedly played a major role in governing the change in China's requests. By October 1938,

22. Bullitt to Roosevelt, August 8, 1938, ibid., pp. 544–45; Roosevelt to Roswell Magill, August 16, 1938, Franklin D. Roosevelt Papers (Franklin D. Roosevelt Library, Hyde Park, New York); Blum, *From the Morgenthau Diaries*, 1:508; memoranda by Hull, August 11 and September 15, 1938, *Foreign Relations, 1938*, 3:546, 559.

23. Morgenthau Diaries, Book 142, p. 176, Henry Morgenthau, Jr. Papers (Franklin D. Roosevelt Library, Hyde Park, New York); memorandum by Herbert Feis, September 22, 1938, *Foreign Relations, 1938*, 3:562–63; Morgenthau Diaries, Book 142, p. 179, Morgenthau Papers. Young discusses the background, from the Chinese perspective, of K. P. Chen's trip and notes that the Chinese hoped to receive currency and commodity support, see Young, *China and the Helping Hand*, pp. 77–79.

Japan controlled all of the large Chinese seaports except Canton, which soon came under attack. The Japanese gains had left China with only three main links to the outside world. One, a highway running from northwest China into Russia, was of little importance as far as American aid was concerned. The second was a railroad from the port of Haiphong through French Indo-China into southwestern China. But since the French were susceptible to Japanese pressure, they were liable to restrict the flow of goods at Tokyo's request. In addition, the railroad had a limited carrying capacity. The final link was the Burma-Yunnan highway which would be ready for use by the end of the year. The road was 650 miles long and was scheduled to be macadamized for all-weather traffic. This route had many advantages over the Indo-China railroad, especially since the United States could count on the cooperation of the English and Burmese governments.[24] China, therefore, had become largely dependent upon truck transportation. To ensure that this system functioned smoothly, she needed adequate supplies of trucks, spare parts, gasoline, and lubricating oils. A primary objective of the Chen mission was to obtain American technical and material assistance for the development of China's truck transportation network.[25]

Roosevelt was aware of China's difficult situation. The president told Chen, above all else "get your transportation organized." To help with the organization, Roosevelt agreed to ask the army to send the Chinese a new military attaché who also happened to be the army's leading expert on transportation. The Americans would place this officer at Chen's disposal.[26] Of greater significance was the tentative arrangement worked out within the Treasury Department in the middle of October. Un-

24. A. Bland Calder, SR No. S–34, "Resume of Military and Political Events in China in 1938," January 24, 1939, File No. 128–X Peiping, RG 151; A. Bland Calder, "New Problems in Maintaining Trade Access Between Chinese Controlled Territory and the Outside World," December 13, 1938, File No. 128–X Peiping, Reports of Commercial Attaché, Hong Kong, ibid.; Henry Morgenthau, Jr. to Roosevelt, December 13, 1938, PSF: China, 1938–1940, Roosevelt Papers.

25. A. Bland Calder, "New Problems in Maintaining Access between Chinese Controlled Territory and the Outside World," December 13, 1938, File No. 128–X Peiping, Reports of Commercial Attaché, Hong Kong, RG 151.

26. Morgenthau Diaries, Book 145, p. 387, Morgenthau Papers.

der this plan, the Chinese government would sell tung oil (needed for paint) to a syndicate of U. S. consumers and would use the proceeds of the sales to purchase American trucks, oil products, and other essential materials. The tung oil sales would extend over a five-year period; but because the Chinese wanted funds immediately, the Treasury Department proposed that the Export-Import Bank loan them 50 percent of the value of the oil they ultimately would deliver. The Chinese government would work through a corporation (Universal Trading Corporation) it had established in the United States to buy materials and to sell Chinese goods.[27]

To help the Chinese Nationalists with technical advice on the best way to ship petroleum products and tung oil into and out of the country, Morgenthau contacted members of the California-Texas Oil Company and the Socony-Vacuum Company to solicit their assistance in organizing China's transportation system. The Treasury Department, moreover, got in touch with the major truck companies to secure their cooperation in lowering prices and making suitable modifications so that the trucks would function properly in the tropics. By October 17, Morgenthau had found solutions for the transportation problems and had received bids for trucks and servicing equipment.[28]

The secretary of the treasury was an enthusiastic supporter of the proposal and believed that the United States stood to gain both commercially and politically from the transaction. U. S. oil companies would be able to "practically get a monopoly for American oil products" in China. In addition, American businessmen would obtain "a complete monopoly on Chinese tung oil," all of which would come to them for redistribution to the world market. Besides these direct economic gains, the United States would obtain China's good will. "The potential economic development of China is admittedly enormous," the secretary reasoned, "and if this country helps China in her time of need, resulting benefit to American trade and business can be counted upon in the years to come." The transaction, furthermore, would provide the Chinese with the outside assistance they needed to continue their struggle against Japan. Whereas a small Ameri-

27. Blum, *From the Morgenthau Diaries*, 2:58–59.
28. Morgenthau Diaries, Book 144, pp. 279, 282–83, 285; Book 145, pp. 248–50; Book 146, p. 66, Morgenthau Papers.

can loan would enable China to fight for a long time, the United States would have to spend far greater sums on naval expansion if China fell. Consequently, Morgenthau insisted that an advance to the Chinese government of the cost of a new battleship was a sound venture even if China could not repay the loan. Continued American inaction had the further disadvantage of aiding communism. "The situation is," the secretary concluded, "no country in the world is giving them [the Chinese] any help except Russia, and in return for that, Russia is just sending their people in and taking control of everything. Is it [the tung oil deal] good business, or anything?"[29]

Not everyone in the Treasury Department, however, thought the transaction was good business. Wayne Taylor, an assistant secretary, argued that the extension of credit from an agency of the American government to a belligerent would signify that the United States favored one combatant over the other. The nuance of loaning to the Chinese government-owned corporation would not alter the fundamentals. Because he believed the transaction would involve responsible officers in a series of acts leading to the use of government funds for financial aid to a belligerent, Taylor opposed extending such credits unless the American people specifically requested them. In the absence of a request, "any executive officer of this Government would stretch to the breaking point any authority hitherto delegated to him by Congress" if he approved credits for combatants engaged in declared or undeclared war.[30]

Despite Taylor's opinion, the tung oil deal moved toward completion. On October 24, Jesse H. Jones notified Morgenthau that the Export-Import Bank was prepared to extend a credit of $20 million to the Universal Trading Corporation.[31] On the following day, Morgenthau went to Roosevelt to obtain his acceptance of the proposal but events in China prompted Roosevelt to withhold approval. Within the preceding three or four days, the Japanese had seized Hankow and Canton, triggering

29. Ibid., Book 144, pp. 282–300; Book 150, pp. 213–16; Book 153, pp. 302–3.
30. Memorandum from Wayne Taylor to Morgenthau, October 20, 1938, attached to Hull to Roosevelt, November 14, 1938, PSF: China, 1938–1940, Roosevelt Papers.
31. Copy of a letter from Jesse H. Jones to Morgenthau, October 24, 1938, OFF 971 Export-Import Bank, 1937–1945, ibid.

rumors that Chiang Kai-shek's government would collapse. Roosevelt thought that it would be embarrassing to make a loan and then be confronted with a new provisional government. Because of the changed situation, he decided to delay and see what statement Chiang Kai-shek made. If the Chinese leader announced that the Nationalists had pulled out of Hankow and Canton for strategic reasons and that he would regroup his forces, and if he could convince the world that his government would not fall, then Roosevelt would be "very glad to promptly approve this loan."[32]

In early November, Roosevelt received satisfactory assurances from Chiang Kai-shek that he would continue to oppose the Japanese. Nonetheless, before Roosevelt approved of the tung oil transaction, he asked Morgenthau to clear the plan with Hull.[33] This request precipitated a full-scale discussion within the State Department about the implications of the deal for America's Far Eastern policy.

In a memorandum written on November 13, Maxwell Hamilton expressed disapproval of the tung oil project. Although he did not wish to see Japan defeat China, he believed that the proposal was impractical and would not have much effect on the outcome of the struggle. To assist China once Japan had nearly completed its positional warfare, Hamilton wrote, "would be of no decisive aid to China and would be a profitless irritant to Japan, *unless the United States is prepared to give really substantial and long-continued assistance to China.* And if that decision be made, it should be made with realization that the course may lead to armed conflict with Japan." Rather than assisting China, he favored a long-range program of applying pressure on Japan. Such action would be of little consequence in the current struggle, but it might produce a situation in which the United States would enjoy a measure of equality of treatment. Finally, this policy would not risk a war.[34]

32. Morgenthau Diaries, Book 147, pp. 435–36, Morgenthau Papers.
33. Ibid., Book 150, p. 200.
34. Emphasis in original, memorandum by Hamilton, November 13, 1938, File No. 893.51/6736 2/8, General Records of the Department of State, RG 59 (National Archives, Washington, D.C.). The memorandum is reprinted without Hamilton's emphasis marks in *Foreign Relations, 1938,* 3:569–72.

Writing on the following day, Stanley Hornbeck addressed himself to the foreign policy aspects of the tung oil project. He argued that it was in the interest of the United States that Japan not gain control of China. Hornbeck warned that unless some other nation stopped the Japanese, the United States and Japan would have a face-to-face confrontation. In an attempt to avert this possibility, he recommended that the American government adopt a plan to halt Japan's advance. A program of this type necessitated the use of material obstacles and pressures, but, if all else failed, it could require the use of armed force. Emphasizing that the United States had to use something stronger than words to achieve its goal, Hornbeck suggested that the American government extend aid to the Chinese while withholding from the Japanese those items which aided their military effort. Accordingly, he proposed the denunciation of the United States-Japan Commercial Treaty of 1911, the placing of embargoes on trade and shipping between Japan and the United States, and the disposal of the fleet in the Pacific. Although the tung oil project would provide assistance to China, Hornbeck advised against it unless the American government was prepared to adopt a comprehensive program similar to the one he had outlined. Hornbeck personally endorsed the adoption of a firm policy and, for that reason, hoped the administration would undertake the proposed transaction.[35]

Hull added the final comments to the debate. Although he too did not want to see Japan overrun China, he was wary about provoking the Japanese. And since he regarded the tung oil deal as being "almost purely political" in nature, he assumed that the transaction would lead to increased Japanese retaliation against American interests in China and perhaps even to war. With so much at stake, Hull did not think that the United States should follow the new policy unless the American people and Congress supported it. Refusing to approve the proposal, the secretary recommended that the administration refrain from any action for a few months and await further developments.[36] On November 15, based on Hull's opposition, Roosevelt postponed making

35. Memorandum by Hornbeck, November 14, 1938, *Foreign Relations, 1938*, 3:572–74.
36. Memorandum by Hull, November 14, 1938, ibid., pp. 574–75.

a decision on the tung oil project. Clearly disturbed by the turn of events, he told Morgenthau he would discuss the matter with Hull.[37]

The great importance which American policymakers attributed to this proposal is significant. They saw it as an overt step by the United States to support China against Japan. Moreover, both Hamilton and Hornbeck believed that it could be effective only as part of a general program to strengthen China and to restrict Japan. All three observers saw the project as the first step in a chain of events which ultimately could lead to a military confrontation between the United States and Japan. If at any time in the future the United States undertook the tung oil transaction, it would be logical to assume that this action represented a hardening of America's Far Eastern policy and that the administration realized the decision involved the risk of war.

Throughout November 1938, the Japanese further clarified their intentions in the Far East. On November 3, the Japanese government announced that it planned to establish a "new order" in East Asia based on a tripartite relationship between Japan, Manchuria, and China. The primary objectives of this relationship were to promote political stability and to facilitate economic cooperation between the three countries. Japan called on the other powers to adapt their policies to the new conditions prevailing in East Asia. In his reply to the American note of October 6, Japanese Foreign Minister Hachiro Arita gave a further indication of the meaning of the "new order." While refuting the American complaints, Arita failed to give assurances that Japan supported the principles of the open door policy. Although the Japanese had always given such assurances in the past, the foreign minister now announced that the new conditions in East Asia demanded new principles and concepts.[38]

On November 19, Arita called on the counselor of the American embassy to discuss Japan's situation in the Far East. There were two ways, he maintained, in which one nation could try to subdue another—military force and economic sanctions. The "new order" would provide Japan with the necessary raw ma-

37. Morgenthau Diaries, Book 151, p. 19A, Morgenthau Papers.
38. Statement by Japanese government and radio speech by Prince Konoye, November 3, 1938, *Foreign Relations: Japan*, 1:477–81; Hachiro Arita to Grew, November 18, 1938, ibid., pp. 797–800.

terials and markets to protect herself against the second possibility. The Japanese had to monopolize various sectors of the Chinese economy in order to attain the same degree of economic freedom which the United States and British empire received from their vast internal markets. Once secure, Japan would guarantee the equality of economic opportunity for others. Arita asserted that Japan no longer could guarantee the open door because she could not reconcile her actual needs and objectives with the principles of this policy. As a consequence, he hoped nations could arrive at a new definition of the open door.[39] With this declaration, Japan issued an outright challenge to the historic Far Eastern policy of the United States. If American leaders acquiesced to the Japanese demands, U. S. interests in East Asia would fall under the control of Japan.

On November 21, Grew informed Arita that the United States would continue to adhere to the principle of equality of commerical opportunity. If all nations observed this principle, he assured Arita, peace and general prosperity would result. Grew further argued that the American government believed "it to be incompatible with the establishment and maintenance of American and world prosperity that any country should endeavor to establish a preferred position for itself in another country." The United States, in addition, opposed attempts by one nation to impose its will upon others.[40]

Morgenthau, meanwhile, continued to seek Roosevelt's approval for the tung oil project. At the end of November, Hull departed for the Lima conference leaving Undersecretary Sumner Welles in charge of the State Department. In an arrangement whereby Morgenthau agreed to help Welles in his dealings with Cuba, the undersecretary promised to talk with Roosevelt about China. After calling the president, Welles told Morgenthau that the deal would go through. The following day, November 30, Roosevelt repeated this decision to Morgenthau.[41]

The situation quickly became more complicated. The same

39. Memorandum by E. H. Dooman, November 19, 1938, ibid., pp. 801–6.

40. Oral statement, Grew to Arita, November 21, 1938, ibid., pp. 808–11.

41. Morgenthau Diaries, Book 153, pp. 300–2, 366–67, Morgenthau Papers.

day Morgenthau received the go-ahead signal from Roosevelt, Welles recommended a postponement of the tung oil project until December 6, when the president (who had left Washington) would return. Having learned that the Japanese government was going to determine which countries it would allow to trade with China, the undersecretary suggested that the United States might wish to state its position clearly, as well as initiate economic actions that would pressure Japan. The administration could include the tung oil transaction as part of its new course of action, but Welles preferred that any decision on an active policy await Roosevelt's return.[42]

The State Department also expressed concern about a particular aspect of the transaction. Because the deal involved the cooperation of the Chinese and American governments to create a virtual monopoly on tung oil exports, it might violate the Nine Power Treaty and the Sino-American Treaty of 1844. To bypass this objection, the treasury arranged to keep both governments out of the contract and to have the contract provide for the purchase of only that proportion of China's tung oil production which the United States had purchased in 1937. Welles explained that the State Department was cautious because the United States was coming squarely to an issue with Japan on whether the Nine Power Treaty was still in force, and the department did not want Japan to have any violation by America to which it could point. A final complication arose on December 4 when Hull indicated that he could not endorse the proposed transaction.[43]

Despite these last-minute snags, the final decision lay with Roosevelt who, since the fall of 1937, had considered a number of ways the United States could try to restrain Japan. The president's predisposition to act, moreover, probably accounted for his willingness to override Hull on this important decision.[44] In

42. Ibid., pp. 366–67.

43. As the entire thrust of America's opposition to Japan was based on the latter's violation of treaties, the Department of State's concern about not violating the Nine Power Treaty and the Sino-American Treaty was quite understandable, Morgenthau Diaries, Book 154, p. 347; Book 155, pp. 76, 116–18, Morgenthau Papers; for Hull's attitude, see Hull to Welles, December 4, 1938, *Foreign Relations, 1938*, 3:577.

44. See Haight, "Roosevelt and a Naval Quarantine of Japan," pp. 203–26; Pratt, "The Anglo-American Naval Conversations on the Far East of January, 1938," pp. 745–63.

any event, when the president came back to the White House, he approved the transaction. On December 13, the Export-Import Bank agreed to extend a credit of $25 million to the Universal Trading Corporation with the understanding that China would repay the credit over a five-year period from the proceeds of the tung oil sales. On December 15, the R.F.C. issued a press release announcing the agreement but describing it as a commercial transaction.[45] To forestall a possible attack on the credit by Senator Arthur Vandenberg of Michigan, a leading isolationist, Morgenthau arranged to have influential individuals from the automobile industry make the senator aware of the benefits which the bank's action had for his state.[46] Four days after the R.F.C.'s announcement, the Treasury Department disclosed that it had extended beyond December 31, 1938, the arrangement of July 9, 1937, which had allowed the Central Bank of China to obtain dollar exchange for stabilization purposes.[47]

With these measures, particularly the Export-Import Bank credit, U. S. officials moved to strengthen China and thus to check Japanese expansion. These steps represented a toughening of policy and indicated that the American government would use material pressure to preserve the open door. As a further clarification of this point, Grew notified Arita on December 30 that the people and government of the United States could not assent to the establishment by any third country of a regime that could deprive them of the long established principle of

45. Agreement between the Export-Import Bank and the Universal Trading Corporation, December 13, 1938, Project No. 217, Universal Trading Corporation, Records of the Export-Import Bank of Washington, RG 275 (National Archives, Washington, D.C.); Welles to Grew, December 15, 1938, *Foreign Relations, 1938*, 3:586–87. Welles thought that by treating the project as an independent and self-contained commercial transaction, the government would not appear to be embarking on an anti-Japanese path. Hull, however, did not believe "that the arrangement would be accepted by American opinion as an isolated commercial transaction and Japanese Government circles will certainly not so regard." Welles to Hull, December 2, 1938, ibid., pp. 575–76; Hull to Welles, December 4, 1938, ibid., p. 577.

46. Morgenthau wanted to do the same thing for the state of Ohio, which would benefit from a large purchase of tires, Morgenthau Diaries, Book 157, p. 211, Morgenthau Papers.

47. Press Release by Treasury Department, December 19, 1938, *Foreign Relations, 1938*, 3:588.

equal opportunity and fair treatment. America's adherence to this principle did not flow solely from a desire to obtain commercial benefits. Rather, the ambassador asserted, the United States had a firm conviction that observance of the equality of opportunity concept would lead to "economic and political stability, which are conducive both to the internal well-being of nations and to mutually beneficial and peaceful relationships between and among nations," as well as to "the opening of trade channels thereby making available the markets, the raw materials and the manufactured products of the community of nations on a mutually and reciprocally beneficial basis." If new situations required any alteration of existing treaties, nations could make changes through the orderly process of negotiation and agreement.[48]

The action by the Export-Import Bank was significant on several counts. Although the amount of the credit was not large enough to be a determining factor in China's struggle with Japan, its importance, both in material and symbolic terms, far transcended its face value. The step which the American government took established a precedent for others to follow. On December 20, the British government announced the extension of a small export credit to China to finance the purchase of trucks, and intimated that further credits would be forthcoming.[49] Chinese leaders reported that, in all, they were able to secure $75 million on the basis of the $25 million which they obtained from the United States.[50]

In addition, the Export-Import Bank's support of the tung oil transaction helped strengthen China. It provided assistance for the Chinese transportation network, which was vital to that nation's ability to continue resisting; and it came at a moment when China faced the prospect of having to curtail sharply foreign purchases due to the depletion of overseas assets. In other

48. Grew to Arita, December 30, 1938, *Foreign Relations: Japan*, 1:820–26.

49. F. C. Jones, *Japan's New Order in East Asia*, p. 139; Young, *China and the Helping Hand*, pp. 84–85. (There is some disagreement between these two over the size of the credit: Jones indicates that it was £450,000 while Young has it as £500,000.) In March 1939, Britain provided a £10 million exchange stabilization fund, see Jones, *Japan's New Order in East Asia*, p. 147.

50. Morgenthau Diaries, Book 156, p. 228, Morgenthau Papers; memorandum by Hull, June 21, 1939, *Foreign Relations, 1939*, 3:675–76.

words, it helped fill the gap left by the exhaustion of China's financial resources. The credit also had an inspirational effect on the Chinese. Nelson Johnson, the ambassador to China, reported that in the aftermath of the bank's action, Chinese morale was at an all-time high so that he doubted Japan would be able to complete the conquest of China. The American aid, furthermore, encouraged the Chinese to believe that more assistance would follow, since the West would not tolerate a Japanese victory.[51]

The Japanese response to the Export-Import Bank credit was another indication of the agreement's significance. While stating that he did not interpret the credit as an unfriendly act, Arita said he regretted the American move which, he believed, would serve only to prolong the hostilities. Nevertheless, Grew noticed that the tone and atmosphere of Arita's conversation were far more conciliatory than in earlier talks. Japanese army officers, moreover, realized that the U. S. aid could become an important element in enabling China to continue the struggle, especially as the combatants began to rely on economic and financial weapons instead of military ones.[52]

The Export-Import Bank and the Universal Trading Corporation signed the final contract in February, 1939, and by May 1, American manufacturers had delivered over 1,300 trucks to Rangoon for use on the Burma Road. Within two or three months, however, Chinese officials asked the United States for additional financial assistance. To repel the Japanese invaders, China needed a large influx of strategic materials and support for its currency system.[53] Although Roosevelt expressed an interest in the Chinese requests, by the fall of 1939, there was little he

51. Young, *China and the Helping Hand*, p. 85; for the ambassador's reaction, see Ickes, *Secret Diary of Harold L. Ickes*, 2:563; Arthur N. Young, *China's Wartime Finance and Inflation, 1937–1945*, p. 103; Jones, *Japan's New Order in East Asia*, p. 140.

52. Grew to Hull, December 19, 1938, *Foreign Relations, 1938*, 3:589–90; Joseph C. Grew, *Turbulent Era*, 2:1208–9; Jones, *Japan's New Order in East Asia*, p. 140.

53. Agreement between Export-Import Bank and Universal Trading Corporation, February 8, 1939, Project No. 217, Universal Trading Corporation, RG 275; Arthur Brady to Hull, May 1, 1939, *Foreign Relations, 1939*, 3:751–52; memorandum by Hull, June 21, 1939, ibid., pp. 675–76; Kung to State Department, July 18, 1939, ibid., p. 692; Bullitt to Hull, July 26, 1939, ibid., pp. 692–94; Hu Shih to Hull, July 29, 1939, ibid., pp. 695–97; Bullitt to Hull, September 13, 1939, ibid., pp. 710–11; Chiang Kai-shek to Roosevelt, December 19, 1939, ibid., p. 717.

could do. The shortage of unallocated funds had severely restricted the bank's activities. In addition, the outbreak of fighting in Europe shifted the administration's attention throughout the remainder of the year to both Europe and Latin America. With the expansion of the bank's lending capacity in 1940, American policymakers opened credits to China totaling $95 million which could be used for the purchase of U. S. goods and to promote currency stabilization.[54]

The bank's action in China in late 1938 helps illuminate a shift in U. S. policy in the Far East. Prior to the Japanese invasion of North China, the bank had been primarily concerned with furthering the expansion of American commercial interests. The Japanese attack created a new situation because it endangered direct American material interests and threatened to destroy the existing framework of Far Eastern relations. U. S. policymakers responded to this threat by providing assistance for China in the belief that by so doing, they would protect this nation's immediate and future interests. Thus, foreign policy considerations, not direct commercial ones, provided the major impetus for the bank's action. The move by the Export-Import Bank contained an implicit warning to Japan that Washington would not redefine or modify its traditional open door policy. Since Hull, Hornbeck, and Hamilton understood that the credit could initiate a chain of events that ultimately would lead to war, they attached a great deal of importance to the measure. As Hornbeck noted, if the United States wanted to protect its interest in China, it would have to resort to the use of weapons stronger than verbal arguments.[55] The Export-Import Bank credit represented one such weapon, as did the severing of the United States-Japan Commercial Treaty of 1911 (on July 26, 1939, Hull notified the Japanese that America would terminate the treaty six months hence) and the other economic sanctions instituted by

54. For an indication of Roosevelt's continued interest in aiding China, see U.S. Congress, Senate, Subcommittee to Investigate the Administration of the Internal Security Act and Other Security Laws of the Judiciary, *Morgenthau Diary (China)*, 89th Cong., 1st sess., 1965, 1:14–16 (as noted in chap. 7, the bank's actions in Latin America were similarly affected by the shortage of funds); Hawthorne Arey, "History of Operations and Policies of Export-Import Bank of Washington," mimeograph, pp. 30, 37–38, 46.

55. Memorandum by Hornbeck, November 14, 1938, *Foreign Relations, 1938*, 3:572–74.

the United States during the period leading to December 7, 1941.[56]

Japan's actions in November 1938 help explain why the administration acted when it did. For the first time, Japan officially had indicated that it would not give assurances as to the preservation of the open door. The initiative then swung to the United States, which could either acquiesce in the Japanese claims or try to uphold the old policy. The bank credit, coupled with Grew's statements of November 21 and December 30, demonstrated that the United States would attempt to sustain its historic Far Eastern policy. By financing the sale of trucks and petroleum products, the Export-Import Bank provided China with important assistance. This action represented the first material pressure the United States government took as it moved to restrain the post-1937 Japanese expansion and thereby safeguard American interests in China.[57]

56. Hull to Kensuke Horinouchi, July 26, 1939, *Foreign Relations: Japan*, 2:189. For an indication of the State Department's reasoning behind the decision to end the trade treaty, see Hamilton, "Narrative of Developments Leading to the Giving of Notice by the United States of an Intention to Terminate the Japanese-American Commercial Treaty of 1911," File No. 711.942/627, RG 59. Hornbeck had recommended all of these actions, as well as some others, see memorandum by Hornbeck, November 14, 1938, *Foreign Relations, 1938*, 3:572–74.

57. During December 1938, the Department of State also carefully considered the possibility of instituting a comprehensive program of economic retaliation against Japan, but concluded that such a plan was too risky at that time. Instead, it recommended that the government continue to discourage credits and loans to Japan and make preparations for the severance of the Treaty of 1911. The consensus was that these steps would not lead to Japanese counteractions, but still would clear the decks for future action. See memorandum by Francis B. Sayre, December 5, 1938, *Foreign Relations, 1938*, 3:406–9; Hornbeck presented his analysis of the memorandum, Hornbeck to Sayre, December 22, 1938, ibid., pp. 425–27.

9

Conclusion

The changing nature of the bank's operations did not go unnoticed by members of Congress. Republican leaders, concerned about the loans to China and Haiti, accused Roosevelt of using the lending powers of the Export-Import Bank to extend U. S. influence abroad. In February 1939, Senator Robert Taft recommended that the institution no longer handle transactions with foreign governments. Arguing along similar lines, Jesse P. Wolcott, head of a special committee of House Republicans, insisted that the bank was potentially dangerous because it could involve the nation in foreign entanglements without having to obtain the consent of Congress.[1]

The rising tide of opposition created two interrelated problems for the administration. First, because the bank's charter was due to lapse in early 1939, Congress would have an opportunity to decide on the institution's future. Secondly, critics who opposed extending loans to foreign governments were attacking an aspect of the bank's operations which American policymakers had recently concluded was a necessary response to disturbed world conditions. Anticipating some of the complaints, Jesse Jones tried to avoid an open debate in Congress by proposing a $125 million loan ceiling. After the Republicans made their charges, Cordell Hull defended the bank as a valuable tool in assisting the nation's foreign commerce. The onset of troubled

1. *New York Times*, February 15, 1939, p. 26; U.S. Congress, Senate, Committee on Banking and Currency, *Hearings, To Continue the Functions of the Commodity Credit Corporation, the Export-Import Bank of Washington, and the Reconstruction Finance Corporation*, 76th Cong., 1st sess., 1939, pp. 37–39; *New York Times*, February 20, 1939, p. 2; press release from the Office of Representative Jesse P. Wolcott of Michigan, February 20, 1939, General Correspondence File, Ex-Im Bk., Part 1, General Records of the Reconstruction Finance Corporation, RG 234 (National Archives, Washington, D.C.).

times, he continued, added to the institution's utility. Picking up the thread of Hull's comments, Jones contended that the country should be prepared to offer liberal credits if it expected to retain its share of South American trade.[2] With most Republicans voting against the bank, the House first defeated Wolcott's amendment to force the Export-Import Bank into liquidation and then extended its life for two years. Nevertheless, the House did place a $100 million ceiling on outstanding obligations. The limitation on loans apparently satisfied most critics in the Senate where the House measure passed easily by a voice vote on February 23.[3]

Within a few months, administration leaders discovered that the congressional ceiling severely restricted the scope of the bank's operations. Following his defeat on a $500 million appropriation bill for loans to foreign governments, Roosevelt asked for a $100 million increase in the bank's lending capacity. The Senate passed a slimmed-down version of the request, but Congress adjourned in August 1939 before the House could act on the bill.[4] The outbreak of fighting during September added to the bank's difficulties, placing new demands on its already limited resources. When the extension of a $10 million credit

2. U.S. Congress, Senate, *Hearings, To Continue the Functions of the Commodity Credit Corporation, the Export-Import Bank of Washington, and the Reconstruction Finance Corporation*, pp. 95–96; memorandum by Feis, April 11, 1939, File No. 821.796 SCA 2/428, General Records of the Department of State, RG 59 (National Archives, Washington, D.C.); *New York Times*, February 21, 1939, pp. 1, 6; and February 22, 1939, p. 3; Hull to Jones, February 20, 1939, File No. 811.516 Export-Import Bank/209A, RG 59.

3. The vote on Wolcott's amendment was 114 in favor, 152 opposed; on the bill itself, the vote was 280 in favor, 77 opposed, U.S. Congress, House, *Congressional Record*, 76th Cong., 1st sess., 1939, 84, pt. 2:1694–96; 1702–4; also see *New York Times*, February 24, 1939, p. 3. Because the loan ceiling would limit the actions of the bank, Arthur Vandenberg and Robert Taft did support the bill. U.S. Congress, Senate, *Congressional Record*, 76th Cong., 1st sess., 1939, 84, pt. 2:1818; *New York Times*, February 24, 1939, p. 27.

4. *New York Times*, June 23, 1939, pp. 1, 4; ibid., July 8, 1939, p. 2; ibid., July 11, 1939, p. 1; ibid., August 7, 1939, p. 4; press conference June 22, 1939, RRF 1-P, Press Conferences, January–June 1939, Vol. 13, Box 233, pp. 436, 442, Franklin D. Roosevelt Papers (Franklin D. Roosevelt Library, Hyde Park, New York); Hawthorne Arey, "History of Operations and Policies of Export-Import Bank of Washington," mimeograph, p. 22.

to Finland at the end of the year virtually exhausted the institution's funds, Roosevelt announced that he would renew his bid for a loan appropriation. In March 1940, the president did obtain an additional $100 million, but not before Congress placed further restrictions on the bank. For the first time, the Export-Import Bank had to adhere to the provisions of the Johnson Act and the Neutrality Act of 1939 (which forbade loans for the purchase of items the president classified as implements of war). Moreover, it could not extend new credits of more than $20 million to one country.[5]

The crisis atmosphere accompanying German victories in the spring and summer of 1940, however, enabled bank supporters to decisively defeat their opponents. Administration spokesmen in Congress argued that the expansion of the bank's resources was an essential element of the nation's defense program: by easing economic distress in the hemisphere, the United States could curb the growth of German influence and maintain continental solidarity. "We have the economic sinews," insisted Senator Robert Wagner, "and we have the sympathies of the democratic peoples of the New World. If we fail to act with resolution and with courage, we may some day find ourselves isolated and exposed to attack from our weakest side. We should take this reasonable measure of preparedness now, for ourselves and our American neighbors, against the uncertain future of a war-torn world."[6] Responding to these arguments, Congress passed legislation raising the loan ceiling to $700 million and extended the bank's life until January 1947. The measure also removed the limit on loans to one nation and rescinded the restriction against financing the sale of war materials. According to the provisions of the bill, the Export-Import Bank could furnish credits to foreign governments and their central banks for the development of resources, the attainment of economic

5. *New York Times*, December 11, 1939, pp. 1–5; ibid., December 13, 1939, p. 8; Raymond Aexis Clarke, "Legislative History of the Export-Import Bank of Washington," in *Study of the Export-Import Bank and World Bank*, U.S. Congress, Senate, Committee on Banking and Currency, 83rd Cong., 2nd sess., 1954, p. 17.

6. U.S. Congress, Senate, *Congressional Record*, 76th Cong., 3rd sess., 1940, 86, pt. 11:11769–75; also see pp. 11834–37. Defenders of the bill in the House used similar arguments, see U.S. Congress, House, *Congressional Record*, 76th Cong., 3rd sess., 1940, 86, pt. 11:10690.

stability, and the orderly marketing of products in the Western Hemisphere. Wartime conditions, therefore, enabled the administration to obtain congressional support for the course of action which the bank had adopted in 1938/39.[7]

The new measure ensured that the Export-Import Bank would play a more prominent role in implementing policy decisions than it had in the past; and to this extent, the institution's actions became a signal of the long-term objectives of Washington officials. At the time of the First World War, U. S. policymakers concluded that the world had become an interrelated unit in which the welfare and stability of each segment was dependent on events occurring elsewhere. Individuals who thought in a systematic fashion about America's relation to the world could concur on this point, even though they often disagreed on such tactical questions as the League of Nations, the World Court, and the tariff. Thus, Wilson and Hughes both thought that the acceptance by other nations of a world-wide commercial system based on equality of opportunity was necessary to satisfy the conditions produced by the geographic division of labor. A competitive structure had the additional advantage of eliminating closed trading spheres, which tended to divide the globe into conflicting power blocs. Finally, since governments would not have to provide continuous support for their nationals, an open world would afford maximum freedom for private enterprise.

In arriving at their conclusions, U. S. officials were influenced, but not controlled, by powerful economic interests. Even though policymakers wanted to establish a pattern of international relations that would benefit American interest groups, they expected these groups to abide by the rules. During the 1920s, business and financial leaders occasionally asked the State Department to provide them with the same degree of support which many European governments furnished their nationals. For the most part, the department rejected these requests, noting that to comply with them would violate the concept of equality of commercial opportunity. Secretary Hughes's obser-

7. Donald Rogers, "Survey of Congressional Committee Hearings Concerning the Export-Import Bank of Washington," in *Study of the Export-Import Bank and World Bank*, U.S. Congress, Senate, Committee on Banking and Currency, pp. 40–41; *New York Times*, September 11, 1940, p. 12; September 16, 1940, p. 28; and September 21, 1940, p. 1.

vation that businessmen were so intent on immediate gain that they ignored the long-run implications of their requests accurately summed up the situation.[8] As officials whose duty it was to integrate all aspects of the nation's foreign policy and to think systematically about international affairs, American policymakers viewed events from a perspective which transcended that of any particular interest.[9]

The depression delivered a potentially fatal blow to the American conception of a viable world order. The economic dislocations triggered a series of revolutions in Latin America, aided the Nazis in their drive to gain control of Germany, and precipitated Japan's attack in Manchuria. Because many nations also adopted restrictive trade systems, the globe was in the process of being divided into spheres which, even more ominously, supported hostile ideologies. The increased regimentation of commercial relations was symptomatic of a general trend in which the state came to make decisions in areas once the preserve of private groups.

Confronted by this complicated set of affairs, leaders of the Roosevelt administration adopted new techniques to arrive at what had become traditional goals. The implementation of those programs, nonetheless, significantly redefined the nation's role

8. Hughes to Coolidge, November 8, 1923, *Foreign Relations, 1923,* 2: 717–18.

9. Drawing heavily on the work of Samuel P. Hays, Thomas J. McCormick has presented a highly suggestive analysis of the interplay between interest groups and those individuals in charge of formulating policy. Policymakers viewed their role as one of integrating the wishes and demands of functional units into a cohesive course of action. This study of the Export-Import Bank lends support to McCormick's contention that interest groups usually did not have a decisive impact on decisions. Even when they appeared to, they had influence only because their goals coincided with those of the decisionmakers. See Thomas J. McCormick, "The State of American Diplomatic History," in *The State of American History,* ed. Herbert J. Bass, pp. 127–29; Samuel P. Hays, "Political Parties and the Community-Society Continuum," in *The American Party System,* ed. William Nisbet Chambers and Walter Dean Burnham, pp. 152–81; Samuel P. Hays, "Introduction—The New Organizational Society," in *Building the Organizational Society,* ed. Jerry Israel, pp. 1–15. For a somewhat different interpretation of the bank, see James M. McHale, "The New Deal and the Origins of Public Lending for Foreign Economic Development, 1933–1945" (Ph.D. dissertation, Univ. of Wisconsin, 1970), passim; James M. McHale, "National Planning and Reciprocal Trade," *Prologue* 6 (Fall 1974): 189–99.

in international relations. Through diplomatic negotiations and the reversal of the Republicans' tariff policy, New Dealers hoped to counter the trend toward regional trade arrangements. The Export-Import Bank exemplified these characteristics: it was a product of the drive to revive foreign commerce within a multilateral framework, and its actions expanded the scope of Washington's participation in the international arena. Whereas Hughes and Hoover had opposed linking loans to the export of American goods, the bank required recipients to spend most of their funds in the United States. The Latin American development projects begun in 1938, moreover, increased America's involvement in the political and economic concerns of those nations. In addition, the troubled world conditions at the end of the decade caused the bank to support transactions designed primarily to achieve diplomatic, rather than purely commercial, goals. To maintain a world order compatible with U. S. interests, New Dealers found themselves having to make commitments which far exceeded the ones earlier administrations had been willing to undertake.

An appreciation of the dual nature of the bank is essential for understanding the significance of its actions. The Export-Import Bank offered government support to foreign traders and gave the administration a means of achieving certain foreign policy objectives. Even though the two goals generally reinforced each other, they occasionally were in conflict. The dualism existed from the moment the two original banks began operations. Roosevelt's decision to make the banks entirely government-controlled enterprises almost guaranteed the split. Similarly, the immediate events which led policymakers to create the banks concerned objectives—an accord with the Soviet Union and the promotion of stability in Cuba—that related only indirectly to the expansion of exports. After establishing the institutions, the administration enlarged their duties to include the support of American commerce throughout the world. The Hull-Peek controversy was another example of the dualism: Peek sought to expand exports by any means possible whereas Hull opposed tactics that would violate the unconditional most-favored-nation policy, the heart of his overall approach to international relations.

An analysis of the Export-Import Bank's activities during the 1930s reveals other cases in which the split nature of the bank was significant. From the beginning, exporters wanted the institution to make without-recourse financing a major part of its lending program. This issue arose particularly with respect to the purchase of obligations of a Latin American government or one of its agencies. Although bank officials tended to side with the exporters, State Department officers preferred to retain the existing policy because they feared the diplomatic ramifications of a debtor-creditor relationship between the U. S. government and the government of another American republic. In addition, the department did not want the bank to participate in transactions that would thaw frozen exchanges by establishing preferential trade arrangements. In the case of Russia, the evidence suggests that some exporters were eager to have the bank extend credit but that Washington decided on inaction because of concern over the general course of United States-Soviet relations.

In 1938/39, the State Department reversed itself and began approving without-recourse loans to Latin American governments for development projects and for support of their exchange systems. It did so, however, for a complex set of reasons. By sharply depressing the prices of primary products, the recession in the last part of the decade had produced an unfavorable balance of payments for many nations in the Western Hemisphere. Besides causing internal unrest, this situation increased the attractiveness of Germany's bilateral trade tactics. The outbreak of fighting in Europe further complicated matters by threatening either the destruction or the major transfiguration of normal commercial patterns. These conditions strengthened the argument of those Latin Americans who believed that economic nationalism offered the best path to prosperity. The combined impact of these events was sufficient to prompt the State Department to reappraise its earlier attitude on bank policy. The increased pressure from exporters, therefore, served more to support decisions already made than to produce decisions.

The bank's involvement in China embraced an entirely different set of circumstances from those found in the Latin American and Soviet episodes. Throughout much of the 1920s, the disruption created by the Chinese revolution discouraged U. S. exporters and financiers from undertaking major projects. The Japanese aggression of the early 1930s added to the difficult situation: besides worrying about the Nationalists' attitude toward foreign interests, American policymakers had to determine whether the Chinese could withstand Japanese pressure. The rather murky picture cleared briefly in early 1937 as the Nationalists extended their control in China, stiffened their resistance against Japan, and sought external assistance for development projects. To achieve the last objective, Chinese officials expressed a willingness to guarantee foreign investment. With this turn of events, American officials approved a large bank commitment for the sale of material to aid in China's modernization program.

The renewed Japanese offensive undercut this movement. By October 1938, American policymakers had learned that Japan's leaders would no longer abide by the open door policy and that they intended to establish a Japanese-dominated sphere of interest. Because the United States government believed the creation of a preferential trade system would be incompatible with American prosperity and would provide a breeding ground for international discord, it was uneasy about the situation in the Far East. When Chiang Kai-shek gave the appearance of being able to resist the Japanese, American officials, acting through the Export-Import Bank and fully aware of the implications, provided him with economic aid.

Thus, in those instances in which the bank's dual nature was apparent, export interests did not play a decisive part in the decision-making machinery. Nevertheless, even though policymakers were not directly controlled by interest groups, over the long haul they may well have been dependent on them. Exporters and financiers could create situations that would cause the government to act in a fashion inconsistent with its principles. This phenomenon occurred with some degree of regularity, especially during the 1920s. Furthermore, if after repeated efforts Washington could not gain the allegiance of other nations to American principles, pressure from domestic groups could force policymakers to adopt a different set of principles. In part, George Peek represented one such challenge as did the leaders of the National Foreign Trade Council, who warned that they might reconsider their support for the reciprocal trade agreement program if nations continued to discriminate against American commerce.

Through its very existence, the Export-Import Bank symbolized the continued belief of American statesmen that the nation had an important stake in the international economy. In addition to aiding the expansion of exports, the bank provided State Department officials with a means of influencing the matrix within which commercial and financial transactions took place. By supplying foreign exchange assistance, by aiding development programs, and by supporting governments whose objectives were consistent with those of America, Washington could attempt to counter the forces which jeopardized the post-World War I world. The creation of the Export-Import Bank also indicated that the experience of the interwar years had strengthened U. S. policymakers' belief in their earlier analysis. They interpreted the depression, the emergence of aggressive totalitarian states, and the growth of economic nationalism as examples of what happened when nations failed to understand that the world was a single economic unit. To stop the drift away from the principles needed for an open world and to guard against countries repeating their earlier mistakes, the Roosevelt administration concluded that Washington would have to adopt a more forceful role in international affairs. The experience of the Second World War and the onset of the Cold War further reinforced this conclusion, so that U. S. officials assumed that only American action could preserve order and stability throughout the world.

Bibliography

I. Manuscript Sources

Davis, Norman H. Library of Congress, Washington, D.C.
Hoover, Herbert C. Herbert Hoover Library, West Branch, Iowa.
Hull, Cordell. Library of Congress, Washington, D.C.
Johnson, Nelson T. Library of Congress, Washington, D.C.
Moore, Ray Walton. Franklin D. Roosevelt Library, Hyde Park, New York.
Morgenthau, Henry, Jr. Franklin D. Roosevelt Library, Hyde Park, New York.
Roosevelt, Franklin D. Franklin D. Roosevelt Library, Hyde Park, New York.

II. Archival Materials

Export-Import Bank Files, U.S. Department of the Treasury, Washington, D.C.
Record Group 20, Records of the Export-Import Bank, S.A.F.T., National Archives, Washington, D.C.
Record Group 40, Records of the Department of Commerce, National Archives, Washington, D.C.
Record Group 59, Records of the Department of State, National Archives, Washington, D.C.
Record Group 151, Records of the Bureau of Foreign and Domestic Commerce, National Archives, Washington, D.C.
Record Group 234, Records of the Reconstruction Finance Corporation, National Archives, Washington, D.C.
Record Group 275, Records of the Export-Import Bank, National Archives, Washington, D.C.

III. Government Publications

Arey, Hawthorne. "History of Operations and Policies of Export-Import Bank of Washington." Washington, D.C.: mimeograph copy, 1953.
Export-Import Bank of Washington. "Annual Report of the Export-

259

Import Bank of Washington" (1936–1939). Washington, D.C.: mimeograph copy.

Export-Import Bank of Washington. "Statement of Loans and Commitments, December 31, 1940." Washington, D.C.: mimeograph copy, 1940.

Hornbeck, Stanley K. *Principles of American Policy in Relation to the Far East.* Washington, D.C.: U.S. Government Printing Office, 1934.

Hull, Cordell. *The Foreign Commercial Policy of the United States.* Department of State, Commercial Policy Series, no. 9. Washington, D.C.: U.S. Government Printing Office, 1935.

————. *International Trade and Domestic Prosperity.* Department of State, Commercial Policy Series, no. 3. Washington, D.C.: U.S. Government Printing Office, 1934.

————. *Recent Developments in Foreign Trade.* Department of State, Commercial Policy Series, no. 51. Washington, D.C.: U.S. Government Printing Office, 1938.

Martin, Charles D. *Foreign Markets for Agricultural Implements.* Department of Commerce, Trade Information Bulletin, no. 488. Washington, D.C.: U.S. Government Printing Office, 1927.

Messersmith, George S. *Some Aspects of the Assistance Rendered by the Department of State and its Foreign Service to American Business.* Department of State, Commercial Policy Series, no. 40. Washington, D.C.: U.S. Government Printing Office, 1937.

Moser, Charles K. *Where China Buys and Sells.* Department of Commerce, Trade Information Bulletin, no. 827. Washington, D.C.: U.S. Government Printing Office, 1935.

Sayre, Francis B. *American Commercial Policy.* Department of State, Commercial Policy Series, no. 6. Washington, D.C.: U.S. Government Printing Office, 1935.

————. *Building for Peace.* Department of State, Commercial Policy Series, no. 33. Washington, D.C.: U.S. Government Printing Office, 1936.

————. *The "Good Neighbor" Policy and Trade Agreements.* Department of State, Commercial Policy Series, no. 34. Washington, D.C.: U.S. Government Printing Office, 1937.

————. *The Hull Agreements and International Trade.* Department of State, Commercial Policy Series, no. 35, Washington, D.C.: U.S. Government Printing Office, 1937.

————. *Liberal Trade Policies the Basis for Peace.* Department of State, Commercial Policy Series, no. 37. Washington, D.C.: U.S. Government Printing Office, 1937.

————. *Most-Favored Nation vs. Preferential Bargaining.* Department of State, Commercial Policy Series, no. 15. Washington, D.C.: U.S. Government Printing Office, 1935.

―――. *Our Relations with Latin America.* Department of State, Latin American Series, no. 14. Washington, D.C.: U.S. Government Printing Office, 1937.

―――. *Trade Agreements and the Farmer.* Department of State, Commercial Policy Series, no. 25. Washington, D.C.: U.S. Government Printing Office, 1936.

―――. *Trade Policies and Peace.* Department of State, Commercial Policy Series, no. 21. Washington, D.C.: U.S. Government Printing Office, 1936.

―――. *The Winning of Peace.* Department of State, Commercial Policy Series, no. 38. Washington, D.C.: U.S. Government Printing Office, 1937.

―――. *Woodrow Wilson and Economic Disarmament.* Department of State, Commercial Policy Series, no. 20. Washington, D.C.: U.S. Government Printing Office, 1936.

―――. *To World Peace through World Trade.* Department of State, Commercial Policy Series, no. 43. Washington, D.C.: U.S. Government Printing Office, 1938.

Stimson, Henry L. *The United States and the Other American Republics.* Department of State, Latin American Series, no. 4. Washington, D.C.: U.S. Government Printing Office, 1931.

U.S. Bureau of the Census. *Historical Statistics of the United States, 1789–1945.* Washington, D.C.: U.S. Government Printing Office, 1949.

U.S. Congress. *Congressional Record.* 76th Congress, 1st session, 1939, 84, pt. 2.

―――. *Congressional Record.* 76th Congress, 3rd session, 1940, 86, pt. 11.

U.S. Congress. House. Committee on Banking and Currency. *Hearings, A Bill to Extend the Functions of the Reconstruction Finance Corporation,* 74th Congress, 1st session, 1935.

―――. *Hearings, To Continue the Functions of the Commodity Credit Corporation, the Export-Import Bank of Washington, and the Reconstruction Finance Corporation,* 76th Congress, 1st session, 1939.

―――. Committee on Appropriations. *Hearings, Legislative Establishment Appropriation Bill for 1938,* 75th Congress, 1st session, 1937.

U.S. Congress. Senate. Committee on Banking and Currency. *Extension of Functions of Reconstruction Finance Corporation.* Report no. 21, 74th Congress, 1st session, 1935.

————. *Hearings, To Extend the Functions of the Reconstruction Finance Corporation.* 74th Congress, 1st session, 1935.

————. *Hearings, To Continue the Functions of the Commodity Credit Corporation, the Export-Import Bank of Washington, and the Reconstruction Finance Corporation,* 76th Congress, 1st session, 1939.

————. *Study of the Export-Import Bank and World Bank.* Senate Document no. 85, pt. 1, 83rd Congress, 2nd session, 1954.

————. Subcommittee to Investigate the Administration of the Internal Security Act and Other Security Laws of the Judiciary. *Morgenthau Diary (China).* 2 vols. 89th Congress, 1st session, 1965.

U.S. Department of Commerce. *Annual Report of the Secretary of Commerce* (1921–1934). Washington, D.C.: U.S. Government Printing Office.

————. *Foreign Commerce and Navigation of the United States for the Calendar Year of . . . .* Washington, D.C.: U.S. Government Printing Office.

————. *Foreign Commerce Yearbook* (1937 and 1939). Washington, D.C.: U.S. Government Printing Office.

————. *The United States in the World Economy.* Economic Series, no. 23. Washington, D.C.: U.S. Government Printing Office, 1943.

————. *World Economic Review 1933.* Washington, D.C.: U.S. Government Printing Office, 1934.

U.S. Department of State. *Papers Relating to the Foreign Relations of the United States.* Washington, D.C.: U.S. Government Printing Office, 1861—. (Referred to in footnotes as *Foreign Relations.*)

————. *Foreign Relations of the United States: The Soviet Union, 1933–1939.* Washington, D.C.: U.S. Government Printing Office, 1952. (Referred to in footnotes as *Foreign Relations: Russia.*)

————. *Foreign Relations of the United States: Japan, 1931–1941.* 2 vols. Washington, D.C.: U.S. Government Printing Office, 1943. (Referred to in footnotes as *Foreign Relations: Japan.*)

Welles, Sumner. *"Good Neighbor" Policy in the Caribbean.* Department of State, Latin American Series, no. 12. Washington, D.C.: U.S. Government Printing Office, 1935.

————. *Inter-American Relations.* Department of State, Latin American Series, no. 8. Washington, D.C.: U.S. Government Printing Office, 1935.

————. *Pan American Cooperation.* Department of State, Latin American Series, no. 10. Washington, D.C.: U.S. Government Printing Office, 1935.

————. *Post-War Commercial Policy.* Department of State, Commercial Policy Series, no. 71. Washington, D.C.: U.S. Government Printing Office, 1941.

————. *Relations Between the United States and Cuba.* Department of State, Latin American Series, no. 7. Washington, D.C.: U.S. Government Printing Office, 1934.

————. *The Roosevelt Administration and its Dealings with the Republics of the Western Hemisphere.* Department of State, Latin American Series, no. 9. Washington, D.C.: U.S. Government Printing Office, 1935.

————. *The Trade-Agreements Program.* Department of State, Commercial Policy Series, no. 2. Washington, D.C.: U.S. Government Printing Office, 1934.

————. *Two Years of the "Good Neighbor" Policy.* Department of State, Latin American Series, no. 11. Washington, D.C.: U.S. Government, 1935.

————. *The Way to Peace on the American Continent.* Department of State, Latin American Series, no. 13. Washington, D.C.: U.S. Government Printing Office, 1936.

IV. Books and Pamphlets

Baker, Ray Stannard. *Woodrow Wilson and World Settlement: Written from His Unpublished and Personal Material.* 3 vols. Reprint ed. Gloucester, Mass.: Peter Smith, 1960.

Bennett, Edward M. *Recognition of Russia: An American Foreign Policy Dilemma.* Waltham, Mass.: Blaisdell Publishers, 1970.

Bennett, Edward W. *Germany and the Diplomacy of the Financial Crisis, 1931.* Cambridge, Mass.: Harvard University Press, 1962.

Bidwell, Percy. *Economic Defense of Latin America.* Boston: World Peace Foundation, 1941.

Bishop, Donald G. *The Roosevelt-Litvinov Agreements: The American View.* Syracuse: Syracuse University Press, 1965.

Blum, John Morton. *From the Morgenthau Diaries.* 3 vols. Boston: Houghton Mifflin Co., 1959–1967.

Bohlen, Charles E. *The Transformation of American Foreign Policy.* Paperback ed. New York: W. W. Norton & Co., 1969.

Borg, Dorothy. *The United States and the Far Eastern Crisis of 1933–1938: From the Manchurian Incident through the Initial Stage of the Undeclared Sino-Japanese War.* Cambridge, Mass.: Harvard University Press, 1964.

Brandes, Joseph. *Herbert Hoover and Economic Diplomacy: Department of Commerce Policy 1921–1928.* Pittsburgh: University of Pittsburgh Press, 1962.

Browder, Robert P. *The Origins of Soviet-American Diplomacy.* Princeton: Princeton University Press, 1952.

Brown, Warren Adams, Jr. *The United States and the Restoration of World Trade: An Analysis and Approval of the ITO Charter and the General Agreement on Tariffs and Trade.* Washington: The Brookings Institution, 1950.

Buckley, Thomas H. *The United States and the Washington Conference, 1921–1922.* Knoxville: University of Tennessee Press, 1970.

Buhite, Russell D. *Nelson T. Johnson and American Policy Toward China, 1925–1941.* East Lansing: Michigan State University Press, 1968.

Burgess, W. Randolph, ed. *Interpretations of Federal Reserve Policy in the Speeches and Writing of Benjamin Strong.* New York: Harper and Brothers, 1930.

Chandler, Lester V. *Benjamin Strong, Central Banker.* Washington: The Brookings Institution, 1958.

Cline, Howard F. *The United States and Mexico.* Revised ed. paperback. New York: Atheneum, 1969.

Cohen, Warren I. *America's Response to China: An Interpretative History of Sino-American Relations.* New York: John Wiley & Sons, 1971.

Commission of Inquiry into National Policy in International Economic Relations. *International Economic Relations: Report of the Commission of Inquiry into National Policy in International Economic Relations.* Minneapolis: University of Minnesota Press, 1934.

Current, Richard. *Secretary Stimson: A Study in Statecraft.* New Brunswick: Rutgers University Press, 1954.

DeConde, Alexander. *Herbert Hoover's Latin American Policy.* Stanford: Stanford University Press, 1951.

Diamond, William. *The Economic Thought of Woodrow Wilson.* Baltimore: The Johns Hopkins University Press, 1943.

Dietrich, Ethel B. *Far Eastern Trade of the United States.* New York: Institute of Pacific Relations, 1940.

Dozer, Donald. *Are We Good Neighbors? Three Decades of Inter-American Relations 1930–1960.* Gainsville: University of Florida Press, 1959.

Duggan, Laurence. *The Americas: The Search for Hemispheric Security.* New York: Henry Holt & Co., 1952.

Ellis, L. Ethan. *Republican Foreign Policy, 1921–1933.* New Brunswick: Rutgers University Press, 1968.

Eudin, Xenia J., and Slusser, Robert M., eds. *Soviet Foreign Policy, 1928–1934: Documents and Materials.* 2 vols. University Park: Pennsylvania State University Press, 1967.

Bibliography

Everest, Allan Seymour. *Morgenthau, the New Deal and Silver: A Story of Pressure Politics*. New York: Columbia University Press, 1950.

Fairbank, John King. *The United States and China*. 3rd rev. ed. paperback. Cambridge, Mass.: Harvard University Press, 1971.

Farnsworth, Beatrice. *William C. Bullitt and the Soviet Union*. Bloomington: Indiana University Press, 1967.

Feis, Herbert. *The Diplomacy of the Dollar, 1919–1932*. Paperback ed. New York: W. W. Norton & Co., 1966.

————. *1933: Characters in Crisis*. Boston: Little, Brown & Co., 1966.

Ferrell, Robert. *American Diplomacy in the Great Depression: Hoover-Stimson Foreign Policy, 1929–1933*. New Haven: Yale University Press, 1957.

Feuerwerker, Albert. *The Chinese Economy, 1912–1949*. Michigan Papers in Chinese Studies, no. 1. Ann Arbor: University of Michigan Press, 1968.

Filene, Peter G. *Americans and the Soviet Experiment, 1917–1933*. Cambridge, Mass.: Harvard University Press, 1967.

Fite, Gilbert. *George N. Peek and the Fight for Farm Parity*. Norman: University of Oklahoma Press, 1954.

Fraser, Herbert. *Foreign Trade and World Politics: A Study of the International Foundations of Prosperity with Particular References to American Conditions*. New York: Alfred A. Knopf, 1926.

Freidel, Frank. *Franklin D. Roosevelt: Launching the New Deal*. Boston: Little, Brown & Co., 1973.

Friedman, Milton and Schwartz, Anna J. *A Monetary History of the United States, 1867–1960*. Princeton: Princeton University Press, 1963.

Frye, Alton. *Nazi Germany and the American Hemisphere, 1933–1941*. New Haven: Yale University Press, 1967.

Fusfeld, Daniel R. *The Economic Thought of Franklin D. Roosevelt and the Origins of the New Deal*. New York: Columbia University Press, 1956.

Gantenbein, James W., ed. *The Evolution of Our Latin American Policy*. New York: Columbia University Press, 1950.

Gardner, Lloyd C. *Achitects of Illusion*. Chicago: Quadrangle, 1970.

————. *Economic Aspects of New Deal Diplomacy*. Madison: University of Wisconsin Press, 1964.

Gellman, Irwin F. *Roosevelt and Batista: Good Neighbor Diplomacy in Cuba, 1933–1945*. Albuquerque: University of New Mexico Press, 1973.

Glad, Betty. *Charles Evans Hughes and the Illusions of Innocence: A*

Study in American Diplomacy. Urbana: University of Illinois Press, 1966.

Green, David. *The Containment of Latin America: A History of the Myths and Realities of the Good Neighbor Policy*. Chicago: Quadrangle, 1971.

Grew, Joseph C. *Ten Years in Japan: A Contemporary Record Drawn from the Diaries and Official Papers of Joseph C. Grew, United States Ambassador to Japan 1932–1942*. New York: Simon & Schuster, 1944.

————. *Turbulent Era: A Diplomatic Record of Forty Years, 1904–1945*. 2 vols. Boston: Houghton Mifflin Co., 1952.

Guerrant, Edward O. *Roosevelt's Good Neighbor Policy*. Alburquerque: University of New Mexico Press, 1950.

Hawley, Ellis. *The New Deal and Problem of Monopoly*. Princeton: Princeton University Press, 1966.

Heinrichs, Waldo. *American Ambassador: Joseph C. Grew and the Development of the United States Diplomatic Tradition*. Boston: Little, Brown & Co., 1966.

Hofstadter, Richard. *The American Political Traditional and the Men Who Made It*. New York: Alfred A. Knopf, 1957.

Hoover, Herbert. *Addresses Upon the American Road, 1940–1941*. New York: Charles Scribner's Sons, 1941.

————. *Addresses Upon the American Road, 1950–1955*. Stanford: Stanford University Press, 1955.

————. *American Individualism*. Garden City, N.Y.: Doubleday, Page & Co., 1922.

————. *The Memoirs of Herbert Hoover*. 3 vols. New York: Macmillan Co., 1951–1952.

Hou Chi-ming. *Foreign Investment and Economic Development in China, 1840–1937*. Cambridge, Mass.: Harvard University Press, 1965.

Hughes, Charles Evans. *Our Relations to the Nations of the Western Hemisphere*. Princeton: Princeton University Press, 1928.

————. *The Pathway of Peace: Representative Addresses Delivered during His Term as Secretary of State (1921–1925)*. New York: Harper & Brothers, 1925.

Hull, Cordell. *The Memoirs of Cordell Hull*. 2 vols. New York: Macmillan Co., 1948.

Ickes, Harold L. *The Secret Diary of Harold L. Ickes*. 3 vols. New York: Simon & Schuster, 1953–1954.

Iriye, Akira. *Across the Pacific: An Inner History of American-East Asian Relations*. Paperback ed. New York: Harcourt, Brace and World, 1967.

————. *After Imperialism: The Search for a New Order in East Asia, 1921–1931.* Paperback ed. New York: Atheneum, 1969.

Jones, F. C. *Japan's New Order in East Asia: Its Rise and Fall, 1937–1945.* London: Oxford University Press, 1954.

Jones, Jesse. *Fifty Billion Dollars: My Thirteen Years with the RFC (1932–1945).* New York: Macmillan Co., 1951.

Kamman, William. *A Search for Stability: United States Diplomacy toward Nicaragua, 1925–1933.* Notre Dame: University of Notre Dame Press, 1968.

Kaufman, Burton I. *Efficiency and Expansion: Foreign Trade Organization in the Wilson Administration, 1913–1921.* Westport, Conn., Greenwood Press, 1974.

Kennan, George F. *Russia and the West under Lenin and Stalin.* Boston: Little, Brown & Co., 1960.

Keynes, John Maynard. *The Economic Consequences of the Peace.* New York: Harcourt, Brace and Howe, 1920.

Klein, Julius. *Frontiers of Trade.* New York: Century, 1929.

Kottman, Richard N. *Reciprocity and the North Atlantic Triangle, 1932–1938.* Ithaca: Cornell University Press, 1967.

Langley, Lester D. *The Cuban Policy of the United States: A Brief History.* New York: John Wiley & Sons, 1968.

League of Nations. *The Course and Phases of the World Economic Depression.* Geneva: League of Nations, 1931.

Leuchtenburg, William E. *Franklin D. Roosevelt and the New Deal 1932–1940.* New York: Harper & Row, 1963.

————. *The Perils of Prosperity, 1914–32.* Chicago: University of Chicago Press, 1958.

Levin, N. Gordon, Jr. *Woodrow Wilson and World Politics: America's Response to War and Revolution.* New York: Oxford University Press, 1968.

Lewis, Cleona. *America's Stake in International Investments.* Washington: The Brookings Institution, 1938.

Lippmann, Walter, and Scroggs, William O. *The United States in World Affairs: An Account of American Foreign Relations 1931.* New York: Harper & Brothers, 1932.

Lochner, Louis. *Herbert Hoover and Germany.* New York: Macmillan Co., 1960.

McCann, Frank D., Jr. *The Brazilian-American Alliance, 1937–1945.* Princeton: Princeton University Press, 1973.

Meyer, Richard H. *Bankers' Diplomacy: Monetary Stabilization in the Twenties.* New York: Columbia University Press, 1970.

Mintz, Ilse. *Cyclical Fluctuations in the Exports of the United States since 1879.* New York: Columbia University Press, 1967.

Moley, Raymond. *After Seven Years.* New York: Harper & Brothers, 1939.

———. *The First New Deal.* New York: Harcourt, Brace and World, 1966.

Moulton, Harold G. *The Reparation Plan: An Interpretation of the Reports of the Expert Committee Appointed by the Reparation Commission November 30, 1923.* New York: McGraw-Hill, 1924.

Moulton, Harold G., and Pasvolsky, Leo. *War Debts and World Prosperity.* New York: Century, 1932.

———. *World War Debt Settlements.* New York: Macmillan Co., 1929.

Murray, Robert K. *The Harding Era: Warren G. Harding and his Administration.* Minneapolis: University of Minnesota Press, 1969.

McClelland, John C. *Nazi Europe and World Trade.* Washington: The Brookings Institution, 1941.

National Foreign Trade Council. *Foreign Trade in 1932: Official Report of the Nineteenth National Foreign Trade Convention and Ninth Pacific Foreign Trade Convention.* New York: India House, 1932.

———. *Report of the American Economic Mission to the Far East: American Trade Prospects in the Orient.* New York: National Foreign Trade Council, 1935.

———. *Report on European Conditions, 1923.* New York: National Foreign Trade Council, 1923.

Neumann, William L. *America Encounters Japan: From Perry to MacArthur.* Paperback ed. Baltimore: The Johns Hopkins University Press, 1969.

Nixon, Edgar B., ed. *Franklin D. Roosevelt and Foreign Affairs.* 3 vols. Cambridge, Mass.: Harvard University Press, 1969.

Norse, Edwin G.; Tyron, Frederick G.; Drury, Horace B.; Leven, Maurice; Moulton, Harold G.; and Lewis, Cleona. *America's Capacity to Produce.* Washington: The Brookings Institution, 1934.

Parrini, Carl. *Heir to Empire: United States Economic Diplomacy, 1916–1923.* Pittsburgh: University of Pittsburgh Press, 1969.

Peek, George N., and Crowther, Samuel. *Why Quit Our Own.* New York: D. Van Nostrand, 1936.

Pratt, Julius. *Cordell Hull, 1933–1934.* 2 vols. New York: Cooper Square, 1964.

Pusey, Merlo. *Charles Evans Hughes.* 2 vols. New York: Macmillan Co., 1951.

Range, Willard D. *Franklin D. Roosevelt's World Order.* Athens: University of Georgia Press, 1959.

Bibliography

Rappaport, Armin. *Henry L. Stimson and Japan, 1931–1933*. Chicago: University of Chicago Press, 1963.

Remer, C. F. *Foreign Investments in China*. Reprint ed. New York: Howard Fertig, 1968.

Roberts, Henry. *Eastern Europe: Politics, Revolution and Diplomacy*. New York: Alfred A. Knopf, 1970.

Roose, Kenneth D. *The Economics of Recession and Revival: An Interpretation of 1937–1938*. New Haven: Yale University Press, 1958.

Roosevelt, Franklin D. *The Public Papers and Addresses of Franklin D. Roosevelt*. Edited by Samuel I. Rosenman. 10 vols. New York: Random House, 1938–1950.

Schlesinger, Arthur M., Jr. *The Age of Roosevelt*, 3 vols. Boston: Houghton Mifflin Co., 1959.

Smith, Robert Freeman. *The United States and Cuba: Business and Diplomacy, 1917–1960*. New York: Bookman Associates, 1960.

———. *The United States and Revolutionary Nationalism in Mexico, 1916–1932*. Chicago: University of Chicago Press, 1972.

Soule, George H.; Efran, David; and Ness, Norman. *Latin America in the Future of the World*. New York: Farrar and Rinehart, 1945.

Soule, George H. *Prosperity Decade From War to Depression: 1917–1929*. Paperback ed. New York: Harper & Row, 1968.

Sternsher, Bernard. *Rexford Tugwell and the New Deal*. New Brunswick: Rutgers University Press, 1964.

Sutton, Antony. *Western Technology and Soviet Economic Development 1917 to 1930*. Hoover Institution on War, Revolution, and Peace, Stanford: Stanford University Press, 1968.

Tausigg, Frank W. *The Tariff History of the United States*. New York: G. P. Putnam & Sons, 1931.

Tugwell, Rexford. *The Brains Trust*. Paperback ed. New York: Viking, 1969.

———. *The Democratic Roosevelt*. Garden City, N.Y.: Doubleday, 1957.

Tulchin, Joseph S. *The Aftermath of War: World War I and U. S. Policy Toward Latin America*. New York: New York University Press, 1971.

Ulam, Adam B. *Expansion and Coexistence: The History of Soviet Foreign Policy, 1917–1967*. Paperback ed. New York: Praeger, 1968.

Warren, Harris Gaylord. *Herbert Hoover and the Great Depression*. Paperback ed. New York: W. W. Norton & Co., 1967.

Welch, William. *American Images of Soviet Foreign Policy: An In-*

quiry into Recent Appraisals from the Academic Community. New Haven: Yale University Press, 1970.

Welles, Sumner. *Seven Decisions That Shaped History.* New York: Harper & Brothers, 1950.

Whitaker, Arthur P., and Jordan, David C. *Nationalism in Contemporary Latin America,* New York: Free Press, 1966.

Wicker, Elmus R. *Federal Reserve Monetary Policy 1917–1933.* New York: Random House, 1966.

Wilbur, Ray L., and Hyde, Arthur M. *The Hoover Policies.* New York: Charles Scribner's Sons, 1937.

Williams, William A. *American-Russian Relations, 1781–1947.* New York: Rinehart and Co., 1952.

————. *The Contours of American History.* Paperback ed. Chicago: Quadrangle, 1966.

Wilson, Joan Hoff. *American Business and Foreign Policy, 1920–1933.* Lexington: University Press of Kentucky, 1971.

————. *Ideology and Economics: U. S. Relations with the Soviet Union, 1918–1933.* Columbia: University of Missouri Press, 1974.

Wilson, Woodrow. *The Messages and Papers of Woodrow Wilson.* Edited by Albert Shaw. 2 vols. New York: Review of Reviews, 1924.

Wirth, John D. *The Politics of Brazilian Development 1930–1945.* Stanford: Stanford University Press, 1970.

Wood, Bryce. *The Making of the Good Neighbor Policy.* Paperback ed. New York: W. W. Norton & Co., 1967.

Young, Arthur N. *China and the Helping Hand, 1937–1945.* Cambridge, Mass.: Harvard University Press, 1963.

————. *China's Wartime Finance and Inflation, 1937–1945.* Cambridge, Mass.: Harvard University Press, 1965.

V. Articles

Abrahams, Paul P. "American Bankers and the Economic Tactics of Peace." *Journal of American History* 56 (December 1969): 572–84.

Aldrich, Winthrop. "Causes of the Present Depression." *Bankers Magazine* 126 (April 1933): 339–44.

Alexander, James S. "Our Foreign Trade and Our Foreign Investment Policy." In *Foreign Trade in 1927: Official Report of the Fourteenth Annual National Foreign Trade Convention,* pp. 23–31. New York: India House, 1927.

Allen, William R. "Cordell Hull and the Defense of the Trade Agreements Program, 1934–1940." In *Isolation and Security,* edited by

Bibliography

Alexander DeConde, pp. 107–32. Durham: Duke University Press, 1957.

———. "The International Trade Philosophy of Cordell Hull, 1907–1933." *American Economic Review* 43 (March 1953): 101–16.

"American Banks and Foreign Trade." *Bankers Magazine* 103 (November 1921): 827–29.

An American Businessman in China. "For Government Support of U.S. Enterprise." *Amerasia* 1 (July 1937): 199–202.

Bergmann, Carl. "Germany and the Young Plan." *Foreign Affairs* 8 (July 1930): 583–97.

Bidwell, Percy W. "Latin America, Germany and the Hull Program." *Foreign Affairs* 17 (January 1939): 374–90.

———. "The New American Tariff: Europe's Answer." *Foreign Affairs* 9 (October 1930): 13–26.

———. "Trade, Tariffs, and the Depression." *Foreign Affairs* 10 (April 1932): 391–401.

Blaiser, Cole. "The United States, Germany, and the Bolivian Revolutionaries (1941–1946)." *Hispanic American Historical Review* 52 (February 1972): 26–54.

Booth, Willis H. "Foreign Trade and the Interior Bank." *Bankers Magazine* 102 (January 1921): 77–83.

Bowers, Robert E. "Hull, Russian Subversion in Cuba, and Recognition of the U.S.S.R." *Journal of American History* 53 (December 1966): 542–54.

———. "Senator Arthur Robinson of Indiana Vindicated: William Bullitt's Secret Mission to Europe." *Indiana Magazine of History* 6 (September 1965): 189–204.

Browder, Robert F. "Soviet Far Eastern Policy and American Recognition, 1932–1934." *Pacific Historical Review* 21 (August 1952): 263–73.

Burck, Gilbert and Silberman, Charles. "What Caused the Great Depression." *Fortune* (February 1955): 94.

Burke, Bernard V. "American Economic Diplomacy and the Weimar Republic." *Mid-America* 54 (October 1972): 211–33.

Burton, Theodore E. "American Foreign Policy: A Republican View." *Foreign Affairs* 3 (September 1924): 35–48.

Castle, William R., Jr. "The Department of State and American Enterprise Abroad." In *Foreign Trade in 1928: Official Report of the Fifteenth Annual National Foreign Trade Convention*, pp. 189–96. New York: India House, 1928.

Clauss, Errol MacGregor. "The Roosevelt Administration and Manchukuo, 1933–1941." *The Historian* 32 (August 1970): 595–611.

Condliffe, J. B. "Vanishing World Trade." *Foreign Affairs* 11 (July 1933): 645–56.

Costigliola, Frank C. "The Other Side of Isolationism: The Establishment of the First World Bank, 1929–1930." *Journal of American History* 59 (December 1972): 602–20.

Cronon, E. David. "Interpreting the Good Neighbor Policy: The Cuban Crisis of 1933." *Hispanic American Historical Review* 39 (November 1959): 538–67.

Davis, Norman H. "Wanted: A Consistent Latin American Policy." *Foreign Affairs* 9 (April 1931): 547–68.

Davis, O. K. "The Relation of Foreign Investment to the Flow of World Trade." *Proceedings of the Academy of Political Science* 12 (January 1928): 811–18.

de Sanchez, J. A. M. "Further Economic Consequences of the Peace." *Foreign Affairs* 1 (September 1922): 158–67.

Dickens, Paul D. "Foreign Capital Issues Publicly Offered in the United States." *Commerce Reports: A Weekly Survey of Foreign Trade* (January 27, 1930): 217.

Drum, John S. "Survey of Economic Conditions." *Journal of the American Bankers' Association* 13 (May 1921): 722–27.

Dulles, John Foster. "Our Foreign Loan Policy." *Foreign Affairs* 5 (October 1926): 33–48.

Edwards, Morris. "Roosevelt Talked Business with Me." *Nation's Business* 20 (December 1932): 14.

Ellsworth, Paul T. "An Economic Foreign Policy for America." *American Economic Review* 30 (February 1941): 301–19.

"Export-Import Bank Loans to Latin America." *Foreign Policy Reports* 17 (June 15, 1941): 82–92.

Falkus, M. E. "United States Economic Policy and the 'Dollar Gap' of the 1920's." *Economic History Review* 29 (November 1971): 599–623.

Farrell, James A. "An American Foreign Trade Policy." In *Foreign Trade in 1922: Official Report of the Ninth Annual National Foreign Trade Convention*, pp. 572–80. New York: India House, 1922.

———. "The Foreign Trade Balance." In *Foreign Trade in 1927: Official Report of the Fourteenth Annual National Foreign Trade Convention*, pp. 478–85. New York: India House, 1927.

———. "The Foreign Trade Outlook." In *Foreign Trade in 1925: Official Report of the Twelfth Annual National Foreign Trade Convention*, pp. 10–18. New York: India House, 1925.

———. "We Need Foreign Trade Too." *Nation's Business* 21 (September 1933): 13–15.

Bibliography

Feis, Herbert. "The Export of American Capital." *Foreign Affairs* 3 (July 1925): 668–86.

Fite, Gilbert. "The Farmers' Dilemma, 1919–1929." In *Change and Continuity in Twentieth Century America: The 1920's*, edited by John Braeman, Robert Bremmer, and David Brody, pp. 67–102. Columbus: Ohio State University Press, 1968.

"Foreign Trade Financing Corporation." *Bankers Magazine* 102 (January 1921): 17–19.

"The Forty-Eighth Annual Convention." *Journal of the American Bankers' Association* 15 (November 1922): 255.

Gannet, Lewis S. "Foreign Investment and Public Policy." *Proceedings of the Academy of Political Science* 12 (January 1928): 861–64.

Gardner, Lloyd C. "The Role of the Commerce and Treasury Departments." In *Pearl Harbor as History: Japanese-American Relations 1931–1941*, edited by Dorothy Borg and Shumpei Okamoto, pp. 261–85. New York: Columbia University Press, 1973.

Gay, Edwin F. "The Great Depression." *Foreign Affairs* 10 (July 1932): 529–40.

George, A. E. "Foreign Loans and Politics in Latin America." *Journal of the American Bankers' Association* 23 (November 1930): 417.

Gilbert, S. Parker. "The Meaning of the 'Dawes Plan'." *Foreign Affairs* 4 (April 1926, special supplement): i–xii.

Glass, Carter. "Government Supervision of Foreign Loans." *Proceedings of the Academy of Political Science* 12 (January 1928): 843–49.

Grady, Henry F. "The Part of Imports in Foreign Trade." In *Foreign Trade in 1929: Official Report of the Sixteenth Annual National Foreign Trade Convention*, pp. 187–96. New York: India House, 1929.

Griffin, Charles. "Welles to Roosevelt: A Memorandum on Inter-American Relations, 1933." *Hispanic American Historical Review* 34 (May 1954): 190–92.

Haight, John McVickar, Jr. "Franklin D. Roosevelt and a Naval Quarantine of Japan." *Pacific Historical Review* 40 (May 1971): 203–26.

Hansen, Alvin T. "Hemisphere Solidarity." *Foreign Affairs* 19 (October 1940): 12–21.

Hays, Samuel P. "Introduction—The New Organizational Society." In *Building the Organizational Society: Essays in Associational Activities in Modern America*, edited by Jerry Israel, pp. 1–15. New York: Free Press, 1972.

———. "Political Parties and the Community-Society Continuum." In *The American Party Systems*, edited by William Nisbet Chambers and Walter Dean Burnham, pp. 152–81. Paperback ed. New York: Oxford University Press, 1967.

Head, Walter. "The Beginning of a New Prosperity." *Journal of the American Bankers' Association* 17 (October 1924): 195–98.

Hecht, R. S. "Premium on the Dollar a Barrier." *Journal of the American Bankers' Association* 14 (September 1921): 107–8.

Helm, William Pickett. "Tariff Walls, Past and Present." *Journal of the American Bankers' Association* 23 (July 1930): 12–13.

Holder, Charles A. "The Place of Foreign Trade Banks in Overseas Trade." *Bankers Magazine* 102 (April 1921): 595–96.

Hornbeck, Stanley K. "A Letter to the Editor." *Amerasia* 1 (March 1937): 16–19.

Inman, Samuel Guy. "Imperialistic America." *Atlantic Monthly* 134 (July 1924): 107–16.

"International Financial Problems." *Bankers Magazine* 104 (January 1922): 2–4.

Iriye, Akira. "Japan's Foreign Policies between World Wars: Sources and Interpretations." Reprinted in *The Origins of the Second World War*, edited by Esmonde M. Robertson, pp. 262–71. London: St. Martin's, 1971.

———. "The Role of the United States Embassy in Tokyo." In *Pearl Harbor as History: Japanese-American Relations 1931–1941*, edited by Dorothy Borg and Shumpei Okamoto, pp. 107–26. New York: Columbia University Press, 1973.

Kaufman, Burton I. "United States Trade with Latin America: The War Years." *Journal of American History* 57 (September 1971): 342–63.

Klein, Herbert S. "American Oil Companies in Latin America: The Bolivian Experience." *Inter-American Economic Affairs* (Autumn 1964): 47–72.

Klein, Julius. "International Cartels." *Foreign Affairs* 6 (April 1928): 448–58.

———. "The Problem of Our Raw Material Supplies." In *Foreign Trade in 1926: Official Report of the Thirteenth Annual National Foreign Trade Convention*, pp. 28–33. New York: India House, 1926.

Kruesi, Paul J. "Building Foreign Trade Through Foreign Loans." In *Foreign Trade in 1926: Official Report of the Thirteenth National Foreign Trade Convention*, pp. 413–20. New York: India House, 1926.

Laders, Arthur A. G. "Foreign Trade and its Relation to Domestic Business." *Bankers Magazine* 103 (July 1921): 73–76.

Lamont, Robert P. "Prospects of United States Foreign Trade." In

Bibliography

Foreign Trade in 1929: Official Report of the Sixteenth Annual National Foreign Trade Convention, pp. 11–20. New York: India House, 1929.

Lamont, Thomas W. "The Final Reparations Settlement." *Foreign Affairs* 8 (April 1930): 336–63.

Laydon, Walter T. "Europe's Future Role in World Trade." *Proceedings of the Academy of Political Science* 12 (January 1928): 947–62.

Leffler, Melvyn. "The Origins of Republican War Debt Policy, 1921–1923: A Case Study in the Applicability of the Open Door Interpretation." *Journal of American History* 59 (December 1972): 585–601.

———. "Political Isolationism: Economic Expansionism or Diplomatic Realism? American Policy toward Western Europe 1921–1933." *Perspectives in American History* 8 (1974): 413–61.

Lodge, Henry Cabot. "Foreign Relations of the United States, 1921–1924." *Foreign Affairs* 2 (June 1924): 525–39.

McAdams, Thomas B. "Address of the President." *Journal of the American Bankers' Association* 15 (November 1922): 263–67.

———. "The Business Outlook for 1922." *Journal of the American Bankers' Association* 14 (January 1922): 495–96.

MacClintock, Samuel. "Foreign Credits." *Bankers Magazine* 102 (February 1921): 257–61.

McCormick, Thomas J. "The State of American Diplomatic History." In *The State of American History*, edited by Herbert J. Bass, pp. 119–41. Chicago: Quadrangle, 1970.

McHale, James M. "National Planning and Reciprocal Trade: The New Deal Origins of Government Guarantees for Private Exporters." *Prologue* 6 (Fall 1974): 189–99.

McHugh, John. "America's Foreign Trade Opportunity." *Bankers Magazine* 102 (January 1921): 19–25.

Maddox, Robert. "Keeping Cool with Coolidge." *Journal of American History* 53 (March 1967): 772–80.

Mills, Ogden L. "Our Foreign Policy: A Republican View." *Foreign Affairs* 6 (July 1928): 555–72.

"Mr. Harriman's Business Platform." *Nation's Business* 20 (July 1932): 20.

Mooney, James D. "Let's Face the Facts about Foreign Trade." *Forbes* 31 (January 15, 1933): 7–9.

Moore, James R. "Sources of New Deal Economic Policy: The International Dimension." *Journal of American History* 61 (December 1974): 728–44.

Morgan, Shephard. "Constructive Functions of the International Bank." *Foreign Affairs* 9 (July 1931): 580–91.

Munro, Dana G. "The American Withdrawal from Haiti, 1929–1934." *Hispanic American Historical Review* 49 (February 1969): 1–26.

Nash, Gerald D. "Herbert Hoover and the Origins of the Reconstruction Finance Corporation." *Mississippi Valley Historical Review* 46 (December 1959): 455–68.

Neumann, William L. "Ambiguity and Ambivalence in Ideas of National Interest in Asia." In *Isolation and Security*, edited by Alexander DeConde, pp. 133–58. Durham: Duke University Press, 1957.

———. "Franklin D. Roosevelt and Japan, 1913–1933." *Pacific Historical Review* 22 (May 1953): 143–53.

"New England Bankers on Business." *Bankers Magazine* 124 (May 1932): 531–32.

Nichols, Jeanette P. "Roosevelt's Monetary Diplomacy in 1933." *American Historical Review* 56 (January 1951): 295–317.

"Our Foreign Trade Banking." *Journal of the American Bankers' Association* 26 (October 1933): 25–26.

Owens, Richard N. "The Hundred Million Dollar Foreign-Trade Financing Corporation." *Journal of Political Economy* 30 (June 1922): 346–62.

"A Panorama of Economic Planning." *Nation's Business* 20 (February 1932): 29–32.

Paterson, Thomas G. "The Abortive American Loan to Russia and the Origins of the Cold War, 1943–1946." *Journal of American History* 56 (June 1969): 70–92.

Patterson, Gardner. "The Export-Import Bank." *Quarterly Journal of Economics* 58 (November 1943): 65–90.

Pierson, Warren L. "Export-Import Bank Operations." *Annals of the American Academy of Political and Social Science* 211 (September 1940): 35–40.

———. "A Report to the American People." *Foreign Commerce Weekly* 4 (August 30, 1941): 3.

Pratt, Lawrence. "The Anglo-American Naval Conversations on the Far East of January 1938." *International Affairs* 47 (October 1971): 745–63.

Radosh, Ronald. "John Spargo and Wilson's Russian Policy, 1920." *Journal of American History* 52 (December 1965): 548–65.

"Record Year for U.S. Exports: World Trade Shows Steady Progress." *Bankers Magazine* 117 (December 1928): 1017–23.

"RFC Aids Foreign Trade." *Business Week* (February 10, 1934), pp. 6–7.

Rhodes, Benjamin D. "Reassessing 'Uncle Shylock': The United States and the French War Debt, 1917–1929." *Journal of American History* 55 (March 1969): 787–803.

Robinson, Henry M. "American Banking and World Rehabilitation." In *Foreign Trade in 1925: Official Report of the Twelfth Annual National Foreign Trade Convention*, pp. 152–62. New York: India House, 1925.

———. "Some Lessons of the Economic Conference." *Foreign Affairs* 6 (October 1927): 14–21.

———. "The United States As a Creditor Nation." *Bankers Magazine* 103 (August 1921): 261–68.

Roosevelt, Franklin D. "Our Foreign Policy: A Democratic View." *Foreign Affairs* 6 (July 1928): 573–86.

———. "Shall We Trust Japan?" *Asia* (July 1923): 475.

Rosen, Elliot. "Intranationalism vs. Internationalism: The Interregnum Struggle for the Sanctity of the New Deal." *Political Science Quarterly* 81 (June 1966): 274–97.

Rothbard, Murray N. "The Hoover Myth." Reprinted in *For a New America: Essays in History and Politics from 'Studies on the Left' 1959–1967*, edited by James Weinstein and David Eakins, pp. 162–79. Paperback ed. New York: Vintage, 1970.

Scroggs, William O. "The American Investment in Latin America." *Foreign Affairs* 10 (April 1932): 502–4.

Sisson, Francis H. "Must We Slow Down if Europe Does Not Come Back?" *Journal of the American Bankers' Association* 16 (January 1924): 414.

Sklar, Martin. "Woodrow Wilson and the Political Economy of Modern United States Liberalism." *Studies on the Left* 1 (Fall 1960): 17–47.

Smith, Robert Freeman. "Businessmen, Bureaucrats, Historians and the Shaping of United States Foreign Policy." *Reviews in American History* 2 (December 1974): 575–81.

———. "The Morrow Mission and the International Committee of Bankers on Mexico: The Interaction of Finance Diplomacy and the New Mexican Elite." *Journal of Latin American Studies* 1, part 2 (November 1969): 149–66.

Snow, Chauncy Depew. "What Will that New Tariff Do?" *Nation's Business* 10 (November 1922): 17–19.

Snyder, Richard J. "William Culbertson and the Formation of Modern American Commercial Policy, 1917–1925." *Kansas Historical Quarterly*, Winter 1969, pp. 396–410.

"A Tariff Holiday." *Bankers Magazine* 123 (August 1931): 126–27.

Tausigg, Frank W. "The Tariff Controversy with France." *Foreign Affairs* 6 (January 1928): 177–90.

Thomas, Eugene P. "The Foreign Trade Outlook." In *Foreign Trade in 1928: Official Report of the Fifteenth Annual National Foreign Trade Convention*, pp. 7–15. New York: India House, 1928.

Thomson, James C., Jr. "The Role of the Department of State." In *Pearl Harbor as History: Japanese-American Relations 1931–1941*, edited by Dorothy Borg and Shumpei Okamoto, pp. 81–106. New York: Columbia University Press, 1973.

Thorne, Christopher. "The Shanghai Crisis of 1932: The Basis of British Policy." *American Historical Review* 75 (October 1970): 1616–39.

Tugwell, Rexford G. "America's Wartime Socialism." *Nation* 124 (April 6, 1927): 364–67.

————. "Hunger, Cold and Candidates." *New Republic* 54 (May 2, 1928): 323–25.

————. "The Paradox of Peace." *New Republic* 54 (April 18, 1928): 262–67.

————. "Wage-Pressure and Efficiency." *New Republic* 55 (July 11, 1928): 196–98.

"Two Roads—Which Shall We Take?" *Bankers Magazine* 126 (February 1933): 116–17.

Ullman, Richard. "The Davies Mission and United States-Soviet Relations, 1937–1941." *World Politics* 9 (January 1957): 220–39.

United Nations Department of Economic and Social Affairs. "The Growth of Foreign Investments in Latin America." Reprinted in *Foreign Investment in Latin America*, edited by Marvin Bernstein, pp. 29–65. Paperback ed. New York: Alfred A. Knopf, 1966.

"United States and Latin America in Ever-Increasing Relations." *Bankers Magazine* 117 (December 1928): 1068.

Van Meter, Robert H., Jr. "American Foreign Policy and the Economic Reconstruction of Europe, 1918–1921." *Topic* 16 (Fall 1968): 47–66.

Vinson, J. Chalmers. "War Debts and Peace Legislation: The Johnson Act of 1934." *Mid-America* 50 (July 1968): 206–22.

Welles, Sumner. "Is America Imperialistic?" *The Atlantic Monthly* 134 (September 1924): 412–23.

"What Business with Russia." *Fortune* 31 (January 1945): 153.

Whittlesey, Charles R. "Five Years of the Export-Import Bank." *American Economic Review* 29 (September 1939): 487–502.

Wicker, Elmus R. "Federal Reserve Monetary Policy, 1923–33: A Re-Interpretation." *Journal of Political Economy* 13 (August 1965): 325–43.

————. "Roosevelt's 1933 Monetary Experiment." *Journal of American History* 57 (March 1971): 864–76.

Bibliography

Williams, William A. "China and Japan: A Challenge and a Choice in the Nineteen Twenties." *Pacific Historical Review* 26 (August 1957): 259–79.

———. "Latin America: Laboratory of American Foreign Policy in the Nineteen-twenties." *Inter-American Economic Affairs* 11 (Autumn 1957): 3–30.

———. "The Legend of Isolationism in the 1920's." *Science and Society* 18 (Winter 1954): 1–20.

———. "What this Country Needs. . . ." *New York Review of Books* 15 (November 5, 1970): 7–11.

Wilson, Joan Hoff. "American Business and the Recognition of the Soviet Union." *Social Science Quarterly* 52 (September 1971): 349–68.

Winkler, Max. "Does It Pay to Lend Abroad?" *Journal of the American Bankers' Association* 23 (June 1931): 962.

Woods, Kenneth F. " 'Imperialistic America': A Landmark in the Development of U.S. Policy toward Latin America." *Inter-American Economic Affairs* 21 (Winter 1967): 55–72.

Youngman, Elmer H. "America's International Banking and Financial Relations." *Bankers Magazine* 103 (September 1921): 401–5.

VI. Unpublished Sources

Batzler, Louis Richard. "The Development of Soviet Foreign Relations with the United States, 1917–1939." Ph.D. dissertation, Georgetown University, 1956.

Bennett, Edward M. "Franklin D. Roosevelt and Russian-American Relations 1933–1939." Ph.D. dissertation, University of Illinois, 1961.

Costigliola, Frank C. "The Politics of Financial Stabilization: American Reconstruction Policy in Europe 1924–30." Ph.D. dissertation, Cornell University, 1973.

Elsasser, Edward O. "The Export-Import Bank and Latin America, 1934–1945." Ph.D. dissertation, University of Chicago, 1954.

Gerberding, William P. "Franklin D. Roosevelt's Conception of the Soviet Union in World Politics." Ph.D. dissertation, University of Chicago, 1959.

Griffin, Donald W. "The Normal Years: Brazilian-American Relations 1930–1939." Ph.D. dissertation, Vanderbilt University, 1962.

Hanson, Betty Crump. "American Diplomatic Reporting from the Soviet Union, 1934–1941." Ph.D. dissertation, Columbia University, 1966.

Hilton, Stanley. "Brazil and Great Power Trade Rivalry in South

America, 1934–1939." Ph.D. dissertation, University of Texas, 1969.

McHale, James M. "The New Deal and the Origins of Public Lending for Foreign Economic Development, 1933–1945." Ph.D. dissertation, University of Wisconsin, 1970.

Maddux, Thomas R. "American Relations with the Soviet Union, 1933–1941." Ph.D. dissertation, University of Michigan, 1969.

Poole, Robert Carlyle. "Charles Evans Hughes and the Protection of American Business Interests Abroad." M.A. thesis: University of Chicago, 1952.

Schatz, Arthur W. "Cordell Hull and the Struggle for the Reciprocal Trade Agreements Program, 1932–1940." Ph.D. dissertation, University of Oregon, 1965.

Index

A

Agricultural Adjustment Administration, 57, 63, 64, 80
Agriculture, Department of, 72, 91, 176, 236
Amau Eiji, 166
American Bankers' Association, 6, 7, 14–15, 74
American Locomotive Corporation, 102, 179, 180n, 183, 183n
American Manufacturers' Export Association, 69, 74
Amtorg Trading Corporation, 101, 105, 113, 114
Andersen Meyer and Company, 183, 183n, 185n
Aranha, Oswaldo, 144, 144n; seeks U. S. aid (1939), 212–13, 214
Argentina, 197, 207; and Export-Import Bank, 204–5, 218, 222
Arita Hachiro, 247; and the New Order, 242–43, 245
Arnold, Julean, 170–71, 176–77, 230; encourages China trade, 175, 177, 180, 182n

B

Bankers, 30, 62–63; seek government aid, 5, 15, 68–69
Bankers Trust Company, 75, 183n
Bank for International Settlements, established by Young Plan, 47–48
Batista, Fulgencio, 137–38, 209–10
Beaulac, Willard, and Export-Import Bank Policy, 142–43, 143n, 158
Berle, Adolph, 200
Bilateral trade arrangements: harmful to U. S., 37, 43, 140, 144–45; favored by Peek, 81–86; opposed by State Department, 90–93,

147–48, 222; NFTC views with favor, 206
Blocked exchanges, 84, 140; State Department's position on, 141–52 passim
Bohlen, Charles, 103, 104
Bolivia, oil expropriation, 189, 210, 222, 224n
Borah, William E., 102, 102n
Brains Trust, 107
Brazil, 92, 143–44, 145n, 147n; and Export-Import Bank, 96, 143–52 passim, 192–93, 196, 196n, 204–5, 212–14 passim, 218, 220, 223; and Germany, 144–45, 145n, 197; and U.S. policy, 143–52 passim, 191, 212–14 passim, 219
Briggs, Ellis O., and Export-Import Bank policy, 211–12
Brüning, Heinrich, 48, 49
Brussels conference, 228, 229n
Bullitt, William C.: background, 108–9; Russian recognition, 109–10, 110n; ambassador to Russia, 111–23 passim, 124n; debt-loan talks, 113–23 passim; aid to China, 236
Burma Road, 237, 247

C

Calder, A. Bland, encourages China trade, 174–78 passim, 178n, 180, 182–83, 183n
California-Texas Oil Company, 185n, 238
Cárdenas, Lázaro, Mexican president, 190
cartel movements, U. S. concern about, 26–27, 26n
Caterpillar Tractor Corporation, 75
Chamberlain, Neville, 229
Chapin, Selden, 200–201, 200n–201n

Index

Export-Import Bank of Washington: created, 66, 70–71; dual purpose of, 71–72, 97, 128, 222–25, 255–57; lending policy of, 71, 77–80 passim, 94–97 passim, 141–59 passim, 191–97 passim, 202–4, 209–10, 212–14 passim, 216–25 passim, 255–58; and exporters, 73–76 passim, 79–80, 141–52 passim, 156–57, 178, 207, 214, 254*n*, 255–58 passim; and Congress, 73, 211, 218–19, 239, 250–53 passim; and Peek (first president), 74–75, 78–81 passim, 93; and German cotton deal, 90–93; and Pierson (second president), seeks liberal lending policy, 94, 158–59, 191–96 passim, 204
—Far East: aid to China, 178, 179, 180*n* 183–87, 185*n*, 235–49 passim, 256–57; as foreign policy tool in, 248–49, 257
—Latin America: Cuba, 71, 96, 138–39, 139*n*, 209–10, 221, 221*n*, 255; and blocked balances, 96, 141–52 passim, 212–18 passim, 220; Brazil, 96, 143–52 passim, 192–93, 196, 196*n*, 204–7 passim, 212–14 passim, 218, 220, 223; lending policy in, 141–58 passim, 191–97, 209–10, 212–14 passim, 223–25 passim, 255–58; Nicaragua, 142–43, 143*n*, 154, 156–57, 215–18, 215*n*, 223; and good neighbor policy, 153, 156, 158, 224–25; and Mexico, 154–57 passim, 155*n*–56*n*, 222; Costa Rica, 154, 220; Chile, 191–92, 204–5, 218, 220, 223; Colombia, 197, 209, 218, 221; Haiti, 198–204 passim, 209, 213, 214, 217, 218, 250; development projects, 198–204 passim, 212–20 passim, 255; Argentina, 204–5, 218, 222; Uruguay, 204–5, 222; Ecuador, 204, 209, 221; I.T.&T., 208, 209; Paraguay, 215–18 passim, 223; Panama, 220; Inter-American Bank, 224
—Soviet Union: created to finance trade with, 112–13, 115; used as economic lever on, 114–28 passim, 127*n*

F

Farrell, James A., 7, 62
Federal Reserve Bank of New York, 20, 52, 145, 185
Federal Reserve System, 32, 39, 52, 68
Feis, Herbert, 63, 135*n*; and Export-Import Bank, 192, 195–96, 208, 210, 236
Finland, and Export-Import Bank, 251–52
Fischer, Louis, 122, 122*n*
Five Power Naval Treaty, 12
Ford, Henry, Russian opportunities, 101
Foreign and Domestic Commerce, Bureau of, 183, 183*n*; trade expansion, 26, 61
Foreign Bondholders' Protective Council, 135, 201, 209
Foreign loans: policy, 29–31; fluctuations in, 33, 39, 68; defaults on, 132
Foreign Trade Financing Corporation, 6–7
Four Power Treaty, 12–13
France, 16–17, 53*n*, 69, 115, 119, 120, 148, 160, 219, 237; and financial crisis of 1931, 51, 51*n*

G

Gantenbein, James, Export-Import Bank policy, 193–95 passim
Garner, James, Far Eastern policy, 227*n*
General Electric, 75
General Motors, 75; export division, 185*n*
Geneva conferences (1927), international economic policy, 27
Germany, 24, 96, 119, 120, 252, 254; and European stability, 15–17, 40, 189; crisis of 1931, 48–51; trade tactics, 69, 206, 256; cotton deal, 90–93; and Russia,

Index

viet Union, 108–27 *passim*; and the Cuban revolution, 137; and the Far East, 166–67, 172–73, 227, 228, 234; and the Export-Import Bank in Latin America, 193–94, 222; at the Lima conference, 207–8; opposed aid to China, 236–44 passim, 245n, 248; defended the Export-Import Bank to Congress, 250–51
Huntington, Ellery C., Jr., lawyer for Dahlberg group, 200
Hutchins, Robert M., 65

I

Inter-American Bank, 224
Interdepartmental Trade Agreements Committee, defends reciprocal trade agreements program, 91–92
International Telephone and Telegraph Corporation, receives aid from Export-Import Bank, 208, 209
Italy, 69, 120, 148, 170, 207
Irving Trust Company, 183, 183n

J

Japan, 36, 69, 148, 160, 161, 254; Manchurian invasion, 52, 163, 254; and the Soviet Union, 105, 112, 118–22, 120n, 124–25; U. S. assessment of Japanese aggression, 164–66 passim, 167n, 226–32 passim, 234–35; North China invasion, 189, 226, 333–40 passim, 242–43, 248–49; U. S. moves to restrain, 242, 245–49 passim, 249n, 257
Johnson, Hugh S., 37
Johnson, Nelson T., 162n, 180, 247; on U. S. opportunities in China, 173–74, 174n, 176–77, 177n
Johnson Act: discussed, 95n; and the Export-Import Bank, 95, 114, 116, 252
Jones, Grosvenor, defends loan controls, 31
Jones, Jesse, and the Export-Im-

port Bank, 73, 94, 152, 184, 186, 223, 239, 250, 251
J. P. Morgan and Company, 17, 20, 183, 183n

K

Kelley, Robert F., 150; and the Soviet Union, 103–13 passim, 108n, 109n
Kellogg, Frank B., Far Eastern policy of, 161–62, 164n
Kellogg-Briand pact, 162, 228
Kennan, George F., and the Soviet Union, 103, 103n
Kent, Fred I., 5, 94, 145
Klein, Julius, 26, 36, 37
Konoye Fumimaro, receives U. S. protest about the New Order, 234
Kreditanstalt für Handel und Gerwebe, 53
Kung, H. H.: seeks U. S. aid for China (1937), 183–87, 184n; presents list of items, 186n
Kuomintang. *See* China

L

Lamont, Thomas, 5; and the Dawes Plan, 17; and China, 171, 176, 182; and Haiti, 200
Lausanne Conference, 53
League of Nations, 4, 8, 27, 120, 253
Lenin, V. I.: New Economic Policy, 100; and Bullitt, 108
Lieu, D. K., analyzes Japan's policy in China, 230, 230n–31n
Lima conference, 207–8, 243
Litvinov, Maxim: and Russian recognition, 110–11, 110n; and debt-loan talks, 113–23 passim, 114n, 120n–24n
Livesey, Frederick, Export-Import Bank policy, 194–95, 195n
Locarno, treaty of, 17–18, 18n
Lodge, Henry Cabot, 8–9
London Economic conference: Hoover and, 53–54, 53n; Roosevelt torpedoes, 58–59

Index

Panay incident, 228
Paraguay, and Export-Import Bank, 215–18 passim, 223
Peek, George N.: background, 37, 64, 80–81; first president Export-Import Bank, 74–75, 78, 81; clashes with State Department, 81–86 passim, 206, 255; favors bilateralism, 141, 143, 147, 147n, 150, 150n, 257; cotton deal, 90–93; resigns, 93
Peru, 132, 204; and Export-Import Bank, 154, 221
Phillips, William, and the Soviet Union, 109, 113
Pierson, Warren L.: second president of Export-Import Bank, 93–94; favors liberal lending policy, 94, 158–59, 159n, 191–95 passim, 204, 221, 223; and Latin America, 152, 191–95 passim, 196n, 202–10 passim, 202n, 215n, 221, 223; and China, 174, 175, 178–81 passim, 180n, 181n, 185, 186, 235
Portugal, and the Export-Import Bank, 126

Q

"Quarantine" speech, 228, 229n

R

RCA Victor Company, and China, 184
Recession of 1921, impact of, 3, 7–8
Recession of 1937, impact of, 188, 188n, 193, 196n, 198, 208, 256
Reconstruction Finance Corporation, 47, 63, 70, 94, 96, 145, 236; and Export-Import Bank, 72–73, 77, 245
Redfield, William C., and trade expansion, 7–8
Reed, Edward L., on Export-Import Bank policy, 157–58
Reparations: unsettled state of, 4–5, 15–16; and Dawes Plan, 16–18; and Young Plan, 47–48; and moratorium, 48–51; and Lausanne conference, 53
Republicans, postwar foreign policy of, 8–37
Robins, Raymond, and the Soviet Union, 102, 102n
Roosevelt, Eleanor, 182
Roosevelt, Franklin D.: and Hoover, 53–54, 54n; role of government, 55–56, 56n; U. S. in world economy, 56–57, 56n, 66; recovery program, 57–67 passim, 188; and London Economic conference, 58–59; trade policy of, 63–67, 80–81, 92–93, 92n; and Export-Import Bank, 66, 72, 79, 80, 139, 147–48, 218, 250–52; relationship with Peek, 80, 82–83, 91–93; and the Soviet Union, 98, 106, 114 passim, 119; Latin American policy, 133–38 passim, 145, 147–48, 189, 200n, 207, 215; and China, 185, 236–44 passim, 247–48; and the Far Eastern war, 189, 227n, 228–29, 228n, 229n, 236–44 passim, 247–48
Roper, Daniel, government lending policy, 171

S

Sackett, Frederic, 49, 50
Saito Hirosi, Japanese ambassador to U. S., 167
Sayre, Francis B., 69, 70; defends reciprocal trade agreements approach, 87, 88, 135, 147–48, 206–7
Sian incident (1936), 168
Simonsen, Roberto, advocate of bilateral trade pacts, 144
Sino-American Treaty of 1844, 244, 244n
Smith, A. Viola, trade commissioner in Shanghai, 233
Smoot, Reed, 22
Social Science Research Council, study of international economic relations, 63
Socony-Vacuum Oil Company, 238

Index

80–86 passim; defended by State Department, 87–93 passim. *See also* Triangular trade patterns
United States Chamber of Commerce, 6, 55, 89
United States-Japanese Commercial Treaty of 1911, U. S. terminates, 241, 248, 249n
United States of America: stake in world economy, 1–3, 13, 20, 33–37 passim, 40, 105n, 129, 169, 169n–70n, 226–27; economic nationalism as threat to, 25, 132–33, 136, 143–44, 159, 189–90, 222–23, 256; impact of depression on trade of, 42–44 passim, 254; moves to protect position in world economy, 222–25, 236–49 passim, 254–58
United States Steel Products Company, 183, 183n
Universal Trading Corporation, 238, 239, 245, 247
Upgren, A. P., Export-Import Bank policy, 141–42
Uruguay, 207; and Export-Import Bank, 204–5, 222

V

Vandenberg, Arthur, 245, 251n
Vanderlip, Frank, 5
Vargas, Getulio, Brazilian president, 143, 144, 145n, 191
Venezuela, 132; and Export-Import Bank, 156, 157, 158, 204–5
Vincent, John C., 184n
Voroshilov, Kliment, 114

W

Wagner, Robert, 252
Wallace, Henry, 236
Warburg, Paul M., 5
War debts, 4–5, 18–20, 19n–20n, 53, 58
Warren, George, 60
Washington conference, 18; and Far Eastern affairs, 11–13, 160–61, 166, 228
Welles, Sumner: and Latin America, 133–34, 136n, 137–38, 147–48, 155–56, 196, 209–10, 209n, 214, 221, 221n; and Export-Import Bank, 147–48, 155–56, 196, 209–10, 209n, 214, 221, 221n; and Far Eastern War, 229n, 243–44, 245n
Westinghouse Electric, 75
Whiting, William F., 35
Whittemore, W. D., on Export-Import Bank policy, 201–2, 212–13
Williams, Frank S., assesses Japan's financial condition, 231
Williams, John S., examines Latin American exchanges, 141n
Wilson, Woodrow, 253; postwar program (and failure of), 3–8 passim; Soviet Union, 98, 108
Wolcott, Jesse P., 250, 251
World War I, impact of, 1, 160, 253
World War II, 258
World War Debt Commission, 18–19

Y

Young Plan, 47–48